SINA ALICA JUNG

International Criminal Law – a promising pathway to promoting global environmental protection?

Beiträge zum Internationalen und
Europäischen Strafrecht

Studies in International and
European Criminal Law and Procedure

Herausgegeben von / Edited by
Prof. Dr. Dr. h.c. Kai Ambos, Richter am Kosovo Sondertribunal
Berater (amicus curiae) Sondergerichtsbarkeit für den Frieden, Bogotá, Kolumbien

Band / Volume 60

International Criminal Law – a promising pathway to promoting global environmental protection?

By

Sina Alica Jung

Duncker & Humblot · Berlin

Unter Beteiligung des Göttinger Vereins zur Förderung der Strafrechtswissenschaft und Kriminologie sowie ihrer praktischen Anwendung e. V.

Die Rechts- und Wirtschaftswissenschaftliche Fakultät/der Fachbereich Rechtswissenschaft der Friedrich-Alexander-Universität Erlangen-Nürnberg hat diese Arbeit im Jahre 2024 als Dissertation angenommen.

Bibliographic information of the German national library

The German national library registers this publication in the German national bibliography; specified bibliographic data are retrievable on the Internet about http://dnb.d-nb.de.

Typesetting: 3w+p GmbH, Rimpar
Printing: Beltz Grafische Betriebe GmbH, Bad Langensalza
Printed in Germany

ISSN 1867-5271
ISBN 978-3-428-19522-0 (Print)
ISBN 978-3-428-59522-8 (E-Book)

Printed on no aging resistant (non-acid) paper
according to ISO 9706 ♾

Duncker & Humblot GmbH, Carl-Heinrich-Becker-Weg 9,
12165 Berlin, Germany | E-Mail: info@duncker-humblot.de
Internet: https://www.duncker-humblot.de

To My Parents

Acknowledgements

My research on this thesis commenced in September 2021 and was accepted as a doctoral dissertation by the Law Faculty of the Friedrich-Alexander University Erlangen-Nuremberg in December 2023.

Cases and literature cover the period up to December 2023. All internet sources referenced in the footnotes were last visited in February 2025.

This thesis would not have been possible without the assistance of numerous people along the way. A very special thank you goes to my supervisor, Professor Dr. Christoph Safferling, LL.M. (LSE), whose guidance and support have been invaluable. I am particularly grateful for his constant availability, prompt and thorough feedback, and approachable nature. His commitment and dedication made the process of completing this thesis feel manageable and enjoyable.

I am sincerely thankful for all of the support that I have received from Dr. Kevin Pike. I am particularly grateful for his assistance in proof-reading the manuscript and providing me with invaluable feedback. If it was not for him and his support throughout the Legal English Certificate Programme at the Friedrich-Alexander-University Erlangen-Nuremberg, I would not have been able to improve my English proficiency to the level needed to write this dissertation in English as a non-native speaker.

I would be remiss if I did not express my appreciation to Professor Dr. Dr. h. c. Kai Ambos for providing me with the opportunity to publish my dissertation in the series "Studies in International and European Criminal Law and Procedure".

I am grateful for the generous financial support that Schmitz-Nüchterlein-Stiftung has provided me with to allow for the publication of this thesis.

Finally, I would like to express my deepest gratitude to my parents whose love and unwavering faith in me have been the foundation of my academic journey. Their constant support has given me the strength to persevere through every challenge. The encouragement from my father – the one and only "Doktorvater" – was an integral part of my decision to begin writing this dissertation. To my friends, thank you for being a steady source of motivation, laughter and inspiration. Your support during the highs and lows of this process has meant more than I can express.

Mykonos, May 2025 *Sina Alica Jung*

Table of contents

A. Introduction

"We are on a highway to climate hell with our foot on the accelerator."[1]
UN Secretary-General, António Guterres

While it took approximately 300,000 years to reach the threshold of one billion humans inhabiting the earth[2], the most recent billion was added within a time span of only 12 years.[3] On 15 November 2022 the world's population officially exceeded the 8 billion-mark and the next billion is expected to be reached in the ensuing 15 years.[4] However, this unprecedented population growth does not come without costs. Population growth is inextricably linked to an expansion of production and consumption. However, while the highest fertility rates are in countries with the lowest income per capita, the highest per capita consumption is in countries with the highest income per capita and not in the countries with the highest population growth.[5] The high standard of living in the world's industrial nations is primarily based on the availability of natural resources. It is estimated that the use of raw materials per capita is four times larger in industrialised countries than in developing countries.[6] This inequality is further exacerbated by the fact that lesser developed countries are typically resource rich. Thus, the bulk of environmental crime is committed by subsidiary companies operating in the Global South where they are largely free to pursue their profits, whereas their partner companies are headquartered in the Global North where strict environmental regulations are in place.[7]

As such, particularly the lack of a consistent global environmental governance system permits multinational corporations to evade liability for widespread ecological destruction. According to the United Nations Environment Programme (UNEP) and Interpol, environmental crime has become the world's fourth largest

---

[1] *Fiona Harvey/Damian Carrington*, World is on 'Highway to Climate Hell', UN Chief Warns at Cop27 Summit, The Guardian, Nov. 7, 2022, https://www.theguardian.com/environment/2022/nov/07/cop27-climate-summit-un-secretary-general-antonio-guterres.

[2] *Craig Welch*, Earth Now has 8 Billion People – and Counting, Where Do We Go From Here?, National Geographic, Nov. 14, 2022, https://www.nationalgeographic.com/environment/article/the-world-now-has-8-billion-people.

[3] United Nations, Day of Eight Billion, https://www.un.org/en/dayof8billion (last visited Feb. 18, 2025).

[4] Id.

[5] Id.

[6] Umweltbundesamt, Resource Use and Its Consequences (2019), https://www.umweltbundesamt.de/en/topics/waste-resources/resource-use-its-consequences (last visited Feb. 18, 2025).

[7] EUROPOL, Environmental Crime in the Age of Climate Change (2022).

crime sector after drug trafficking, crimes of counterfeiting and human trafficking, increasing at a 5% to 7% rate per year, thereby exceeding the global economic growth rate by two to three times.[8] UNEP and Interpol broadly describe 'environmental crime' as "a collective term to describe illegal activities harming the environment and aimed at benefitting individuals or groups or companies from the exploitation of, damage to, trade or theft of natural resources, including serious crimes and transnational organised crime"[9]. Thus, besides illegal logging and deforestation, illegal fishing and trade, illegal mining, illegal discharging of hazardous waste, wildlife poaching and trade, environmental crime is also deeply intertwined with tax fraud, money laundering, forgery and terrorism.[10] Environmental crime is estimated to generate illicit profits ranging between 110 and 281 billion USD per year.[11] At the same time the annual global loss resulting from environmental crime is estimated to reach 80 to 230 billion EUR.[12] To put it in a nutshell, the most vulnerable countries, which have traditionally contributed the least to the environmental crisis, are at the same time the most affected by its repercussions. This striking inequality signals the need for a global environmental governance system ensuring that environmental crime does not go unpunished.

This thesis aims to assess the legal lacunae in international law rendering current global environmental protection inadequate (Chapter B.) prior to discussing two possible legal means of promoting global environmental protection. In Chapter C., the possibility of incorporating a fifth crime of ecocide into the Rome Statute will be examined, and in Chapter D. the adoption of an International Environmental Convention, which could either be indirectly enforced through national courts or directly enforced through an International Environmental Court, will be assessed with regards to the desired goal of promoting global environmental protection.

---

[8] European Commission, Question and Answers on the Revised EU Directive on Environmental Crime, https://ec.europa.eu/commission/presscorner/detail/en/QANDA_21_6745 (last visited Feb. 18, 2025).

[9] UNEP, The Rise of Environmental Crime, A Growing Threat to Natural Resources, Peace, Development and Security 17 (2016).

[10] Id. at 30.

[11] INTERPOL, INTERPOL Makes Public Appeal to Help Track Environmental Fugitives (2019), https://www.interpol.int/News-and-Events/News/2019/INTERPOL-makes-public-appeal-to-help-track-environmental-fugitives (last visited Feb. 18, 2025).

[12] European Commission, European Green Deal: Strengthening EU Law to Combat Environmental Crime (2021).

B. Legal lacunae in current global environmental protection

Although environmental protection is afforded by several bodies of international law, including international environmental law, international humanitarian law, human rights law and international criminal law, international law currently fails to afford effective global environmental protection. In the following, the legal lacunae under international law which render current global environmental protection inadequate will be examined.

I. International environmental law

The field of law primarily concerned with environmental protection is international environmental law.[1] While international environmental law has developed into a distinct area of public international law, it is also closely linked to numerous other fields of international law such as international economic law, human rights law or international humanitarian law.[2] In this section, a brief overview over the historical development of international environmental law will be given prior to an analysis of the current legal lacunae in this field of law.

1. History of international environmental law

International environmental law is a rapidly growing area of law whose history is longer than some might expect. While the idea of environmental regulation goes back to Ancient Rome, where environmental regulations were adopted to ensure the city's water supplies[3], modern international environmental law did not emerge until the second half of the 19th century.[4] Prior to the late 1960s environmental destruction did not occur on a large scale, states hesitated to interfere with the sovereignty of other states over their resources and environmental harm was not perceived as a

---

[1] *Frédéric Mégret*, The Problem of an International Criminal Law of the Environment, 36 Colum. J. Envtl. L. 195, 218 (2011).

[2] *Philippe Sands/Jacqueline Peel*, Principles of International Environmental Law 4, 811–926 (4th ed., 2018).

[3] Encyclopedia Britannica, Environmental Law https://www.britannica.com/topic/environmental-law (last visited Feb. 18, 2025).

[4] *Philippe Sands/Jacqueline Peel*, Principles of International Environmental Law 21 (2018).

potential threat to the international community.[5] However, in the late 1960s severe incidents of environmental damage, such as the disposal of hazardous waste on the high seas, oil spills or global warming caught the attention of the public.[6] Thus, early bilateral conventions primarily focusing on the protection of wildlife were introduced at the regional and global level.[7] Yet, these conventions only targeted specific sectoral environmental problems, such as oil pollution or nuclear testing, either responding to certain environmental incidents or the emergence of new scientific evidence.[8] States are generally reluctant to adopt transnational environmental regulations due to the strong recognition of states' "permanent sovereignty over their natural wealth and resources".[9] At this point in time most conventions did not contain any implementation techniques or mechanisms to ensure compliance and an international organisation having the overall authority to coordinate and direct international environmental governance did not exist.[10]

However, in the following years, two events in particular – the Stockholm Conference in 1972 and the Rio Earth Summit in 1992 – accelerated the development of modern international environmental law. The growing international interest in constraining man-made environmental destruction through legal means at the global level culminated in the first world conference on environmental matters, the United Nations Conference on the Human Environment[11], which was held in Stockholm in 1972 and is widely considered the birthplace of modern international environmental law.[12] The Conference resulted, *inter alia*, in the adoption of the Stockholm Declaration[13], which contained a set of twenty-six general principles intending to "inspire and guide the peoples of the world in the preservation and enhancement of the human environment"[14]. Despite being non-binding in nature,

[5] *Mohammed Saif-Alden Wattad*, The Rome Statute & Captain Planet: What Lies Between 'Crimes Against Humanity' and the 'Natural Environment'?, 19 (2) Fordham Environmental Law Review 265, 279, 280 (2009).

[6] Id. at 280.

[7] *Philippe Sands/Jacqueline Peel*, Principles of International Environmental Law 22–26 (2018); *Karen Hulme*, War Torn Environment: Interpreting the Legal Threshold 6–9 (2004).

[8] *Philippe Sands/Jacqueline Peel*, Principles of International Environmental Law 22–29 (2018).

[9] G.A. Res. 1803 (XVII), ¶ 1 (Dec. 14, 1962).

[10] *Philippe Sands/Jacqueline Peel*, Principles of International Environmental Law 29 (2018).

[11] Report of the UN Conference on the Human Environment, at 3, U.N. Doc. A/CONF.48/Rev.1 (1972).

[12] *Marc Pallemaerts*, International Environmental Law from Stockholm to Rio: Back to the Future, 1 (3) Rev. Eur. Comp. & Int'l Envtl. L. 254, 255 (1992).

[13] Declaration of the United Nations Conference on the Human Environment, Report of the UN Conference on the Human Environment, at 3–5, U.N. Doc. A/CONF.48/Rev.1 (1972).

[14] Id. at 3.

the Stockholm Declaration[15] constitutes a foundational document for modern international environmental law.[16] In particular, Principle 21/Principle 1[17] governing state responsibility for transboundary environmental damage was later transformed into hard law and thus became binding.[18]

After the Stockholm Conference, environmental lawmaking gained momentum both at the regional and global level, which resulted in the adoption of numerous conventions and treaties forming the basic legal framework in international environmental law.[19] This also included the establishment of the United Nations Environment Programme (UNEP) in 1972, the first UN body exclusively tasked with the coordination of environmental matters.[20] In 1991, this was followed by the creation of the Global Environment Facility (GEF), which is the world's largest funder of global environmental protection.[21] Precisely twenty years after the Stockholm Conference, the UN Conference on Environment and Development (UNCED)[22], better known as the Rio Earth Summit, was convened by the UN in 1992. The object behind this conference was to "promote the further development of international environmental law [...by] elaborating general rights and obligations of States [...] in the field of the environment"[23]. The summit produced three non-binding documents, including the Rio Declaration[24] which encompasses twenty-seven principles. While the Stockholm Declaration exclusively aimed at the restriction of environmental destruction, the Rio Declaration demanded a reorientation in international

[15] For a detailed analysis of the Conference and the Declaration, see *Louis B. Sohn*, The Stockholm Declaration on the Human Environment, 14 Harvard International Law Journal 423 (1973).

[16] *Marc Pallemaerts*, Rev. Eur. Comp. & Int'l Envtl. L., 255 (1992); *Philippe Roch/Franz Xaver Perrez*, International Environmental Governance: The Strive Towards a Comprehensive, Coherent, Effective and Efficient International Environmental Regime, 16 (1) Colorado Journal of International Environmenal Law and Policy 1, 7 (2005).

[17] Principle 21/Principle 1 of the Stockholm Declaration reads as follows: "States have [...] the sovereign right to exploit their own resources pursuant to their own environmental policies, and the responsibility to ensure that activities within their jurisdiction or control do not cause damage to the environment of other States or of areas beyond the limits of national jurisdiction."

[18] *Marc Pallemaerts*, Rev. Eur. Comp. & Int'l Envtl. L., 255 (1992).

[19] *Philippe Sands/Jacqueline Peel*, Principles of International Environmental Law 33–41 (2018).

[20] UNEP, About UN Environment Programme, https://www.unep.org/about-un-environment (last visited Feb. 18, 2025).

[21] GEF, https://www.thegef.org/who-we-are (last visited Feb. 18, 2025).

[22] G.A. Res. 44/228 (Dec. 22, 1989).

[23] G.A. Res. 44/228, at 153 (Dec. 22, 1989).

[24] Report of the United Nations Conference on Environment and Development, at 3–8, Annex I, U.N. Doc. A/CONF.151/26/Rev.1 (Vol. I) (1992).

environmental lawmaking. The Rio Declaration[25] understood international environmental law as part of a new field of 'international law of sustainable development'[26] and thereby demanded that environmental matters should no longer be regarded distinctly but had to be considered in relation to sustainable development, requiring a balance between economic and environmental matters.[27]

Although some[28] feared this might constitute the end of international environmental law as a distinct field of international law, the opposite occurred. In the following years after the Rio Summit, flesh was added to the bones formed by the Stockholm and Rio Declarations, which resulted in the adoption of numerous new issue-specific conventions concerning particular environmental issues, such as climate change[29], biodiversity[30] or desertification.[31] Nevertheless, as Palmer stated, the existing methods for lawmaking in international environmental law were "slow, cumbersome, expensive, uncoordinated and uncertain".[32]

In the 21st century the rate of legislating slowed considerably due to a declining political will and the fact that environmental matters are increasingly intertwined with economic and human rights considerations and thus collided with the UN development agenda.[33] Additionally, the primary object over the past two decades was not to add new environmental regulations, but to implement effective compliance mechanisms in international environmental law.[34] Nevertheless, despite the decline in the rate of lawmaking, to date international environmental law has virtually exploded in a "mushrooming growth"[35] to a mosaic of over 500 international treaties.[36]

---

[25] See for a detailed analysis of the Rio Declaration: *David A. Wirth*, The Rio Declaration on Environment and Development: Two Steps Forward and One Back, or Vice Versa, 29 (3) Georgia Law Review 599 (1995).

[26] See Principle 27 of the Rio Declaration: "States and people shall cooperate […] in the further development of international law in the field of sustainable development".

[27] *Philippe Sands/Jacqueline Peel*, Principles of International Environmental Law 41 (2018); *Marc Pallemaerts*, Rev. Eur. Comp. & Int'l Envtl. L., 264 (1992).

[28] *Marc Pallemaerts*, Rev. Eur. Comp. & Int'l Envtl. L., 264 (1992); contra *David Freestone*, The Road from Rio: International Environmental Law After the Earth Summit, 6 (2) Journal of Environmental Law 193, 216 (1994).

[29] United Nations Framework Convention on Climate Change, May 9, 1992, S. Treaty Doc. No. 102–38, 1771 U.N.T.S. 107.

[30] Convention on Biological Diversity, June 5, 1992, 1760 U.N.T.S. 79.

[31] United Nations Convention to Combat Desertification in Those Countries Experiencing Serious Drought and/or Desertification, Particularly in Africa, Oct. 14, 1994, 1954 U.N.T.S. 3.

[32] *Geoffrey Palmer*, New Ways to Make International Environmental Law 86 (2) The American Journal of International Law 259, 259 (1992).

[33] *Philippe Sands/Jacqueline Peel*, Principles of International Environmental Law 50 (2018).

[34] Id. at 190.

[35] *Philippe Roch/Franz Xaver Perrez*, Colorado Journal of International Environmenal Law and Policy 6 (2005).

2. Legal lacunae in international environmental law

Although international environmental law has developed into an extremely detailed and complex legal architecture and has thereby raised global awareness for the unlimited exploitation of nature, its effectiveness is severely hampered by numerous legal lacunae which will be examined below.

a) Normative fragmentation

International environmental law is characterised by normative fragmentation hindering effective protection of the environment. With respect to the sources of international environmental law, international conventions are the predominant sources of law as customary international environmental law[37] is scarce.[38] Instead of having adopted one single consolidated legal instrument governing the general principles of international environmental law, a patchwork of over 500 international conventions, each of which addresses issue-specific environmental issues, has been passed.[39] This piecemeal approach generally entails a lack of coherence and certain types of environmental harm remain unaddressed.[40] Furthermore, consensus-based lawmaking is becoming increasingly difficult as the number of states engaging in international environmental law constantly proliferates and environmental matters often affect economic interests of other countries.[41]

b) Inadequate domestic implementation and compliance

Furthermore, multilateral environmental treaties are often inadequately implemented at the national level for various reasons, including the absence of institutional, human and financial resources, differing interpretations concerning the meaning of obligations or simply a lack of political will.[42] Yet, international environmental agreements are only effective when adequately enshrined in domestic

[36] U.N. Secretary-General, Gaps in International Environmental Law and Environmental-Related Instruments, Towards a Global Pact for the Environment, at 4, U.N. Doc. A/73/419 (2018); see ECOLEX, https://www.ecolex.org (last visited Feb. 18, 2025).

[37] See further on the existence of customary international environmenal law *Daniel Bodansky*, Customary (and Not So Customary) International Environmental Law 3 (1) Indiana Journal of Global Studies 105 (1995).

[38] U.N. Secretary-General, Gaps in International Environmental Law at 4, U.N. Doc. A/73/419 (2018).

[39] Id.

[40] Id. at 4, 43.

[41] *Philippe Sands/Jacqueline Peel*, Principles of International Environmental Law 938 (2018).

[42] Id. at 147, 148; U.N. Secretary-General, Gaps in International Environmental Law at 45, U.N. Doc. A/73/419 (2018); see further *David G. Victor*, et al., The Implementation and Effectiveness of International Environmental Commitments, Theory and Practice (1998).

laws as otherwise national courts struggle to enforce the environmental obligations.[43] Besides being weakly implemented, environmental obligations are further inadequately complied with as domestic public authorities lack resources and the political commitment to ensure compliance with international environmental obligations.[44] Additionally, developing countries in particular fail to comply with their reporting obligations concerning domestic implementation measures.[45]

c) Lack of liability for environmental damage

Additionally, international environmental law lacks liability rules concerning the occasioning of environmental damage. State liability as well as civil liability rules are largely uncodified and require further development in international environmental law.[46]

In general, international law state liability is a well-established principle with Article 1 ILC Responsibility of States for Internationally Wrongful Acts (2001) stating that "[e]very internationally wrongful act of a State entails the international responsibility of that State". The existence of an internationally wrongful act requires the violation of an obligation under general international law or a treaty.[47] Several judicial and arbitral decisions[48] affirmed the customary "international obligation for every State to ensure that activities within its territory or control do not cause damage to the environment of other States or of areas beyond the limits of national jurisdiction"[49].[50] This general obligation for states was also confirmed in soft-law, namely in Principle 21 of the Stockholm Declaration and Principle 2 of the Rio Declaration. In this regard, state liability entails the obligation to cease the commission of cross-boundary environmental harm and provide reparation.[51] However, state liability for cross-boundary environmental harm is thus not predi-

[43] *Philippe Sands/Jacqueline Peel*, Principles of International Environmental Law 148 (2018); U.N. Secretary-General, Gaps in International Environmental Law at 36, U.N. Doc. A/73/419 (2018).

[44] *Philippe Sands/Jacqueline Peel*, Principles of International Environmental Law 148–151 (2018).

[45] Id. at 152, 153.

[46] Id. at 735; U.N. Secretary-General, Gaps in International Environmental Law at 39–42, U.N. Doc. A/73/419 (2018).

[47] Article 2 ILC Responsibility of States for Internationally Wrongful Acts (2001).

[48] See for instance Legality of the Threat or Use of Nuclear Weapons, Advisory Opinion, 1996 I.C.J. Rep., ¶ 29 (July 8).

[49] U.N. Secretary-General, Gaps in International Environmental Law at 40, U.N. Doc. A/73/419 (2018).

[50] *Philippe Sands/Jacqueline Peel*, Principles of International Environmental Law 740 (2018).

[51] U.N. Secretary-General, Gaps in International Environmental Law at 40, U.N. Doc. A/73/419 (2018); *Philippe Sands/Jacqueline Peel*, Principles of International Environmental Law 762–769 (2018).

cated on an 'internationally wrongful act', as only very few treaties contain state liability for cross-boundary environmental damage in relation to specific activities.[52] The absence of state liability in this particular field of law stems from the states' unwillingness to face excessive costs.[53]

Contrary to state liability, a growing number of issue-specific conventions, particularly in relation to oil pollution and nuclear activities, address civil liability of natural and legal persons for cross-boundary environmental damage.[54] Nevertheless, many civil liability regimes have not yet entered into force and some probably never will.[55] Furthermore, many environmentally-harmful activities are not covered by civil liability rules and the most polluting countries often evade liability by not having ratified the treaties.[56]

Hence, aside from oil pollution and nuclear activities liability for transboundary environmental damage is largely underdeveloped in current international environmental law.[57]

d) Institutional fragmentation and lack of an international environmental court

Furthermore, international environmental law lacks coherence due to institutional fragmentation and the lack of a uniform international judicial system. Subsequent to the creation of the UNEP as the leading global authority for environmental matters after the Stockholm Conference, another estimated 200 international environmental institutions were established over the following two decades.[58] This institutional fragmentation is exacerbated by the absence of a single, overarching UN specialised agency tasked with environmental protection, similar to international economic institutions such as the WTO.

Furthermore, the lack of a uniform international judicial system in the form of an international environmental court fuels inconsistent jurisprudence regarding envi-

---

[52] U.N. Secretary-General, Gaps in International Environmental Law at 40, U.N. Doc. A/73/419 (2018); *Philippe Sands/Jacqueline Peel*, Principles of International Environmental Law 762–769 (2018).

[53] *Philippe Sands/Jacqueline Peel*, Principles of International Environmental Law 736 (2018).

[54] U.N. Secretary-General, Gaps in International Environmental Law at 41, U.N. Doc. A/73/419 (2018); *Philippe Sands/Jacqueline Peel*, Principles of International Environmental Law 771 (2018).

[55] *Philippe Sands/Jacqueline Peel*, Principles of International Environmental Law 771 (2018).

[56] Id. at 804.

[57] Id. at 803; U.N. Secretary-General, Gaps in International Environmental Law at 44, 45 U.N. Doc. A/73/419 (2018).

[58] U.N. Secretary-General, Gaps in International Environmental Law at 33, U.N. Doc. A/73/419 (2018).

ronmental disputes and promotes 'forum-shopping'.[59] Due to the paucity of a uniform international environmental court international environmental disputes are adjudicated by a plethora of international courts and tribunals, including the Court of Justice of the European Union, the International Court of Justice, the International Tribunal for the Law of the Sea, the WTO Dispute Settlement Body as well as the Permanent Court of Arbitration or human rights tribunals.[60]

In the following, a brief overview over the existing international courts and tribunals capable of adjudicating on international environmental disputes will be provided. In particular, it will be examined why these courts and tribunals only afford very limited global environmental protection.

aa) Court of Justice of the European Union

Within the European Union, the Court of Justice of the European Union (*hereinafter* CJEU) has extensive competence and experience in hearing environmental cases. Concerning disputes arising from the interpretation or implementation of EU law, the CJEU hears cases submitted by EU Member States, organs of the EU, individuals, companies or organisations.[61] Although the CJEU has extensive experience in adjudicating on environmental cases[62], its jurisdiction is geographically restricted to the EU and thus cannot promote *global* environmental protection.[63] Nevertheless, the CJEU contributes to the further evolvement of European environmental law[64] and serves in many aspects as a model for effective adjudication of international environmental disputes.[65]

---

[59] *Philippe Sands/Jacqueline Peel*, Principles of International Environmental Law 191 (2018).

[60] Id.; U.N. Secretary-General, Gaps in International Environmental Law at 38, U.N. Doc. A/73/419 (2018).

[61] EU, Court of Justice of the European Union (CJEU), https://european-union.europa.eu/institutions-law-budget/institutions-and-bodies/institutions-and-bodies-profiles/court-justice-european-union-cjeu_en (last visited Feb. 18, 2025).

[62] *Philippe Sands/Jacqueline Peel*, Principles of International Environmental Law 187–189 (2018); see for an overview of environmental cases adjudicated by the CJEU in 2019, *Richard Moules*, Significant EU Environmental Cases: 2019, 32 (1) Journal of Environmental Law 161 (2020).

[63] *Sean Murphy*, Does the World Need a New International Environmental Court?, 32 (3) Geo. Wash. J. Int'l L. & Econ. 333, 340 (2000); *Alfred Rest*, Enhanced Implementation of the Biological Diversity Convention by Judicial Control, 29 (1) Envtl. Pol'y & L. 32, 38 (1999).

[64] *Alfred Rest*, Envtl. Pol'y & L., 38 (1999).

[65] *Tim Stephens*, International Courts and Environmental Protection 52, 53 (2009).

bb) International Tribunal for the Law of the Sea

With respect to the protection of the marine environment, State Parties to the 1982 UN Convention on the Law of the Sea (UNCLOS)[66] can refer disputes regarding the interpretation and implementation of the Convention to the International Tribunal for the Law of the Sea (*hereinafter* ITLOS). UNCLOS provides compulsory dispute resolution, however, the Convention enables State Parties to choose between ITLOS, the International Court of Justice or arbitral tribunals.[67] In this regard, ITLOS has adjudicated upon numerous environmental cases.[68] Nevertheless, the subject matter competence of ITLOS is limited to disputes concerning the marine environment. Hence, ITLOS cannot serve as a general adjudicator of environmental crimes.

cc) WTO Dispute Settlement Body

Since many environmental matters are closely intertwined with trade matters, it is not surprising that to date numerous international disputes involving environmental issues have been submitted to the WTO dispute settlement system[69] and therefore the WTO Dispute Settlement Body significantly contributes to the evolvement of international environmental law.[70] However, with its exclusive focus on trade issues, the WTO Dispute Settlement Body is unquestionably biased in favour of international trade[71], which was evidenced, *inter alia*, in its *Shrimp-Turtle* decision.[72]

---

[66] U.N. Convention on the Law of the Sea, Dec. 10, 1982, 1833 U.N.T.S. 397.

[67] U.N. Convention on the Law of the Sea art. 287, Dec. 10, 1982, 1833 U.N.T.S. 397.

[68] Amongst relevant cases are the Southern Bluefin Tuna Cases (New Zealand v. Japan; Australia v. Japan), Case No. 3,4, Provisional Measures, 1999 ITLOS Rep. (Aug. 27).

[69] Amongst relevant decisions by the WTO Appellate Body are Appellate Body World Trade Organization, EC Measures Concerning Meat and Meat Products (Hormones), WT/DS26/AB/R; WT/DS48/AB/R (1998); Appellate Body World Trade Organization, United States – Import Prohibition of Certain Shrimp and Shrimp Products, WT/DS58/AB/RW (2001).

[70] *Philippe Sands/Jacqueline Peel*, Principles of International Environmental Law 186, 187 (2018); *Tim Stephens*, International Courts and Environmental Protection 49 (2009).

[71] *Kenneth F. McCallion/H. Rajan Sharma*, Environmental Justice Without Borders: The Need for an International Court of the Environment to Protect Fundamental Environmental Rights, 32 (3) Geo. Wash. J. Int'l L. & Econ. 351, 364 (2000); *Sean Murphy*, Geo. Wash. J. Int'l L. & Econ. 343 (2000).

[72] *Peggy Rodgers Kalas*, International Environmental Dispute Resolution and the Need for Access by Non-State Entities, 12 Colorado Journal of International Environmenal Law and Policy 191, 225, 226 (2001).

dd) International Court of Justice

The International Court of Justice (*hereinafter* ICJ), the UN's main judicial body seated in The Hague, is well equipped to adjudicate on environmental disputes. In terms of jurisdiction, the ICJ has both binding jurisdiction over contentious cases between states as well as the competence to issue non-binding advisory opinions on legal questions at the request of states, the UN General Assembly, the Security Council or other UN organs or specialised agencies.[73] However, advisory opinions are non-binding and no legal question concerning an environmental matter has yet been the subject of an advisory opinion.[74]

Nonetheless, at the behest of the Republic of Vanuatu and a coalition of over 80 states, including Germany, a draft resolution entitled "Request for an advisory opinion of the International Court of Justice on the obligations of States in respect of climate change" was proposed to the UN General Assembly on 1 March 2023.[75] In response, the UN General Assembly adopted by consensus a milestone resolution on 29 March 2023 requesting that the ICJ provide an advisory opinion on the following two questions:

"(a) What are the obligations of States under international law to ensure the protection of the climate system and other parts of the environment from anthropogenic emissions of greenhouse gases for States and for present and future generations;

(b) What are the legal consequences under these obligations for States where they, by their acts and omissions, have caused significant harm to the climate system and other parts of the environment, with respect to:

(i) States, including, in particular, small island developing States, which due to their geographical circumstances and level of development, are injured or specially affected by or are particularly vulnerable to the adverse effects of climate change?

(ii) Peoples and individuals of the present and future generations affected by the adverse effects of climate change?"[76]

After the resolution was transmitted to the ICJ on 12 April 2023, all States which are authorised to appear before the Court are now allowed to submit written statements to the Court concerning the abovementioned legal questions by 22 January 2024.[77]

---

[73] *Philippe Sands/Jacqueline Peel*, Principles of International Environmental Law 180, 182 (2018).

[74] Id. at 182.

[75] U.N. GAOR, 77th Sess., U.N. Doc. A/77/L.58 (Mar. 1, 2023).

[76] G.A., Request for an advisory opinion of the International Court of Justice on the obligations of States in respect of climate change, U.N. Doc. A/RES/77/276 (April 29, 2023).

[77] International Court of Justice, Obligations of States in Respect of Climate Change, Press Release No. 2023/44 (2023), https://www.icj-cij.org/sites/default/files/case-related/187/187-20230901-pre-01-00-en.pdf (last visited Feb. 18, 2025).

The resolution further requests the ICJ to render an opinion "on the legal consequences under these obligations for States where they, by their acts and omissions, have caused significant harm to the climate system and other parts of the environment, with respect to States, and in particular, small island developing States, and people of present and future generations".[78]

Thus far, the ICJ has contributed considerably to the development of general principles in international environmental law by adjudicating on numerous significant environmental cases, including the *Gabčíkovo-Nagymaros* case[79], the *Pulp Mills* case[80] and its Advisory Opinion on the Legality of the Threat or Use of Nuclear Weapons in 1996[81].

However, the ICJ has been criticised on several occasions for its anthropocentric rather than ecocentric approach to environmental disputes. In the context of environmental protection two approaches may be distinguished, namely anthropocentric and ecocentric approaches.[82] While anthropocentric approaches[83] directly focus on protecting human life (human environment), ecocentric approaches aim at protecting the environment per se, irrespective of its relation to human life (natural environment).[84]

For instance, with respect to the *Gabčikovo* decision Sands questioned "whether the ICJ has missed an opportunity to indicate a real willingness to show its environmental credentials?"[85]. Regarding the *Pulp Mills* case Judges Al-Khasawneh and Simma criticised the ICJ in a joint dissenting opinion for not having applied a more preventive approach to the ecological hazards emanating from the mill.[86] Additionally, although the ICJ has reiterated the significance of environmental protection

---

[78] United Nations, General Assembly Adopts Resolution Requesting International Court of Justice Provide Advisory Opinion on States' Obligations Concerning Climate Change (2023), https://press.un.org/en/2023/ga12497.doc.htm (last visited Feb. 18, 2025).

[79] Gabčíkovo-Nagymaros Project (Hungary v. Slovakia), Judgment, 1997 I.C.J. Rep. (Sept. 25).

[80] Pulp Mills on the River Uruguay (Argentina v. Uruguay), Judgment, 2010 I.C.J. Rep. (Apr. 20).

[81] Legality of the Threat or Use of Nuclear Weapons, Advisory Opinion, 1996 I.C.J. Rep. (July 8).

[82] *Jessica C. Lawrence/Kevin Jon Heller*, The First Ecocentric Environmental War Crime: The Limits of Article 8 (2) (b) (iv) of the Rome Statute, 20 (1) Geo. Int'l Envtl. L. Rev. 61, 64, 65 (2007); *Stephen C. McCaffrey*, Criminalization of Environmental Protection, in: International Criminal Law 1013, 1014 (Cherif M. Bassiouni ed., 2008).

[83] See for instance, Principle 1 of the Rio Declaration: "Human beings are at the centre of concerns for sustainable development. They are entitled to a healthy and productive life in harmony with nature."

[84] *Stephen C. McCaffrey*, Criminalization of Environmental Protection 1013, 1014 (2008).

[85] *Philippe Sands*, International Environmental Litigation and its Future, 32 (5) U. Rich. L. Rev. 1619, 1633 (1999).

[86] Pulp Mills on the River Uruguay (Argentina v. Uruguay), Join Dissenting Opinion of Judges Al-Khasawneh and Simma, 2010 I.C.J. Rep., ¶ 25 (Apr. 20).

on several occasions, it concluded in its Advisory Opinion on the Legality of Nuclear Weapons that the use of nuclear weapons cannot be prohibited on the basis of environmental considerations.[87]

Furthermore, in 1993, the ICJ established a Chamber for Environmental Matters, however, not a single environmental case had been referred to the Chamber in its 13 years of existence until 2006.[88] Due to two major impediments regarding the adjudication of environmental crimes, the ICJ cannot afford effective environmental protection. Firstly, pursuant to Article 34 (1) ICJ Statute the Court's jurisdiction is limited to disputes between states thereby excluding individuals, corporations, and other non-governmental organisations from having *locus standi*.[89] Thus, only one state which has sustained major environmental harm is able to sue the responsible state. This almost occurred in 2005 when Tuvalu threatened to sue the US for damages before the International Court of Justice due to its contribution to climate change.[90] However, environmental degradation is sometimes caused or at least condoned by states.[91] Thus, in the environmental context, the exclusion of NGOs, who are often the most committed supporters of environmental protection, of individual and transnational corporations appears particularly problematic.[92] Since the extension of the Court's personal jurisdiction to non-state actors would require states to relinquish their sovereignty, it would appear to be rather unrealistic for this to happen in the foreseeable future.[93]

Secondly, the ICJ's contentious jurisdiction only arises by agreement, requiring either a special agreement of both litigant states, the inclusion of a compromissory clause in an international treaty or the general recognition of the ICJ's compulsory

[87] *Ole W. Pedersen*, An International Environmental Court and International Legalism, 24 (3) Journal of Environmental Law 547, 550 (2012).

[88] International Court of Justice, Chambers and Committees, https://www.icj-cij.org/en/chambers-and-committees (last visited Feb. 18, 2025); *Philippe Sands/Jacqueline Peel*, Principles of International Environmental Law 180, 181 (2018); *Stephen Hockman*, An International Court for the Environment, 1, 1 Envtl. L. Rev. 1, 2, 3 (2008).

[89] *Alfred Rest*, Envtl. Pol'y & L., 38 (1999); *Mark Drumbl*, International Human Rights, International Humanitarian Law and Environmental Security: Can the International Criminal Court Bridge the Gaps?, 6 (2) ILSA J. INT'L & COMP. L. 305, 327 fn. 84 (2000); *Kenneth F. McCallion/H. Rajan Sharma*, Geo. Wash. J. Int'l L. & Econ. 359 (2000).

[90] See *Rebecca Elizabeth Jacobs*, Treading Deep Waters: Substantive Law Issues in Tuvalu's Threat to Sue the United States in the International Court of Justice, 14 Pac. Rim L & Pol'y J. 103 (2005).

[91] *Peggy Rodgers Kalas*, Colorado Journal of International Environmenal Law and Policy 208 (2001).

[92] Id.

[93] *Alfred Rest*, Envtl. Pol'y & L., 38 (1999); *Peggy Rodgers Kalas*, Colorado Journal of International Environmenal Law and Policy 208 (2001).

jurisdiction.[94] However, the recognition of the ICJ's compulsory jurisdiction is rather the exception than the rule.[95] Instead, referring a dispute to the ICJ usually requires the consent of all state parties in each individual case.[96] However, concerning environmental disputes it appears unlikely for polluting states to voluntarily subject themselves to the jurisdiction of the ICJ.[97] Sands even goes as far as to say that the consent requirement is the reason why the establishment of the Chamber for Environmental Matters ultimately proved unsuccessful.[98]

ee) Permanent Court of Arbitration (PCA)

Established in 1899, the Permanent Court of Arbitration (*hereinafter* PCA) is an intergovernmental organisation with currently 122 Contracting Parties[99], which is the oldest international forum for resolving international disputes.[100] As dispute resolution services the PCA offers three of the dispute resolution methods listed in Article 33 UN Charta, including arbitration, mediation and conciliation.[101] While mediation and conciliation produce non-binding decisions enabling the parties to reject the suggested settlement, arbitration adopts legally binding decisions.[102] The PCA is a popular forum for environmental dispute resolution for multilateral treaties and other agreements pertaining to natural resources and the environment[103] and intends to actively promote and participate in the evolvement of international environmental law.[104] In 2001, the PCA adopted the PCA Optional Rules for Arbitration of Disputes Relating to the Environment and/or Natural Resources and in 2002 the PCA Optional Rules for Conciliation of Disputes Relating to the Environment and/or Natural Resources, which is the most comprehensive set of proce-

---

[94] Statute of the International Court of Justice art. 36 (1) and (2), Oct. 24, 1945, 1 U.N.T.S. XVI; *Philippe Sands/Jacqueline Peel*, Principles of International Environmental Law 181 (2018).

[95] *Philippe Sands/Jacqueline Peel*, Principles of International Environmental Law 181 (2018).

[96] Id.; *Peggy Rodgers Kalas*, Colorado Journal of International Environmenal Law and Policy 207, 208 (2001).

[97] *Mark Drumbl*, ILSA J. INT'L & COMP. L. 327 fn. 84 (2000).

[98] *Philippe Sands/Jacqueline Peel*, Principles of International Environmental Law 190 (2018).

[99] Permanent Court of Arbitration, Contracting Parties, https://pca-cpa.org/en/about/introduction/contracting-parties/ (last visited Feb. 18, 2025).

[100] *Sean Murphy*, Geo. Wash. J. Int'l L. & Econ. 348 (2000).

[101] Permanent Court of Arbitration, Dispute Resolution Services, https://pca-cpa.org/en/services/ (last visited Feb. 18, 2025).

[102] *Philippe Sands/Jacqueline Peel*, Principles of International Environmental Law 167, 178 (2018).

[103] Permanent Court of Arbitration, Environmental Dispute Resolution, https://pca-cpa.org/en/services/arbitration-services/environmental-dispute-resolution/ (last visited Feb. 18, 2025).

[104] Id.

dural rules for environmental dispute resolution currently available.[105] However, both sets of rules are optional and only apply upon the explicit consent of both parties or through incorporation in an agreement.[106] These Environmental Rules provide the Parties with an optional panel of specialised arbitrators with expertise in environmental law as well as a panel of environmental experts as potential expert witnesses.[107] The Environmental Rules apply to disputes between states, international organisations, and private parties, including NGOs and corporations.[108]

Due to its flexibility, the PCA offers numerous advantages in contrast to the rigid system of judicial settlement of the ICJ. By offering several dispute resolution services, the PCA provides the parties to the dispute with the choice to design their own arbitration process.[109] Although judicial settlement and arbitration are similar to the extent that both forms of dispute resolution produce a binding decision, international environmental treaties evidence a strong tendency towards the more flexible arbitration.[110] Furthermore, the state's willingness to cooperate and comply with decisions is significantly lower in the case of judicial settlement.[111] Particularly the flexibility of the place of arbitration at the PCA is beneficial in the environmental context, as this can facilitate the production of evidence.[112] Furthermore, unlike the ICJ, the PCA's competence is not limited to states, but also includes international organisations and private parties.[113] Additionally, due to the Environmental Rules for Arbitration the parties have access to a panel of highly specialised arbitrators and experts in environmental law, which guarantees a higher level of expertise compared to court proceedings before the ICJ, where judges are not experts in environmental law.

Due to this higher level of flexibility, particularly in contrast to the ICJ, some scholars envisage the PCA as a suitable interim forum for the resolution of environmental disputes pending the establishment of an International Environmental Court.[114]

---

[105] Id.

[106] PCA Optional Rules for Arbitration of Disputes Relating to Natural Resources and/or the Environment art. 1 (1), adopted in 2001; PCA Optional Rules for Conciliation of Disputes Relating to the Environment and/or Natural Resources art. 1 (2), adopted in 2002; *Tim Stephens*, International Courts and Environmental Protection 31, 32 (2009).

[107] Permanent Court of Arbitration, Environmental Dispute Resolution, https://pca-cpa.org/en/services/arbitration-services/environmental-dispute-resolution/ (last visited Feb. 18, 2025).

[108] *Alfred Rest*, Envtl. Pol'y & L., 40 (1999).

[109] Id.

[110] *Tim Stephens*, International Courts and Environmental Protection 28, 29 (2009).

[111] Id. at 34.

[112] *Alfred Rest*, Envtl. Pol'y & L., 40 (1999).

[113] Id.

[114] Id. at 40, 41; *Sean Murphy*, Geo. Wash. J. Int'l L. & Econ. 347–349 (2000).

However, the high flexibility and adaptability rendering arbitration an attractive dispute settlement mechanism, at the same time impedes its suitability as an adjudicator for environmental disputes. Firstly, similar to the ICJ, the PCA's jurisdiction is not compulsory but rather based on explicit agreement from both parties.[115] However, the lack of compulsory jurisdiction enables any party to evade the Court's jurisdiction. Secondly, although arbitration has become much closer to judicial settlement over the years, arbitration is still primarily envisaged as a form of private settlement exclusively intended to attain justice between the parties.[116] However, environmental disputes are rarely confined to the parties of the dispute, but mostly involve the interests of other actors.[117] Furthermore, the fact that the arbitration process predominantly focuses on the dispute resolution between the relevant parties rather than focusing on the environmental issue as such, impedes the normative development of international environmental law.[118] This is also exacerbated by the fact that the decisions produced in the *inter partes* process remain completely confidential unless otherwise agreed upon.[119] By contrast, permanent international courts are more independent in rendering a decision which not only focuses on the disputants' interests but also on the public interest of contributing to the evolvement of international environmental law.[120]

Hence, particularly due to the lack of compulsory jurisdiction, the PCA only inadequately affords global environmental protection. Similarly, the International Court of Environmental Arbitration and Conciliation (ICEAC), designed to settle environmental disputes submitted by states, natural or legal persons through conciliation and arbitration, lacks compulsory jurisdiction and requires the parties to the dispute to consent to its jurisdiction and is, therefore, an inadequate general adjudicator for international environmental disputes.[121]

ff) Conclusion

Despite the plethora of international forums capable of resolving international environmental disputes, none of the pre-existing forums is sufficiently equipped to adjudicate on *transboundary* environmental disputes.[122] While the CJEU's juris-

[115] *Alfred Rest*, Envtl. Pol'y & L., 40 (1999); *Stephen Hockman*, Envtl. L. Rev. 2 (2008).

[116] *Tim Stephens*, International Courts and Environmental Protection 35 (2009).

[117] Id.

[118] Id. at 35, 36.

[119] *Ole W. Pedersen*, Journal of Environmental Law 552 (2012); *Stephen Hockman*, Envtl. L. Rev. 2 (2008); *Tim Stephens*, International Courts and Environmental Protection 35 (2009).

[120] *Tim Stephens*, International Courts and Environmental Protection 36 (2009).

[121] *Susan M. Hinde*, The International Environmental Court: Its Broad Jurisdiction as a Possible Fatal Flaw, 32 Hofstra L. Rev. 727, 746 (2003); *Peggy Rodgers Kalas*, Colorado Journal of International Envirοnmenal Law and Policy 213, 214 (2001).

[122] Similar *Peggy Rodgers Kalas*, Colorado Journal of International Environmenal Law and Policy 242 (2001).

diction is geographically limited, ITLOS and the WTO Dispute Settlement Body appear inadequate adjudicators of environmental disputes due to their limited subject matter jurisdiction or clear bias in favour of international trade. Thus, the two most relevant international forums concerning the adjudication of international environmental disputes are the ICJ and the PCA. However, both institutions lack compulsory jurisdiction and thus fully rely upon the consent of both parties. Additionally, the ICJ only grants states *locus standi* excluding private party, such as individuals, corporations or NGOs from its jurisdiction.

3. Research findings

In conclusion, international environmental law is, due to institutional and normative fragmentation, not a uniform body of law. Weak implementation and compliance at the national level as well as the lack of an international judicial system hamper effective global environmental protection. This is particularly exacerbated by the lack of liability regimes for transboundary environmental damage. Thus, despite significant progress over the past century, the environment is at stake now more than ever and its inadequate protection through modern international environmental law is becoming more and more apparent.

II. International humanitarian law

Environmental protection is further afforded by international humanitarian law. International humanitarian law, also referred to as '*jus in bello*', encompasses all rules of international law regulating the protection of non-belligerent actors as well as the limitation of the means and methods of warfare.[123] Concerning the sources of law, international humanitarian law primarily consists of treaty law and customary rules.[124] In the environmental context, international humanitarian law becomes particularly relevant as military activities during armed conflicts often incur significant environmental harm, which has been evidenced by conflicts such as in Vietnam or Afghanistan.[125] Under international humanitarian law, two conventions specifically relating to environmental harm during armed conflicts particularly require a mention.

[123] *Mary Ellen O'Connell*, Historical Development and Legal Basis, in: The Handbook of International Humanitarian Law 20, 21 (Dieter Fleck ed., 2021).

[124] ICRC, Advisory Service on International Humanitarian Law (2004), https://www.icrc.org/en/doc/assets/files/other/what_is_ihl.pdf (last visited Feb. 18, 2025).

[125] *Philippe Sands/Jacqueline Peel*, Principles of International Environmental Law 828 (2018).

Firstly, the 1977 Convention on the Prohibition of Military or Any Hostile Uses of Environmental Modification (*hereinafter* ENMOD Convention)[126] and secondly, the 1977 Additional Protocol I to the 1949 Geneva Conventions[127] (*hereinafter* AP I). Article I (1) ENMOD Convention prohibits signatory States "to engage in military or any other hostile use of environmental modification techniques having widespread, long-lasting or severe effects as the means of destruction, damage or injury to any other State Party"[128]. By 'environmental modification techniques' the Convention means "any technique for changing – through the deliberate manipulation of natural processes – the dynamics, composition or structure of the earth, including its biota, lithosphere, hydrosphere and atmosphere, or of outer space"[129]. The ENMOD Convention was established in reaction to the Vietnam War where the US army deployed large amounts of chemical defoliants and contemplated deploying further military tactics aimed at modifying the environment, such as provoking tsunamis or earthquakes.[130] As such, by only applying to the very specific situation of military environmental modification techniques the subject matter of the ENMOD Convention is very limited and does not cover today's prevalent forms of industrial environmental destruction.[131] Thus, it only affords very limited environmental protection.

In 1977, a war crime establishing individual criminal liability for environmental destruction during warfare was enshrined in Articles 35 (3), 55 (1) AP I, prohibiting the use of "methods or means of warfare which are intended, or may be expected, to cause widespread, long-term and severe damage to the natural environment"[132]. Due to the wide recognition amongst State Parties, Articles 35 (3) and 55 (1) AP I are understood as rules of international customary law.[133] While Article 35 (3) AP I prohibiting "methods or means of warfare which are intended, or may be expected, to cause widespread, long-term and severe damage to the natural environment", is considered the first inherently ecocentric provision[134], Article 55 (1) AP I includes an anthropocentric reference by requiring environmentally detrimental warfare to

[126] Convention on the Prohibition of Military or Any Hostile Uses of Environmental Modification, Dec. 10, 1976, 1108 U.N.T.S. 151.

[127] See Protocol Additional to the Geneva Conventions of 12 August 1949, and Relating to the Protection of Victims of International Armed Conflicts (Protocol I), adopted on June 8, 1977, 1125 U.N.T.S. 3.

[128] Art. I (1) ENMOD Convention.

[129] Art. II ENMOD Convention.

[130] UNEP, Protecting the Environment During Armed Conflict: An Inventory and Analysis of International Law 12 (2009).

[131] Id.

[132] Art. 35 (3) AP I.

[133] *Philippe Sands/Jacqueline Peel*, Principles of International Environmental Law 835 (2018).

[134] UNEP, Protecting the Environment 11 (2009).

"prejudice the health or survival of the population".[135] The reasoning and repercussions concerning the mixed ecocentric and anthropocentric approach in Article 35 (3) and 55 (1) AP I are disputed.[136]

In contrast to Article I (1) ENMOD Convention, which only requires 'widespread, long-lasting *or* severe' damage in alternative fashion, Articles 35 (3), 55 (1) AP I cumulatively presuppose 'widespread, long-lasting *and* severe' damage to the natural environment. This discrepancy is due to the fact that the Additional Protocol I not only criminalises intentional environmental destruction, but also incidental, albeit foreseeable, environmental damage, as opposed to the ENMOD Convention, which only proscribes intentional environmental degradation.[137] By requiring the triple standard cumulatively the Protocol sets a significantly higher threshold excluding all but the most egregious cases of environmental harm.[138]

This is further exacerbated by the ambiguity evolving around the three criteria, which are left undefined under the Protocol.[139] Thus, Articles 35 (3) and 55 (1) AP I only afford very limited environmental protection due to their significantly high and ambiguous material threshold.[140] Additionally, Articles 35 (3), 55 (1) AP I are restricted to international armed conflicts[141], thereby leaving environmental damage during peacetime or non-international armed conflicts unaddressed. This appears particularly problematic in the environmental context, as non-international conflicts are the prevalent type of conflicts these days[142] and most incidents of large-scale environmental harm occur during peacetime.[143]

---

[135] *Michael Bothe*, Protection of the Environment in Relation to Armed Conflicts, in: The Handbook of International Humanitarian Law 346 (Dieter Fleck ed., 2021).

[136] Id.

[137] *Gerhard Werle/Florian Jeßberger*, Principles of International Criminal Law para. 1450 (4th ed., 2020); *Yoram Dinstein*, Protection of the Environment in International Armed Conflict, 5 Max Planck Yearbook of United Nations Law 523, 540, 541 (2001); *Ines Peterson*, The Natural Environment in Times of Armed Conflict: A Concern for International War Crimes Law?, 22 (2) Leiden Journal of International Law 325, 329 (2009).

[138] *Michael N. Schmitt*, Green War: An Assessment of the Environmental Law of International Armed Conflict, 22 Yale Journal of International Law 1, 71 (1997); UNEP, Protecting the Environment 11 (2009).

[139] *Michael N. Schmitt*, Yale Journal of International Law, 71 (1997); UNEP, Protecting the Environment 11 (2009).

[140] *Michael Bothe*, Protection of the Environment in Relation to Armed Conflicts 346 (2021).

[141] See Art. 1 (3) AP I in conjunction with Geneva Convention Relative to the Protection of Civilian Persons in Time of War art. 2, Aug. 12, 1949, 75 U.N.T.S. 287. No equivalent provision is provided by Protocol II pertaining to non-international armed conflicts.

[142] UNEP, Protecting the Environment 4 (2009); *Carl E. Bruch*, All's Not Fair in (Civil) War: Criminal Liability for Environmental Damage in Internal Armed Conflict, 25 (3) Vermont Law Review 695, 720, 739 (2001); *Jessica C. Lawrence/Kevin Jon Heller*, Geo. Int'l Envtl. L. Rev. 85 (2007).

Hence, both Article I (1) ENMOD Convention as well as Articles 35 (3) and 55 (1) AP I are weak legal instruments which only inadequately afford global environmental protection. In addition to that, no international court is tasked with the enforcement of these two legal instruments.

III. International human rights law

Environmental protection is further afforded by international human rights law. The 1972 Stockholm Declaration first emphasised the interconnectedness between a healthy environment and human rights by having proclaimed that "[b]oth aspects of a man's environment, the natural and the man-made, are essential to his well-being and to the enjoyment of basic human rights – even the right to life itself"[144]. In Principle 1, the Stockholm Declaration further declared that: "Man has the fundamental right to freedom, equality and adequate conditions of life, in an environment of a quality that permits a life of dignity and well-being, and he bears a solemn responsibility to protect and improve the environment for present and future generations". Principle 1 of the Rio Declaration further held an anthropocentric approach by stating that "Human beings are at the centre of concerns for sustainable development. They are entitled to a healthy and productive life in harmony with nature."[145] Additionally, the 1998 Aarhus Convention recognised in its Preamble "that every person has the right to live in an environment adequate to his or her health and well-being".[146] In 2019, the UN Special Rapporteur on Human Rights and the Environment revealed that 80 per cent of the UN Member States, that is 156 out of 193, enshrined the right to a safe, clean, healthy and sustainable environment in their constitutions.[147] The 2008 Ecuadorian Constitution went even further by ascribing the environment itself rights stipulating that "Nature, or Pacha Mama, where life is reproduced and occurs, has the right to integral respect for its existence and for the maintenance and regeneration of its life cycles, structure, functions and evolutionary processes"[148]. More recently, on 28 July 2022 the UN General As-

---

[143] *Mohammed Saif-Alden Wattad*, Fordham Environmental Law Review 281, 282 (2009); *Liemertje Julia Sieders*, The Battle of Realities: the Case for and Against the Inclusion of 'Ecocide' in the ICC Rome Statute, RIDP 29, 34 (2020).

[144] Declaration of the United Nations Conference on the Human Environment, Report of the UN Conference on the Human Environment, at 3, U.N. Doc. A/CONF.48/Rev.1 (1972).

[145] Principle 1 Rio Declaration on Environment and Development, at 1, U.N. Doc. A/CONF.151/26 (Vol. I) (1992).

[146] Convention on Access to Information, Public Participation in Decision-Making and Access to Justice in Environmental Matters, June 25, 1998, 2161 U.N.T.S. 447.

[147] G.A., Report of the Special Rapporteur on the Issue of Human Rights Obligations Relating to the Enjoyment of a Safe, Clean, Healthy and Sustainable Environment, at para. 13, U.N. Doc. A/HRC/43/53 (2019).

[148] Constitución Política de la República del Ecuador [Constitution], Oct. 20, 2008, Title II, Ch. 7, art. 71 (Ecuador).

sembly declared in a historic resolution "access to a clean, healthy and sustainable environment, a universal human right"[149]. Despite being not legally binding, the resolution is expected to act as a catalyst for more institutions to enshrine such a right.

However, even if the resolution were binding, an international human rights court to globally enforce a right to a clean and healthy environment does not exist. Thus, enforcing human rights is entrusted to human rights courts based on regional human rights conventions, including the European Court of Human Rights, the Inter-American Court of Human Rights and the African Court of Human and Peoples' Rights. However, only the European Court of Human Rights appears to have *sustainably* addressed environmental matters so far.[150]

In accordance with Articles 33 and 34 of the European Convention on Human rights (*hereinafter* ECHR)[151], the European Court of Human Rights hears applications submitted by states, individuals, non-governmental organisations and groups of individuals concerning alleged violations of the ECHR. Although Article 37 of the Charter of Fundamental Rights of the European Union stipulates that "[a] high level of environmental protection and the improvement of the quality of the environment must be integrated into the policies of the Union", the ECHR currently lacks a right to a healthy environment. Thus, the case law of the European Court of Human Rights, which is particularly rich in environmental matters, only refers to existing human rights such as Article 2 (right to life) or Article 8 (privacy).[152] However, on 29 September 2021, the Parliamentary Assembly of the Council of Europe proposed a draft new protocol to the ECHR including the right to a safe, clean, healthy and sustainable environment.[153] According to the European Parliament, 19 out of 27 EU Member States have incorporated this right into their con-

---

[149] United Nations, UN General Assembly Declares Access to Clean and Healthy Environment a Universal Human Right (2022), https://news.un.org/en/story/2022/07/1123482 (last visited Feb. 18, 2025).

[150] See the most relevant environmental cases ruled by the European Court of Human Rights, European Court of Human Rights, Factsheet, Environment and the Eurpoean Convention on Human Rights (2022); *Philippe Sands/Jacqueline Peel*, Principles of International Environmental Law 189 (2018).

[151] Convention for the Protection of Human Rights and Fundamental Freedoms, Nov. 4, 1950, Europ. T.S. No. 5, 213 U.N.T.S. 221.

[152] European Court of Human Rights, Guide to the Case-Law of the European Court of Human Rights (2022); European Court of Human Rights, Factsheet (2022).

[153] Parliamentary Assembly Council of Europe, The Right to a Healthy Environment: PACE Proposes Draft of a New Protocol to the European Convention on Human Rights (2021), https://pace.coe.int/en/news/8452/the-right-to-a-healthy-environment-pace-proposes-draft-of-a-new-protocol-to-the-european-convention-on-human-rights- (last visited Feb. 18, 2025).

stitutions.[154] The remaining 8 Member States, including Austria and Germany have ratified the Aarhus Convention, which also contains this right.[155] In its June 2021 resolution on the EU biodiversity strategy for 2030, the European Parliament considered "that the right to a healthy environment should be recognised in the Charter and that the EU should lead the initiative to recognise a similar right internationally".[156] Thus, it is to be hoped that the EU will incorporate a right to a safe, clean, healthy and sustainable environment into the ECHR, following this international trend. However, the scope of the jurisdiction of the European Court of Human Rights is severely limited as it requires the previous exhaustion of all local remedies prior to an individual application to the Court.[157]

Furthermore, the available regional human rights courts are all restricted to a specific regional territory and thus cannot promote global environmental protection.[158] Thus, human rights law lacks an institutional court enforcing environmental human rights, such as the access to a clean, healthy and sustainable environment. Furthermore, human rights law holds a strictly anthropocentric view only affording environmental protection as a means of safeguarding human beings.[159]

In conclusion, international human rights law only inadequately affords global environmental protection.

IV. International Criminal Law

Environmental protection is further afforded by criminal law. However, this thesis will not assess the extent to which domestic criminal law affords environmental protection, as effective *global* environmental protection can only be afforded at the international level. At the time the Stockholm Declaration was adopted, it was already recognised that environmental issues were a global concern[160] which do not

---

[154] European Parliament, A Universal Right to a Healthy Environment (2021), https://www.europarl.europa.eu/RegData/etudes/ATAG/2021/698846/EPRS_ATA(2021)698846_EN.pdf (last visited Feb. 18, 2025).

[155] Id.

[156] European Parliament Resolution of 9 June 2021 on the EU Biodiversity Strategy for 2030: Bringing Nature Back into our Lives, Eur, Parl. Res. P9_TA(2012)0277, ¶ 143 (June 9, 2021).

[157] See Article 35 (1) ECHR.

[158] *Ricardo Pereira*, After the ICC Office of the Prosecutor's 2016 Policy Paper on Case Selection and Prioritisation: Towards an International Crime of Ecocide?, 31 Criminal Law Forum 179, 206 (2020).

[159] *Tim Stephens*, International Courts and Environmental Protection 53 (2009); *Anastacia Greene*, The Campaign to Make Ecocide an International Crime: Quixotic Quest or Moral Imperative?, 30 (3) Fordham Environmental Law Review 1, 46 (2019).

[160] See Preamble (7) of the Stockholm Declaration: "A growing class of environmental problems, because they are regional or global in extent or because they affect the common

respect territorial borders and thus can only be effectively addressed at the international level.[161] As stated by INTERPOL and UNEP, "[e]nvironmental crime cannot be tackled in isolation: it calls for global and cooperative effort".[162] This becomes particularly obvious with transboundary environmental damage, such as transboundary pollution.[163] Due to their ubiquitous impacts environmental crimes are international crimes *par excellence.*[164] However, even environmental harm confined to a certain territory eventually entails global impacts.[165] For instance, although the deforestation of the Amazonian rainforest for the purposes of cattle farming and soya growing is restricted to this particular region, its repercussions are, indubitably, global.[166] Additionally, the majority of environmental harm is perpetrated in the Global South by subsidiary companies of multinational corporations headquartered in the Global North necessitating international criminalisation.[167] For these reasons, it is evident that domestic criminalisation of large-scale environmental damage is insufficient. Instead, international criminalisation of environmental degradation is necessary. However, with respect to *substantive* criminal law at the international level, two categories can be distinguished, namely international criminal law and transnational criminal law. In the following the distinction between both categories will be explained prior examining the extent to which both categories of criminal law afford environmental protection.

1. International Criminal Law vs. Transnational Criminal Law

With respect to substantive criminal law at the international level, there are two types of international crime: (1) crimes involving transboundary harm directly

---

international realm, will require extensive co-operation among nations and action by international organizations in the common interest"; *Frédéric Mégret*, Colum. J. Envtl. L. 239 (2011).

[161] *Philippe Sands/Jacqueline Peel*, Principles of International Environmental Law 4 (2018).

[162] INTERPOL/UNEP, Strategic Report, Environment, Peace and Security, A Convergence of Threats 8 (2016).

[163] Documents of the Forty-Eighth Session, [1996] 2 Y.B. Int'l L. Comm'n 24 ¶ 32, U.N. Doc. A/CN.4/SER.A/1996/Add.1 (Part 1).

[164] *Frédéric Mégret*, Colum. J. Envtl. L. 241 (2011); *Audrey Crasson*, The Case of Chevron in Ecuador: The Need for an International Crime Against the Environment?, 9 (3) Amsterdam Law Forum 29, 45 (2017).

[165] Documents of the Forty-Eighth Session, [1996] 2 Y.B. Int'l L. Comm'n 24 ¶ 32, U.N. Doc. A/CN.4/SER.A/1996/Add.1 (Part 1).

[166] *Matt Sandy*, The Amazon Rainforest Is Nearly Gone, We Went to the Front Lines to See If It Could Be Saved, Time, Sept. 12, 2019, https://time.com/amazon-rainforest-disappearing/.

[167] *Frédéric Mégret*, Colum. J. Envtl. L. 240 (2011); EUROPOL, Environmental Crime in the Age of Climate Change 7 (2022).

established under international law and (2) crimes involving transboundary harm which are enshrined in domestic law pursuant to international law.[168]

Although the distinction between these two groups of international crimes is widely acknowledged, both categories or crime are referred to by a variety of terms.[169] For the purpose of clarity, in this thesis international offences enshrined in domestic law pursuant to international law will be referred to as 'transnational crimes' (transnational criminal law), whereas international offences criminalised and enforced directly under international law will be referred to as 'crimes under international law' or 'core crimes' (international criminal law). This distinction is also in line with other languages, such as German ('*Völkerstrafrecht*' as opposed to '*Internationales Strafrecht*') or French ('*droit international penal*' and '*droit penal international*').[170] In accordance with the Preamble of the Rome Statute, both categories of crimes will be dealt with under the general heading of "international crimes"[171] in this thesis. Nevertheless, the distinction between transnational crimes and crimes under international law is fluid, as transnational crimes may become crimes under international law upon incorporation into international criminal law.[172]

Transnational criminal law consists of a variety of international treaties containing transboundary crimes, such as, for instance, environmental treaties under international environmental law, which obligate states to transpose these crimes into

---

168 *Gerhard Werle/Florian Jeßberger*, Principles of International Criminal Law para. 164 (2020).

169 *Kai Ambos/Anina Timmermann*, Neue transnationale Verbrechen für das VStGB?, in: Völkerstrafrechtspolitik 306 (Christoph Safferling/Stefan Kirsch eds., 2014) ("völkerrechtliche Kernverbrechen" and "transnationale Verbrechen"); *Gerhard Werle/Florian Jeßberger*, Principles of International Criminal Law para. 164 (2020) ("crimes under international law" and "treaty-based crimes"); *Robert Cryer*, The Doctrinal Foundations of International Criminalization, in: International Criminal Law 107 (Cherif M. Bassiouni ed., 2008) ("core crimes" and "transnational crimes"); *Robert Cryer*, et al., An Introduction to International Criminal Law and Procedure 4 (4th ed., 2019) ("core crimes" and "transnational crimes"); *Claus Kreß*, International Criminal Law (2009), https://opil.ouplaw.com/view/10.1093/law:epil/9780199231690/law-9780199231690-e1423#law-9780199231690-e1423 (last visited Feb. 18, 2025) ("international criminal law stricto sensu" and "supranational criminal law"); *William A. Schabas*, An Introduction to the International Criminal Court 75 (6th ed., 2020) ("transnational/treaty crimes" and "crimes within the jurisdiction of the International Criminal Court"); *Antonio Cassese*, et al., Cassese's International Criminal Law 21 (3rd ed., 2013) (generally referring to "international crimes").

170 *Robert Cryer*, et al., An Introduction to International Criminal Law and Procedure 5, 6 (2019).

171 The Preamble of the Rome Statute coins the term 'international crimes' and thereby refers to the core crimes as well as other transnational crimes going beyond Article 5 Rome Statute (Rome Statute Preamble (6), July 17, 1998, 2187 U.N.T.S. 3); similar *Gerhard Werle/Florian Jeßberger*, Principles of International Criminal Law para. 164 (2020).

172 *Carsten Stahn*, A Critical Introduction to International Criminal Law 21 (2019).

domestic criminal law.[173] Thus, transnational crimes are prosecuted under domestic law.[174] Concerning the implementation of the crimes in domestic law, the state obligations included in these treaties vary greatly depending on the time they were concluded and the respective parties who concluded the treaty.[175]

By contrast, international criminal law encompasses crimes directly enshrined in international treaties, without further need of domestic implementation.[176] International criminal law is a relatively new field of public international law combining two fields of law, international law and criminal law.[177] Since both areas of law could not be more different, this combination gives rise to tension.[178] Whereas international law governs the relations of states as legal entities[179], criminal law establishes individual criminal liability.[180] International criminal law draws upon criminal law as it establishes individual criminal liability, the crimes, however, are derived from international law.[181] International criminal law as a distinct field of law has its birthplace in Nuremberg in the aftermath of the Second World War.[182] In 2002, the first permanent court, the International Criminal Court (*hereinafter* 'ICC'), was established in The Hague marking a historical turning point in the history of international criminal law.[183] The creation of the ICC was based on the Rome Statute, which constitutes the main legal source of modern international

---

[173] *Antonio Cassese*, et al., Cassese's International Criminal Law 19 (2013); *Robert Cryer*, The Doctrinal Foundations of International Criminalization 109 (2008); *Claus Kreß*, International Criminal Law (2009), https://opil.ouplaw.com/view/10.1093/law:epil/9780199231690/law-9780199231690-e1423#law-9780199231690-e1423 (last visited Feb. 18, 2025); *Robert Cryer*, et al., An Introduction to International Criminal Law and Procedure 5, 6 (2019).

[174] *Robert Cryer*, et al., An Introduction to International Criminal Law and Procedure 319, 320 (2019).

[175] *Cherif M. Bassiouni*, International Crimes: The Ratione Materiae of International Criminal Law, in: International Criminal Law 158 (Cherif M. Bassiouni ed., 2008).

[176] *Claus Kreß*, International Criminal Law (2009), https://opil.ouplaw.com/view/10.1093/law:epil/9780199231690/law-9780199231690-e1423#law-9780199231690-e1423 (last visited Feb. 18, 2025); *Robert Cryer*, The Doctrinal Foundations of International Criminalization 108 (2008).

[177] *Robert Cryer*, et al., An Introduction to International Criminal Law and Procedure 3 (2019).

[178] *Christoph Safferling*, Internationales Strafrecht § 4 para. 4 (2011); *Robert Cryer*, et al., An Introduction to International Criminal Law and Procedure 3 (2019).

[179] *Robert Jennings/Arthur Watts*, Oppenheim's International Law 5–7 (9th ed., 2008).

[180] *Christoph Safferling*, Internationales Strafrecht § 4 para. 1 (2011); *Robert Cryer*, et al., An Introduction to International Criminal Law and Procedure 3 (2019).

[181] *Gerhard Werle/Florian Jeßberger*, Principles of International Criminal Law para. 97 (2020); *Antonio Cassese*, et al., Cassese's International Criminal Law 3 (2013).

[182] *Mark Drumbl*, Atrocity, Punishment and International Law 3 (2007); *Antonio Cassese*, et al., Cassese's International Criminal Law 4 (2013); see on the creation of the ICC *William A. Schabas*, An Introduction to the International Criminal Court 1–23 (2020); *Cenap Çakmak*, A Brief History of International Criminal Law and International Criminal Court (2017).

[183] *Christoph Safferling*, Internationales Strafrecht § 4 para. 60 (2011).

criminal law comprising the four core crimes, namely war crimes (Article 8), crimes against humanity (Article 7), genocide (Article 6) and crime of aggression (Article 8 bis).[184] Thus, in contrast to transnational criminal law, international criminal law is composed of a uniform body of law, the Rome Statute, which is enforced through an international court, the ICC.

2. Environmental protection under Transnational Criminal Law

With respect to transnational criminal law, the majority of modern international environmental conventions forming part of international environmental law, including, for instance, the Convention on International Trade in Endangered Species (*hereinafter* "CITES") include penal provisions mandating the signatory parties to create respective criminal provisions in domestic law.[185] This is also the current approach taken by the EU in terms of environmental protection. On 19 November 2008, the EU Crime Directive[186] on the protection of the environment through criminal law was adopted intending to tackle environmental protection more effectively than currently afforded by international environmental law or civil law. By requiring EU Member States to implement a minimum standard of environmental crimes at the national level, the Environmental Crime Directive[187] was the first significant supranational, albeit regional, legal document to harmonise domestic environmental criminal law across the EU. The EU Crime Directive ensured that a corresponding set of environmental crimes was implemented as crimes in all EU Member States.[188] However, the Directive only required Member States to "take the necessary measures to ensure that the offences […] are punishable by effective, proportionate and dissuasive criminal penalties"[189] and thus did not require the

[184] *Gerhard Werle/Florian Jeßberger*, Principles of International Criminal Law para. 82 (2020).

[185] See Convention on International Trade in Endangered Species of Wild Fauna and Flora art. VIII ¶ 1, Mar. 3, 1973, 993 U.N.T.S. 243; see further Basel Convention on the Control of Transboundary Movements of Hazardous Wastes and Their Disposal art. 9 (5), Mar. 22, 1989, 1673 U.N.T.S. 57; International Convention for the Regulation of Whaling article IX (1), Dec. 2, 1946, 161 U.N.T.S. 72; see for further examples, *Cho Byung-Sun*, Emergence of an International Environmental Criminal Law?, 19 (1) UCLA Journal of Environmental Law and Policy 11, 15 fn. 8, 16 fn. 9 (2000).

[186] Directive 2008/99/EC, of the European Parliament and of the Council of 19 November 2008 on the Protection of the Environment Through Criminal Law, art. 3, Nov. 19, 2008, 2008 O.J. (L 328).

[187] See for more information on the EU Environmental Crime Directive: *Ricardo Pereira*, Towards Effective Implementation of the EU Environmental Crime Directive? The Case of Illegal Waste Management and Trafficking Offences, 26 (2) Rev. Eur. Comp. & Int'l Envtl. L. 147 (2017).

[188] Directive 2008/99/EC, art. 3.

[189] Id. art. 5.

implementation of specific penalties. As such, sanction levels vary greatly amongst the EU States.[190]

Nevertheless, an evaluation of the 2008 EU Crime Directive conducted in 2019 and 2020 revealed significant limitations and enforcement gaps.[191] Consequently, the European Commission proposed a revised[192] EU Crime Directive on 15 December 2021 replacing the 2008 EU Crime Directive with the intention of enhancing the investigation and prosecution of environmental crimes. In this regard, the revised EU Crime Directive will contain an updated list of 20 environmental offences and provide harmonised levels of sanctions for individuals and legal persons, including, *inter alia,* prison terms, criminal fines as well as the reinstatement of the environment.[193] This proposal by the Commission forms part of the European Green Deal[194], yet hitherto the revised EU Crime Directive has not entered into force and is still being negotiated by the European Parliament and the European Council.[195] In the course of evaluating the 2008 EU Crime Directive, a preparatory survey conducted in the EU revealed that "87% of respondents agree that criminalisation of environmental offences is an effective way to ensure compliance with environmental law and that criminalisation should complement administrative sanctions and preventive measures".[196] On 12 May 2021, as part of the EU policy cycle to combat serious and organised crime the EU Council renewed its goal to prioritise

[190] Communication from the Commission to the European Parliament and the Council on Stepping Up the Fight Against Environmental Crime, at 2, COM (2021) 814 final (Dec. 15, 2021).

[191] See Commission Staff Working Document, Evaluation of the Directive 2008/99/EC of the European Parliament and of the Council of 19 November 2008 on the Protection of the Environment through Criminal Law (Environmental Crime Directive), SWD (2020) 259 final (part 1/2) (Oct. 28, 2020).

[192] Commission Proposal for a Directive of the European Parliament and of the Council on the Protection of the Environment through Criminal Law and Replacing Directive 2008/99/EC, COM (2021) 851 final (Dec. 15, 2021).

[193] European Council, Council Agrees Its Negotiating Mandate on the Environmental Crime Directive (2022), https://www.consilium.europa.eu/en/press/press-releases/2022/12/09/council-agrees-its-negotiating-mandate-on-the-environmental-crime-directive/ (last visited Feb. 18, 2025).

[194] European Commission, A European Green Deal, https://ec.europa.eu/info/strategy/priorities-2019-2024/european-green-deal_en (last visited Feb. 18, 2025).

[195] European Council, Council Agrees Its Negotiating Mandate on the Environmental Crime Directive (2022), https://www.consilium.europa.eu/en/press/press-releases/2022/12/09/council-agrees-its-negotiating-mandate-on-the-environmental-crime-directive/ (last visited Feb. 18, 2025).

[196] Commission Staff Working Document, Evaluation of the Directive 2008/99/EC of the European Parliament and of the Council of 19 November 2008 on the Protection of the Environment through Criminal Law (Environmental Crime Directive), at 133, SWD (2020) 259 final (part 2/2) (Oct. 28, 2020).

the fight against environmental crime for 2022 to 2025.[197] The recent developments in Europe mirror the increased political appetite to criminalise large-scale industrial environmental destruction through establishing treaty-based environmental crimes. However, international environmental treaties have been adopted in a piecemeal approach and only address specific environmental issues leaving many other environmental issues unaddressed. Furthermore, the adequate *implementation* of the crimes in domestic law as well as the *enforcement* of the crimes is entrusted to the states, which promotes inconsistent environmental regulations amongst the different states.[198] Thus, competing environmental laws allow corporations to evade stringent environmental standards by choosing to operate in countries with less stringent environmental laws and thereby promotes "ecological dumping"[199].[200]

Hence, primarily due to the lack of a generic environmental crime established in an international environmental treaty and the lack of an international judicial body to enforce transnational crimes, current transnational criminal law only inadequately affords global environmental protection.

3. Environmental protection under the current Rome Statute

In the following, the extent to which international criminal law, i. e. the current Rome Statute, affords global environmental protection will be examined.

Since the current Rome Statute lacks any distinct crime against the environment, environmental destruction can only be prosecuted by the ICC if the conduct in question amounts to of one of the four core crimes of the Rome Statute, including the crime of genocide (Article 6), crimes against humanity (Article 7), war crimes (Article 8) and the crime of aggression (Article 8 bis). However, due to its leadership requirement and its limitation to the use of armed force by a state against another state, the crime of aggression only plays a subordinate role in the context of environmental harm.[201] Hence, only the remaining three core crimes will be examined in this section.

In 2016, the Office of the ICC Prosecutor (*hereinafter* OTP) published a Policy Paper on Case Selection and Prioritisation[202] according to which the prosecution of

---

197 Council Conclusions Setting the EU's Priorities for the Fight Against Serious and Organised Crime for EMPACT 2022–2025, at 10, Council Conclusions 8665/2 (May 12, 2021).

198 *Frédéric Mégret*, Colum. J. Envtl. L. 238 (2011); *Robert Cryer*, et al., An Introduction to International Criminal Law and Procedure 321 (2019).

199 See on environmental dumping, *Michael Rauscher*, On Ecological Dumping, 46 Oxford Economic Papers 822 (1994).

200 *Frédéric Mégret*, Colum. J. Envtl. L. 238 (2011).

201 See *Matthew Gillett*, Eco-Struggles, in: Environmental Protection and Transitions from Conflict to Peace: Clarifying Norms, Principles, and Practices 227, 228 (Carsten Stahn, et al. eds., 2017).

202 Office of the Prosecutor, Policy Paper on Case Selection and Prioritisation (2016).

environmentally destructive activities falling under the scope of one of the four core crimes would be prioritised. In this document, the OTP stated that it "will give particular consideration to prosecuting Rome Statute crimes that are committed *by means of*, or that *result in*, *inter alia*, the destruction of the environment, the illegal exploitation of natural resources or the illegal dispossession of land".[203] Thus, environmental matters under the current Rome Statute may be addressed in two ways: firstly, to prosecute the core crimes committed '*by means of* [...] the destruction of the environment'; and secondly, to prosecute the core crimes which '*result* in [...] the destruction of the environment'. While in the former, the environment is used as a weapon causing human harm, in the latter the nature itself falls victim. Hence, the former scenario upholds an anthropocentric approach protecting human values, whereas the latter takes an ecocentric perspective aiming at protecting the environment itself.[204] Thus, the 2016 Policy Paper upholds the traditional distinction between anthropocentric and ecocentric perspectives. Although the 2016 Policy Paper did not expand the ICC's jurisdiction to a new generic environmental crime, it demonstrates the OTP's inclination to address environmental issues and contributed to the overall 'greening' of the current Rome Statute.[205]

a) Environmental war crime, Article 8 (2) (b) (iv) Rome Statute

According to the Preamble of the Rome Statute, the ICC was established "for the sake of the present and future generations"[206]. It goes without saying that large-scale environmental degradation is one of the most challenging topics for the present and future generations. Thus, it is surprising that Article 8 (2) (b) (iv) Rome Statute is the only provision under the current Rome Statute directly referring to conduct *resulting in* damage to the natural environmental as a crime under international criminal law. As such, Article 8 (2) (b) (iv) Rome Statute is the first ecocentric war crime taking a step forward compared to its predecessors Articles 35 (3), 55 (1) AP I and Article 1 ENMOD which were largely anthropocentric.[207] Since Article 8

---

[203] Id. at para. 41 (emphasis added).

[204] *Eliana Teresa Cusato*, Beyond Symbolism, 15 JICJ 491, 494 (2017).

[205] *Rosemary Mwanza*, Enhancing Accountability For Environmental Damage Under International Law: Ecocide As a Legal Fulfillment of Ecological Integrity, 19 (2) Melb. Journal of International Law 1, 13 (2018).

[206] Preamble (9) of the Rome Statute.

[207] *Michael N. Schmitt*, Yale Journal of International Law, 13, 14, 70 (1997) argues that the ENMOD convention holds an anthropocentric perspective as it only criminalises the use of the environment as a method of warfare but not the commission of environmental damage. While Article 55 (1) AP I is strictly anthropocentric requiring environmental damage intended or expected to "prejudice the health or survival of the population", Article 35 (3) AP I was the first provision which was not linked to human interests and thus for the first time introduced an ecocentric approach; *Yoram Dinstein*, Max Planck Yearbook of United Nations Law 531 (2001); *Jessica C. Lawrence/Kevin Jon Heller*, Geo. Int'l Envtl. L. Rev. 66, 67 (2007); *Ines Peterson*, Leiden Journal of International Law 334 (2009).

(2) (b) (iv) Rome Statute ensures environmental protection irrespective of harm to human interests and acknowledges the intrinsic[208] value of the environment itself, the provision is considered ecocentric.

Article 8 (2) (b) (iv) Rome Statute, second alternative, proscribes the act of "intentionally launching an attack in the knowledge that such attack will cause [...] widespread, long-term and severe damage to the natural environment, which would be clearly excessive in relation to the concrete and direct overall military advantage anticipated". However, neither Article 8 (2) (b) (iv) Rome Statute nor the Elements of Crime specify the meaning of 'natural environment'. The term 'natural environment' was derived from Articles 35 (3), 55 (1) AP I, which, however, did not include any definition thereof. Surprisingly, to date even international environmental law does not provide a general agreed-upon definition of 'environment'.[209] A perusal of environmental treaties displays that the protection of the 'environment' encompasses "flora and fauna, air, soil, water, vegetation, habitat, forests, marine living resources, ecosystems, organisms, climate and agriculture"[210]. However, the term 'environment' in its widest sense refers not only to the natural world, but also its interconnectedness to human life.[211] Yet, at first sight the inclusion of the add-on 'natural' in Article 8 (2) (b) (iv) Rome Statute gives rise to question as to whether its scope is restricted to natural elements precluding artificially modified natural elements by humans.[212] However, this assumption is to be refuted. According to the commentary pertaining to Article 55 AP I, "the concept of the natural environment should be understood in the widest sense to cover the biological environment in which a population is living".[213] Further, background materials concerning Article 26 of the Draft Code of Crimes, which also included the term 'natural environment', reveal that "the words 'natural environment' should be taken broadly to cover the environment of the human race and where the human race develops, as well as areas the preservation of which is of fundamental importance in protecting the environment." [214] Thus these words cover "the seas, the atmosphere, climate, forests and other plant cover, fauna, flora and other biological elements."[215]

---

[208] See *Michael N. Schmitt*, Yale Journal of International Law, 6 (1997).

[209] *Karen Hulme*, War Torn Environment 12 (2004); *Philippe Sands/Jacqueline Peel*, Principles of International Environmental Law 14–16 (2018); *Ines Peterson*, Leiden Journal of International Law 328 (2009).

[210] *Karen Hulme*, War Torn Environment 12 (2004).

[211] *Philippe Sands/Jacqueline Peel*, Principles of International Environmental Law 14 (2018); *Karen Hulme*, War Torn Environment 12 (2004).

[212] *Ines Peterson*, Leiden Journal of International Law 328 (2009).

[213] *Claude Pilloud/Jean De Preux*, Article 55, in: Commentary on the Additional Protocols of 8 June 1977 to the Geneva Conventions of 12 August 1949, para. 2126 (Yves Sandoz, et al. eds., 1987).

[214] Report of the Commission to the General Assembly on the Work of its Forty-Third Session, [1991] 2 Y.B. Int'l L. Comm'n 107 ¶ 4, U.N. Doc. A/CN.4/SER.A/1991/Add.1 (Part 2); see also *Yoram Dinstein*, Max Planck Yearbook of United Nations Law 534 (2001).

Hence, the term 'natural environment' in Article 8 (2) (b) (iv) Rome Statute does not exclusively refer to natural elements, but also to the inextricable link between living organisms and their surrounding inanimate environment and thus also includes artificially modified nature.[216]

aa) Limitations

Despite the strong symbolic value of recognising the intrinsic value of the environment as such, Article 8 (2) (b) (iv) Rome Statute is subjected to several limitations which severely restrict the afforded environmental protection.[217]

(1) International armed conflicts

The most severe restriction arises from the fact that the provision is confined to international armed conflicts. Thus, environmental destruction during non-international conflicts or peacetime is not prosecutable as an environmental war crime under Article 8 (2) (b) (iv) Rome Statute. Although this limitation is in line with customary international humanitarian law[218], excluding environmental destruction during non-international armed conflicts appears to be problematic, since nowadays non-international armed conflicts are the prevalent type of conflict.[219] In the context of environmental destruction this is further complicated by the reciprocal interconnectedness of environmental harm and non-international armed conflicts. The environment not only falls victim in armed conflicts[220], but at the same time the

[215] Report of the Commission to the General Assembly on the Work of its Forty-Third Session, [1991] 2 Y.B. Int'l L. Comm'n 107 ¶ 4, U.N. Doc. A/CN.4/SER.A/1991/Add.1 (Part 2); see also *Yoram Dinstein*, Max Planck Yearbook of United Nations Law 534 (2001).

[216] *Karen Hulme*, War Torn Environment 13 (2004); *Ines Peterson*, Leiden Journal of International Law 329 (2009); *Claude Pilloud/Jean De Preux*, Article 55 Art. 35 para. 1451 (1987).

[217] See generally *Jessica C. Lawrence/Kevin Jon Heller*, Geo. Int'l Envtl. L. Rev. (2007).

[218] *Gerhard Werle/Florian Jeßberger*, Principles of International Criminal Law para. 1455 (2020). This also corresponds to Sec. 11 (3) of the German Code of Crimes Against International Law [Völkerstrafgesetzbuch, VStGB], which only prohibits disproportionate environmental destruction during international armed conflicts.

[219] UNEP, Protecting the Environment 4 (2009); *Carl E. Bruch*, Vermont Law Review 720, 739 (2001); *Jessica C. Lawrence/Kevin Jon Heller*, Geo. Int'l Envtl. L. Rev. 85 (2007).

[220] This was already stated in Principle 24 of the Rio Declaration: "Warfare is inherently destructive of sustainable development. States shall therefore respect international law providing protection for the environment in times of armed conflict and cooperate in its further development, as necessary"; see for an analysis of the impacts of armed conflicts on the environment, UNEP, From Conflict to Peacebuilding: The Role of Natural Resources and the Environment (2009); see also *Regina Rauxloh*, The Role of International Criminal Law in Environmental Protection, in: Natural Resource Investment and Africa's Development 426–428 (Francis N. Botchway ed., 2011).

environment often gives reason for conflict.[221] The latter has been monitored by the UNEP having revealed in 2009 that at least 40% of all intrastate conflicts in the preceding 60 years had been linked to natural resources.[222] Most importantly, competition over natural resources complicated by resource scarcity due to environmental destruction and climate change coupled with rapid population growth ignites and prolongs non-international armed conflicts.[223] Thus, the exploitation of natural resources causing large-scale environmental degradation contributes not only to the outbreak, but also to the perpetuation of conflicts and the undermining of peacebuilding prospects.[224] This is further evidenced by the UN resolution titled "The role of diamonds in fuelling conflict: breaking the link between the illicit transaction of rough diamonds and armed conflict as a contribution to prevention and settlement of conflicts", which was adopted by the UN General Assembly on 12 February 2007.[225] The nexus between resource exploitation and non-international armed conflicts has also been recognised in several judgments of the ICC. In *Lubanga*, for instance, the ICC determined that resource exploitation in the Ituri region initiated the non-international armed conflict.[226] Similarly, the ICC's Office of the Prosecutor contended in *Ntaganda* that the protracted non-international armed conflict in the district of Ituri was fuelled by competition over the resources in this area.[227]

Since the global population is continuously increasing, the demand for resources steadily grows and environmental destruction occurs at an unprecedented pace, the number of non-international armed conflicts over natural resources is expected to proliferate in the near future. However, these cases will fall outside the premises of Article 8 (2) (b) (iv) Rome Statute. Hence, some propose the inclusion of an environmental war crime into Article 8 (2) (e) Rome Statute, which is applicable to non-

---

[221] See United Nations, Briefing UN Security Council on Humanitarian Effects of Environmental Degradation on Peace and Security (2020), https://www.unccd.int/news-stories/statements/briefing-un-security-council-humanitarian-effects-environmental-degradation (last visited Feb. 18, 2025); *Philippe Sands/Jacqueline Peel*, Principles of International Environmental Law 836, 837 (2018).

[222] UNEP, From Conflict to Peacebuilding 30 (2009).

[223] See United Nations, Briefing UN Security Council on Humanitarian Effects of Environmental Degradation on Peace and Security (2020), https://www.unccd.int/news-stories/statements/briefing-un-security-council-humanitarian-effects-environmental-degradation (last visited Feb. 18, 2025); UNEP, From Conflict to Peacebuilding 8, 9 (2009).

[224] UNEP, From Conflict to Peacebuilding 8–14 (2009).

[225] UN General Assembly, The Role of Diamonds in Fuelling Conflict: Breaking the Link Between the Illicit Transaction of Rough Diamonds and Armed Conflict as a Contribution to Prevention and Settlement of Conflicts, U.N. Doc. A/RES/61/28 (Feb. 12, 2007).

[226] Prosecutor v. Lubanga, ICC-01/04-01/06, Judgment Pursuant to Article 74 of the Statute, ¶ 71, 72 (Mar. 14, 2012).

[227] Prosecutor v. Ntaganda, ICC-01/04-02/06, Public Redacted Version of "Prosecution's Pre-Trial Brief", ICC-01/04-02/06-503-Conf-AnxA, ¶ 7 (Sept. 1, 2015).

international armed conflicts.[228] However, even the establishment of an environmental crime applicable to non-international armed conflicts would leave the majority of environmental damage caused by industrial activities during peacetime unpunished.

(2) 'Widespread, long-term and severe' environmental damage

Nonetheless, even environmental destruction occurring during an international armed conflict is only prohibited to a very limited extent. Article 8 (2) (b) (iv) Rome Statute requires an attack resulting in 'widespread, long-term and severe' environmental damage. Although such an 'attack' includes all types of attacks, and the provision does not require the occurrence of actual damage to the natural environment but the mere launching of an attack in the knowledge that this attack will cause widespread, long-term and severe damage to the natural environment[229], the *actus reus* of Article 8 (2) (b) (iv) Rome Statute is severely constrained by the triple cumulative standard of 'widespread, long-term and severe' environmental damage.

The criteria 'widespread, long-term and severe' are derived from Articles 35 (3) and 55 (1) AP I.[230] However, neither the Rome Statute nor the Elements of Crime specify the terms 'widespread, long-term and severe'. Hence, recourse needs to be taken to other related international agreements, including the 1977 ENMOD Convention and the 1977 Additional Protocol I.[231] Nonetheless, it is noteworthy that Article 8 (2) (b) (iv) Rome Statute and Articles 35 (3), 55 (1) AP I carry a much higher threshold than the ENMOD Convention. While Article I (1) of the ENMOD Convention requires 'widespread, long-lasting, *or* severe' environmental damage in alternative fashion, Article 8 (2) (b) (iv) Rome Statute and Articles 35 (3), 55 (1) AP I cumulatively presuppose 'widespread, long-lasting, *and* severe' damage to the natural environment. This discrepancy is due to the fact that the Rome Statute and the Additional Protocol I not only criminalise intentional environmental destruction, but also incidental, albeit foreseeable, environmental damage, as opposed to the ENMOD Convention, which only proscribes intentional environmental degradation.[232]

---

[228] See considerations concerning the inclusion of an environmental war crime into Article 8 (2) (e) of the Rome Statute, *Matthew Gillett*, Eco-Struggles 234–248 (2017).

[229] *Knut Dörmann*, Preparatory Commission for the International Criminal Court: The Elements of War Crimes, Part II, 83 International Review of the Red Cross 461, 470, 471 (2001).

[230] *Stefan Wehrenberg*, Article 8, War Crimes, in: Rome Statute of the International Criminal Court para. 252 (Kai Ambos ed., 2022).

[231] See Article 21 (1) (b) Rome Statute, which expressly allows such recourse.

[232] *Michael Bothe*, Protection of the Environment in Relation to Armed Conflicts 347 (2021); *Gerhard Werle/Florian Jeßberger*, Principles of International Criminal Law para. 1450 (2020); *Yoram Dinstein*, Max Planck Yearbook of United Nations Law 540, 541 (2001); *Ines Peterson*, Leiden Journal of International Law 329 (2009).

However, interpreting the criteria 'widespread', 'long-term' and 'severe' is complicated by virtue of the fact that the ENMOD Convention and AP I ascribe deviant meanings to identical terms. According to an Understanding relating to Article I of the ENMOD convention, environmental damage is considered 'widespread' if it extends to an area of several hundred square kilometers; 'long-lasting if it lasts for a period of months, or approximately a season; and 'severe' if it entails serious or significant disruption or harm to human life, natural and economic resources or other assets.[233] In any event, the Understanding expressly stated that "the interpretation set forth above is intended exclusively for this Convention and is not intended to prejudice the interpretation of the same or similar terms if used in connexion with any other international agreement"[234] and thus cannot be transferred to Articles 35 (3) and 55 AP I[235] or Article 8 (2) (b) (iv) Rome Statute.[236] While the *travaux préparatoires* to the Additional Protocol I remain silent on the exact meaning of 'widespread' and 'severe', 'long-term' is defined as environmental damage lasting at least two or three decades.[237] The diverging interpretations of 'long-term' imply that the Additional Protocol I carries a much higher threshold than the ENMOD Convention.[238] In this regard, 'widespread' is expected to cover natural damage exceeding ENMOD's threshold of several hundred square kilometers.[239] With regards to the term 'severe' it is argued that 'severe' environmental damage necessitates, at a minimum, the prejudicing of the survival or health of the human population.[240] Since 'severe' environmental harm requires human harm, it can be argued that Article 35 (3) AP I despite lacking any explicit reference to human injury as opposed to Article 55 (1) AP I is not exclusively ecocentric in nature.[241] However, the International Tribunal for the Former Yugoslavia (*hereinafter* 'ICTY') measured 'long-term' "in years rather than months"[242].

[233] G.A., Report of the Conference of the Committee on Disarmament, at 91 (Annex I), U. N. Doc. A/31/27 (Vol. I) (1976).

[234] Id.

[235] *Gerhard Werle/Florian Jeßberger*, Principles of International Criminal Law para. 1451 (2020); *Ines Peterson*, Leiden Journal of International Law 330 (2009); *Yoram Dinstein*, Max Planck Yearbook of United Nations Law 542 (2001).

[236] *Gerhard Werle/Florian Jeßberger*, Principles of International Criminal Law para. 1451 (2020).

[237] *Stefan Wehrenberg*, Article 8 para. 252 (2022); *Eliana Teresa Cusato*, JICJ 496 (2017); *Jessica C. Lawrence/Kevin Jon Heller*, Geo. Int'l Envtl. L. Rev. 73 (2007).

[238] *Karen Hulme*, War Torn Environment 92 (2004).

[239] *Stefan Wehrenberg*, Article 8 para. 252 (2022); *Karen Hulme*, War Torn Environment 92, 98 (2004).

[240] *Stefan Wehrenberg*, Article 8 para. 252 (2022); *Karen Hulme*, War Torn Environment 95–98 (2004).

[241] *Karen Hulme*, War Torn Environment 96 (2004).

[242] ICTY, Final Report to the Prosecutor by the Committee Established to Review the Nato Bombing Campaign Against the Federal Republic of Yugoslavia, at para. 15 (2000).

Hence, it can be seen that even after having taken recourse to the Understanding of the ENMOD Convention and the *traveaux préparatoires* to Additional Protocol I the exact meanings of the terms 'widespread', 'long-term' and 'severe' remain ambiguous. In this regard, UNEP proposes to transfer the definitions set out in the Understanding relating to Article 1 of the ENMOD Convention verbatim to Articles 35 (3), 55 (1) AP I[243] and Wehrenberg even goes as far as to argue that these definitions may as well be applied to Article 8 (2) (b) (iv) Rome Statute.[244]

In conclusion, the triple cumulative standard of 'widespread, long-term and severe' environmental damage severely limits Article 8 (2) (b) (iv)'s scope of application. Firstly, the triple cumulative standard restricts the crime's scope to the most egregious cases of environmental destruction during international armed conflicts excluding most cases of incidental battlefield damage.[245] Secondly, determining the criteria of 'widespread, long-term and severe' environmental harm is further complicated by scientific difficulties concerning the measurement of environmental destruction.[246] For instance, with regards to the 'long-term' requirement it is difficult to assess the longevity of environmental damage against the backdrop of nature's ability to regenerate.[247] In this regard, the 1990–1991 Gulf War serves as an excellent example. According to the U.S. Department of Defense after having reviewed the Gulf War, the intentional burning of over 600 oil drums in Kuwait by the Iraqi army would have only constituted widespread and severe environmental damage in accordance with Articles 35 (3), 55 (I) AP I, if Additional Protocol I had been applicable at that time.[248] The environmental damage, however, could not have been classed as 'long-term', as it was not clear that the damage would last for several decades.[249] Additionally, in the case of environmental destruction during wartime it proves difficult to prove the causal link between the ecological harm sustained and the wartime actions.[250] Thirdly, the determination of the *actus reus* is further complicated by its ambiguity, which appears particularly problematic in light of the principle of legality requiring the crimes to be defined as clearly as

243 UNEP, Protecting the Environment 5 (2009).

244 *Stefan Wehrenberg*, Article 8 para. 252 (2022).

245 Id.; *Michael N. Schmitt*, Yale Journal of International Law 71 (1997).

246 *Tara Weinstein*, Prosecuting Attacks that Destroy the Environment: Environmental Crimes or Humanitarian Atrocities, 17 (4) Geo. Int'l Envtl. L. Rev. 697, 708 (2005); *Jessica C. Lawrence/Kevin Jon Heller*, Geo. Int'l Envtl. L. Rev. 75 (2007).

247 *Tara Weinstein*, Geo. Int'l Envtl. L. Rev. 708 (2005); *Ines Peterson*, Leiden Journal of International Law 335 (2009).

248 United States, Department of Defense Report to Congress on the Conduct of the Persian Gulf War – Appendix on the Role of the Law of War, 31 (3) International Legal Materials 612, 636, 637 (1992).

249 Id.

250 *Tara Weinstein*, Geo. Int'l Envtl. L. Rev. 708 (2005).

possible.[251] Due to the lack of clarity, the introduction of the terms 'widespread, long-term and severe' has already met with major opposition during the drafting of Additional Protocol I.[252] Thus, as long as the ASP does not establish exact definitions, it is up to the ICC to elucidate the specific meaning of the terms 'widespread, long-term and severe' in future decisions, which, however, is likely to add yet more uncertainty to the provision.[253]

(3) Proportionality test

The already narrow scope of Article 8 (2) (b) (iv) Rome Statute is further limited by requiring the environmental damage not only to be 'widespread, long-term and severe', but also 'clearly excessive to the concrete and direct overall military advantage anticipated'. According to the Elements of Crime, the perpetrator needs to be able to foresee the military advantage which may or may not be temporally or geographically related to the object at the relevant time.[254] However, it will be difficult for the perpetrator to assess *ex ante* at the relevant time the expected environmental damage and the anticipated military advantage and compare both.[255] Thus, due to these difficulties perpetrators are granted a degree of discretion in this assessment which, however, *ex post* severely impedes judicial scrutiny.[256] By including this proportionality test, which allows environmental harm to be justified by military advantage, the scope of Article 8 (2) (b) (iv) Rome Statute is narrower[257] than the absolute prohibition in Articles 35 (3), 55 (1) AP I proscribing collateral environmental harm even if required by military circumstances.[258] The principle of proportionality is a principle of customary international law prohibiting "injury or damage disproportionate to the military advantage sought by an action"[259].

Further, the words 'clearly' and 'overall' were inserted requiring environmental harm not only to be just excessive, but to be 'clearly' excessive to the concrete and direct overall military advantage.[260] In its report on the NATO bombing, the ICTY

---

[251] *Gerhard Werle/Florian Jeßberger*, Principles of International Criminal Law para. 135 (2020).

[252] *Michael N. Schmitt*, Yale Journal of International Law 71 (1997).

[253] *Jessica C. Lawrence/Kevin Jon Heller*, Geo. Int'l Envtl. L. Rev. 89 (2007).

[254] ICC Elements of Crimes, Art. 8 (2) (b (iv), para. 2 n. 36.

[255] *Stefan Wehrenberg*, Article 8 para. 252 (2022).

[256] Id.

[257] See *Gerhard Werle/Florian Jeßberger*, Principles of International Criminal Law para. 1453 fn. 766 (2020), doubting that the inclusion of the proportionality test represents a further limitation as assumably 'widespread, long-term and severe' environmental damage will not be able to be justified by military advantage; similar *Ines Peterson*, Leiden Journal of International Law 341 (2009).

[258] *Stefan Wehrenberg*, Article 8 para. 252 (2022); *Eliana Teresa Cusato*, JICJ 497 (2017); *Antonio Cassese*, et al., Cassese's International Criminal Law 81, 82 (2013).

[259] *Michael N. Schmitt*, Yale Journal of International Law 55 (1997).

[260] *Eliana Teresa Cusato*, JICJ 497 (2017); *Stefan Wehrenberg*, Article 8 para. 252 (2022).

reaffirmed that the insertion of the word 'clearly' ensured that perpetrators could only be held criminally liable in cases where the excessiveness was obvious.[261] However, similar to the triple standard 'widespread, long-term and severe' the proportionality test lacks clarity, which again raises concerns regarding the principle of legality.[262]

Hence, only the most obviously disproportionate attacks on the natural environment are prosecutable under this provision.

(4) Knowledge and intent

In the absence of a built-in mental threshold contained in Article 8 (2) (b) (iv) Rome Statute, Article 30 Rome Statute regulating the subjective side of the core crimes is to be applied. Pursuant to Article 30 (1) Rome Statute the mental element consists of intent and knowledge. Thus, the attack has to be launched with intent and knowledge that the attack *will* cause widespread, long-term and severe environmental damage and, *will* be clearly excessive to the overall military advantage anticipated.

Although Article 30 (1) Rome Statute requires that "the material elements are committed with intent and knowledge", the requisite mental threshold differs depending on the respective material element it relates to. With respect to the criminalised conduct, the perpetrator has to act with intent (Article 30 (2) (a) Rome Statute), whereas regarding the consequences of the conduct, the perpetrator has to act with intent and knowledge (Article 30 (2) (b) and (3) Rome Statute). With respect to the criminalised conduct, the perpetrator has intent if he "means to engage in the conduct"[263]. Thus, at a minimum, the perpetrator must act voluntarily excluding involuntary behaviour.[264] In the context of environmental harm this appears to be unproblematic.

With respect to consequences of the crime, the perpetrator has intent if he "means to cause that consequence or is aware that it will occur in the ordinary course of events"[265]. Hence, concerning the consequences of the crime, the perpetrator must act either with direct ("means to cause that consequence") or indirect

---

[261] ICTY, Final Report to the Prosecutor by the Committee Established to Review the Nato Bombing Campaign Against the Federal Republic of Yugoslavia, at para. 21 (2000).

[262] *Jessica C. Lawrence/Kevin Jon Heller*, Geo. Int'l Envtl. L. Rev. 78 (2007); *Tara Weinstein*, Geo. Int'l Envtl. L. Rev. 709 (2005).

[263] Art. 30 (2) (a) Rome Statute.

[264] *Donald K. Piragoff/Darryl Robinson*, Article 30, Mental Element, in: Rome Statute of the International Criminal Court para. 21 (Kai Ambos ed., 2022); *William A. Schabas*, The International Criminal Court: A Commentary on the Rome Statute 631 (2nd ed., 2016); *Gerhard Werle/Florian Jeßberger*, Principles of International Criminal Law para. 571 (2020); *Albin Eser*, Mental Elements – Mistake of Fact and Mistake of Law, in: The Rome Statute of the International Criminal Court: A Commentary 913 (Antonio Cassese, et al. eds., 2002).

[265] Art. 30 (2) (b) Rome Statute.

("is aware that it will occur in the ordinary course of events") intent.[266] Direct intent, also known as *dolus directus in the first degree* is characterised by a strong volitional element[267], requiring the "will or desire to produce an outcome"[268]. In this case the volitional element outweighs the cognitive element.[269] By contrast, indirect intent or *dolus directus in the second degree* is characterised by a cognitive element, requiring the awareness "that [the] consequence will occur in the ordinary course of events"[270]. In this case, the cognitive element is prevalent over the volitional element.[271] Pursuant to Article 30 (3) Rome Statute, with regards to the consequences of the conduct the perpetrator also has to act with knowledge, meaning the "awareness that [...] a consequence will occur in the ordinary course of events". However, since indirect intent already includes the exact same cognitive element, knowledge only plays a distinct role in the case of direct intent.[272]

Thus, direct intent only covers cases of environmental harm where environmental destruction was the desired goal of the perpetrator. During wartime, intentional environmental destruction is often deployed as a weapon to subdue resistance or achieve a strategic advantage by, for instance, polluting water wells, defoliating forests or poisoning soil.[273] The defoliation of Vietnam's forests by having sprayed the dioxin-containing herbicide Agent Orange over large parts of Vietnam during the Vietnam War by the US army or the burning of oil wells in Kuwait during the 1991 Gulf War may serve as examples of intentional environmental harm.[274] Nevertheless, although intentional environmental destruction exists as a war strategy, the bulk of environmental harm during times of armed conflicts is collateral and thus largely unintended.[275] Collateral environmental harm is, *inter alia*, caused by debris and chemicals resulting from bomb damage, landmines, movement of military troops or unexploded ordnance.[276]

Since in these cases the perpetrators would lack direct intent, it would have to be proved that they were aware that environmental harm *will* occur in the ordinary

[266] *Donald K. Piragoff/Darryl Robinson*, Article 30 paras. 23–25 (2022).

[267] *Albin Eser*, Mental Elements 914 (2002).

[268] Id. at para. 23.

[269] Prosecutor v. Bemba, ICC-01/05-01/13, Judgment Pursuant to Article 74 of the Statute, ¶ 29 (Oct. 19, 2016); *William A. Schabas*, The International Criminal Court: A Commentary on the Rome Statute 629 (2016).

[270] Art. 30 (2) (b) and (3) Rome Statute; *Donald K. Piragoff/Darryl Robinson*, Article 30 para. 1 (2022).

[271] Prosecutor v. Bemba, ICC-01/05-01/13, Judgment Pursuant to Article 74 of the Statute, ¶ 29 (Oct. 19, 2016); *Albin Eser*, Mental Elements 915 (2002); *William A. Schabas*, The International Criminal Court: A Commentary on the Rome Statute 629 (2016).

[272] *Albin Eser*, Mental Elements 916 (2002).

[273] UNEP, From Conflict to Peacebuilding 15 (2009).

[274] Id.

[275] Id.

[276] Id.

course of events (indirect intent) to establish criminal liability under Article 8 (2) (b) (iv) Rome Statute. While in terms of indirect intent it is undisputed that the perpetrator must act with awareness, it is disputed how likely the occurrence of environmental harm must be so that it 'will occur in the ordinary course of events'.[277] At the lowest end of the spectrum of probabilities, it is rightly held that unlikely risks and low probabilities do not satisfy the 'will occur' standard.[278] Thus, concepts of *dolus eventualis* or recklessness[279], that is, "awareness of the existence of a mere likelihood or possibility"[280], and negligence[281], under which low probabilities are deemed sufficient, are excluded from Article 30 (2) (b) and (3) Rome Statute.[282] It is argued that if the concepts of *dolus eventualis* or recklessness were meant to be included into Article 30 (2) (b) and (3) Rome Statute, the phrases "may occur"[283] or "might occur in the ordinary course of events"[284] would have been used instead of 'will occur'.[285] However, from the future tense 'will occur', read together with 'in the ordinary course of events', the jurisprudence deduced in several decisions that the required probability of the occurrence of the consequence must be close to certainty, yet not absolute certainty.[286] The ICC reiterated that the phrase

[277] *Donald K. Piragoff/Darryl Robinson*, Article 30 paras. 1, 26 (2022).

[278] Id. at paras. 26, 27.

[279] See Chapter C. V. 2. b).

[280] Prosecutor v. Katanga, ICC-01/04-01/07, Judgment Pursuant to Article 74 of the Statute, ¶ 775 (Mar. 7, 2014).

[281] See Chapter C. V. 2. c).

[282] Prosecutor v. Bemba, ICC-01/05-01/13, Judgment Pursuant to Article 74 of the Statute, ¶ 29 (Oct. 19, 2016); Prosecutor v. Bemba, ICC-01/05-01/08, Decision Pursuant to Article 61(7)(a) and (b) of the Rome Statute on the Charges of the Prosecutor Against Jean-Pierre Bemba Gombo, ¶ 360, 369 (June 15, 2009); Prosecutor v. Lubanga, ICC-01/04-01/06 A 5, Judgment on the Appeal of Mr. Thomas Lubanga Dyilo Against His Conviction, ¶ 449 (Dec. 1, 2014); Prosecutor v. Lubanga, ICC-01/04-01/06, Judgment Pursuant to Article 74 of the Statute, para. 1011 (Mar. 14, 2012); *Donald K. Piragoff/Darryl Robinson*, Article 30 para. 26 (2022); *Gerhard Werle/Florian Jeßberger*, Principles of International Criminal Law para. 573 (2020); *William A. Schabas*, The International Criminal Court: A Commentary on the Rome Statute 631, 632 (2016); *Albin Eser*, Mental Elements 915, 916 (2002).

[283] Prosecutor v. Lubanga, ICC-01/04-01/06, Judgment Pursuant to Article 74 of the Statute, ¶ 1011 (Mar. 14, 2012); see Prosecutor v. Lubanga, ICC-01/04-01/06 A 5, Judgment on the Appeal of Mr. Thomas Lubanga Dyilo Against His Conviction, ¶ 447 (Dec. 1, 2014); *William A. Schabas*, The International Criminal Court: A Commentary on the Rome Statute 632 (2016).

[284] Prosecutor v. Bemba, ICC-01/05-01/08, Decision Pursuant to Article 61(7)(a) and (b) of the Rome Statute on the Charges of the Prosecutor Against Jean-Pierre Bemba Gombo, ¶ 363 (June 15, 2009).

[285] *William A. Schabas*, The International Criminal Court: A Commentary on the Rome Statute 631, 632 (2016); *Albin Eser*, Mental Elements 915 (2002); *Gerhard Werle/Florian Jeßberger*, 'Unless Otherwise Provided': Article 30 of the ICC Statute and the Mental Element of Crimes under International Criminal Law, 3 (1) JICJ 35, 41 (2005).

[286] Prosecutor v. Katanga, ICC-01/04-01/07, Judgment Pursuant to Article 74 of the Statute, ¶ 776 (Mar. 7, 2014); Prosecutor v. Bemba, ICC-01/05-01/08, Decision Pursuant to Ar-

'will occur in the ordinary course of events' requires the "virtual certainty"[287] or almost inevitability[288] of the occurrence of the consequence. However, there is a not inconsiderable spectrum of probabilities between low probabilities excluded from Article 30 Rome Statute, and the virtual certainty of events, which has been inadequately explored by the jurisprudence.[289] In this regard, for instance, it remains open to interpretation whether "probable or highly probable"[290] consequences fall within the ambit of indirect intent. Thus, in order to act with indirect intent, the perpetrator would not only have to be aware of the virtually certain occurrence of widespread, long-term and severe environmental harm at the time of committing the environmentally harmful conduct[291], but also of its clear excessiveness to the anticipated overall military advantage. With regards to the excessiveness of the environmental damage, the perpetrator has to make a value judgment in deviation to the general rule[292] stipulated in the Elements of Crimes.[293] This value judgment, or normative evaluation, requires the perpetrator to be aware of the factual circumstances rendering the widespread, long-term and severe environmental damage clearly excessive.[294] Perpetrators would therefore most likely claim in their defence that they could have not foreseen the consequences of their actions to a virtual certainty at the time of their commission in order to evade criminal liability.[295] Nonetheless, the court will infer from the factual circumstances of the conduct perpetrated whether the perpetrator was aware that his actions will result in widespread, long-term and severe environmental harm.[296] Hence, at least in cases where the causation of environmental harm was evident at the time of its commission, this defence will not

---

ticle 61(7)(a) and (b) of the Rome Statute on the Charges of the Prosecutor Against Jean-Pierre Bemba Gombo, ¶ 362 (June 15, 2009).

[287] Prosecutor v. Bemba, ICC-01/05-01/13, Judgment Pursuant to Article 74 of the Statute, ¶ 29 (Oct. 19, 2016); Prosecutor v. Lubanga, ICC-01/04-01/06 A 5, Judgment on the Appeal of Mr. Thomas Lubanga Dyilo Against His Conviction, ¶ 447 (Dec. 1, 2014); Prosecutor v. Katanga, ICC-01/04-01/07, Judgment Pursuant to Article 74 of the Statute, ¶ 776 (Mar. 7, 2014); Prosecutor v. Bemba, ICC-01/05-01/08, Decision Pursuant to Article 61(7)(a) and (b) of the Rome Statute on the Charges of the Prosecutor Against Jean-Pierre Bemba Gombo, ¶ 362 (June 15, 2009).

[288] Prosecutor v. Bemba, ICC-01/05-01/08, Decision Pursuant to Article 61(7)(a) and (b) of the Rome Statute on the Charges of the Prosecutor Against Jean-Pierre Bemba Gombo, ¶ 359 (June 15, 2009).

[289] *Donald K. Piragoff/Darryl Robinson*, Article 30 para. 27 (2022).

[290] Id.

[291] *Albin Eser*, Mental Elements 930 (2002).

[292] ICC Elements of Crimes, General Introduction, para. 4.

[293] ICC Elements of Crimes, Art. 8 (2) (b) (iv) para. 3 n. 37; *Albin Eser*, Mental Elements 922, 923 (2002).

[294] *Albin Eser*, Mental Elements 923 (2002); see *Donald K. Piragoff/Darryl Robinson*, Article 30 para. 34 (2022).

[295] *Polly Higgins*, et al., Protecting the Planet: A Proposal for a Law of Ecocide, 59 Crime, Law and Social Change 251, 262 (2013).

[296] *Antonio Cassese*, et al., Cassese's International Criminal Law 57 (2013).

necessarily be successful. Nevertheless, cases of large-scale environmental degradation where the occurrence of widespread, long-term and severe environmental harm or its clear excessiveness to the expected military advantage was not virtually certain, but only (highly) probable would be excluded from criminal liability. Furthermore, major environmental accidents, such as the Deepwater Horizon oil spill, would also be excluded form criminal liability under Article 8 (2) (b) (iv) Rome Statute.[297]

bb) Conclusion

In conclusion, the scope of Article 8 (2) (b) (iv) Rome Statute is too narrow as to be able to afford effective environmental protection. Firstly, Article 8 (2) (b) (iv) Rome Statute is limited to environmental damage which has occurred during international armed conflicts, excluding times of non-international armed conflict and peace where the bulk of environmental harm is committed nowadays. Secondly, by cumulatively requiring the environmental harm to be 'widespread, long-term and severe', the provision is restricted to the most egregious forms of environmental destruction. Thirdly, any environmental harm can, at least in theory[298], be justified by military advantages and, fourthly, environmental harm which was at the time of its commission not foreseeable as a virtual certainty falls outside the scope of Article 8 (2) (b) (iv) Rome Statute. Due to these strict requirements, it is hardly surprising that, to date, not a single perpetrator has been prosecuted for an environmental war crime in accordance with Article 8 (2) (b) (iv) Rome Statute.[299]

Thus, some propose redrafting Article 8 (2) (b) (iv) Rome Statute by, *inter alia*, providing definitions of 'widespread, long-term and severe' and making the crime both applicable to international and non-international armed conflicts.[300] However, even if the provision were to be redrafted it would still only apply to armed conflicts, whether international or non-international, and would thus leave the bulk of large-scale environmental harm occurring during peacetime unaddressed. Additionally, the significantly high objective standard of 'widespread, long-term and severe' environmental damage would continue to exclude most cases of environmental harm. Furthermore, particularly with regards to Article 30 Rome Statute, it appears unlikely that the high mental threshold would be lowered.

---

[297] *Ricardo Pereira*, Criminal Law Forum 195 (2020).

[298] See *Gerhard Werle/Florian Jeßberger*, Principles of International Criminal Law para. 1453 fn. 766 (2020), doubting that 'widespread, long-term and severe' environmental damage can be justified by military advantage; similar *Ines Peterson*, Leiden Journal of International Law 341 (2009).

[299] *Rachel Killean*, From Ecocide to Eco-Sensitivity: 'Greening' Reparations at the International Criminal Court, 25 (2) International Journal of Human Rights 323, 328 (2021); two Nazi officials were prosecuted for environmental destruction during wartime by the Nuremberg IMT, see *Carl E. Bruch*, Vermont Law Review 716 (2001).

[300] *Jessica C. Lawrence/Kevin Jon Heller*, Geo. Int'l Envtl. L. Rev. 88–94 (2007).

With regard to war crimes, it is to be noted that besides Article 8 (2) (b) (iv) Rome Statute, conduct *resulting in* environmental harm is also indirectly prohibited by other war crimes, partially applicable to international and non-international armed conflicts.[301] In case law, particularly the act of pillaging during non-international armed conflicts, pursuant to Article 8 (2) (e) (v) Rome Statute, has gained increased attention in the context of environmental destruction, since environmental harm is often linked to the exploitation of natural resources.[302] However, irrespective of whether it be applicable during international or non-international armed conflicts, war crimes remain restricted to armed conflicts and therefore do not apply to environmental destruction during peacetime. Additionally, these provisions are anthropocentric only *indirectly* addressing environmental harm as a side-effect.[303] Thus, these war crimes only play a subordinate role in the promotion of global environmental protection.

b) Genocide

Instead of prosecuting attacks on the environment as such under Article 8 (2) (b) (iv) Rome Statute, according to the 2016 OTP Policy Paper, environmental crime can also be addressed by prosecuting crimes against humanity and crimes of genocide committed *by means of* environmental destruction[304] irrespective of the existence of armed conflicts. In this case, the environmental harm was caused in order to perpetrate another atrocity, such as genocide or crimes against humanity. In contrast to Article 8 (2) (b) (iv) Rome Statute, crimes against humanity and the crime of genocide are inherently anthropocentric and thus do not protect the environment per se but only to the extent that environmental destruction violates human interests. In this regard, the *Akayesu* case can serve as a precedent for prosecuting an act conducted as a means of committing another atrocity by having considered rape as a tool to commit genocide.[305] This approach also corresponds to the case of *Al Bashir*, where the former Sudanese President Al Bashir was alleged to have committed genocide.[306] His Armed Forces were alleged to have destroyed "all the target

[301] See *Matthew Gillett*, Eco-Struggles 230–233 (2017); UNEP, Protecting the Environment 30, 31 (2009); *Carl E. Bruch*, Vermont Law Review 718, 719 (2001).

[302] See for instance Prosecutor v. Ntaganda, ICC-01/04-02/06, Judgment, ¶ 440, 1199 (July 8, 2019). However, this judgment proves the secondary importance of environmental harm within this provision since Ntganda was only convicted of pillaging items but not natural resources although the Trial Chamber confirmed the UPC's intention to illegally exploit natural resources.

[303] *Jessica C. Lawrence/Kevin Jon Heller*, Geo. Int'l Envtl. L. Rev. 93 (2007).

[304] Office of the Prosecutor, Policy Paper on Case Selection and Prioritisation para. 41 (2016); *Stefan Wehrenberg*, Article 8 para. 252 (2022).

[305] See Prosecutor v. Akayesu, Case No. ICTR-96–4-T, Judgment (Sept. 2, 1998); *Tara Weinstein*, Geo. Int'l Envtl. L. Rev. 714 (2005).

[306] See Situation in Darfur, ICC-02/05–157-AnxA, Public Redacted Version of the Prosecutor's Application under Article 58 (July 14, 2008).

group's means of survival, poison[ed] sources of water including communal wells, destroy[ed] water pumps, [stolen] livestock and stripp[ed] the towns and villages of household and community assets".[307] In a second decision, the Pre-Trial Chamber of the ICC issued an arrest warrant contending that "the acts of contamination of water pumps and forcible transfer coupled by resettlement by member[s] of other tribes, were committed in furtherance of the genocidal policy, and that the conditions of life inflicted on the Fur, Masalit and Zaghawa groups were calculated to bring about the physical destruction of a part of those ethnic groups".[308] In doing so, the ICC recognised the underlying environmental degradation (water contamination) as a means of committing genocide.[309]

Hence, although Article 6 Rome Statute does not explicitly refer to environmental harm, it is possible to envisage environmentally destructive conduct, such as water contamination or extractive activities, as acts of genocide when the existence of a particular group is endangered by ecological degradation.[310] Firstly, environmentally destructive activities may be identified as acts of genocide 'causing serious bodily or mental harm' pursuant to Article 6 (b) Rome Statute.[311] According to the Elements of Crime, "this conduct may include, *but is not necessarily restricted to*, acts of torture, rape, sexual violence or inhuman or degrading treatment"[312] implying that other activities such as environmental degradation may also be subsumed under this provision.[313]

Secondly, and most importantly, environmentally harmful activities "deliberately inflicting on the group conditions of life calculated to bring about its physical destruction in whole or in part" may constitute acts of genocide in accordance with Article 6 (c) Rome Statute. According to the Elements of Crime, these *conditions of life* "may include, but [are] not necessarily restricted to, deliberate deprivation of resources indispensable for survival, such as food or medical services, or systematic expulsion from homes".[314] Thus, it appears possible to envisage severe environmental degradation as the reason for the forcible displacement of people from their native territory or for deteriorating health conditions.[315] The nexus of environmental

[307] Id. at ¶ 14.

[308] Prosecutor v. Al Bashir, ICC-02/05-01/09, Second Decision on the Prosecution's Application for a Warrant of Arrest, ¶ 38 (July 12, 2010).

[309] *Eliana Teresa Cusato*, JICJ 499 (2017); *Ricardo Pereira*, Criminal Law Forum 216 (2020); UNEP, Protecting the Environment 31 (2009).

[310] *Marcos Orellana*, Criminal Punishment for Environmental Damage: Individual and State Responsibility at a Crossroad, 17 (4) Geo. Int'l Envtl. L. Rev. 673, 692 (2005).

[311] UNEP, Protecting the Environment 31 (2009).

[312] ICC Elements of Crimes, Art. 6 (b) para. 1 n. 3 (emphasis added).

[313] *Alessandra Mistura*, Is There Space for Environmental Crimes Under International Criminal Law? The Impact of the Office of the Prosecutor Policy Paper on Case Selection and Prioritization on the Current Legal Framework, Colum. J. Envtl. L. 181, 205 (2018).

[314] ICC Elements of Crimes, Art. 6 (c) para. 4 n. 4.

[315] *Alessandra Mistura*, Colum. J. Envtl. L. 205 (2018).

degradation and genocide is particularly relevant for indigenous people whose existence directly depends on their natural habitat.[316] In some cases, indigenous people are forcibly expelled from their native territories in order to make room for industrial extraction sites, in other cases their natural habitat is severely contaminated by toxic waste leading to fatal diseases amongst their population.[317] For instance, in *Al Bashir* acts of water contamination coupled with the forcible displacement and resettlement of indigenous tribes were considered 'conditions of life calculated to bring about the physical destruction of an ethnic group'.[318]

However, although environmental harm can constitute a crime of genocide, the nexus between environmental degradation and genocide remains strictly theoretical in nature. In practice, establishing criminal liability under the crime of genocide for environmental degradation faces one major problem: proving the specific intent requirement set out in Article 6 Rome Statute.[319] The crime of genocide requires the perpetrator to act "with intent to destroy, in whole or in part, a national, ethnical, racial or religious group"[320] thereby distinguishing the crime of genocide from all other core crimes.[321] Thus, the Prosecutor would have to prove that the environmentally destructive act was aimed at destroying a particular group. However, while it is not difficult to envisage a corporation knowingly discharging toxic wastes leading to the displacement or killing of an indigenous population, it appears highly unlikely that one would be able to prove the business leader's intent to destroy a particular group of people. This is particularly relevant in the case of environmental devastation resulting from industrial activities, as these environmentally destructive activities mainly occur for the purpose of development and economic profit and not with the intent to destroy a certain protected group.[322]

In general, the major hurdle of proving the special intent requirement is the reason why genocide convictions by international courts and tribunals are so scarce. The ICC has only charged someone with the crime of genocide on one occasion,

---

[316] *Carl E. Bruch*, Vermont Law Review 727 (2001); *Alessandra Mistura*, Colum. J. Envtl. L. 205 (2018); *Marcos Orellana*, Geo. Int'l Envtl. L. Rev. 692 (2005); *Regina Rauxloh*, The Role of International Criminal Law in Environmental Protection 434 (2011).

[317] *Damien Short*, Redefining Genocide, Settler Colonialism, Social Death and Ecocide 172 (2016); *Alessandra Mistura*, Colum. J. Envtl. L. 205–207 (2018).

[318] Prosecutor v. Al Bashir, ICC-02/05-01/09, Second Decision on the Prosecution's Application for a Warrant of Arrest, ¶ 37, 38 (July 12, 2010).

[319] *Ricardo Pereira*, Criminal Law Forum 215 (2020); *Alessandra Mistura*, Colum. J. Envtl. L. 207 (2018); *Marcos Orellana*, Geo. Int'l Envtl. L. Rev. 692 (2005); *Carl E. Bruch*, Vermont Law Review 727 (2001).

[320] Art. 6 Rome Statute.

[321] *Robert Cryer*, et al., An Introduction to International Criminal Law and Procedure 205 (2019); *William A. Schabas*, An Introduction to the International Criminal Court 90 (2020).

[322] *Eliana Teresa Cusato*, JICJ 499 (2017); *Peter Sharp*, Prospects for Environmental Liability in the International Criminal Court, 18 (2) Virginia Environmental Law Journal 217, 234 (1999).

namely, in the second arrest warrant of *Al Bashir* after the Pre-Trial Chamber had initially dismissed the charge of genocide.[323] However, in some national jurisdictions, particularly in Germany, the number of genocide convictions has perceptibly increased, since German courts tend to generally interpret the special intent requirement more expansively than international courts or tribunals.[324] Germany hereby claims universal jurisdiction over crimes of genocide, as the genocidal acts in question were perpetrated in other countries than Germany by non-German perpetrators.[325]

However, most prosecutions of environmental harm as crimes of genocide by the ICC will fail due to the significantly high mental threshold. Hence, it appears more likely for environmentally destructive conduct to fall within the ambit of crimes against humanity containing a perceptibly lower mental threshold, which will be discussed next.

c) Crimes against Humanity

Similar to genocide, environmental destruction is not explicitly listed as a crime against humanity in Article 7 (1) (a)–(k) Rome Statute. However, environmental destruction could become indirectly relevant, if environmental harm were to be used as a tool to perpetrate one of the crimes enumerated in Article 7 Rome Statute.

aa) Environmental degradation as a crime against humanity

Firstly, large-scale environmental harm can be deployed as a tool to commit an act of 'extermination' in accordance with Article 7 (1) (b) Rome Statute.[326] In contrast to murder, extermination is characterised by the killing of one or more persons within the context of a mass killing.[327] Pursuant to Article 7 (2) (b) Rome

---

[323] Prosecutor v. Al Bashir, ICC-02/05-01/09, Second Decision on the Prosecution's Application for a Warrant of Arrest, ¶ 39 (July 12, 2010).

[324] *William A. Schabas*, Genocide in International Law: The Crime of Crimes 438 (2nd ed., 2009).

[325] Id. at 435–439.

[326] *Ricardo Pereira*, Criminal Law Forum 211 (2020); *Alessandra Mistura*, Colum. J. Envtl. L. 208 (2018); *Eliana Teresa Cusato*, JICJ 499 (2017); *Caitlin Lambert*, Environmental Destruction in Ecuador: Crimes Against Humanity Under the Rome Statute?, 30 Leiden Journal of International Law 707, 726 (2017); *Luigi Prosperi/Jacopo Terrosi*, Embracing the 'Human Factor': Is There New Impetus at the ICC for Conceiving and Prioritizing International Environmental Harms as Crimes Against Humanity?, 15 (3) JICJ 509, 518 (2017).

[327] ICC Elements of Crimes, Art. 7 (1) (b) para. 2; *Carsten Stahn*, Article 7, Crimes Against Humanity, in: Rome Statute of the International Criminal Court para. 44 (Kai Ambos ed., 2022); *Gerhard Werle/Florian Jeßberger*, Principles of International Criminal Law para. 1027 (2020); *Robert Cryer*, et al., An Introduction to International Criminal Law and Procedure 243 (2019).

Statute, the crime of extermination covers the direct as well as the indirect killing[328] through "the intentional infliction of conditions of life, *inter alia* the deprivation of access to food and medicine, calculated to bring about the destruction of part of a population"[329]. Thus, the conduct required is borrowed from the above-mentioned crime of genocide pursuant to Article 6 (c) Rome Statute[330], however, with the difference of not presupposing any specific intent to destroy a particular group.[331] The withholding of access to food or medicine can undoubtedly result from the environmental contamination or the exploitation of natural resources such as water.[332] This was, for instance, confirmed in *Al Bashir,* where the Prosecution alleged the commission of the crime of extermination by, *inter alia*, the "destruction of the means of livelihood"[333].

Secondly, the deportation or forcible transfer[334] of people pursuant to Article 7 (1) (d) Rome Statute could be committed by means of severe ecological damage.[335] This requires the "forcible displacement of the persons concerned by expulsion or other coercive acts from the area in which they are lawfully present, without grounds permitted under international law".[336] *Other coercive acts* incurring the involuntary displacement of victims may include the devastation of the population's homeland through environmental harm caused by, *inter alia*, infrastructure projects including highways, land-grabs, extractive activities or dams.[337] In this sense, environmental harm could easily be considered a "coercive environment"[338]. At this juncture, it is primarily indigenous tribes that are forcibly displaced for economic

---

[328] *Gerhard Werle/Florian Jeßberger*, Principles of International Criminal Law para. 1030 (2020); *Robert Cryer*, et al., An Introduction to International Criminal Law and Procedure 243 (2019); *William A. Schabas*, The International Criminal Court: A Commentary on the Rome Statute 174 (2016).

[329] Art. 7 (2) (b) Rome Statute; see also ICC Elements of Crimes, Art. 7 (1) (b) para. 1 n. 9.

[330] *Carsten Stahn*, Article 7 para. 46 (2022); *Gerhard Werle/Florian Jeßberger*, Principles of International Criminal Law para. 1029 (2020); *William A. Schabas*, The International Criminal Court: A Commentary on the Rome Statute 174 (2016).

[331] *William A. Schabas*, The International Criminal Court: A Commentary on the Rome Statute 174 (2016).

[332] *Matthew Gillett*, Eco-Struggles 226 (2017); *Caitlin Lambert*, Leiden Journal of International Law 726 (2017); *Luigi Prosperi/Jacopo Terrosi*, JICJ 518 (2017).

[333] Prosecutor v. Al Bashir, ICC-02/05-01/09, Second Decision on the Prosecution's Application for a Warrant of Arrest, ¶ 35 (July 12, 2010).

[334] See for the different meanings of 'deportation' and 'forcible transfer' *Robert Cryer*, et al., An Introduction to International Criminal Law and Procedure 245 (2019).

[335] *Carsten Stahn*, Article 7 para. 62 (2022); *Eliana Teresa Cusato*, JICJ 499 (2017); *Matthew Gillett*, Eco-Struggles 226 (2017); *Caitlin Lambert*, Leiden Journal of International Law 726 (2017); UNEP, Protecting the Environment 31 (2009).

[336] Art. 7 (2) (d) Rome Statute.

[337] *Carsten Stahn*, Article 7 para. 62 (2022); see *Caitlin Lambert*, Leiden Journal of International Law (2017).

[338] *Luigi Prosperi/Jacopo Terrosi*, JICJ 519, 520 (2017).

reasons as their native territory often proves to be profitable land.[339] In the *Al Bashir* case, for instance, attacks on the group's means of survival, including the poisoning and destruction of water supplies leading to the forcible displacement of at least 2.7 million people were charged as crimes against humanity in accordance with Article 7 (1) (d) Rome Statute.[340] In general, the number of 'environmental refugees', that is people being forcibly displaced due to environmental conditions, is expected to rise in the future due to deteriorating environmental conditions as a result of climate change.[341] However, the crime of deportation and forcible transfer is constrained by the fact that it only covers displacements impermissible under international law.[342]

Thirdly, serious environmental destruction could be deployed in order to persecute an identifiable group.[343] The crime of persecution pursuant to Article 7 (1) (h) Rome Statute prohibits the "intentional and severe deprivation of fundamental rights contrary to international law by reason of the identity of the group or collectivity".[344] Causing resource scarcity or preventing access to food and clean water by means of severe environmental degradation certainly breaches fundamental human rights and thus could constitute persecution.[345] In this regard, it is of importance that the UN General Assembly recently declared access to a clean and healthy environment a universal human right.[346]

However, the crime of persecution is constrained in a number of ways. For one, persecution is characterised by its discriminatory element requiring the deprivation of rights on discriminatory grounds[347], including political, cultural, ethnical or "other grounds that are universally recognised as impermissible under international law"[348]. In this regard, the intentional targeting of indigenous tribes based on their identity impeding, for instance, extractive activities, may constitute persecu-

---

[339] *Caitlin Lambert*, Leiden Journal of International Law 727 (2017).

[340] Situation in Darfur, Sudan, ICC-02/05, Summary of Prosecutor's Application under Article 58, ¶ 14, 15 (July 14, 2008).

[341] *Philippe Sands/Jacqueline Peel*, Principles of International Environmental Law 837 (2018).

[342] *Gerhard Werle/Florian Jeßberger*, Principles of International Criminal Law para. 1056 (2020).

[343] *Luigi Prosperi/Jacopo Terrosi*, JICJ 520–523 (2017); *Eliana Teresa Cusato*, JICJ 499 (2017); *Caitlin Lambert*, Leiden Journal of International Law 727 (2017); *Alessandra Mistura*, Colum. J. Envtl. L. 209 (2018).

[344] Art. 7 (2) (g) Rome Statute; see also ICC Elements of Crimes, Art. 7 (1) (h) para. 1.

[345] *Eliana Teresa Cusato*, JICJ 499, 500 (2017).

[346] United Nations, UN General Assembly Declares Access to Clean and Healthy Environment a Universal Human Right (2022), https://news.un.org/en/story/2022/07/1123482 (last visited Feb. 18, 2025).

[347] *Robert Cryer*, et al., An Introduction to International Criminal Law and Procedure 252, 253 (2019).

[348] Article 7 (1) (h) Rome Statute.

tion.[349] Additionally, persecution is the only crime against humanity which requires an additional discriminatory intent besides the ordinary mental element[350], that is, "the intent to target a person or group on prohibited grounds of discrimination".[351] Furthermore, its scope of application is further narrowed by the fact that the act of persecution must be perpetrated in conjunction with another act listed in Article 7 Rome Statute or any other crime within the jurisdiction of the Court.[352]

Fourthly, environmentally destructive behaviour may constitute "other acts of similar character intentionally causing great suffering, or serious injury to body or to mental or physical health" pursuant to Article 7 (1) (k) Rome Statute.[353] This catch-all provision covers conduct otherwise left unaddressed by Article 7 Rome Statute[354] and thus provides the opportunity of expanding the scope of crimes against humanity beyond the original drafters' understanding.[355] However, in light of *nullum crimen sine lege*, the residual clause of Article 7 (1) (k) Rome Statute requires (1) the conduct to be of similar nature and gravity compared to the other acts enumerated in Article 7 Rome Statute[356] and, (2) presupposes the causation of "great suffering, or serious injury to body or to mental or physical health".[357] Accordingly, 'other inhumane acts' include "serious violations of international customary law and the basic rights pertaining to human beings, drawn from the norms of international human rights law, which are of a similar nature and gravity to the

---

[349] *Caitlin Lambert*, Leiden Journal of International Law 727 (2017).

[350] Prosecutor v. Kordić, Case No. IT-95-14/2-T, Judgment, ¶ 212 (Feb. 26, 2001).

[351] *Robert Cryer*, et al., An Introduction to International Criminal Law and Procedure 254 (2019).

[352] See Art. 7 (1) (h) Rome Statute; ICC Elements of Crimes, Art. 7 (1) (h) para. 4; *Robert Cryer*, et al., An Introduction to International Criminal Law and Procedure 253, 254 (2019); *Gerhard Werle/Florian Jeßberger*, Principles of International Criminal Law para. 1111 (2020).

[353] *Ricardo Pereira*, Criminal Law Forum 211 (2020); *Eliana Teresa Cusato*, JICJ 499 (2017); *Matthew Gillett*, Eco-Struggles 226 (2017); *Caitlin Lambert*, Leiden Journal of International Law 727 (2017); *Luigi Prosperi/Jacopo Terrosi*, JICJ 523 (2017); *Mohammed Saif-Alden Wattad*, Fordham Environmental Law Review 282 (2009); *Tara Weinstein*, Geo. Int'l Envtl. L. Rev. 720 (2005); *Carl E. Bruch*, Vermont Law Review 729 (2001).

[354] Prosecutor v. Katanga, ICC-01/04-01/07, Decision on the Confirmation of Charges, ¶ 452 (Sept. 30, 2008); Prosecutor v. Muthaura., ICC-01/09-02/11, Decision on the Confirmation of Charges Pursuant to Article 61 (7) (a) and (b) of the Rome Statute, ¶ 269 (Jan. 23, 2012).

[355] See the International Committee of the Red Cross (*hereinafter* ICRC) commenting on common Article 3 of the Geneva Conventions: "However great the care taken in drawing up a list of all the various forms of infliction, it would never be possible to catch up with the imagination of future torturers who wished to satisfy their bestial instincts; and the more specific and complete a list tries to be, the more restrictive it becomes" (cited in Prosecutor v. Kupreškić, Case No. IT-95-16-T, Judgement, ¶ 563 (Jan. 14, 2000)); *Caitlin Lambert*, Leiden Journal of International Law 729 (2017).

[356] ICC Elements of Crimes, Art. 7 (1) (k) para. 2.

[357] Art. 7 (1) (k) Rome Statute.

acts referred to in [A]rticle 7 (1) of the Statute."[358] Thus, determining the scope of 'other inhumane acts' requires a recourse to human rights law, since the category of crimes against humanity is largely based on international human rights law.[359] However, only human rights violations of similar nature and gravity to the other acts enumerated in Article 7 (1) Rome Statute can constitute 'other inhumane acts'. The gravity of the conduct and its comparability must be determined on a case-by-case analysis.[360] In the environmental context, it is certainly possible to envisage the destruction of natural food sources or the contamination of drinking water directly causing severe physical or mental harm to the local population as 'other inhumane acts'.[361]

bb) Limitations

Although serious environmental harm can constitute one of the acts pursuant to Article 7 (1) (b), (d), (h) or (k) Rome Statute, envisaging environmental degradation as crimes against humanity faces several limitations.

(1) Contextual element

Firstly, the environmentally destructive conduct must be committed "as part of a widespread or systematic attack directed against any civilian population"[362] in order to elevate it to the level of a crime of international concern. This contextual element serves to distinguish domestic crimes from crimes under international law.[363] Thus, isolated acts of environmental damage not occurring as part of a widespread or systematic attack can only constitute grave human rights violations or, under certain circumstances, war crimes, however they do not reach the threshold of crimes against humanity.[364]

An 'attack directed against any civilian population' requires "a course of conduct involving the multiple commission of acts referred to in paragraph 1 against any

---

[358] Prosecutor v. Katanga, ICC-01/04-01/07, Decision on the Confirmation of Charges, ¶ 448 (Sept. 30, 2008).

[359] *Antonio Cassese*, et al., Cassese's International Criminal Law 92 (2013).

[360] *Gerhard Werle/Florian Jeßberger*, Principles of International Criminal Law para. 1138 (2020); *Iris Haenen*, Classifying Acts as Crimes Against Humanity in the Rome Statute of the International Criminal Court, 14 (7) German American Law Journal 796, 820 (2013).

[361] *Ricardo Pereira*, Criminal Law Forum 211 (2020); *Matthew Gillett*, Eco-Struggles 226 (2017); *Carl E. Bruch*, Vermont Law Review 729 (2001).

[362] Art. 7 (1) Rome Statute.

[363] *Kai Ambos*, Article 7, Crimes Against Humanity, in: Rome Statute of the International Criminal Court para. 13 (Kai Ambos ed., 2022); *Gerhard Werle/Florian Jeßberger*, Principles of International Criminal Law para. 987 (2020).

[364] See *Antonio Cassese*, et al., Cassese's International Criminal Law 93 (2013); *Antonio Cassese*, et al., The Rome Statute of the International Criminal Court: A Commentary 360 (2002).

civilian population, pursuant to or in furtherance of a State or organisational policy to commit such attack"[365]. The 'multiple commission of acts', however, does not necessarily require the perpetration of more than one act enumerated in Article 7 Rome Statute, but the multiple commission of the same act is also deemed sufficient.[366] With regards to environmental degradation, for instance, the multiple perpetration of single acts of toxic waste disposal would suffice if the disposal of toxic waste constituted, for instance, 'other inhumane act'.[367] In the context of Article 7 Rome Statute, it is noteworthy that an 'attack' does not denote a military attack[368] but rather pertains to any maltreatment of a civilian population.[369] Thus, environmentally destructive acts, such as water contamination or the destruction of food sources through industrial activity could easily amount to an 'attack directed against any civilian population'.[370]Additionally, environmental degradation will most likely be directed against 'any civilian population', especially if perpetrated in times of peace. Since crimes against humanity require an attack directed against 'any' civilian population, this type of crime is perceptibly broader than genocide which is restricted to particular groups.[371]

Since crimes against humanity can both be perpetrated in times of war and peace[372], their scope of application is broader than the environmental war crime pursuant to Article 8 (2) (b) (iv) Rome Statute which is restricted to international armed conflicts. Nevertheless, the conduct in question must be perpetrated as part of a 'widespread or systematic' attack in order to be able to constitute a crime against humanity. However, it is imperative to note that "[o]nly the attack, not the individual acts of the accused, must be widespread or systematic"[373]. The individual act

---

[365] Art. 7 (2) (a) Rome Statute.

[366] *Gerhard Werle/Florian Jeßberger*, Principles of International Criminal Law para. 997 (2020).

[367] *Caitlin Lambert*, Leiden Journal of International Law 721 (2017).

[368] ICC Elements of Crimes, Article 7 Introduction para. 3.

[369] Prosecutor v. Katanga, ICC-01/04-01/07, Judgment Pursuant to Article 74 of the Statute, ¶ 1101 (Mar. 7, 2014) ("the attack need not necessarily be military in nature, and it may involve any form of violence against a civilian population"); *Kai Ambos*, Article 7 para. 16 (2022); *Gerhard Werle/Florian Jeßberger*, Principles of International Criminal Law para. 998 (2020).

[370] *Caitlin Lambert*, Leiden Journal of International Law 721 (2017).

[371] *Gerhard Werle/Florian Jeßberger*, Principles of International Criminal Law para. 973 (2020).

[372] Prosecutor v. Tadić, Case No. IT-94-T, Decision on the Defence Motion on Jurisdiction, ¶ 80, 81 (Aug. 10, 1995); *Robert Cryer*, et al., An Introduction to International Criminal Law and Procedure 231, 232 (2019); *William A. Schabas*, The International Criminal Court: A Commentary on the Rome Statute 168–171 (2016).

[373] Prosecutor v. Kordić, Case No. IT-95–14/2-A, Judgment, ¶ 94 (Dec. 17, 2004); Prosecutor v. Blaškić, Case No. IT-95-14-A, Judgement, ¶ 101 (July 29, 2004).

itself then must be 'part of' this widespread or systematic attack directed against any civilian population.[374]

Despite initial disagreement, these two criteria were ultimately included as disjunctive prerequisites: thus, the attack needs to be either widespread or systematic.[375] The 'widespread' criterion pertains to the quantitative nature of the attack[376] concerning the "large-scale nature of the attack and the number of victims"[377]. The 'systematic' criterion, in turn, pertains to the qualitative nature of the attack and thus to "the organised nature of the acts of violence and to the improbability of their random occurrence"[378]. Thus, in order to qualify as systematic, the attack must be characterised by organisation and by following a certain pattern.[379] In general, both criteria are aimed at precluding random and isolated acts from constituting crimes against humanity.[380] In the context of environmental harm, it seems possible to envisage environmental harm as part of a widespread as well as a systematic attack. Environmental degradation causing large-scale environmental degradation and affecting large numbers of victims through, for instance, water or soil contamination could easily be identified as part of 'widespread' attack. At the same time, the continuous discharging of toxic wastes by multinational corporations could be recognised as a systematic policy.[381]

---

[374] Article 7 (1) Rome Statute; *William A. Schabas*, The International Criminal Court: A Commentary on the Rome Statute 166, 167 (2016).

[375] *Gerhard Werle/Florian Jeßberger*, Principles of International Criminal Law para. 1000 (2020).

[376] *Kai Ambos*, Article 7 para. 20 (2022); *Gerhard Werle/Florian Jeßberger*, Principles of International Criminal Law para. 1001 (2020); *Hans Vest*, Humanitätsverbrechen – Herausforderung für das Individualstrafrecht?, 113 (3) ZStW 457, 468 (2001).

[377] Prosecutor v. Kunarac, Case No. IT-96-23-T & IT-96-23/1-T, Judgement, ¶ 428 (Feb. 22, 2001); see also Prosecutor v. Al Bashir, ICC-02/05-01/09, Decision on the Prosecution's Application for a Warrant of Arrest against Omar Hassan Ahmad Al Bashir, ¶ 81 (Mar. 4, 2009); Prosecutor v. Blašić, Case No. IT-95-14-T, Judgement, ¶ 206 (Mar. 3, 2000); Prosecutor v. Tadić, Case No. IT-94-1-T, Opinion and Judgment, ¶ 648 (May 7, 1997); Prosecutor v. Akayesu, Case No. ICTR-96-4-T, Judgement, ¶ 580 (Sept. 2, 1998); Prosecutor v. Bemba, ICC-01/05-01/08, Decision Pursuant to Article 61(7)(a) and (b) of the Rome Statute on the Charges of the Prosecutor against Jean-Pierre Bemba Gombo, ¶ 83 (June 15, 2009).

[378] Prosecutor v. Al Bashir, ICC-02/05-01/09, Decision on the Prosecution's Application for a Warrant of Arrest against Omar Hassan Ahmad Al Bashir, ¶ 81 (Mar. 4, 2009); Prosecutor v. Katanga, ICC-01/04-01/07, Decision on the Confirmation of Charges, ¶ 394 (Sept. 30, 2008).

[379] *Gerhard Werle/Florian Jeßberger*, Principles of International Criminal Law para. 1002 (2020); *William A. Schabas*, The International Criminal Court: A Commentary on the Rome Statute 165 (2016).

[380] Prosecutor v. Al Bashir, ICC-02/05-01/09, Decision on the Prosecution's Application for a Warrant of Arrest against Omar Hassan Ahmad Al Bashir, ¶ 81 (Mar. 4, 2009); Prosecutor v. Katanga, ICC-01/04-01/07, Decision on the Confirmation of Charges, ¶ 394 (Sept. 30, 2008).

[381] *Caitlin Lambert*, Leiden Journal of International Law 725 (2017).

Additionally, such an attack needs to be perpetrated "pursuant to or in furtherance of a State or organizational policy to commit such attack"[382]. This so-called 'policy element' was included as a compromise for having incorporated 'widespread' and 'systematic' in the alternative instead of in a cumulative fashion.[383] In early decisions, the ad hoc Tribunals necessitated a "preconceived plan or policy"[384] in order to deem the policy element fulfilled, whereas nowadays neither a formally adopted nor an explicitly declared policy is required.[385] These days, "planned, directed or organized – as opposed to spontaneous or isolated acts of violence" are deemed sufficient.[386] While a certain degree of organisation is immanent to a systematic attack, a widespread attack is not necessarily organised or pre-planned, which is why the policy element becomes particularly relevant in the case of a 'widespread' attack.[387] At first glance, the wording 'State or organizational policy' insinuates that such a policy may be equally established by states and by non-state actors, which is particularly important in the context of environmental harm as this is most likely to be perpetrated by non-state actors such as corporate CEOs acting upon an organisational policy. Although some require a state policy in order to consider the policy element fulfilled[388], the ICC's jurisprudence is uniform in only requiring a "regular pattern"[389]. Accordingly, the policy must not be formalised and

---

[382] Article 7 (2) (a) Rome Statute.

[383] *Gerhard Werle/Florian Jeßberger*, Principles of International Criminal Law para. 1004 (2020); *Robert Cryer*, et al., An Introduction to International Criminal Law and Procedure 234 (2019).

[384] Prosecutor v. Akayesu, Case No. ICTR-96-4-T, Judgement, ¶ 580 (Sept. 2, 1998) (citing Report of the International Law Commission on the Work of its Forty-Eight Session, U.N. GAOR Supp. No.10, at 47, U.N. Doc. A/51/10 (1996)).

[385] Prosecutor v. Blaškić, Case No. IT-95-14-T, Judgement, ¶ 204 (Mar. 3, 2000); Prosecutor v. Tadić, Case No. IT-94-1-T, Opinion and Judgment, ¶ 653 (May 7, 1997); *Gerhard Werle/Florian Jeßberger*, Principles of International Criminal Law para. 1007 (2020); *Robert Cryer*, et al., An Introduction to International Criminal Law and Procedure 236–238 (2019).

[386] Prosecutor v. Bemba, ICC-01/05-01/08, Decision Pursuant to Article 61(7)(a) and (b) of the Rome Statute on the Charges of the Prosecutor against Jean-Pierre Bemba Gombo, ¶ 81 (June 15, 2009); see also Prosecutor v. Katanga, ICC-01/04-01/07, Decision on the Confirmation of Charges, ¶ 396 (Sept. 30, 2008).

[387] Prosecutor v. Katanga, ICC-01/04-01/07, Decision on the Confirmation of Charges, ¶ 396 (Sept. 30, 2008).

[388] Situation in the Republic of Kenya, Decision Pursuant to Article 15 of the Rome Statute on the Authorization of an Investigation into the Situation in the Republic of Kenya, ICC-01/09-19-Corr, Dissenting Opinion of Judge Hans-Peter Kaul, ¶ 51 (Mar. 31, 2010) (contending that "even though the constitutive elements of statehood need not be established those 'organizations' should partake of some characteristics of a State. Those characteristics eventually turn the private 'organization' into an entity which may act like a State or has quasi-State abilities").

[389] Prosecutor v. Bemba, ICC-01/05-01/08, Decision Pursuant to Article 61(7)(a) and (b) of the Rome Statute on the Charges of the Prosecutor Against Jean-Pierre Bemba Gombo, ¶ 81 (June 15, 2009); Prosecutor v. Katanga, ICC-01/04-01/07, Decision on the Confirmation of Charges, ¶ 396 (Sept. 30, 2008).

must not necessarily be the policy of a state, but it is rather sufficient for a policy to be made by "any organization with the capability to commit a widespread or systematic attack against a civilian population"[390] irrespective of its nature or organisation.[391] This broad interpretation of an 'organizational policy' corresponds to the wording of the provision implying that the drafters would not have included this term if they had only intended to refer to state actors.[392]Additionally, this interpretation is in line with the purpose of the policy element to preclude isolated and random acts perpetrated upon an individual's own initiative.[393] Accordingly, multinational corporations repeatedly causing large-scale environmental degradation, and thereby severely affecting the civilian population, undoubtedly operate in furtherance of an organisational policy.[394] However, it is noteworthy that according to the Elements of Crime the policy to commit such an attack requires the state or organisation to "actively promote or encourage such an attack against a civilian population"[395] or to deliberately fail to take action "which is consciously aimed at encouraging such attack"[396]. This, in turn, leads to the assumption that any environmental harm "simply tolerated or condoned by a state or an organization"[397] is excluded from criminal liability. In this vein, the Elements of Crime determine that the existence of a policy cannot be solely deduced from the paucity of state or organisational action.[398] Since the Rome Statute does not specify when a policy is

---

[390] Prosecutor v. Bemba, ICC-01/05-01/08, Decision Pursuant to Article 61(7)(a) and (b) of the Rome Statute on the Charges of the Prosecutor Against Jean-Pierre Bemba Gombo, ¶ 81 (June 15, 2009); see also Prosecutor v. Katanga, ICC-01/04-01/07, Decision on the Confirmation of Charges, para. 396 (Sept. 30, 2008); situation in the Republic of Kenya, Decision Pursuant to Article 15 of the Rome Statute on the Authorization of an Investigation into the Situation in the Republic of Kenya, ¶ 92 (Mar. 31, 2010); Prosecutor v. Tadić, Case No. IT-94-1-T, Opinion and Judgment, ¶ 654 (May 7, 1997).

[391] Situation in the Republic of Kenya, Decision Pursuant to Article 15 of the Rome Statute on the Authorization of an Investigation into the Situation on the Republic of Kenya, ICC-01/09, ¶ 90 (Mar. 31, 2010); quoted in Prosecutor v. Muthaura, ICC-01/09-02/11, Decision on the Confirmation of Charges pursuant to Article 61(7)(a) and (b) of the Rome Statute, ¶ 112 (Jan. 23, 2012); see also Situation in the Republic of Côte d'Ivoire, ICC-02/11, ¶ 46 (Oct. 3, 2011) (listing a number of criteria which may be considered when determining whether a group qualifies as an 'organisation').

[392] Situation in the Republic of Kenya, Decision Pursuant to Article 15 of the Rome Statute on the Authorization of an Investigation into the Situation in the Republic of Kenya, ¶ 92 (Mar. 31, 2010); quoted in Prosecutor v. Muthaura, ICC-01/09-02/11, Decision on the Confirmation of Charges Pursuant to Article 61(7)(a) and (b) of the Rome Statute, ¶ 112 (Jan. 23, 2012).

[393] *Robert Cryer*, et al., An Introduction to International Criminal Law and Procedure 238 (2019); *Kai Ambos*, Article 7 para. 4 (2022).

[394] See *Caitlin Lambert*, Leiden Journal of International Law 722, 723 (2017).

[395] ICC Elements of Crimes, Art. 7 Introduction para. 3.

[396] ICC Elements of Crimes, Art. 7 Introduction, para. 3 n. 6.

[397] *Antonio Cassese*, et al., Cassese's International Criminal Law 107 (2013).

[398] ICC Elements of Crimes, Art. 7 Introduction, para. 3 n. 6.

actively promoted or encouraged, this requirement must be determined on a case-by-case analysis.

The perpetrator has to further act "with knowledge of the attack"[399]. However, according to the Elements of Crime, the accused is not required to have knowledge of "all characteristics of the attack or the precise details of the plan or policy of the State or organization"[400]. Instead, the accused is meant to be aware of the existence of a widespread and systematic attack and that his individual act is part thereof.[401] Thus, crimes against humanity have a perceptibly lower mental threshold than the crime of genocide. This lower mental threshold facilitates the prosecution of environmental harm since environmental destruction during peacetime is mostly an unwanted but condoned side-effect of industrial activities, which does not amount to genocidal intent in the majority of cases.

(2) Inherently anthropocentric perspective

However, the main limitation concerning environmental harm is the inherently anthropocentric perspective of crimes *against humanity*.[402] Crimes against humanity, such as extermination or the deportation of a population, require the *direct* causation of human harm.[403] Thus, environmental harm only constitutes a crime against humanity if it *directly* causes human harm. Hence, the environment as such remains unprotected and can only gain indirect relevance if human harm is *directly* caused *by means of* environmental harm.

(3) Conclusion

While, in theory, environmental destruction can fall within the ambit of Article 7 Rome Statute, environmentally destructive conduct can only be prosecuted as a crime against humanity if it is committed as part of a widespread or systematic attack directed against any civilian population following a state or organisational policy. Hence, random and isolated acts resulting in large-scale environmental degradation are not prosecutable as crimes against humanity. Most importantly, however, crimes against humanity are inherently anthropocentric requiring the *direct* causation of human harm by means of environmental harm.

---

[399] Art. 7 (1) Rome Statute.

[400] ICC Elements of Crimes, Art. 7 Introduction para. 2.

[401] *Gerhard Werle/Florian Jeßberger*, Principles of International Criminal Law para. 1020 (2020); *Antonio Cassese*, et al., Cassese's International Criminal Law 98 (2013); *Antonio Cassese*, et al., The Rome Statute of the International Criminal Court: A Commentary 373 (2002).

[402] *Rosemary Mwanza*, Melb. Journal of International Law 12 (2018); *Caitlin Lambert*, Leiden Journal of International Law 713 (2017).

[403] *Emanuela Fronza*, Towards a New Crime of Ecocide: The Moving Frontiers of International Criminal Law, in: Strafrecht und Systemunrecht 100 (Florian Jeßberger, et al. eds., 2022).

For these reasons, it is not advisable to include a new environmental crime as a crime against humanity into Article 7 Rome Statute, not only because of its strictly anthropocentric legal view but also because of its limited scope of application due to its contextual requirement.[404] However, prosecuting environmental destruction as crimes against humanity within its current ambit could serve as an intermediate step towards the establishment of a legal precedent concerning the prosecution of environmental harm irrespective of human harm.[405]

Notwithstanding, to date Sudanese President Al Bashir is the only person who has been charged with several crimes against humanity involving environmental harm, yet he is still at large, and the case is thus stuck in the Pre-Trial stage.[406] Nonetheless, the ICC has already been asked to investigate cases involving environmental harm allegedly constituting crimes against humanity on several occasions. In October 2014, a Communication[407] was filed with the ICC Prosecutor requesting her to investigate the situation in Ecuador where the oil company Chevron was alleged to have committed crimes against humanity after having discharged tons of oil and toxic wastes into the environment resulting in severe contamination of soil and water and not having adhered to the court order mandating the company to clean up the toxic contamination in the Amazon.[408] However, in 2015 the Communication was ultimately dismissed by the Prosecutor both on *lex temporalis* and evidentiary grounds.[409] Additionally, in October 2014, a Communication pursuant to Article 15 Rome Statue was filed with the ICC Prosecutor alleging mass human rights violations due to systematic land-grabbing committed by Cambodian officials amounting to crimes against humanity.[410] However, to date the OTP

---

[404] *Prisca Merz/Cabanes Valérie, et al.*, Ending Ecocide, The Next Necessary Step In International Law at 16 (2014); *Kevin Jon Heller*, Skeptical Thoughts on the Proposed Crime of "Ecocide" (That Isn't), OpinioJuris (June 23, 2021), https://opiniojuris.org/2021/06/23/skeptical-thoughts-on-the-proposed-crime-of-ecocide-that-isnt/ (last visited Feb. 18, 2025).

[405] *Tara Weinstein*, Geo. Int'l Envtl. L. Rev. 713, 722 (2005).

[406] International Criminal Court, Al Bashir Case, https://www.icc-cpi.int/darfur/albashir (last visited Feb. 18, 2025).

[407] *Pablo Fajardo Mendoza/Eduardo Bernabé Toledo*, Communication, Situation in Ecuador, https://chevroninecuador.org/assets/docs/2014-icc-complaint.pdf (last visited Feb. 18, 2025).

[408] Id.; see *Audrey Crasson*, Amsterdam Law Forum (2017); *Caitlin Lambert*, Leiden Journal of International Law (2017).

[409] The Office of the Prosecutor, Letter from M.P. Dillon, Head of the Information & Evidence Unit, Office of the Prosecutor, Reference No. OTP2014/036752 (Mar. 16, 2015), available at: http://freebeacon.com/wp-content/uploads/2015/04/ICC-letter.pdf (last visited Feb. 18, 2025); *Audrey Crasson*, Amsterdam Law Forum 38 (2017).

[410] Since the communication still remains classified, only an executive summary is accessible here: Global Diligence, Communication under Article 15 of the Rome Statute of the International Criminal Court (2020), https://www.fidh.org/IMG/pdf/executive_summary-2.pdf (last visited Feb. 18, 2025); see for a detailed analysis of this Communication, *Franziska Maria Oehm*, Land Grabbing in Cambodia as a Crime Against Humanity, Approaches, in: International Criminal Law 48 (4), Verfassung und Recht in Übersee 469 (2015).

has not initiated preliminary examinations.[411] More recently, in 2021, the ICC became engaged with environmental harm in the context of crimes against humanity, when a communication was filed with the ICC requesting the preliminary examination into Brazilian President Bolsonaro's governance having promoted the unprecedented deforestation of the Amazon's rainforest, which is alleged to amount to crimes against humanity, including the murder, forced displacement and persecution of indigenous people.[412] However, so far, the OTP has not conducted a respective preliminary examination.[413]

V. Research findings

In theory, large-scale environmental devastation can be prosecuted as war crimes, genocide, or crimes against humanity under the current Rome Statute. However, despite the 2016 OTP Policy Paper no preliminary examination concerning environmental harm in the context of war crimes, crimes against humanity or genocide has been instigated since 2016.[414]

In practice, the ICC is unlikely to prosecute environmental harm as a crime of genocide due to the significantly high evidentiary burden of having to prove the perpetrator's intent to destroy a particular group. Even if the Prosecutor succeeds in proving the knowing destruction of ecosystems, in the majority of cases the conduct in question will have occurred for economic reasons and not with the intention of destroying a particular group of people.

Thus, it seems far more feasible to prosecute environmental destruction as a crime against humanity or as a war crime as both do not require genocidal intent. However, a successful prosecution as a war crime pursuant to Article 8 (2) (b) (iv) Rome Statute requires the environmental harm to occur in the context of an international armed conflict excluding conduct occurring during non-international armed conflict or in peacetime. Since most environmental devastation is caused by

---

[411] International Criminal Court, Preliminary Examinations, https://www.icc-cpi.int/situations-preliminary-examinations (last visited Feb. 18, 2025).

[412] *Flàvia Milhorance*, Jair Bolsonaro Could Face Charges in The Hague Over Amazon Rainforest, The Guardian, Jan. 23, 2021, https://www.theguardian.com/world/2021/jan/23/jair-bolsonaro-could-face-charges-in-the-hague-over-amazon-rainforest.

[413] International Criminal Court, Preliminary Examinations, https://www.icc-cpi.int/situations-preliminary-examinations (last visited Feb. 18, 2025).

[414] See The Office of the Prosecutor, Report on Preliminary Examination Activities (2020); The Office of the Prosecutor, Report on Preliminary Examination Activities (2019) (With regards to the preliminary examinations concerning the alleged environmental destruction committed by Chinese nations in the Philippines, the ICC concluded that the alleged crimes fall outside the territorial or personal jurisdiction of the Court, see para. 51); The Office of the Prosecutor, Report on Preliminary Examination Activities (2018); The Office of the Prosecutor, Report on Preliminary Examination Activities (2017); The Office of the Prosecutor, Report on Preliminary Examination Activities (2016).

corporate activities during peacetime, Article 8 (2) (b) (iv) Rome Statute does not afford effective global environmental protection, despite being the only ecocentric provision under the current Rome Statute. Furthermore, not only the significantly high material standard of 'widespread, long-term and severe' environmental damage, but also the high mental standard excluding all forms of reckless and negligent conduct, precludes all but the most egregious forms of environmental harm. Additionally, all types of environmental harm, not matter how serious, can at least in theory be justified by military advantage.

Hence, particularly with regards to peacetime environmental destruction prosecuting environmental harm as crimes against humanity appears to be the sole option, as crimes against humanity are not restricted to international armed conflicts and have a considerably lower mental threshold than the crime of genocide, while at the same time many of the same acts are covered. Nevertheless, the environmental harm in question must form part of a widespread or systematic attack pursuant to or in furtherance of an organisational policy excluding random and isolated acts of environmental damage. Although most large-scale environmental harm, especially if committed by multinational corporations following a particular pattern, would satisfy this contextual element, crimes against humanity hold an exclusively anthropocentric perspective. Thus, environmental destruction only constitutes a crime against humanity if it *directly* causes human harm. Should environmental harm not *directly* cause human harm by killing, displacing, violating universal human rights or inflicting great suffering or serious bodily or mental harm, it would not be prosecutable as a crime against humanity. The environment as such is thus left unprotected. The fact that crimes against humanity and genocide both only afford *indirect* environmental protection lessens the potential deterrent effect and symbolic value of possible convictions for environmental degradation.[415] Thus, it is not surprising that beyond academic debate, promoting environmental protection under the rubric of genocide or crimes against humanity has received very little attention so far.[416]

In conclusion, these findings manifest that environmental protection afforded under the current Rome Statute is riddled with gaps. Nevertheless, not only international criminal law but more accurately the entire current legal framework including international environmental law, international humanitarian law, human rights law as well as international criminal law is not equipped to halt large-scale environmental destruction and to afford global environmental protection. This, however, stands in stark contrast to Principle 10 of the Rio Declaration requiring that "[e]ffective access to judicial and administrative proceedings, including redress and remedy, shall be available". Hence, this signals the need to establish new legal tools to promote global environmental protection. In this thesis, a proposal to promote global environmental protection through criminal law by establishing a

[415] *Matthew Gillett*, Eco-Struggles 226, 227 (2017).

[416] *Ricardo Pereira*, Rev. Eur. Comp. & Int'l Envtl. L., 217 (2017).

generic international crime against the environment will be advanced. In the following two chapters, two possibilities of establishing such a crime against the environment will be discussed. First, the incorporation of a fifth core crime into the Rome Statute and, secondly, the establishment of an International Environmental Convention containing such a crime, which could either be indirectly enforced through national courts or directly enforced through an International Environmental Court, which is yet to be established.

C. Incorporation of a fifth crime of ecocide into the Rome Statute

> "Experience has shown that the existing systems of penalties have not been sufficient to achieve complete compliance with the laws for the protection of the environment. Such compliance can and should be strengthened by the availability of criminal penalties, which demonstrate a social disapproval of a qualitatively different nature compared to administrative penalties or a compensation mechanism under civil law."[1]

Due to the inadequate environmental protection currently afforded by international law, some propose to incorporate a fifth core crime into the Rome Statute proscribing large-scale environmental harm.[2] By stipulating individual criminal liability for environmentally harmful conduct with the inherent threat of being sent to prison, international criminal law is of a completely different qualitative nature than administrative or civil law. As Philippe Sands rightly stated, "Nothing concentrates the mind better than the prospect of an individual being found criminally liable"[3]. The debate of whether to incorporate a fifth environmental crime is conducted under the heading of a possible new *crime of ecocide*.[4]

Section C will serve to analyse whether the establishment of a stand-alone crime of ecocide under the Rome Statute could promote global environmental protection. Firstly, the meaning of the term 'ecocide' will be outlined (I.). Secondly, the history of ecocide will be presented (II.). Thirdly, the potentials of including a fifth core crime will be discussed (III.). Fourthly, the characteristics of crimes under international criminal law will be presented in order to examine whether large-scale environmental harm could qualify as a crime under international law (IV.). Fifthly, possible definitions of such a generic crime of ecocide will be assessed and evaluated (V.). Sixthly, the requirements to amend the Rome Statute will be outlined

---

[1] Directive 2008/99/EC, Preamble (3).

[2] *Polly Higgins*, Eradicating Ecocide: Laws and Governance to Stop the Destruction of the Planet (2nd ed., 2015); *Prisca Merz/Cabanes Valérie*, et al., Ending Ecocide, The Next Necessary Step In International Law (2014); *Polly Higgins*, et al., Crime, Law and Social Change (2013); *Anja Gauger*, et al., The Ecocide Project – Ecocide Is the Missing 5th Crime Against Peace (2012); *Mark Allan Gray*, The International Crime of Ecocide, 26 Cal. W. Int'l L.J. 215 (1996).

[3] *India Bourke*, Philippe Sands on why "Ecocide" Should Be a Crime, The New Statesman, Feb. 16, 2021, https://www.newstatesman.com/world/2021/02/philippe-sands-why-ecocide-should-be-crime.

[4] *Polly Higgins*, Eradicating Ecocide: Laws and Governance to Stop the Destruction of the Planet 61 (2015); *Mark Allan Gray*, Cal. W. Int'l L.J. (1996); *Laurent Neyret*, Des écocrimes à l'écocide: le droit pénal au secours de l'environnement 343 (2015).

(VI.), prior to discussing the impediments to the enforcement of a possible crime of ecocide under the Rome Statute (VII.).

I. The term ecocide

Broadly speaking, *ecocide* denotes "the destruction of the natural environment"[5] according to Prisca Merz, initiator of the European Citizens' Initiative 'End Ecocide in Europe'. In terms of etymology the term *ecocide* combines two terms: 'eco' and 'cide'. 'Eco' is derived from 'oikos', the Greek word for house or home; and 'cide' is derived from 'caedere', the Latin verb for killing.[6] Thus, *ecocide* literally denotes "killing our home"[7].

According to the Stop Ecocide International Foundation, the following environmentally harmful conduct could qualify as ecocide[8]:

- *ocean damage* caused by industrial fishery (overfishing/deep sea bottom trawling), oil spills[9], plastic pollution or deep-sea mining;
- *deforestation* due to industrial farming[10] (cattle farming/soya growing), mineral extraction, oil drilling or palm oil and wood manufacturing;
- *land and water contamination* caused by oil spills[11], mining[12], tar sands[13], fracking, the disposal of textile chemicals, industrial agricultural chemicals and monocrop practices; and

---

[5] *Prisca Merz*, Ecocide: Prisca Merz Argues It Is Now Time to Act Against the Large-Scale Damage or Destruction of Ecosystems, Socialist Lawyer 16, 17 (2014).

[6] *Anastacia Greene*, Fordham Environmental Law Review 31 (2019).

[7] Id.

[8] See for possible cases of ecocide, Stop Ecocide International, What is Ecocide?, https://www.stopecocide.earth/what-is-ecocide (last visited Feb. 18, 2025).

[9] The largest oil spill in history occurred at the BP Deepwater Horizon in the Gulf of Mexico in April 2010. Twelve years after the tragedy no BP employee has yet been convicted under U.S. criminal law (see *Jonathan Stempel*, No Prison Terms for Gulf Spill As Final Defendant Gets Probation, Reuters, Apr. 6, 2016, https://www.reuters.com/article/us-bp-spill-sentencing-idUSKCN0X3241).This incident could have been a case for an international crime of 'ecocide'.

[10] President Bolsonaro could be tried for ecocide for the ongoing deforestation of the Amazonian rainforest (see *Georgina Rannard*, Amazon Deforestation, Record High Destruction of Trees in January, BBC News, Feb. 11, 2022, https://www.bbc.com/news/science-environment-60333422).

[11] A case could be Shell's oil spills and gas flaring in the Niger Delta which continue despite having been prohibited by a national court in 2005 and exacerbate the climate change crisis in this area (see *Mélissa Godin*, Lawyers Are Working to Put 'Ecocide' On Par with War Crimes, Could an International Law Hold Major Polluters to Account?, Time, Feb. 19, 2021, https://time.com/5940759/ecocide-law-environment-destruction-icc/).

[12] A possible ecocide case is the mountaintop removal mining in the Appalachia (see *Sarah Saadoun*, The Coal Mine Next Door, How the US Government's Deregulation of Mountaintop

– *air pollution* due to chemical disasters[14], chemical weapons, nuclear accidents[15], nuclear testing, nuclear weapons and industrial emissions.

As demonstrated, numerous highly environmentally detrimental activities which could qualify as ecocide are taking place all over the world in this very moment. Yet, with regards to a new fifth crime under the Rome Statute, the term ecocide appears problematic.

The neologism 'ecocide' draws upon the word 'genocide' comprising the Greek word 'genos', meaning race or tribe and the Latin 'caedere' for killing, which was coined by Polish jurist and Holocaust survivor Rafael Lemkin during the Second World War.[16]

Since 'genocide' emerged in response to the atrocities perpetrated against European Jews by the Nazis, Lemkin's concept of genocide is largely dominated by the Holocaust.[17] Lemkin's work paved the way for the adoption of the Genocide Convention[18] in 1948 whose definition of the crime of genocide was later incorporated verbatim into the ICTY, ICTR[19] and ICC Statutes.

While the definition of genocide under the Rome Statute is very restrictive, particularly with regard to its significantly high subjective element, the term 'genocide' is much more loosely used in international politics to relate to any severe human rights infringement irrespective of whether such behaviour would actually

---

Removal Threatens Public Health, Human Rights Watch, Dec. 10, 2018, https://www.hrw.org/report/2018/12/10/coal-mine-next-door/how-us-governments-deregulation-mountaintop-removal-threatens).

[13] A case could be the Athabasca tar sands located in Alberta, Canada, which are currently the largest tar sands (see *Stephen Leahy*, This Is The World's Most Destructive Oil Operation – And It's Growing, National Geographic, Apr. 11, 2019, https://www.nationalgeographic.com/environment/article/alberta-canadas-tar-sands-is-growing-but-indigenous-people-fight-back).

[14] The worst chemical disaster in history took place in Bhopal in 1984, having killed thousands of people, which resulted in the conviction of eight former Union Carbide employees in 2010 who were sentenced to two years in prison (see *Ashutosh Shukla*, Bhopal Gas Tragedy Convict Dead, 37 Years Later, Court Fight Drags On, The Times of India, Oct. 12, 2021, https://timesofindia.indiatimes.com/city/bhopal/bhopal-gas-tragedy-convict-dead-37-years-later-court-fight-drags-on/articleshow/86954663.cms). Less lenient sentences could have been served if an international crime of ecocide had been in force.

[15] Another possible ecocide case could have been the Fukishima nuclear accident in 2011 for which nobody was held criminally liable (see *Yating Wang*, Fukushima Nuclear Disaster Aftermath: No One Was Found Criminally Liable, Fordham Environmental Law Review (Dec. 3, 2019), https://fordhamlawelr.org/?p=686).

[16] *Raphael Lemkin*, Axis Rule in Occupied Europe 79 (1944).

[17] *Damien Short*, Redefining Genocide, Settler Colonialism, Social Death and Ecocide 2 (2016).

[18] Convention on the Prevention and Punishment of the Crime of Genocide, Dec. 9, 1948, 78 U.N.T.S. 277.

[19] ICTR stands for the International Criminal Tribunal for Rwanda.

constitute a crime of genocide pursuant to Article 6 Rome Statute.[20] This was recently evidenced when Russia invaded the Ukraine under the pretense of an alleged genocide committed against the Russian population in Luhansk and Donetsk in the East of Ukraine. In this regard, the ICJ issued a provisional order for Russia to "immediately suspend the military operations commenced on 24 February 2022"[21] due to a lack of evidence concerning the Russian allegation of genocide pursuant to the Genocide Convention.[22] The Security Council published a statement on behalf of the Russian Federation, in which the Russian Federation clarified that "[a] reference to genocide is not equal to the invocation of the Convention [...] since the notion of genocide exists in customary international law independently of the Convention"[23].

This, in turn, demonstrates that the term 'genocide' is highly politicised and is widely utilised by politicians to accuse states of grave human rights violations.[24]

Thus, referring to large-scale environmental destruction as 'ecocide' and thereby cross-referencing to genocide, the "crime of crimes"[25], undoubtedly generates attention. However, drawing from the term 'genocide' also entails numerous problems.

First, by equating severe environmental destruction with genocide, the crime of genocide may be trivialised and victims of the Holocaust or the Rwandan or Srebrenican genocide may thus be dishonoured.[26] While the crime of genocide primarily, if not exclusively, protects the existence of a certain national, ethnical, racial

[20] *Christoph Safferling*, Internationales Strafrecht § 6 para. 2 (2011); see *Robert Cryer*, et al., An Introduction to International Criminal Law and Procedure 206 (2019).

[21] Allegations of Genocide Under the Convention on the Prevention and Punishment of the Crime of Genocide (Ukraine v. Russian Federation), Provisional Measures, Order, para. 5a, I. C.J. Reports 2022 (Mar. 16).

[22] Id. at paras. 55–60.

[23] U.N. Security Council, Letter Dated 24 February 2022 from the Permanent Representative of the Russian Federation to the United Nations Addressed to the Secretary-General, at para. 20, U.N. Doc. S/2022/154 (2022).

[24] Another example of states deploying the term 'genocide' to accuse a State of severe human rights infringements is the alleged genocide perpetrated by China against the Uighurs, see *Edward Wong/Chris Buckley*, U.S. Says China's Repression of Uighurs Is 'Genocide', The New York Times, Jan. 19, 2021, https://www.nytimes.com/2021/01/19/us/politics/trump-china-xinjiang.html.

[25] Prosecutor v. Kambanda, Case No. ICTR 97-23-S, Judgement and Sentence, ¶ 16 (Sept. 4, 1998); Prosecutor v. Serushago, Case No. ICTR 98-39-S, Sentence, ¶ 15 (Feb. 5, 1999); see also Proscecutor v. Al Bashir, ICC-02/05-01/09, Decision on the Prosecution's Application for a Warrant of Arrest Against Omar Hassan Ahmad Al Bashir, ¶ 133 (Mar. 4, 2009); *William A. Schabas*, Genocide in International Law: The Crime of Crimes 15 (2009).

[26] See *Mark Notaras*, Should Ecocide Be Deemed a Crime Against Peace?, Our World, Mar. 5, 2010, https://ourworld.unu.edu/en/should-ecocide-be-deemed-a-crime-against-peace; *Wesley Smith*, Ecocide: A Crime Against Peace?, The Weekly Standard, May 10, 2010, https://www.washingtonexaminer.com/weekly-standard/ecocide-a-crime-against-peace.

or religious group[27], a crime of ecocide intends to protect the environment as such, not specific species. Hence, it could be argued that by referring to genocide, the term ecocide equates severe environmental destruction with the extinction of certain groups of people. Secondly, the reference to 'genocide' might allude to the fact that a crime of 'ecocide' requires a similarly high mental threshold, which renders most genocide prosecutions unsuccessful. Thirdly, similar to genocide, ecocide might turn, if it has not already done so, into a highly political term to describe any serious environmental damage, irrespective of whether the conduct in question constitutes a crime under international criminal law.

Hence, as the debate concerning the incorporation of a fifth environmental crime into the Rome Statute has always been conducted under the general heading of a 'crime of ecocide', in this thesis the term will be used to generally refer to the criminalisation of large-scale environmental destruction under international criminal law. However, for the abovementioned reasons it is not advisable to introduce a generic crime of large-scale environmental harm under the heading of a 'crime of ecocide'. Instead, to eschew similar problems experienced with the crime of genocide, it is suggested to resort to alternative terms such as 'crimes against the environment'[28], instead of using terms such as 'ecocide'[29] or 'geocide'[30].

II. History of ecocide

Prior to assessing the creation of a fifth crime of ecocide under the Rome Statute it is imperative to comprehend the historical origins of the concept of ecocide which shed light on the current legal gaps concerning environmental protection under the Rome Statute. In any event, the idea of identifying environmentally destructive behaviour as a crime under international criminal law is not a new concept and has already persisted for over 50 years.

1. Origin of 'ecocide' – Vietnam War

The term ecocide was first coined by Prof. Arthur Galston in 1970 to describe the environmental harm inflicted upon South Vietnam during the Vietnam war where the US military had sprayed more than ten percent of South Vietnam with a defo-

[27] *Gerhard Werle/Florian Jeßberger*, Principles of International Criminal Law paras. 890–894 (2020); *Christoph Safferling*, Internationales Strafrecht § 6 paras. 9, 10 (2011).

[28] *Regina Rauxloh*, The Role of International Criminal Law in Environmental Protection 447 (2011); *Alfred Rest*, Envtl. Pol'y & L., 39 (1999).

[29] *Polly Higgins*, Eradicating Ecocide: Laws and Governance to Stop the Destruction of the Planet 61 (2015); *Mark Allan Gray*, Cal. W. Int'l L.J. (1996); *Laurent Neyret*, Des écocrimes à l'écocide: le droit pénal au secours de l'environnement 343 (2015).

[30] *Lynn Berat*, Defending the Right to a Healthy Environment: Toward a Crime of Geocide in International Law, B.U. INT'l L. J. 327 (1993).

liant herbicide called 'Agent Orange'.[31] This herbicide contained the toxic chemical dioxin, which was used to defoliate forests and mangroves and which caused long-term soil and air contamination as well as human suffering.[32] Thus, the debate as to whether the US was committing ecocide was provoked. At the Conference on War and National Responsibility in Washington in 1970, Galston, a US biologist, "proposed a new international agreement to ban ecocide"[33] after discovering that his Ph. D. findings had been used in the development of Agent Orange.[34] However, Galston's primary intention was to prohibit chemical warfare, such as the use of Agent Orange, rather than drafting a crime of ecocide.[35] He subsequently initiated the investigation of the impacts of Agent Orange on human beings by the Department of Defense which published a report revealing the detrimental effects on the reproductive system of laboratory rats and which then urged President Nixon to instantly outlaw Agent Orange in 1971.[36]

After ecocide was first mentioned by Galston, the term rapidly spread across the news and legal academia. However, due to its first emergence in the context of the Vietnam war, the concept of ecocide was originally limited to wartime.[37]

2. 1970s–1980s: Draft Ecocide Convention and proposals to revise the Genocide Convention

In his speech at the Stockholm Conference in 1972, Swedish Prime Minister Olof Palme referred to the US warfare in Vietnam as ecocide, stating:

> "The immense destruction brought about by indiscriminate bombing, by large scale use of bulldozers and herbicides is an outrage sometimes described as ecocide, which requires urgent international attention [...]. It is of paramount importance [...] that ecological warfare cease immediately."[38]

---

[31] See further on 'Agent Orange' *Michael G. Palmer*, The Case of Agent Orange, 29 Contemporary Southeast Asia 172 (2007).

[32] *Richard A. Falk*, Environmental Warfare and Ecocide, 4 (1) Bulletin of Peace Proposals 80, 85 (1973); *Karen Hulme*, War Torn Environment 5 (2004).

[33] New York Times, Febr. 26, 1970, cited in *Barry Weisberg*, Ecocide in Indochina, The Ecology of War (1970).

[34] *Anastacia Greene*, Fordham Environmental Law Review 8 (2019).

[35] See *Damien Short*, Redefining Genocide, Settler Colonialism, Social Death and Ecocide 41 (2016); *Anastacia Greene*, Fordham Environmental Law Review 9 (2019).

[36] *Jeremy Pearce*, Arthur Galston, Agent Orange Researcher, Is Dead at 88, The New York Times, June 23, 2008, https://www.nytimes.com/2008/06/23/us/23galston.html.

[37] *Damien Short*, Redefining Genocide, Settler Colonialism, Social Death and Ecocide 40 (2016).

[38] *Olof Palme*, Outrage of Ecocide, Bulletin of the Atomic Scientists 44, 44, 45 (1972).

In 1973, Professor Richard Falk published a draft International Convention on the Crime of Ecocide[39] introducing a list of acts which can constitute ecocide when committed "with intent to disrupt or destroy, in whole or in part, a human ecosystem" (Article II). Falk thereby drew a comparison to the Genocide Convention, which arose in the aftermath of the Second World War. He argued, that "just as the Genocide Convention came along to formalise part of what has already been carried and punished at Nuremberg, so an Ecocide Convention could help carry forward into the future a legal condemnation of environmental warfare in Indochina"[40]. Although the draft Ecocide Convention was applicable both in times of peace and war (Article I), the list of acts predominantly pertained to environmental harm in the context of war or military actions. Ultimately, Falk's draft Ecocide Convention was never adopted.

However, the perceptibly growing inclination to curb military tactics adversely affecting the environment in reaction to the Vietnam war resulted in the adoption of the aforementioned ENMOD Convention[41] in 1977. Nonetheless, it is particularly noteworthy that a breach of the Convention did not incur individual criminal liability. Hence, with regards to international criminal law, the ENMOD Convention can only serve as an interpretive aid for the Rome Statute provisions. In 1977, however, a war crime establishing individual criminal liability for environmental destruction was enshrined in Articles 35 (3), 55 (1) AP I, prohibiting the use of "methods or means of warfare which are intended, or may be expected, to cause widespread, long-term and severe damage to the natural environment"[42]. Nevertheless, the provisions only apply to international armed conflicts.[43]

Besides the idea of establishing a crime of ecocide as a stand-alone crime, the notion of including a crime of ecocide into the Genocide Convention was also contemplated. However, a UN study assessing the potential incorporation of a crime of ecocide into the Genocide Convention rejected this idea in 1978. The Special Rapporteur argued that ecocide is regarded as a war crime after having been included in the Additional Protocol I to the Geneva Conventions[44], and thus "an exaggerated extension of the idea of genocide to cases of ecocide which can only have a very distant connexion with that idea is liable to prejudice the effectiveness

[39] *Richard A. Falk*, Bulletin of Peace Proposals, 93, Appendix I (1973).

[40] Id. at 84.

[41] Convention on the Prohibition of Military or Any Hostile Uses of Environmental Modification, Dec. 10, 1976, 1108 U.N.T. S. 151.

[42] Art. 35 (3) AP I.

[43] See Art. 1 (3) AP I in conjunction with Geneva Convention Relative to the Protection of Civilian Persons in Time of War art. 2, Aug. 12, 1949, 75 U.N.T.S. 287. No equivalent provision is provided by Protocol II pertaining to non-international armed conflicts.

[44] *Nicodème Ruhashyankiko* (Special Rapporteur on Prevention and Punishment of the Crime of Genocide), Study of the Question of the Prevention and Punishment of the Crime of Genocide, at paras. 470–474, U.N. Doc. E/CN.4/Sub.2/416 (1978).

of the 1948 Genocide Convention very seriously" [45]. In 1985, the UN-study was updated and the inclusion of ecocide into the Genocide Convention was reconsidered.[46] While some members of the Sub-Commission proposed including a crime of ecocide in the genocide definition as "adverse alterations, often irreparable, to the environment – for example, through nuclear explosions, chemical weapons, serious pollution and acid rain, or destruction of the rain forest – which threaten the existence of entire populations, whether deliberately or with criminal negligence"[47], others opined that ecocide should rather be considered a crime against humanity than genocide.[48] The Sub-Commission's final report included a recommendation for the Special Rapporteur Whitaker to further investigate the inclusion of ecocide into the Genocide Convention.[49] However, ultimately a crime of ecocide was never incorporated into the Genocide Convention.[50]

Even though consensus regarding the criminalisation of ecocide was never reached in the 1970s and 1980s, the concept of ecocide has broadened in two ways. First, the concept of ecocide was no longer exclusively constrained to wartime, but included peacetime industrial activities such as serious pollution, acid rain and the destruction of the rain forest. Secondly, environmental crime no longer needed to be intended but could also be committed negligently.

3. 1980s–2000s: Early drafts of the Rome Statute including ecocide

Even though a distinct Ecocide Convention was never adopted, and a crime of ecocide was never included in the Genocide Convention, the idea of criminalising environmental destruction persisted. In 1947, after having acknowledged the need to establish a permanent international criminal court in the aftermath of the Second World War, the International Law Commission (*hereinafter* ILC) was mandated by the United Nations General Assembly with preparing a code of crimes against peace and security of mankind[51], a code which would later become the Rome Statute. Although the ILC had prepared two draft statutes in 1951 and 1953, the General Assembly adjourned the drafting of the Code to a later date due to legal disputes

[45] Id. at para. 478.

[46] See *Benjamin Whitaker* (Special Rapporteur on Prevention and Punishment of the Crime of Genocide), Revised and Updated Report on the Question of the Prevention and Punishment of the Crime of Genocide, U.N. Doc. E/CN.4/Sub.2/1985/6 (1985).

[47] Id. at para. 33.

[48] Id.

[49] U.N. Subcommission on Prevention of Discrimination and Protection of Minorities, Report of the Sub-Commission on Prevention of Discrimination and Protection of Minorities on its Thirty-Eight Session, at para. 45, U.N. Doc. E/CN.4/1986/5 (1985).

[50] *Damien Short*, Redefining Genocide, Settler Colonialism, Social Death and Ecocide 44 (2016).

[51] G.A., Formulation of the Principles Recognized in the Charter of the Nürnberg Tribunal and in the Judgment of the Tribunal, U.N. Doc. A/RES/177(II) (Nov. 21, 1947).

concerning the definition of the crime of aggression.[52] The drafting of the Code, however, was reconsidered in 1982 and culminated in its adoption in 1996.[53] In the time between 1984 and 1996 the ILC debated as to whether to include "acts causing serious damage to the environment"[54] into the Code and particularly whether such a crime required intent.[55]

In 1991, the ILC adopted on first reading the draft Code of Crimes against the Peace and Security of Mankind including an autonomous environmental crime in Article 26 stipulating, "[a]n individual who wilfully causes or orders the causing of widespread, long-term and severe damage to the natural environment shall, on conviction thereof, be sentenced"[56]. However, it is noteworthy that the ILC never expressly referred to 'ecocide'.[57] According to the ILC, the definition of Article 26 was derived from the aforementioned Articles 35 (3), 55 (1) AP I with the major difference that Article 26 is not restricted to armed conflicts.[58] Besides the distinct environmental crime in Article 26, the Draft Code also included an environmental war crime in Article 22 (2) (d), criminalising the employment of "methods or means of warfare which are intended or may be expected to cause widespread, long-term and severe damage to the natural environment".[59] However, some members of the Commission criticised the inconsistency concerning the mental element of Article 26 and Article 22. While Article 26 required intent excluding deliberate or negligent behaviour, perpetrators could already be held criminally liable under Article 22 (2) (d) if the employment of warfare "may be expected" to cause large-scale environmental damage. Thus, some countries demanded the mental threshold in Article 26 be lowered so as to coincide with the one in Article 22, as ecocide during peacetime is predominantly committed for economic motives and not with the primary intention of harming the environment, which is why most cases would fall outside the scope of Article 26.[60]

---

[52] *Damien Short*, Redefining Genocide, Settler Colonialism, Social Death and Ecocide 44 (2016).

[53] Id.

[54] Report of the Commission to the General Assembly on the Work of its Thirty-Sixth Session, [1984] 2 Y.B. Int'l L. Comm'n ¶ 30, U.N. Doc. A/CN.4/SER.A/1984/Add.1 (Part 2).

[55] Id. at ¶ 96.

[56] Report of the Commission to the General Assembly on the Work of its Forty-Third Session, [1991] 2 Y.B. Int'l L. Comm'n, at 97, U.N. Doc. A/CN.4/SER.A/1991/Add.1 (Part 2).

[57] *Damien Short*, Redefining Genocide, Settler Colonialism, Social Death and Ecocide 45 (2016).

[58] Report of the Commission to the General Assembly on the Work of its Forty-Third Session, [1991] 2 Y.B. Int'l L. Comm'n, at 107, U.N. Doc. A/CN.4/SER.A/1991/Add.1 (Part 2).

[59] Id. at 105.

[60] See Documents of the Forty-Fifth Session, [1993] 2 Y.B. Int'l L. Comm'n, at 66 ¶ 50 (Australia), U.N. Doc. A/CN.4/SER.A/1993/Add.1 (Part 1); Documents of the Forty-Fifth Session, [1993] 2 Y.B. Int'l L. Comm'n, at 68 ¶ 30 (Austria), U.N. Doc. A/CN.4/SER.A/1993/

Nonetheless, instead of having adapted the subjective threshold in Article 26, the provision was removed from the Draft Code of Crimes against the Peace and Security of Mankind altogether in 1996.[61] At the 47th session in 1995, Special Rapporteur Thiam suggested removing Article 26 for fear that it overextended the confines of the offences established at the Nuremberg trial.[62] Since most states did not concur with the proposed removal of Article 26[63], the ILC decided to establish a further working group mandated with examining the possibilities of including "the issue of wilful and severe damage to the environment"[64] into the Draft Code. In 1996, the working group issued a 'Document on crimes against the environment'[65] recommending the incorporation of environmental crimes either as (1) a separate provision under Article 26, (2) a crime against humanity under Article 21 or (3) a war crime under Article 22.[66] However, at the 48th session (2430th meeting) in 1996, the chairman of the ILC unilaterally decided to "leave aside draft article 26" [67]. Thus, at the ensuing 2431st meeting the Commission only voted upon the decision of whether to refer the question of wilful and severe damage to the environment to the Drafting Committee in the context of Article 21 or Article 22.[68] However, Mr. Szekely immediately objected that the Commission had not yet voted upon the referral of Article 26.[69] At the previous 2430th meeting the members of the Commission had not reached consensus regarding the question as to whether to refer

Add.1 (Part 1); Documents of the Forty-Eighth Session, [1996] 2 Y.B. Int'l L. Comm'n, at 18 ¶ 27 (Belgium), U.N. Doc. A/CN.4/SER.A/1996/Add.1 (Part 1).

[61] See Draft Code of Crimes Against the Peace and Security of Mankind (1996), reprinted in [1996] 2 Y.B. Int'l L. Comm'n, ¶ 30–50 (Australia), U.N. Doc. A/CN.4/SER.A/1996/Add.1 (Part 2).

[62] Documents of the Forty-Eight Session, [1996] 2 Y.B. Int'l L. Comm'n, at 17 ¶ 2, U.N. Doc. A/CN.4/SER.A/1996/Add.1 (Part 1).

[63] Id. at 19, 20 ¶ 10.

[64] Id. at 16 ¶ 1.

[65] Id. at 15–27.

[66] The proposed provisions read as follows:

Art. 22 (War Crimes): 2 (a) (iii) (bis): "Employing methods or means of warfare which are intended or may be expected to cause such widespread, long-term and severe damage to the natural environment that the health or survival of a population will be gravely prejudiced";

Art. 21 (Crimes against Humanity): 2 (h) (bis): "Wilfully causing such widespread, long-term and severe damage to the natural environment that the health or survival of a population will be gravely prejudiced";

Art. 26 (Wilful and severe damage to the environment): "An individual who wilfully causes such widespread, long-term and severe damage to the natural environment that the health or survival of a population will be gravely prejudiced, shall, on conviction thereof, be sentenced to…", Summary Records of the Meetings of the Forty-Eighth Session, [1996] 1 Y. B. Int'l L. Comm'n, at 7 ¶ 3, U.N. Doc. A/CN.4/SER.A/1996.

[67] Id. at 13 ¶ 62.

[68] Id. at 13 ¶ 1.

[69] Id. at 14 ¶ 7.

Article 26 to the Drafting Commission.[70] In this regard, Christian Tomuschat, member of the working group, stated that "decisions to send texts to the Drafting Committee were traditionally taken by consensus, but there was no obligation to do so".[71] Ultimately, Article 26 was never referred to the Drafting Committee or voted upon by the General Assembly and thus was not included in the final Code. However, the underlying reasons for the sudden removal of Article 26 from the Draft Code are barely documented. According to Mr. Thiam, Special Rapporteur of the Code, the removal was owing to a few governments having generally opposed the incorporation of Article 26 in 1993.[72] Similarly, Sands, who participated in the drafting of the Preamble of the Rome Statute, claimed that Article 26 was removed due to it lacking political support.[73] Tomuschat argued that governments rejected the inclusion of Article 26 for fear of being held criminally liable for nuclear testing during peacetime.

In an article published in 1996 Tomuschat stated: "One cannot escape the impression that nuclear arms played a decisive role in the minds of many of those who opted for the final text which now has been emasculated to such an extent that its conditions of applicability will almost never be met even after humankind would have gone through disasters of the most atrocious kind as a consequence of conscious action by persons who were completely aware of the fatal consequences their decisions would entail"[74].

Although records of the 2430th meeting did not reveal any relation to nuclear arms[75], Tomuschat stated in the 'Document on crimes against the environment' that there are "good reasons to assume" that atmospheric nuclear testing would constitute a crime against the environment.[76] Thus, ultimately only Article 21 and Article 22 were put to a vote. While the ILC voted against the inclusion of environmental destruction as a crime against humanity under Article 21[77], it voted in favour

---

[70] Id. at 13 ¶ 58.

[71] Id. at 13 ¶ 58.

[72] *Doudou Thiam* (Special Rapporteur), Thirteenth Report on the Draft Code of Crimes Against the Peace and Security of Mankind, at 35 ¶ 8, 10, U.N. Doc. A/CN.4/466 (Mar. 24, 1995), reprinted in Documents of the Forty-Seventh Session, [1995] 2 Y.B. Int'l L. Comm'n, at 33–51, U.N. Doc. A/CN.4/SER.A/1995/Add. 1 (Part 1).

[73] *Mélissa Godin*, Lawyers Are Working to Put 'Ecocide' On Par with War Crimes, Could an International Law Hold Major Polluters to Account?, Time, 2021.

[74] *Christian Tomuschat*, Crimes Against the Environment, 26 (6) Envtl. Pol'y & L. 242, 243 (1996).

[75] Summary Records of the Meetings of the Forty-Eighth Session, [1996] 1 Y.B. Int'l L. Comm'n, at 7–13, U.N. Doc. A/CN.4/SER.A/1996; *Anastacia Greene*, Fordham Environmental Law Review 17 (2019).

[76] Documents of the Forty-Eight Session, [1996] 2 Y.B. Int'l L. Comm'n, at 27 ¶ 50, U.N. A/CN.4/SER.A/1996/Add. 1 (Part 1).

[77] Summary Records of the Meetings of the Forty-Eighth Session, [1996] 1 Y.B. Int'l L. Comm'n, at 14 ¶ 14, U.N. Doc. A/CN.4/SER.A/1996.

of incorporating large-scale environmental harm as a war crime under Article 22 in the Draft Code[78], which later became Article 8 (b) (iv) Rome Statute under the perceptibly narrower Rome Statute. On 1 July 2002, when the Rome Statute entered into force, Article 8 (b) (iv) thereof became the only provision explicitly referring to large-scale environmental destruction as a crime under international law to this day. Nevertheless, as seen above, the crime is restricted to international armed conflicts and intentional damage. Despite the failure to introduce a crime of ecocide applicable during peacetime into the Rome Statute, it is noteworthy that large-scale environmental destruction was considered at least serious enough to be included into the 1991 draft Code of Crimes Against the Peace and Security of Mankind alongside war crimes and crimes against humanity.

4. Since 2010: Polly Higgins' legacy to include a fifth crime of ecocide into the Rome Statute

It was not until 2010 that UK barrister Polly Higgins reignited the debate concerning the inclusion of a fifth crime of ecocide into the Rome Statute by having proposed the following definition of ecocide to the UN Law Commission: "Ecocide is the extensive damage to, destruction of or loss of ecosystem(s) of a given territory, whether by human agency or by other causes, to such an extent that peaceful enjoyment by the inhabitants of that territory has been severely diminished".[79] Higgin's proposal gained much attention and was followed by the emergence of several campaigns promoting the idea of creating an international crime of ecocide under the Rome Statute.

On 30 September 2011 a mock ecocide trial was held at the UK's Supreme Court at the end of which industrial leaders of fossil fuel corporations were convicted of the crime of ecocide.[80] Two European Citizen's Initiatives called "End Ecocide in Europe: A Citizen's Initiative to give the Earth Rights" registered in 2012 and 2013 requesting the European Commission criminalise ecocide at the regional level were withdrawn after having failed to attain the requisite one million signatures.[81] After the failure of the European Citizen's Initiatives the "End Ecocide on Earth" campaign emerged in 2014, which presented 170,000 signatures to the European Par-

[78] Id. at 14 ¶ 6.

[79] *Polly Higgins*, et al., Crime, Law and Social Change, 257 (2013); *Polly Higgins*, Eradicating Ecocide: Laws and Governance to Stop the Destruction of the Planet 63 (2015).

[80] *Damian Carrington*, Test Trial Convicts Fossil Fuel Bosses of 'Ecocide', The Guardian, Oct. 5, 2011, https://www.theguardian.com/environment/damian-carrington-blog/2011/sep/29/ecocide-oil-criminal-court.

[81] European Citizens' Initiative, End Ecocide in Europe: A Citizens' Initiative to Give the Earth Rights, https://europa.eu/citizens-initiative/initiatives/details/2012/000012_en (last visited Feb. 18, 2025).

liament requesting the creation of an international crime of ecocide at the regional level.[82]

In 2017, the European Green Party released a Draft Resolution advocating the international recognition of the crime of ecocide.[83] This was followed by the Maldives and Vanuatu, one of the regions most affected by climate change, demanding the inclusion of a fifth crime of ecocide into the Rome Statute at the 18th session of the Assembly of States Parties in 2019.[84]

In response to the increased appetite to criminalise environmental destruction at the international level, an international expert panel convened by the international 'Stop Ecocide Foundation' proposed a definition for a potential fifth crime of ecocide under the Rome Statute in June 2021.[85] Globally, the proposed definition received wide support.

Until now, the criminalisation of large-scale environmental destruction has become a matter of interest both politically and legally in at least 24 ICC Member States.[86] In August 2021, France, as the first European country, introduced a domestic *délit* of ecocide into the French environmental code.[87] However, it was widely criticised that the French government fell short of the Citizen's Climate Assembly's original proposal to enact a crime of ecocide by adopting a civil offence

---

[82] *Ian Johnston*, Campaign to Out Ecocide on a Par with Genocide in Attempt to Curb Environmental Destruction, The Independent, Oct. 12, 2014, https://www.independent.co.uk/climate-change/news/campaign-to-put-ecocide-on-a-par-with-genocide-in-attempt-to-curb-environmental-destruction-9789297.html.

[83] Global Greens & European Greens Congress 2017, Draft EGP Resolution, On an International Recognition of the Crime of Ecocide: For a Binding International Environmental Law Architecture (Mar. 30 – Apr. 2, 2017), available at: https://europeangreens.eu/sites/europeangreens.eu/files/9%20On%20Ecocide%20-%20EGP%20Congress%20Liverpool%20_0.pdf (last visited Feb. 18, 2025).

[84] Government of the Republic of Vanuatu, General Debate of the 18th Session of the Assembly of States Parties to the Rome Statute of the International Criminal Court, Statement by H.E. John H. Licht (2019); Republic of Maldives, 18th Session of the Assembly of State Parties to the Rome Statute of the International Criminal Court, Written Statement of the Republic of Maldives (2019).

[85] *Haroon Siddique*, Legal Experts Worldwide Draw Up 'Historic' Definition of Ecocide, The Guardian, June 22, 2021, https://www.theguardian.com/environment/2021/jun/22/legal-experts-worldwide-draw-up-historic-definition-of-ecocide.

[86] Stop Ecocide International, What We Do, https://www.stopecocide.earth/what-we-do (last visited Feb. 18, 2025).

[87] See French Environmental Code, art. L.231–3 (Aug. 22, 2021): "The offenses provided for in Article L.231-1 constitute ecocide when the actions are committed intentionally. The offenses provided for in Article L.231-2, committed intentionally also constitute ecocide when they lead to serious and lasting damage to health, flora, fauna or the quality of the air, soil or water […]."

instead, even though the civil offence entails a prison sentence for up to ten years.[88] Additionally, the Belgian parliament adopted a Resolution in 2021 requesting the Belgian government to both include a crime of ecocide into the Belgian penal code and to propose an amendment of the Rome Statute to incorporate a fifth crime of ecocide.[89] On 5 November 2022 the Belgian Minister for the Environment announced that the Belgian government intends to include a crime of ecocide in its domestic Penal Code defined as "the intentional perpetration of an illegal act that causes serious, widespread and long-term damage to the environment while knowing that these acts result in this damage", which is punishable with a term of imprisonment of between 10 and 20 years.[90] In its Resolution of 20 May 2021 the European Parliament took note of "the Member States' increasing commitment to working towards the recognition of ecocide at national and international level [and requested] the Commission to study the relevance of ecocide to EU law and EU diplomacy".[91] At the 20th Assembly of State Parties on 7 December 2021 in The Hague, three ICC Member States, Bangladesh, Samoa and Vanuatu, which are currently experiencing the adverse impacts of environmental destruction at first hand, advocated the establishment of such a fifth crime.[92]

Later, on 17 February 2022, the European Parliament appealed in its annual human rights report to "the EU and its Member States to promote the recognition of ecocide as an international crime under the Rome Statute of the ICC".[93]

However, the idea of incorporating a crime of ecocide into the Rome Statute is not only supported by civil societies[94] or political institutions, but also by economic organisations, such as the International Corporate Governance Network (ICGN) which has assets amounting to over 59 trillion US Dollars, that addressed governments in a statement at the UN Climate Change Conference in Glasgow on 20 October 2021 to "[m]andate regulations and collaborate internationally to crimi-

---

[88] *Liz Alderman/Constant Méheut*, Going Green, or Greenwashing? A Proposed Climate Law Divides France, The New York Times, May 19, 2021, https://www.nytimes.com/2021/05/19/business/macron-france-climate-bill.html.

[89] Chambre Des Représentants de Belgique, Proposition De Résolution, Doc. 55 1429/006 (Dec. 2, 2021).

[90] *Kevin Jon Heller*, Belgium Set to Criminalise Ecocide (Kinda Sorta), Opinio Juris (Nov. 8, 2022), http://opiniojuris.org/2022/11/08/belgium-set-to-criminalise-ecocide-kinda-sorta/ (last visited Feb. 18, 2025); *Zakia Khattabi*, Zakia Khattabi Gets the Crime of Ecocide Written into the Criminal Code (2022), https://khattabi.belgium.be/en/pr-zakia-khattabi-gets-crime-ecocide-written-criminal-code (last visited Feb. 18, 2025).

[91] European Parliament Resolution of 20 May 2021 on the Liability of Companies for Environmental Damage, Eur, Parl. Res. P9_TA(2021)0259 (May 20, 2021).

[92] Link to the full recorded meeting: https://www.youtube.com/watch?v=JHYf89GH2d0 (last visited Feb. 18, 2025).

[93] European Parliament Resolution of 17 February 2022 on Human Rights and Democracy in the World and the European Union's Policy on the Matter – Annual Report 2021, Eur. Parl. Res. P9_TA(2022)0041 (Feb. 17, 2022).

[94] See, for instance, End Ecocide on Earth, Stop Ecocide Foundation International.

nalise ecocide"[95]. In this regard, the economy may become the driver of politics as conducting industrial activities requires a viable and resource-rich environment.

III. Potentials of establishing a fifth crime of ecocide

After having revealed the inadequacy of current global environmental protection, the question arises as to whether international criminal law would be an appropriate legal tool to fill this void. In this regard, it is helpful to assess the purposes of punishment in international criminal law. Concerning the rationales of punishment in international criminal law[96] the Rome Statute lacks any respective specification. However, the long-lasting debate in domestic criminal law has produced a nuanced range of punishment theories, including deterrence, retribution, social reintegration and positive general prevention. Since none of the rationales of punishment taken alone can fully justify criminal liability, most domestic criminal justice systems are not predicated on a single purpose but rather on a mix of forward-looking and backward-looking penological objectives.[97] Hence, the question arises as to whether these traditional punishment theories derived from national criminal law can be transferred to the international level (the domestic analogy).[98] International criminal law governs macro-criminality[99], which vastly differs from ordinary criminality in relation to the perpetrator, the victims and the nature of the crimes. Macro-criminality is characterised by a "collective nature of the violence, the deflection of authority within groups, the pressure of following orders, and the normalisation of

[95] ICGN, ICGN Statement of Shared Climate Change Responsibilities to the United Nations Climate Change Conference of the Parties 27 (Oct. 20, 2021).

[96] See generally on the purposes of punishment in international criminal law the contributions in *Florian Jeßberger/Julia Geneuss*, Why Punish Perpetrators of Mass Atrocities? Purposes of Punishment in International Criminal Law (Florian Jeßberger/Julia Geneuss eds., 2020); *Robert Cryer*, et al., An Introduction to International Criminal Law and Procedure 28–43 (2019); *Carsten Stahn*, A Critical Introduction to International Criminal Law 174–181 (2019).

[97] *Robert Cryer*, et al., An Introduction to International Criminal Law and Procedure 30 (2019).

[98] See the following contributions *Kai Ambos*, Not Much, but Better than Nothing – Purposes of Punishment in International Criminal Law, in: Why Punish Perpetrators of Mass Atrocities? (Florian Jeßberger/Julia Geneuss eds., 2020); *Elies Van Sliedregt*, Punishment and the Domestic Analogy, in: Why Punish Perpetrators of Mass Atrocities? (Florian Jeßberger/Julia Geneuss eds., 2020); *Klaus Günther/Vasco Reuss*, Legitimation des Völkerstrafrechts in Deutschland – Völkerstrafrecht als Bürgerstrafrecht?, in: Völkerstrafrechtspoltik (Christoph Safferling/Stefan Kirsch eds., 2014); *Frank Neubacher*, Kriminologische Grundlagen einer internationalen Strafgerichtsbarkeit (2005); *Christina Möller*, Völkerstrafrecht und Internationaler Strafgerichtshof (2003).

[99] The term "macro-criminality" was first used by Herbert Jäger and is translated from the German "Makrokriminalität", see *Herbert Jäger*, Makrokriminalität (1989).

violence under rubrics of self-defence or group survival"[100]. Thus, macro-crimes occur in the context of collective action often initiated by states or de facto states and are committed by persons, who as a member of the group do not act socially deviant, but in accordance with superior orders.[101] In terms of gravity, crimes under international criminal law only pertain to the "most serious crimes of concern to the international community as a whole"[102].

Nonetheless, with respect to the rationales of criminal punishment the unique character[103] of international criminal law should not be overexaggerated. For one, there are not only differences but also similarities between macro-criminality and ordinary criminality, especially with domestic organised crime.[104] Furthermore, due to the principle of complementarity, international criminal law is intended to be largely implemented and enforced at the national level.[105] Additionally, determining the rationales of criminal punishment is a classic issue of criminal law, irrespective of whether it is applied at the international or national level. Thus, international criminal law should benefit from the vast theoretical development of the purposes of punishment in domestic criminal law by transferring these traditional domestic penological objectives rather than reinventing the wheel.[106]

However, despite the vast amount of literature concerning the possible rationales of punishment in international criminal law, this debate remains strictly academic in nature. International courts and tribunals have a long history of simply reiterating the traditional domestic punishment theories to justify their sentences without ever questioning their transferability to international criminal law.[107] Some court deci-

---

[100] *Mark Drumbl*, International Punishment from 'Other' Perspectives, in: Research Handbook on the International Penal System 386 (Roisin Mulgrew & Denis Abels eds., 2016).

[101] *Florian Jeßberger/Julia Geneuss*, Introduction: The Need for a Robust and Consistent Theory of International Punishment, in: Why Punish Perpetrators of Mass Atrocities? 2 (Florian Jeßberger/Julia Geneuss eds., 2020).

[102] Preamble of the Rome Statute (4) and (9), Art. 5 of the Rome Statute.

[103] See *Robert Sloane*, The Expressive Capacity of International Punishment: The Limits of the National Law Analogy and the Potential of International Criminal Law, 43 Stanford Journal of International Law 39, 40–42 (2007).

[104] *Elies Van Sliedregt*, Punishment and the Domestic Analogy 92, 100 (2020).

[105] *Robert Cryer*, et al., An Introduction to International Criminal Law and Procedure 29 (2019).

[106] *Jochen Bung*, Is International Criminal Law Special?, in: Why Punish Perpetrators of Mass Atrocities? 132 (Florian Jeßberger/Julia Geneuss eds., 2020); *Kai Ambos*, Not Much, but Better than Nothing 106 (2020); *Stephen C. McCaffrey*, Criminalization of Environmental Protection 1017 (2008); critical *Elies Van Sliedregt*, Punishment and the Domestic Analogy (2020); *Sergey Vasiliev*, Punishment Rationales in International Criminal Jurisprudence, in: Why Punish Perpetrators of Mass Atrocities? (Florian Jeßberger/Julia Geneuss eds., 2020).

[107] See for instance, Prosecutor v. Bemba, ICC-01/05-01/08, Decision on Sentence Pursuant to Article 76 of the Statute, ¶ 10, 11 (June 21, 2016); Prosecutor v. Katanga, ICC-01/04-01/07, Decision on Sentence Pursuant to Article 76 of the Statute, ¶ 37 (May 23, 2014); Prosecutor v. Al Mahdi, ICC-01/12-01/15, Judgment and Sentence, ¶ 66, 67 (Sept. 27, 2016);

sions even lack any reference to the underlying punishment modalities.[108] Thus, in practice, the sentence factors are much more important than the rationales of punishment. Nonetheless, assessing the objectives of criminal punishment sheds light on the potentials of a fifth crime of ecocide in distinction to the pre-existing civil and administrative remedies. Hence, in the following, the purposes of criminal punishment which could become relevant in the environmental context, including retribution, deterrence, positive general prevention and the discovery of truth, will be assessed.

1. Retribution[109] and deterrence

As stated in the Preamble of the Rome Statute, "the most serious crimes of concern to the international community as a whole must not go unpunished"[110] and international criminal law intends "to put an end to impunity of the perpetrators of these crimes and thus to contribute to the prevention of such crimes"[111]. By explicitly referring to the "prevention of such crimes" the Preamble appears to allude that the primary objective of sentencing in international criminal law is deterrence. However, the ICC[112] as well as the ICTY[113] reiterated that deterrence and retribution are equally important purposes of international criminal punishment.

Retributivist approaches can be traced back to the philosophy of Immanuel Kant and demand criminal punishment simply on the basis that criminals deserve to be punished for having violated societal norms irrespective of potential future advantages of prosecution.[114] In this regard, criminal sentences serve to express the public condemnation of the offences committed.[115] Due to threatening the international community as such, crimes under international law incur an even higher level of

---

see *Sergey Vasiliev*, Punishment Rationales in International Criminal Jurisprudence 54–73 (2020).

[108] See for instance, Prosecutor v. Rugambarara, Judgment, Case No. ICTR-00-59-T (Nov. 16, 2007).

[109] For retributivist motivations see generally *Alexander K.A. Greenawalt*, International Criminal Law for Retributivists, 35 (4) University of Pennsylvania Journal of International Law 969 (2014).

[110] Preamble of the Rome Statute (4).

[111] Preamble of the Rome Statute (5).

[112] Prosecutor v. Bemba, ICC-01/05-01/13, Decision on Sentence Pursuant to Article 76 of the Statute, ¶ 19 (Mar. 22, 2017); Prosecutor v. Al Mahdi, ICC-01/12-01/15, Judgment and Sentence, ¶ 66 (Sept. 27, 2016); Prosecutor v. Katanga, ICC-01/04-01/07, Decision on Sentence pursuant to Article 76 of the Statute, ¶ 37, 38 (May 23, 2014).

[113] Prosecutor v. Kupreškić, Case No. IT-95-16-T, Judgement, ¶ 848 (Jan. 14, 2000); Prosecutor v. Naletilić, Case No. IT-98-34-T, Judgement, ¶ 739 (Mar. 31, 2003).

[114] *Robert Cryer*, et al., An Introduction to International Criminal Law and Procedure 30 (2019).

[115] Prosecutor v. Al Mahdi, ICC-01/12-01/15, Judgment and Sentence, ¶ 67 (Sept. 27, 2016).

societal condemnation than domestic offences.[116] Put simply, sentences are imposed because perpetrators of mass atrocities deserve to be punished.[117] However, retribution must not be confused with revenge but is rather to be understood as "just deserts" [118]. Thus, sentences need to be just and proportionate in relation to the gravity of the criminal act, the harm inflicted and the perpetrator's culpability.[119] However, in international criminal law the imposition of custodial sentences may never be able to match the egregious gravity of crimes[120], as the duration of imprisonment is restricted by the perpetrator's human rights.[121] Hence, an international criminal conviction for environmental destruction would express the social condemnation of large-scale environmental harm by the international community. The inclusion of a fifth environmental crime of ecocide would therefore convey the message that large-scale environmental harm must not go unpunished.

In distinction from retribution, deterrence focuses on the future benefits of criminal prosecution.[122] According to deterrence-based theories, criminal punishment serves to deter both the convicted (specific deterrence) as well as other potential perpetrators (general deterrence) from (re-)offending.[123] In this regard, criminal punishment ultimately aims at preventing the commission of further crimes by reducing the absolute number of crimes. In international criminal law the primary focus typically lies upon general deterrence.[124] This is due to the fact that once the specific situation which typically gave rise to the criminal conduct, for instance an armed conflict, terminates, the perpetrator does not need to be deterred from

[116] *Mohammed Saif-Alden Wattad*, Is Terrorism a Crime or an Aggravating Factor in Sentencing?, 4 (5) JICJ 1017, 1022 (2006).

[117] *Mark Drumbl*, We're Exhausting Ourselves, Let's Get Busy Instead, in: Why Punish Perpetrators of Mass Atrocities? 197 (Florian Jeßberger/Julia Geneuss eds., 2020).

[118] Prosecutor v. Erdemović, Case No. IT-96-22-T, Sentencing Judgement, ¶ 65 (Nov. 29, 1996); quoted in Prosecutor v. Kordič, Case No. IT-95-14/2-A, Judgment, ¶ 1075 (Dec. 17, 2004).

[119] Prosecutor v. Al Mahdi, ICC-01/12-01/15, Judgment and Sentence, ¶ 67 (Sept. 27, 2016); Prosecutor v. Katanga, ICC-01/04-01/07, Decision on Sentence Pursuant to Article 76 of the Statute, ¶ 38 (May 23, 2014).

[120] *Mark Drumbl*, We're Exhausting Ourselves, Let's Get Busy Instead 198 (2020); *Frank Neubacher*, Criminology of International Crimes, in: Why Punish Perpetrators of Mass Atrocities? 27 (Florian Jeßberger/Julia Geneuss eds., 2020); *Robert Cryer*, et al., An Introduction to International Criminal Law and Procedure 31 (2019); *Klaus Günther/Vasco Reuss*, Legitimation des Völkerstrafrechts 147 (2014).

[121] See *Mark Drumbl*, Atrocity 15 (2007); *Gerhard Werle/Florian Jeßberger*, Principles of International Criminal Law para. 185 (2020).

[122] *Robert Cryer*, et al., An Introduction to International Criminal Law and Procedure 32 (2019).

[123] Prosecutor v. Al Mahdi, ICC-01/12-01/15, Judgment and Sentence, ¶ 67 (Sept. 27, 2016); *Robert Cryer*, et al., An Introduction to International Criminal Law and Procedure 32 (2019); *Mark Drumbl*, Atrocity 61 (2007).

[124] Prosecutor Serushago, Case No. ICTR 98-39-S, Sentence, para. 20 (Feb. 5, 1999); *Mark Drumbl*, Atrocity 61 (2007).

recidivism rendering specific deterrence obsolete.[125] However, environmental crimes are mostly committed for economic purposes over extended periods of time and not due to a specific situation. Thus, in the environmental context, specific deterrence is equally significant as general deterrence. In terms of specific deterrence, it is particularly noteworthy that perpetrators of environmental harm acting out of economic purposes tend to be far more responsive to the threat of reputational damage and financial loss due to a criminal conviction than the typical war criminals acting out of hate and political motives.[126]

However, deterrence depends on a high likelihood of being prosecuted and on the severity of sanctions.[127] In accordance with Article 77 (1) Rome Statute, the primary criminal sanction in international criminal law is imprisonment. The prospect of being incarcerated certainly entails a strong deterrent effect, especially on corporate officials. As Geis rightly stated, "Jail terms have a self-evident deterrent impact upon corporate officials, who belong to a social group that is exquisitely sensitive to status deprivation and censure".[128] However, according to empirical studies the likelihood of prosecution is much more important than the severity of applicable sanctions in terms of creating a deterrent effect.[129] Nonetheless, in international criminal law the prospect of being actually prosecuted is significantly low due to a high selectivity[130] impeding its potential deterrent effect.[131] Furthermore, the deterrent effect of criminal punishment has never been empirically proven but is rather assumed to exist.[132] The fact that some of the worst atrocities, such as the Srebrenica massacre (1995) or the ethnic cleaning in Kosovo (1998) were committed whilst international tribunals and courts such as the ICTY were opera-

[125] *Klaus Günther/Vasco Reuss*, Legitimation des Völkerstrafrechts 148, 149 (2014); *Christoph Safferling*, Internationales Strafrecht § 4 para. 72 (2011).

[126] *Frédéric Mégret*, Colum. J. Envtl. L. 234, 235 (2011); *Stephen C. McCaffrey*, Criminalization of Environmental Protection 1016 (2008).

[127] *Audrey Crasson*, Amsterdam Law Forum 41 (2017); *Carsten Stahn*, A Critical Introduction to International Criminal Law 175 (2019); *Mark Drumbl*, Atrocity 169, 170 (2007).

[128] *Gilbert Geis*, On White-Collar Crime 53 (1982).

[129] *Dieter Dölling*, Generalprävention durch Strafrecht: Realität oder Illusion?, 1 (102) ZStW 1, 8 (1990).

[130] See generally on selectivity in international criminal law, *Harmen Van der Wilt*, Selectivity in International Criminal Law, in: Why Punish Perpetrators of Mass Atrocities? (Florian Jeßberger/Julia Geneuss eds., 2020).

[131] *Carsten Stahn*, A Critical Introduction to International Criminal Law 175 (2019); *Klaus Günther/Vasco Reuss*, Legitimation des Völkerstrafrechts 149 (2014); *Christoph Safferling*, Internationales Strafrecht § 4 para. 71 (2011); *Mark Drumbl*, Atrocity 169–173 (2007).

[132] *Kai Ambos*, Protecting the Environment Through International Criminal Law?, EJIL: Talk! (June 29, 2021), https://www.ejiltalk.org/protecting-the-environment-through-internation al-criminal-law/ (last visited Feb. 18, 2025); *Robert Cryer*, et al., An Introduction to International Criminal Law and Procedure 468 (2019); *Carsten Stahn*, A Critical Introduction to International Criminal Law 176 (2019); *Dieter Dölling*, ZStW 8 (1990).

tive, appear to contradict the theory of deterrence in international criminal law.[133] However, this scepticism should not be overexaggerated.[134] It remains unknown whether even worse atrocities would have been committed if international criminal tribunals and courts had not existed.[135] In general, it appears more likely that the existence of criminal sanctions diminishes the occurrence of crimes through deterrence than its absence.[136] Obstacles such as selective enforcement and lack of empirical data concerning the alleged deterrent effect only hamper deterrence but do not render it obsolete.

In particular due to the ongoing environmental destruction at an unprecedented scale, deterrence and thus prevention of further harm appears to be one of the primary goals of criminal punishment in the environmental context. The prevention of further environmental damage is particularly significant with regards to the irreversibility of many types of environmental harm, such as the extinction of whole species.[137] With respect to the desired goal of promoting global environmental protection the potential deterrent effect of criminal punishment renders criminal sanctions much more meaningful and effective than civil or administrative remedies. Although administrative penalties, such as revocation, suspension or the prohibition of licences entail serious consequences, administrative remedies are barely used in the environmental context.[138] The most popular means to address environmental disputes are civil remedies. For instance, human rights law, which also affords environmental protection to a certain but very limited extent, only provides civil remedies to sue states for damages rather than establishing individual criminal liability, such as in international criminal law.[139] In this regard, Decaux rightly observed that there is a striking difference between "a justice system affording civil redress for damage suffered by victims by holding states responsible, in the manner of the European Court of Human Rights, and [...] a justice system based on [individual] criminal responsibility of the perpetrators of international crimes"[140]. Another well-established avenue for resolving international environmental disputes is tort law. In this vein, particularly the U.S. Alien Tort Statute (ATS) deserves a mention, which enables non-US citizens ('aliens') to file civil claims in US courts

---

133 *Mark Drumbl*, Atrocity 169 (2007).

134 See *Jakob Holtermann*, 'Can I Be Brought Before the ICC?', in: Why Punish Perpetrators of Mass Atrocities? (Florian Jeßberger/Julia Geneuss eds., 2020).

135 *Mark Drumbl*, Atrocity 169 (2007).

136 *Jakob Holtermann*, 'Can I Be Brought Before the ICC?' 143, 144 (2020).

137 Gabčíkovo-Nagymaros Project (Hungary v. Slovakia), Judgment, 1997 I.C.J. Rep. ¶ 140 (Sept. 25); *Stephen C. McCaffrey*, Criminalization of Environmental Protection 1034 (2008).

138 *Audrey Crasson*, Amsterdam Law Forum 42 (2017).

139 *Ricardo Pereira*, Criminal Law Forum 206 (2020).

140 *Emmanuel Decaux*, The Place of Human Rights Courts and International Criminal Courts in the International System, 9 (3), JICJ 597, 597 (2011).

for human rights violations, even if the harm was sustained outside the US.[141] Numerous international environmental claims have already been filed with US district courts on the basis of the ATS. For instance, in *Agent Orange*, Vietnamese nationals sued chemical companies alleging personal injuries and property damage sustained by chemical defoliants produced and sold to the US and eventually deployed during the Vietnam War.[142] Outside the context of armed conflict, in *Beanal* plaintiffs filed civil claims against a multinational mining company alleging human rights infringements, environmental destruction and cultural genocide at its mine in Indonesia.[143] Furthermore, in *Flores*, plaintiffs sued a US copper mining company alleging that sulphur dioxide pollution emanating from the company's operations in Peru caused fatal respiratory diseases.[144]

Nevertheless, "[c]ivil fines are essentially financial penalties which lack the moral overtones of comparable criminal sentences".[145] Thus, civil fines do not express societal condemnation of the behaviour and thus do not incur reputational damage to the same extent as criminal sanctions. Corporations often perceive civil fines as incidental costs, which can eventually be passed on to consumers.[146] Given that civil fines are often modest in comparison to the financial profit of corporations[147], corporations find it cheaper to pay civil damages and continue infringing upon environmental regulations rather than abiding by the rules. Thus, civil fines are viewed as costly inconveniences rather than incentives to adapt corporate policies.[148] For instance, in the legal settlement ensuing from the Exxon Valdez oil spill, Exxon agreed to pay a 100 million US Dollars in criminal fines as well as 900 million US dollars in civil damages.[149] Apart from the 100 million in criminal fines,

[141] Alien Tort Statute, § 1350, 28 U.S.C. (June 25, 1948): "The district courts shall have original jurisdiction of any civil action by an alien for a tort only, committed in violation of the law of nations or a treaty of the United States"; International Commission of Jurists, Report of the International Commission of Jurists Expert Legal Panel on Corporate Complicity in International Crimes, Volume 3 (2008).

[142] Agent Orange Product Liability Litigation, Re, Vietnam Association For Victims Of Agent Orange/Dioxin v. Dow Chemical Company, 373 F.Supp.2d 7, 15 (E.D.N.Y. 2005), ILDC 123 (US 2005); *Mark A. Drumbl*, Accountability for Property Crimes and Environmental War Crimes: Prosecution, Litigation, and Development, ICTJ 1, 11, 12 (2009).

[143] Beanal v. Freeport-McMoran, Inc., 197 F.3d 161, 163 (5th Cir. 1999); *Mark A. Drumbl*, International Center for Transitional Justice 13 (2009).

[144] Flores v. Southern Peru Copper Co., 414 F.3d 233, 237 (2nd Cir. 2003); *Mark A. Drumbl*, International Center for Transitional Justice 13 (2009).

[145] *Michael Watson*, The Enforcement of Environmental Law: Civil or Criminal Penalties?, 17 (1), Environmental Law and Management 3, 6 (2005).

[146] *Susan Hedman*, Expressive Functions of Criminal Sanctions in Environmental Law 59 (4), Geo. Wash. Int'l. Rev. 889, 894 (1990).

[147] *Audrey Crasson*, Amsterdam Law Forum 42 (2017).

[148] *Regina Rauxloh*, The Role of International Criminal Law in Environmental Protection 438 (2011).

[149] *Keith Schneider*, The Nation, The New York Times, Mar. 17, 1991, https://www.nytimes.com/1991/03/17/weekinreview/the-nation-423191.html.

the whole legal settlement was able to be written off by Exxon as business expenses.[150] In response to the legal settlement, Lawrence G. Rawl, former chairman of Exxon, later stated: "We're talking about stretching a bill out over 10 years [...] It will not curtail any of our plans."[151] This demonstrates that monetary fines alone, whether civil or criminal, do not sufficiently deter corporate officials from engaging in further criminal conduct. However, in international criminal law criminal fines can only be imposed in addition to imprisonment, which certainly entails a much higher deterrent effect than civil fines taken alone.

Hence, by expressing the societal condemnation of large-scale environmental harm perpetrators are potentially deterred (re-)offending for fear of reputational harm. Thus, criminal sanctions, especially non-monetary criminal sanctions, convey a different message than civil remedies and therefore carry far more potential to incentivise corporations to adopting a more environmentally friendly policy.

2. Positive general prevention (expressivism)

Besides punishing perpetrators because they deserve it or are deterred by it, sentencing in international criminal law also intends to reinforce the faith of the general public in the rule of law by morally educating the international community that breaching international criminal law does not remain unpunished.[152] As Hedman puts it, criminal law intends to "give force and symbolic representation to moral values by conveying condemnation and disgrace"[153]. Thus, the addressee of these so-called expressivist motives is the international community as such.[154] From the expressivist perspective, punishment proactively promotes universal acceptance and awareness of international criminal law by internalising its provisions and enticing the general public to voluntarily comply with these.[155] It is hoped that punishing thereby contributes to the prevention of future crimes ("positive general prevention").[156] However, similar to the aforementioned negative deterrent effect,

[150] Id.

[151] Id.

[152] Prosecutor v. Rajić, Case No. IT-95-12-S, Sentencing Judgment, ¶ 69 (May 8, 2006); Prosecutor v. Kordić, Case No. IT-95-14/2-A, Judgment, ¶ 1082 (Dec. 17, 2004); Prosecutor v. Kupreškić, Case No. IT-95-16-T, Judgment, ¶ 848 (Jan. 14, 2000); *Carsten Stahn*, A Critical Introduction to International Criminal Law 181 (2019); *Mark Drumbl*, Atrocity 61, 173 (2007).

[153] *Susan Hedman*, Geo. Wash. Int'l. Rev. 896 (1990).

[154] *Mark Drumbl*, Atrocity 12 (2007).

[155] Prosecutor v. Kordić, Case No. IT-95-14/2-A, Judgment, ¶ 1080 (Dec. 17, 2004); *Gerhard Werle/Florian Jeßberger*, Principles of International Criminal Law para. 129 (2020); *Mark Drumbl*, Atrocity 173, 174 (2007).

[156] *Gerhard Werle/Florian Jeßberger*, Principles of International Criminal Law para. 129 (2020).

such a positive general preventive effect has not yet been empirically proven.[157] International criminal law thus establishes a minimum standard of human rights reciprocally acknowledged by the international community superseding national standards.[158] In terms of positive general prevention, international punishment therefore strives to encourage people to live in compliance with these fundamental human rights standards set out by international criminal law.[159] However, in some cases the addition of an international normative system to the preexisting domestic systems gives rise to tension, as citizens now have two legal, at times contradicting, systems to comply with, which can result in norm collision in case of deviation.[160] Thus, at times international criminal law forces citizens to disobey their national legal system in order to abide by international criminal law.[161] This, in turn, requires civic courage, whose development among the general public some consider the primary goal of punishment in international criminal law.[162] According to Günther, positive general prevention in the international context therefore means that "citizens shall trust in the validity of human rights and distrust their own domestic legal order".[163]

In the current legal debate concerning the rationales of punishment, positive general prevention, also referred to as expressivist motives[164], is gaining increased attention and seems to have developed into the "ultimate, catch-all objective"[165] of sentencing.[166] It is argued that the mere fact that it is debated whether the term

[157] *Kai Ambos*, EJIL: Talk! (June 29, 2021), https://www.ejiltalk.org/protecting-the-environment-through-international-criminal-law/ (last visited Feb. 18, 2025).

[158] See *Gerhard Werle/Florian Jeßberger*, Principles of International Criminal Law paras. 178–184 (2020); *Gerhard Werle*, Menschenrechtsschutz durch Völkerstrafrecht, 109 (4) ZStW 808 (1997).

[159] *Klaus Günther/Vasco Reuss*, Legitimation des Völkerstrafrechts 150, 151 (2014); *Vasco Reuss*, Zivilcourage als Strafzweck des Völkerstrafrechts 8 (2012); *Christina Möller*, Völkerstrafrecht und Internationaler Strafgerichtshof 527, 528 (2003).

[160] *Klaus Günther*, Positive General Prevention and the Idea of Civic Courage in International Criminal Law, in: Why Punish Perpetrators of Mass Atrocities? 219 (Florian Jeßberger/Julia Geneuss eds., 2020).

[161] Id. at 220; *Gerhard Werle/Florian Jeßberger*, Principles of International Criminal Law para. 130 (2020); *Vasco Reuss*, Zivilcourage 15, 76 (2012).

[162] *Vasco Reuss*, Zivilcourage (2012); *Klaus Günther*, Positive General Prevention (2020); *Klaus Günther/Vasco Reuss*, Legitimation des Völkerstrafrechts (2014); see Möller considering the emergence of civic courage as unrealistic, *Christina Möller*, Völkerstrafrecht und Internationaler Strafgerichtshof (2003).

[163] *Klaus Günther*, Positive General Prevention 224 (2020).

[164] *Mark Drumbl*, Atrocity 61, 173 (2007); *Carsten Stahn*, A Critical Introduction to International Criminal Law 181 (2019).

[165] *Kai Ambos*, Not Much, but Better than Nothing 107 (2020).

[166] Prosecutor v. Obrenović, Case No. IT-02-60/2-S, Sentencing Judgement, ¶ 54 (Dec. 10, 2003) ("In conclusion, the Trial Chamber endorses these principles of punishment that readily lend themselves to promoting the rule of law and the realisation that violations thereof will not be tolerated").

genocide may be used in the context of certain events demonstrates the expressive function of international criminal punishment.[167] In this regard, it may also be contended that the proposal to label a new environmental crime 'ecocide', thereby drawing upon the international crime of genocide, emphasises the expressive function of criminal punishment.

Although, at first glance, expressive rationales of punishment seem to be a plausible legitimisation of international criminal law, they appear to be vague[168] and susceptible to being hampered by selective enforcement[169]. Nonetheless, in the context of environmental destruction, expressivism may be the strongest rationale for punishing under international criminal law.[170] Prosecuting environmental crimes exposes wrongdoing and labels large-scale environmental harm as criminal.[171] In doing so, prosecuting environmental crimes assists in connecting the related yet distinct areas of international criminal law and international human rights law.[172] The recent declaration of access to a clean, healthy, and sustainable environment as a universal human right by the UN General Assembly has yet again proved what had already been recognised in the 1972 Stockholm Declaration: the increasing interdependence of human and environmental health. By incorporating a fifth environmental crime into the Rome Statute, the need for environmental protection in relation to human health would become part of the minimum human rights standards set out by international criminal law. By this, corporate officials operating in environmentally sensitive areas would be enticed to conduct their businesses in an environmentally friendly and sustainable manner so as to avoid international criminal liability. Thus, corporate officials would have to comply with international standards of environmental protection, even if the respective country they operate in allows the exploitation of natural resources at all costs.

Hence, by evoking a positive general preventive effect transcending a mere (negative) deterrent effect, it is hoped a change in consciousness concerning environmental protection will be brought about. The criminal punishment of large-scale environmental harm would carry a significant symbolic value which non-criminal penalties miss.[173]

---

[167] *Robert Cryer*, et al., An Introduction to International Criminal Law and Procedure 37 (2019); see *Diane Marie Amann*, Group Mentality, Expressivism, and Genocide, 2 (2) International Criminal Law Review 93 (2002).

[168] *Florian Jeßberger/Julia Geneuss*, Concluding Remarks 385 (2020).

[169] *Mark Drumbl*, Atrocity 17 (2007); *Kai Ambos*, Not Much, but Better than Nothing 111 (2020).

[170] *Mark A. Drumbl*, International Center for Transitional Justice, 22 (2009); *Eliana Teresa Cusato*, JICJ 505 (2017).

[171] *Mark A. Drumbl*, International Center for Transitional Justice, 22 (2009).

[172] Id.

[173] *Joel Feinberg*, The Expressive Function of Punishment, 49 (3) The Monist 397, 400 (1970).

3. The discovery of truth

Besides the traditional punishment theories operative in the domestic context, international criminal justice also intends to ascertain the truth by dismantling justificatory narratives.[174] By determining the underlying facts in relation to the individual criminal liability of the offender, international criminal trials contribute to exposing the truth by recording the historical event.[175] Establishing international criminal liability for environmental harm could thus assist in discovering the true facts that led to the environmental destruction, which may facilitate the prevention of similar environmental disasters in the future. By contrast, for instance, *inter partes* arbitration procedures before the PCA, which often remain completely confidential[176], predominantly focus on reaching a legal settlement between the parties[177] and not on discovering all the relevant facts regarding the environmental issue.

4. Conclusion

In conclusion, incorporating a fifth crime of ecocide into the Rome Statute has the potential to promote global environmental protection for several reasons. Establishing international criminal liability would express the societal condemnation for large-scale environmental destruction in the international community. Labelling large-scale environmental harm as being criminal signals that environmental crimes do not go unpunished (retribution). Thus, for fear of reputational damage and financial loss resulting from the prospect of being incarcerated, corporate officials are likely to be deterred from causing (further) environmental harm. Although this (negative) deterrent effect has not yet been empirically proven, criminal sanctions have a different moral overtone than civil remedies, which are only perceived as collateral inconveniences but not as an incentive to curb environmental destruction by adopting environmental-friendly policies. Thus, particularly corporate officials who are typically sensitive to their reputation are more likely to refrain from engaging in criminal conduct for fear of reputational damage than typical war criminals. Furthermore, creating a fifth crime of ecocide under the Rome Statute would reinforce the awareness amongst the general public that large-scale environmental damage does not go unpunished. Thus, criminalisation of large-scale environmental

---

[174] Prosecutor v. Erdemović, Case No. IT-96-22-T*bis*, Sentencing Judgment, ¶ 21 (Mar. 5, 1998); *Klaus Günther*, Positive General Prevention 224 (2020); *Robert Cryer*, et al., An Introduction to International Criminal Law and Procedure 38–41 (2019); *Frank Neubacher*, Strafzwecke und Völkerstrafrecht, NJW 966, 969 (2006).

[175] *Daniela Demko*, An Expressive Theory of International Punishment for International Crimes, in: Why Punish Perpetrators of Mass Atrocities? 193 (Florian Jeßberger/Julia Geneuss eds., 2020).

[176] *Ole W. Pedersen*, Journal of Environmental Law 552 (2012); *Stephen Hockman*, Envtl. L. Rev. 2 (2008); *Tim Stephens*, International Courts and Environmental Protection 35 (2009).

[177] *Tim Stephens*, International Courts and Environmental Protection 35, 36 (2009).

damage may initiate a change in consciousness in the international community regarding environmental protection. In this vein, international criminal law has the potential to incentivise people to comply with these international environmental standards to avoid criminal liability (positive general prevention). However, similar to the negative deterrent effect, a positive preventive effect has not yet been empirically proven. Thus, it could be argued that unreasonably high expectations are set for what international criminal law can do. Nonetheless, the same criticism could be voiced in relation to domestic criminal law, yet this has not resulted in widespread calls to abolish domestic criminal law. In conclusion, criminal sanctions at least have a considerably higher potential to incentivise people to refrain from causing environmental harm than civil or administrative penalties, which are mostly accepted as inevitable side-effects. Additionally, conducting criminal trials before the ICC concerning environmental crimes would assist in discovering the true facts that caused the environmental harm, which may assist in preventing similar cases of environmental destruction (discovery of truth).

To conclude, elevating large-scale environmental harm to the same level as war crimes, crimes against humanity and genocide by including a stand-alone fifth crime against the environment would be of much higher symbolic value than merely ordering multinational corporations to pay civil damages for environmental destruction. Criminal law expresses not only the moral condemnation of a constituted society but is to a certain extent "*the very constitution of that society*"[178]. As Jojo Mehta, co-founder of Stop Ecocide, stated: "If something's a crime, we place it below a moral red line"[179]. Given that large-scale environmental destruction during armed conflicts has long been placed below a moral red line by having established Article 8 (2) (b) (iv) Rome Statute, the time is ripe to apply the same level of societal condemnation to environmental harm during peacetime

IV. Characteristics of crimes under international law

Furthermore, it needs to be examined whether, in theory, large-scale environmental harm could constitute a crime under international criminal law and could thus be conceptualised as a stand-alone fifth crime against the environment within the jurisdiction of the ICC. In this regard, the characteristics of crimes under international law will be analysed below. While determining the characteristics of crimes under international law has only received limited academic attention so far, different approaches have been taken and these will be examined in the following.

---

[178] *Frédéric Mégret*, Colum. J. Envtl. L. 256 (2011).

[179] *Sophie Yeo*, Ecocide, Should Killing Nature Be a Crime?, BBC, Nov. 6, 2020, https://www.bbc.com/future/article/20201105-what-is-ecocide.

1. Abstract criteria

The Appeals Chamber in the *Tadić* case developed a set of four abstract criteria, which must be fulfilled for an offence to be prosecutable by the ICTY[180]:

(1) *the violation must constitute an infringement of a rule of international humanitarian law;*

(2) *the rule must be customary in nature or, if it belongs to treaty law, the required conditions must be met;*

(3) *the violation must be "serious", that is to say, it must constitute a breach of a rule protecting important values, and the breach must involve grave consequences for the victim; and*

(4) *the violation of the rule must entail, under customary or conventional law, the individual criminal responsibility of the person breaching the rule.*

The task of establishing abstract criteria to determine the characteristics of international crimes was only attended to by very few scholars.[181] Amongst them, Ambos and Timmermann[182] developed a set of three distinguishing characteristics of crimes under international law: [183]

(1) *the violation must constitute an infringement of a rule of international law.*[184]

(2) *the violation must be serious, meaning that it must infringe upon important universal values.*[185]

---

[180] Prosecutor v. Tadić, Case No. IT-94-1, Decision on the Defence Motion for Interlocutory Appeal on Jurisdiction, ¶ 94 (Oct. 2, 1995).

[181] Scholars having dealt with the characteristics: *Antonio Cassese*, et al., Cassese's International Criminal Law 20 (2013) (four criteria); *Kai Ambos/Anina Timmermann*, Neue transnationale Verbrechen für das VStGB? 308 (2014) (three criteria); *Gerhard Werle/Florian Jeßberger*, Principles of International Criminal Law para. 101 (2020) (three criteria); *Cherif M. Bassiouni*, International Crimes: The Ratione Materiae of International Criminal Law 133 (2008) (five criteria); *Terje Einarsen*, The Concept of Universal Crimes in International Law 236 (2012) (five criteria).

[182] *Kai Ambos/Anina Timmermann*, Neue transnationale Verbrechen für das VStGB? 308, 309 (2014).

[183] Similar *Gerhard Werle/Florian Jeßberger*, Principles of International Criminal Law para. 101 (2020) (criterion 3); *Terje Einarsen*, The Concept of Universal Crimes in International Law 236 (2012) (criterion 5).

[184] Similar *Antonio Cassese*, et al., Cassese's International Criminal Law 20 (2013) (criterion 1 with emphasis on international customary law); *Terje Einarsen*, The Concept of Universal Crimes in International Law 236 (2012) (criterion 4); *Gerhard Werle/Florian Jeßberger*, Principles of International Criminal Law para. 101 (2020) (criterion 2).

[185] Similar *Antonio Cassese*, et al., Cassese's International Criminal Law 20 (2013) (criterion 2); *Cherif M. Bassiouni*, International Crimes: The Ratione Materiae of International Criminal Law 133 (2008) (criteria 1, 2, 4); *Terje Einarsen*, The Concept of Universal Crimes in International Law 236 (2012) (criteria 1, 3); *Gerhard Werle/Florian Jeßberger*, Principles of International Criminal Law paras. 107, 108 (2020); *Robert Cryer*, et al., An Introduction to

(3) *the violation must directly entail individual criminal responsibility of the person breaching the rule*[186]*, irrespective of whether the conduct in question is proscribed under domestic criminal law.*

Thus, Ambos and Timmermann agree with the ICTY to the extent that there must be (1) a pre-existing international (customary) provision proscribing the conduct in question, (2) which entails a serious infringement of universal values of the international community and (3) stipulates individual criminal responsibility in the event of violation.

Since the ICTY and most scholars seem to concur at least with these three core prerequisites[187], in the following it will be examined whether a potential fifth crime against the environment would meet these requirements and could thus be elevated to a crime under international law.

a) Violation of a rule of international (customary) law

Firstly, a generic crime against the environment would have to infringe upon international (customary) law. This, in turn, would require the existence of a glob-

International Criminal Law and Procedure 6 (2019); *Claus Kreß*, International Criminal Law (2009), https://opil.ouplaw.com/view/10.1093/law:epil/9780199231690/law-9780199231690-e1423#law-9780199231690-e1423 (last visited Feb. 18, 2025).

[186] Similar *Claus Kreß*, International Criminal Law (2009), https://opil.ouplaw.com/view/10.1093/law:epil/9780199231690/law-9780199231690-e1423#law-9780199231690-e1423 (last visited Feb. 18, 2025); *Gerhard Werle/Florian Jeßberger*, Principles of International Criminal Law para. 101 (2020) (criterion 1).

[187] *Gerhard Werle/Florian Jeßberger*, Principles of International Criminal Law para. 101 (2020); *Terje Einarsen*, The Concept of Universal Crimes in International Law 236 (2012); *Antonio Cassese*, et al., Cassese's International Criminal Law 20 (2013). Cassese presupposes an additional fourth criterion, namely "if the perpetrator has acted in an official capacity, i.e. as a *de jure* or *de facto* state official, the state on whose behalf he has performed the prohibited act is *barred* from claiming the immunity from the civil or criminal jurisdiction of foreign states accruing under customary international law to state officials acting in the exercise of their functions" (*Cassese*, et al., Cassese's International Criminal Law 20 (2013)). However, this criterion pertains to the consequences of international criminal liability and does not constitute a prerequisite of a crime under international law (Similar, *Einarsen*, The Concept of Universal Crimes in International Law 152 (2012)). In general, it has to be noted that immunity of state officials only plays a subordinate role in the context of environmental harm, as only very few cases of environmental harm are directly caused by state officials (*Pereira*, Criminal Law Forum 191 (2020)). In contrast to the aforementioned scholars, Bassiouni took a much broader approach (*Bassiouni*, International Crimes: The Ratione Materiae of International Criminal Law 133 (2008)), which, however, is deemed too wide (Similar, Ambos & Timmermann, Neue transnationale Verbrechen für das VStGB? 308 n.18 (2014)). Particularly requirements such as 'conduct shocking the conscience of humanity', are highly subjective and their determination remains a matter of judgment (See *Cryer*, The Doctrinal Foundations of International Criminalization 125, 126 (2008)).

ally accepted definition of an international crime against the environment[188] either set out in international treaty law or international customary law.[189] Although international environmental law has developed into a mosaic of over 500 treaties, these treaties, such as, for instance, the CITES[190], are restricted to very specific types of environmentally harmful conduct such as illegal logging or illegal fishing. However, at present, a generic crime against the environment is not enshrined in any international environmental treaty.[191] Nonetheless, as Tomuschat rightly stated during the drafting of the Rome Statute, the Rome Statute "is not meant to enforce international environmental legislation"[192]. Due to the incoherence and incompleteness of international environmental law, requiring the existence of a violation of international environmental treaty law as a prerequisite for establishing a crime under international law, would only risk creating further lacunae in international criminalisation.[193] It appears much more meaningful to fill the legal lacunae in international environmental law by establishing a generic crime against the environment under international criminal law.

Thus, the question arises as to whether large-scale environmental harm is prohibited under customary international law. Pursuant to Article 38 (1) (b) Statute of the ICJ, international customary law is composed of two elements: state practice and *opinio juris.*[194] However, both elements are difficult to prove especially concerning international environmental obligations where little empirical research has been undertaken in this regard.[195] Given the considerable number of ratifications and states supporting Articles 35 (3), 55 (1) AP I, these rules of international humanitarian law are considered rules of international customary law.[196] However, the war crime establishing individual criminal liability for widespread, long-term and

---

[188] *Kai Ambos/Anina Timmermann*, Neue transnationale Verbrechen für das VStGB? 308 (2014).

[189] Prosecutor v. Tadic, Case No. IT-94-1, Decision on the Defence Motion for Interlocutory Appeal on Jurisdiction, ¶ 94 (Oct. 2, 1995); *Antonio Cassese*, et al., Cassese's International Criminal Law 20 (2013).

[190] Convention on International Trade in Endangered Species of Wild Fauna and Flora, Mar. 3, 1973, 993 U.N.T.S. 243.

[191] *Anastacia Greene*, Fordham Environmental Law Review 1 (2019).

[192] Documents of the Forty-Eight Session, [1996] 2 Y.B. Int'l L. Comm'n, at 25 ¶ 35, U.N. A/CN.4/SER.A/1996/Add. 1 (Part 1).

[193] See id.

[194] See also Legality of the Threat or Use of Nuclear Weapons, Advisory Opinion, 1996 I. C.J. Rep., ¶ 64 (July 8); *Philippe Sands/Jacqueline Peel*, Principles of International Environmental Law 119 (2018).

[195] *Philippe Sands/Jacqueline Peel*, Principles of International Environmental Law 120, 121 (2018); see *Daniel Bodansky*, Indiana Journal of Global Studies (1995).

[196] *Philippe Sands/Jacqueline Peel*, Principles of International Environmental Law 835 (2018).

severe damage to the natural environment is limited to international armed conflicts.[197]

Furthermore, in the 1996 Advisory Opinion on the Legality of the Threat or Use of Nuclear Weapons, the ICJ acknowledged the customary status of Principle 21/ Principle 2 of the Stockholm Declaration[198] stipulating that "[s]tates have […] the responsibility to ensure that activities within their jurisdiction or control do not cause damage to the environment of other States or of areas beyond the limits of national jurisdiction"[199]. In the 1996 Advisory Opinion on the Legality of the Threat or Use of Nuclear Weapons the ICJ further stated that Article I (1) ENMOD Convention and Articles 35 (3), 55 (1) AP I taken together "embody a general obligation to protect the natural environment against widespread, long-term and severe environmental damage".[200] Similarly, in *Pulp Mills*, the ICJ confirmed the customary status of the principle of prevention, that is the states' obligation to prevent environmental harm by reducing, limiting and controlling activities capable of causing such damage having originated from the due diligence required of a state within its territory.[201] In *Pulp Mills*, the ICJ further stated that the states' obligation to "undertake an environmental impact assessment where there is a risk that the proposed industrial activity may have a significant adverse impact in a transboundary context" is considered "a requirement under general international law".[202] However, both the preventive principle as well as Principle 21 entail state obligations and do not establish individual criminal liability. Notwithstanding, as ruled in *Tadić*, the violation of the rule must entail, under customary or conventional law, the individual criminal responsibility of the person breaching the rule.[203]

---

[197] See Art. 1 (3) AP I in conjunction with Geneva Convention Relative to the Protection of Civilian Persons in Time of War art. 2, Aug. 12, 1949, 75 U.N.T.S. 287. No equivalent provision is provided by Additional Protocol II which pertains to non-international armed conflicts.

[198] *Philippe Sands/Jacqueline Peel*, Principles of International Environmental Law 121, 206 (2018).

[199] Principle 21/Principle 2 of the Stockholm Declaration.

[200] Legality of the Threat or Use of Nuclear Weapons, Advisory Opinion, 1996 I.C.J. Rep., ¶ 31 (July 8).

[201] Pulp Mills on the River Uruguay (Argentina v. Uruguay), Judgment, 2010 I.C.J. Rep., ¶ 101 (Apr. 20); *Philippe Sands/Jacqueline Peel*, Principles of International Environmental Law 211 (2018).

[202] Pulp Mills on the River Uruguay (Argentina v. Uruguay), Judgment, 2010 I.C.J. Rep., ¶ 204 (Apr. 20).

[203] Prosecutor v. Tadić, Case No. IT-94-1, Decision on the Defence Motion for Interlocutory Appeal on Jurisdiction, ¶ 94 (Oct. 2, 1995); similar *Gerhard Werle/Florian Jeßberger*, Principles of International Criminal Law para. 101 (2020); *Kai Ambos/Anina Timmermann*, Neue transnationale Verbrechen für das VStGB? 308 (2014); *Claus Kreß*, International Criminal Law (2009), https://opil.ouplaw.com/view/10.1093/law:epil/9780199231690/law-9780199231690-e1423#law-9780199231690-e1423 (last visited Feb. 18, 2025).

Hence, a generic crime of ecocide applicable during times of war and peace incurring individual criminal liability is not recognised under customary international law.[204] However, although customary international law is considered "the thrust of the Rome Statute"[205], in some cases the Rome Statute "arguably goes beyond customary law"[206]. For instance, Article 8 (2) (b) (iii), (iv) and (viii) Rome Statute did not form part of customary international law at the time the Rome Statute was adopted.[207] Furthermore, at the Review Conference in 2010 the crime of aggression was criticised for not having reflected customary international law.[208] In response to this, an enclosed Understanding emphasised that in accordance with Article 10 Rome Statute these amendments must "not be interpreted as limiting or prejudicing in any way existing or developing rules of international law for purposes other than this Statute".[209] Thus, Article 10 Rome Statute proves that the ICC Statute does not strictly reflect but can go beyond customary international law.[210]

Furthermore, Article 21 (1) (a) Rome Statute, which defines the applicable sources of law, gives the Rome Statute precedence over customary international law. This, however, would not make sense if the Rome Statute were only designed to reflect customary international law.[211] Thus, while the ad hoc tribunals are bound by customary international law due to the principle of *nullum crime sine lege*[212], the ICC's primary source of law is its Statute, which does not necessarily have to reflect customary law.[213] As Jennings already stated in 1981: "Perhaps it is time to face squarely the fact that the orthodox tests of custom-practice and *opinio juris* – are

---

204 *Ryan M. Scoville*, Finding Customary International Law, 101 Iowa L. Rev. 1893, 1914, 1936 (2016).

205 *William A. Schabas*, The International Criminal Court: A Commentary on the Rome Statute 335 (2016).

206 *Alexander Heinze*, Article 10, in: Rome Statute of the International Criminal Court 773 para. 19 (Kai Ambos ed., 2022); *Marko Milanović*, Is the Rome Statute Binding on Individuals? (And Why We Should Care), 9 (1) JICJ 25, 30 (2011).

207 *William A. Schabas*, An Introduction to the International Criminal Court 122 (2020).

208 Review Conference of the Rome Statute of the International Criminal Court (May 31–June 11, 2010) at 47, ¶ 16, Official Records RC/11.

209 Resolution RC/Res.6 of the Review Conference of the Rome Statute, Annex III, at 22, ¶ 4 (June 11, 2010).

210 *Alexander Heinze*, Article 10 para. 2 (2022); *Norman Farrell*, Attributing Criminal Liability to Corporate Actors: Some Lessons from the International Tribunals, 8 (3) JICJ 873, 887 (2010).

211 *Marko Milanović*, JICJ 31 (2011).

212 Prosecutor v. Bagilishema, Case No. ICTR-95-1 A-A, Judgement, ¶ 34 (July 3, 2002); U.N. Security Council, Report of the Secretary-General Pursuant to Paragraph 2 of Security Council Resolution 808, at 8, ¶ 29, U.N. Doc. S/25704 (1993); *Simon M. Meisenberg*, Auf dem Wege zu einem Unternehmensvölkerstrafrecht? Eine kritische Würdigung der "New TV S.A.L."-Entscheidung des Sondergerichtshofs für den Libanon 61 (2016).

213 *Norman Farrell*, JICJ 887 (2010); see *Frank Meyer*, Multinationale Unternehmen und das Völkerstrafrecht, 131 (1) Schweizerische Zeitschrift für Strafrecht 56, 77 (2013).

often not only inadequate but even irrelevant for the identification of much new law today"[214].

Thus, a new crime against the environment does not necessarily have to be recognised as a rule of (customary) international law prior to its incorporation into the Rome Statute.[215] Instead, by incorporating a new core crime into the Rome Statute, the State Parties would establish a new crime under (conventional) international criminal law, which may be recognised a rule of customary international law in the future.

b) Serious infringement of universal values of the international community

Secondly, large-scale environmental degradation must be serious meaning that it must infringe upon important universal values.[216] According to the Preamble of the Rome Statute, international criminal law intends to protect the "peace, security and well-being of the world"[217]. However, over the course of time protecting internationally enshrined human rights has gained significant importance.[218] In May 2022, the G7 Foreign Ministers explicitly acknowledged that environmental degradation, climate change and biodiversity loss "pose a threat to international peace and stability"[219]. It was argued that since the environment is shared by all, the nations' peace and security are interdependent.[220] Moreover, since grave environmental harm threatens human life, for instance, by causing resource and food scarcity,

---

[214] Cited in *Daniel Bodansky*, Indiana Journal of Global Studies, 112 (1995).

[215] Dapo Akande, Customary International Law and the Addition of New War Crimes to the Statute of the ICC, EJIL: Talk! (Jan. 2, 2018), https://www.ejiltalk.org/customary-international-law-and-the-addition-of-new-war-crimes-to-the-statute-of-the-icc/ (last visited Feb. 18, 2025); similar with respect to the incorporation of corporate criminal liability into the Rome Statute, *Frank Meyer*, Schweizerische Zeitschrift für Strafrecht 77 (2013).

[216] Prosecutor v. Tadić, Case No. IT-94–1, Decision on the Defence Motion for Interlocutory Appeal on Jurisdiction, ¶ 94 (Oct. 2, 1995); *Kai Ambos/Anina Timmermann*, Neue transnationale Verbrechen für das VStGB? 308 (2014); *Gerhard Werle/Florian Jeßberger*, Principles of International Criminal Law paras. 107, 108 (2020); *Antonio Cassese*, et al., Cassese's International Criminal Law 20 (2013); *Terje Einarsen*, The Concept of Universal Crimes in International Law 236 (2012); *Cherif M. Bassiouni*, International Crimes: The Ratione Materiae of International Criminal Law 133 (2008); *Robert Cryer*, et al., An Introduction to International Criminal Law and Procedure 6, 7 (2019); *Claus Kreß*, International Criminal Law (2009), https://opil.ouplaw.com/view/10.1093/law:epil/9780199231690/law-9780199231690-e1423#law9780199231690-e1423 (last visited Feb. 18, 2025).

[217] Preamble of the Rome Statute (3).

[218] *Christoph Safferling*, Internationales Strafrecht § 4 para. 67 (2011); *Claus Kreß*, International Criminal Law (2009), https://opil.ouplaw.com/view/10.1093/law:epil/9780199231690/law-9780199231690-e1423#law-9780199231690-e1423 (last visited Feb. 18, 2025).

[219] Federal Foreign Office, G7 Foreign Minister's Statement on Climate, Environment, Peace and Security (2022), https://www.auswaertiges-amt.de/en/newsroom/news/-/2531240 (last visited Feb. 18, 2025).

[220] Id.

affected populations have to fight for their right to life, which, in turn, promotes conflicts and thus endangers international peace and security.[221] As the UN already warned in 2007, extreme weather conditions, including floodings and droughts, intensifying resource competition and famine are expected to promote environmental-related migration in the future, which further threatens international peace and security.[222]

Furthermore, on 28 July 2022 the UN General Assembly declared in a historic resolution "access to a clean, healthy and sustainable environment, a universal human right".[223] Hence, by being a threat to international peace and security and violating the universal human right to access to a clean, healthy and sustainable environment, large-scale environmental harm potentially violates the universal values of the international community and could thus be considered a crime under international law.[224] However, a definition of a potential fifth crime of ecocide would have to contain a gravity threshold ensuring that only grave environmental harm likely to infringe upon universal values is covered by the crime.

c) Individual criminal responsibility under international law

Thirdly, the underlying international (customary) rule would have to directly entail individual criminal responsibility of the person breaching the rule, irrespective of whether the conduct in question is proscribed under domestic criminal law.[225] However, as stated above, although presently such an international environmental crime neither exists in international treaty law nor in international customary law, the ICC Statute is not bound by customary international law but can go beyond it. Incorporating a distinct crime of ecocide into the Rome Statute would automatically establish individual criminal liability under Article 25 (1) and (2) Rome Statute for the perpetrator of the crime. As such, the crime would be prosecutable by the ICC

[221] Documents of the Forty-Eighth Session, [1996] 2 Y.B. Int'l L. Comm'n 22 ¶ 18, U.N. Doc. A/CN.4/SER.A/1996/Add.1 (Part 1).

[222] United Nations, Security Council Holds First-Ever Debate on Impact of Climate Change on Peace, Security, Hearing over 50 Speakers (2007), https://press.un.org/en/2007/sc9000.doc.htm (last visited Feb. 18, 2025); *Philippe Sands/Jacqueline Peel*, Principles of International Environmental Law 837 (2018).

[223] United Nations, UN General Assembly Declares Access to Clean and Healthy Environment a Universal Human Right (2022), https://news.un.org/en/story/2022/07/1123482 (last visited Feb. 18, 2025).

[224] *Ricardo Pereira*, Criminal Law Forum 191, 192 (2020); *Antonio Cassese*, et al., Cassese's International Criminal Law 21 (2013).

[225] Prosecutor v. Tadić, Case No. IT-94-1, Decision on the Defence Motion for Interlocutory Appeal on Jurisdiction, ¶ 94 (Oct. 2, 1995); *Claus Kreß*, International Criminal Law (2009), https://opil.ouplaw.com/view/10.1093/law:epil/9780199231690/law-9780199231690-e1423#law-9780199231690-e1423 (last visited Feb. 18, 2025); *Gerhard Werle/Florian Jeßberger*, Principles of International Criminal Law para. 101 (2020); *Kai Ambos/Anina Timmermann*, Neue transnationale Verbrechen für das VStGB? 308 (2014).

irrespective of whether the conduct in question is proscribed under domestic criminal law. Thus, in contrast to transnational crimes, the enforcement of the crime would not be entrusted to the states.

d) Conclusion

In conclusion, it appears difficult to agree upon a set of abstract criteria characterising crimes under international law. While it appears right to require the crime to exceed a certain threshold of gravity to be elevated to a crime under international law, it seems inappropriate to demand the pre-existence of an international (customary) rule stipulating individual criminal responsibility for the conduct in question. In this regard, it should be considered that the lack of an international environmental crime was the reason for contemplating the establishment of a crime of ecocide under the Rome Statute in the first place.

With regard to the aforementioned abstract criteria, it is particularly noteworthy that although the characteristics of crimes under international law are far from self-evident, none of the aforementioned scholars ever elaborated on the reasons as to why they chose this particular set of criteria.[226] This is further exacerbated by the fact that each scholar perceives the scope of the two different categories of international crimes, crimes under international law and transnational crimes, differently and refers to them differently. For instance, Cassese established the set of criteria in relation to 'international crimes' comprising not only the four core crimes under the Rome Statute but also the crime of international terrorism, which is not included in the Rome Statute.[227] Similar to Cassese, Bassiouni developed the criteria in relation to "*jus cogens*" crimes encompassing not only the four core crimes but also a number of transnational crimes, such as torture, piracy and apartheid, which are not enshrined in the Rome Statute.[228] By contrast, Werle established the characteristics of 'crimes under international law' and thereby only refers to the four core crimes under the Rome Statute.[229]

Thus, since the sets of criteria were developed by different scholars in relation to different international crimes, these abstract criteria are not well-suited to determine the characteristics of crimes under international law in delineation to transnational crimes in order to examine whether a new crime of ecocide could qualify as a crime under international criminal law. Furthermore, history displays that neither international criminal law nor transnational criminal law evolved gradually and coher-

---

[226] *Terje Einarsen*, The Concept of Universal Crimes in International Law 152, 153 (2012).

[227] *Antonio Cassese*, et al., Cassese's International Criminal Law 21 (2013).

[228] *Cherif M. Bassiouni*, International Crimes: The Ratione Materiae of International Criminal Law 138 (2008).

[229] *Gerhard Werle/Florian Jeßberger*, Principles of International Criminal Law para. 100 (2020).

ently, but rather emerged in reaction to particular egregious events.[230] In fact, states have never applied any of those abstract formulae during the process of establishing new international crimes.[231] Consequently, Cryer, for instance, does not distinguish crimes under international law from transnational crimes by establishing a list of criteria, but very pragmatically, by the fact of whether the crime falls within the ambit of an international criminal court.[232] Thus, simply by incorporating a crime into the Rome Statute a transnational crime becomes a crime under international law.[233] However, prior to contemplating the inclusion of a fifth core crime into the Rome Statute those abstract criteria might prove helpful to determine the comparability with the pre-existing core crimes.[234] Although it is strictly forbidden, in accordance with Article 22 (2) Rome Statute, to extend the ICC's jurisdiction by analogy, it appears reasonable to argue in favour of criminalising certain conduct which is similar to the pre-existing crimes.[235]

2. Seriousness

When contemplating the extension of the ICC's jurisdiction to a fifth core crime, it needs to be considered that criminal law, whether at the domestic or international level, is the last resort[236] and thus may not be resorted to too lightly. However, the Preamble of the Rome Statute emphasises that the ICC only has jurisdiction over "the most serious crimes of concern to the international community as a whole"[237] as opposed to ordinary criminality. Elsewhere in the Rome Statute, the four core crimes are described as "unimaginable atrocities that deeply shock the conscience of humanity"[238] or "the most serious crimes of international concern"[239].

With respect to the international criminalisation of large-scale environmental destruction thus the question arises as to whether such conduct meets the required gravity threshold in order to be able to be deemed a crime under international criminal law. In this context it was once argued: "The main difficulty in concluding

[230] *Robert Cryer*, The Doctrinal Foundations of International Criminalization 119 (2008).

[231] Id. at 127.

[232] *Robert Cryer*, et al., An Introduction to International Criminal Law and Procedure 5 (2019).

[233] *Terje Einarsen*, The Concept of Universal Crimes in International Law 160 (2012).

[234] *Robert Cryer*, The Doctrinal Foundations of International Criminalization 127 (2008).

[235] Id.

[236] See Council of Europe, Committee of Ministers, Resolution (77) 28 on the Contribution of Criminal Law to the Protection of the Environment, Preamble ¶ 3 (Sept. 28, 1977) ("Considering that while recourse to the criminal law in this field should be a last resort, nevertheless use must be made of it when other measures are not observed or are ineffective or inadequate").

[237] Preamble of the Rome Statute (4), (9); Art. 5 Rome Statute.

[238] Preamble of the Rome Statute (2).

[239] Art. 1 Rome Statute.

that wilful and severe damage to the environment is an international crime, is that in most cases such damage will be caught by other crimes, such as aggression or war crimes, and where that is not the case, there may be doubts as to whether it achieves the threshold of gravity for an international crime"[240].

During the drafting of the Rome Statute, it was unanimously agreed by the ILC that crimes against the peace and security of mankind are characterised by its seriousness.[241] It was agreed that "[t]hese are crimes which affect the very foundations of human society"[242]. In this regard, either the nature of the conduct in question or the magnitude of its implications indicate the seriousness of the crime.[243] With regards to environmental destruction, at least the gravest forms of environmental destruction appear to be capable of undermining the very foundations of the international community.[244]

However, the parameter against which the seriousness of the crime is measured is human life[245], not the environment itself, which mirrors the mainly anthropocentric approach of the Rome Statute. Nonetheless, some provisions of the Rome Statute, including Article 8 (2) (b) (iv) Rome Statute or the crime of aggression, do not directly protect human interests.[246] Hence, seriousness does not necessarily require the *direct* causation of human harm in terms of an attack on the physical integrity.[247] Acts may rather be deemed sufficiently grave if they "undermine the substantive bases of life in conditions of good health and individual and collective dignity"[248]. Thus, although the seriousness of the environmental damage is not directly determined by the causation of human harm, environmental protection through international criminal law would only occur for the reason to secure "the

[240] *Patrick Robinson*, The Missing Crimes, in: The Rome Statute of the International Criminal Court: A Commentary 523 (Antonio Cassese, et al. eds., 2002).

[241] Report of the Commission to the General Assembly on the Work of its Thirty-Ninth Session, [1987] 2 Y.B. Int'l L. Comm'n 13 ¶ 66 (2), U.N. Doc. A/CN.4/SER.A/1987/Add.1 (Part 2); see Schabas according to whom seriousness is "a qualitative criterion for inclusion of crimes within the Rome Statute", *William A. Schabas*, The International Criminal Court: A Commentary on the Rome Statute 41 (2016).

[242] Report of the Commission to the General Assembly on the Work of its Thirty-Ninth Session, [1987] 2 Y.B. Int'l L. Comm'n 13 ¶ 66 (2), U.N. Doc. A/CN.4/SER.A/1987/Add.1 (Part 2).

[243] Id.; Documents of the Forty-Eighth Session, [1996] 2 Y.B. Int'l L. Comm'n 21 ¶ 14, U. N. Doc. A/CN.4/SER.A/1996/Add.1 (Part 1).

[244] Documents of the Forty-Eighth Session, [1996] 2 Y.B. Int'l L. Comm'n 21 ¶ 15, U.N. Doc. A/CN.4/SER.A/1996/Add.1 (Part 1).

[245] Id. at 21 ¶ 14.

[246] Id. at 21 ¶ 16, 17.

[247] Id. at 22 ¶ 18.

[248] Id. at 22 ¶ 18.

survival of humankind from a long-term perspective"[249] and not to safeguard the viability of the environment as such.[250]

Thus, in order to be elevated to a crime under international law, environmental harm needs to ultimately threaten human interests, albeit only *indirectly*.[251] However, as a healthy environment is essential for human life, it appears almost impossible to envisage a case of severe environmental destruction which does not ultimately affect human life. This assertion is confirmed by the recent decision of the UN General Assembly which recognised access to a clean, healthy and sustainable environment a universal human right.[252] Even if severe environmental harm does not immediately and directly incur human harm, it will inevitably impact human interests in the long-term, for instance, by causing generic alterations, incurable diseases or rendering entire regions uninhabitable.[253]

Hence, the abovementioned assertion that most cases of environmental harm are covered by the pre-existing core crimes, especially aggression and war crimes, has to be refuted, and apart from that it is doubtful as to whether environmental harm meets the gravity threshold for an international crime.[254] As seen above, the existing core crimes only insufficiently protect the environment. While the crime of aggression only plays a subordinate role in environmental protection, war crimes only cover large-scale environmental harm occurring during an international armed conflict. However, peacetime environmental destruction, which is the most prevalent form of environmental harm these days, is left mainly unaddressed. Isolated acts of grave environmental destruction which do not form part of a widespread or systematic attack have the same serious environmental repercussions as environmental degradation which form part of such an attack, but do not fall under the scope of crimes against humanity. Furthermore, crimes against humanity, such as extermination or the deportation of a population, require the *direct* causation of human harm.[255] Although the Rome Statute is predominately anthropocentric, a fifth crime of ecocide could be designed in an ecocentric fashion. Thus, large-scale environmental destruction not directly but only *indirectly* causing human harm could be criminalised. Hence, this lacuna in current international criminal law could be filled by establishing a fifth crime of ecocide.

---

[249] Id. at 24 ¶ 29.

[250] Id. at 24 ¶ 29; *Frédéric Mégret*, Colum. J. Envtl. L. 208, 209 (2011).

[251] *Emanuela Fronza*, Towards a New Crime of Ecocide 100 (2022).

[252] United Nations, UN General Assembly Declares Access to Clean and Healthy Environment a Universal Human Right (2022), https://news.un.org/en/story/2022/07/1123482 (last visited Feb. 18, 2025).

[253] Documents of the Forty-Eighth Session, [1996] 2 Y.B. Int'l L. Comm'n 22 ¶ 18, U.N. Doc. A/CN.4/SER.A/1996/Add.1 (Part 1).

[254] *Patrick Robinson*, The Missing Crimes 523 (2002).

[255] *Emanuela Fronza*, Towards a New Crime of Ecocide 100 (2022).

As severe environmental harm infringes upon universal values by threatening international peace and security and violating basic human interests, large-scale environmental harm is serious enough to be elevated to a crime under international law.[256] However, a definition of a potential fifth crime of ecocide would have to include a respective gravity threshold ensuring that only grave environmental harm is covered by the crime.

3. Impunity in domestic jurisdiction

Instead of focusing on the gravity of the conduct, Schabas argues that impunity in domestic jurisdictions is the reason for establishing criminal liability under international law.[257] In the context of the four core crimes he argues that most of the crimes are perpetrated by states, which is why they go widely unpunished in domestic judicial systems.[258]

In the environmental context, so far only 11 states have incorporated a generic crime of ecocide in their domestic criminal codes.[259] Vietnam was the first country to enact a crime of ecocide in domestic law in 1990 in response to the environmental harm sustained during the Vietnam War.[260] After the collapse of the Soviet Union in 1991, Vietnam was followed by Russia[261] and former USSR Republics, including Armenia[262], Belarus[263], Republic of Moldova[264], Ukraine[265], Georgia[266], Kazakhstan[267], Kyrgyzstan[268] and Tajikistan[269]. Thus, large-scale environmental destruction largely goes unpunished due to the lack of appropriate domestic laws. This is further exacerbated by the fact that most environmental destruction is caused by multinational corporations which significantly influence states both politically and eco-

[256] See Chapter C. IV. 1. b).

[257] *William A. Schabas*, An Introduction to the International Criminal Court 91 (2020).

[258] Id.

[259] Ecocide law, Ecocide Law in National Jurisdictions, https://ecocidelaw.com/existing-ecocide-laws/ (last visited Feb. 18, 2025).

[260] Penal Code Vietnam (1990) art. 278: "Ecocide or destroying the natural environment", whether committed during war or peace, constitutes a crime against humanity. In 1999 the crime of ecocide was included in Art. 342 of the Penal Code Vietnam, No. 15/1999/QH10 (1999).

[261] The Criminal Code of the Russian Federation art. 358, No. 63-FZ (June 13, 1996).

[262] Criminal Code of the Republic of Armenia art. 394, Law HO-528-N (Apr. 18, 2003).

[263] Criminal Code of the Republic of Belarus art. 131, No. 275-Z (July 9, 1999).

[264] The Criminal Code of the Republic of Moldova art. 136, No. 985-XV (Apr. 18, 2002).

[265] Criminal Code of the Republic of Ukraine art. 441, No. 2341-III (Sept. 1, 2001).

[266] Criminal Code of Georgia art. 409, No. 2287 (July 22, 1999).

[267] Criminal Code of the Republic of Kazakhstan art. 169, No. 226-V ZRK (July 3, 1997).

[268] Criminal Code of the Kyrgyz Republic art. 374, No. 68 (Oct. 1, 1997).

[269] Penal Code of the Republic of Tajikistan art. 400 (May 21, 1998).

nomically by providing employment and revenue and requiring full impunity in return.[270]

4. Values protected by international criminal law

In similar fashion, other scholars determine the characteristics of international crimes by assessing the values protected by international criminal law.[271] Cryer argues that "international crimes are considered to be those which are of concern to the international community as a whole (a description which is not of great precision), or acts which violate a fundamental interest protected by international law".[272] In line with the Preamble of the Rome Statute[273], international peace and security were originally deemed the fundamental values behind international criminal law.[274] However, more recently, the protection of human rights has gained significance.[275] As such, international criminal law not only protects collective values such as international peace and security, but also individual rights, such as universally recognised human rights.[276] As stated above, grave environmental harm is both likely to interfere with international peace and security as well as with universal human rights[277] such as the access to a clean, healthy and sustainable environment and would thus fit within the framework of values protected by international criminal law.

[270] Fafo & International Peace Academy, Business and International Crimes: Assessing the Liability of Business Entities for Grave Violations of International Law, at 22, Fafo-Report 467 (2005); *Regina Rauxloh*, The Role of International Criminal Law in Environmental Protection 441 (2011).

[271] *Robert Cryer*, et al., An Introduction to International Criminal Law and Procedure 6, 7 (2019); *Carsten Stahn*, A Critical Introduction to International Criminal Law 16 (2019).

[272] *Robert Cryer*, et al., An Introduction to International Criminal Law and Procedure 6 (2019); also *Claus Kreß*, International Criminal Law (2009), https://opil.ouplaw.com/view/10.1093/law:epil/9780199231690/law-9780199231690-e1423#law-9780199231690-e1423 (last visited Feb. 18, 2025); *Gerhard Werle/Florian Jeßberger*, Principles of International Criminal Law paras. 107, 108 (2020).

[273] See Preamble of the Rome Statute (3) ("Recognizing that such grave crimes threaten the peace, security and well-being of the world").

[274] *Claus Kreß*, International Criminal Law (2009), https://opil.ouplaw.com/view/10.1093/law:epil/9780199231690/law-9780199231690-e1423#law-9780199231690-e1423 (last visited Feb. 18, 2025).

[275] Id.; *Christoph Safferling*, Internationales Strafrecht § 4 para. 67 (2011).

[276] *Claus Kreß*, International Criminal Law (2009), https://opil.ouplaw.com/view/10.1093/law:epil/9780199231690/law-9780199231690-e1423#law-9780199231690-e1423 (last visited Feb. 18, 2025); *Christoph Safferling*, Internationales Strafrecht § 4 para. 67 (2011).

[277] See Chapter C.IV.1.b).

5. Conclusion

In conclusion, it appears possible to elevate large-scale environmental harm to a crime under international law. While establishing sets of abstract characteristics of crimes under international criminal law is not to be advised, three main characteristics have to be considered when contemplating the creation of a new core crime. First, the potential new core crime has to be serious enough to be referred to as one of the 'most serious crimes of concern to the international community as a whole'. Secondly, in order to be deemed serious enough, the proscribed conduct has to be likely to threaten the international peace and security or violate fundamental human rights. Thirdly, the absence of domestic criminalisation of the proscribed conduct speaks in favour of international criminalisation.

Since the environment is shared by all and the repercussions of environmental harm are ubiquitous, environmental degradation poses a threat to international peace and stability. However, it also poses a threat to human life itself by causing resource and food scarcity, which, in turn, promotes and protracts conflicts. As a consequence, environment-related migration will be one of the most daunting challenges for the international community in the future. Thus, large-scale environmental harm is one of the 'most serious crimes of concern to the international community as a whole'. This is further exacerbated by the fact that generic crimes of ecocide have only been enshrined in ten states so far. Hence, large-scale environmental harm largely goes unpunished and is, if at all, only addressed by civil remedies which lack the moral overtone of criminal sanctions and which carry the potential of deterring and thus preventing further harm. This, in turn, signals the need to establish an international crime of ecocide. However, the definition of a potential fifth crime of ecocide under the Rome Statute would have to contain a gravity threshold ensuring that only grave environmental harm, which should be elevated to a crime under international law, is covered by the crime. In this regard, it is particularly noteworthy that although Article 23 of the Draft Code was deliberately excluded from the Draft Code, the existence of Article 10 Rome Statute proves that this decision cannot be used to argue against the subsequent inclusion of a fifth crime of ecocide.[278]

In the following, it will be assessed how such a fifth crime of ecocide could be defined.

---

[278] *Alexander Heinze*, Article 10 para. 18 (2022).

V. The definition of a crime of ecocide

As argued by the President of the Monsanto Tribunal, Tulkens[279]: "[t]his offence still does not exist and in order for that to happen, it first has to be *precisely* defined."[280] Despite years of legal debate, so far, no official definition of a potential crime of ecocide has yet been agreed upon for the purpose of an international prohibition of environmentally destructive activities in a legally binding instrument. However, a definition is needed if a crime of ecocide is to be incorporated into the Rome Statute. In the process of defining a crime of ecocide, two elements are the most contentious: the gravity threshold and the mental element. Both elements can either render the crime too broad, risking the loss of political support, or too narrow, excluding substantial environmental degradation from its scope of application.

In the following, it will be examined how the material and mental elements[281] of a potential crime of ecocide could best be formulated to provide effective environmental protection, whilst, at the same time, adhering to the peculiarities of international criminal law. In a third step the newly proposed ecocide definition of 2021 will be evaluated against the backdrop of the findings reached with regards to the material and mental elements.

1. The material elements of the crime

Although the Rome Statute does not contain a distinct provision pertaining to the material elements of a crime, it can be deduced from Article 30 (2) and (3) thereof that the objective side pertains to the criminalised conduct, the consequences and the circumstances which thus constitute the material elements of a crime.[282] However, with regards to defining a potential crime of ecocide, only the criminalised conduct and the consequences will be of concern and will therefore be discussed below. On the objective side, it is particularly important to clearly define the criminalised conduct as well as the consequences of the crime.

---

[279] See also *Marco Colacurci*, The Draft Convention Ecocide and the Role for Corporate Remediation, Some Insights from the International Monsanto Tribunal and a Recent Research Proposal, 21 International Criminal Law Review 154 (2021).

[280] *Emanuela Fronza*, Towards a New Crime of Ecocide 102 (2022).

[281] With respect to the structure of crimes under international criminal law, the Rome Statute distinguishes between material elements and mental elements (see Art. 30 Rome Statute; ICC Elements of Crimes, General Introduction para. 2). However, the ICC also refers to material elements as 'actus reus' or 'objective elements' and to mental elements as 'mens rea' or 'subjective elements' (see for instance Prosecutor v. Bemba, ICC-01/05-01/08, Decision Pursuant to Article 61 (7)(a) and (b) of the Rome Statute on the Charges of the Prosecutor Against Jean-Pierre Bemba Gombo, ¶ 130 (June 15, 2009)).

[282] *Donald K. Piragoff/Darryl Robinson*, Article 30 para. 11 (2022); *Gerhard Werle/Florian Jeßberger*, Principles of International Criminal Law para. 541 (2020); *Antonio Cassese*, et al., Cassese's International Criminal Law 38, 39 (2013).

a) The criminalised conduct

With respect to the principle of legality (*nullum crimen sine lege*) stipulated in Article 22 Rome Statute, it is particularly important to define the proscribed conduct as clearly as possible to avoid any ambiguity.[283] Although the Rome Statute lacks any issue-specific provision regulating culpable omissions, the criminalised conduct may include positive acts as well as omissions.[284] With respect to proscribing environmental harm, there are generally two approaches which can be taken.

First, the criminalised conduct can be defined by enumerating certain acts which constitute a crime under the respective provision. For instance, Articles 6, 7 and 8 of the Rome Statute have been defined according to such an enumerative approach. However, while some lists of conduct are exhaustive, such as, for instance, Article 6 Rome Statute, others are non-exhaustive often by including a catch-all clause, such as, for instance, Article 7 (1) (k) Rome Statute. As one of the first to draft a potential international crime of ecocide, Richard Falk proposed a definition of ecocide for his draft Convention on the Crime of Ecocide in 1973.[285] By taking an enumerative approach, Falk provided a list of six environmentally destructive activities, including, *inter alia*, the usage of chemical herbicides or the use of techniques to modify weather conditions for military purposes.[286] Nevertheless, the creation of such exhaustive lists of environmentally destructive activities creates the risk of excluding relevant behaviour from criminal liability and thus impedes environmental protection. With ongoing technological progress, new forms of environmentally destructive activities will inevitably emanate which may be precluded from the crime's scope unless the provision is constantly amended. Thus, in the event of choosing an enumerative approach, it is sensible to include a catch-all clause. In this vein, Neyret defined the crime of ecocide by referring to a list of specific environmentally detrimental activities, such as the discharging of hazardous substances into the environment, while including a catch-all clause proscribing "other acts of similar nature which are committed intentionally and threaten the security of the planet".[287] By including this catch-all provision it is ensured to include equally destructive conduct. However, in this particular case, the question arises as to whether environmentally destructive behaviour, such as deforestation or extractive activities, could qualify as 'other acts of similar nature' as the enumerated acts in Neyret's definition primarily pertain to environmental destruction caused by the discharging of hazardous substances. Hence, Neyret's definition displays that even non-ex-

---

[283] *Gerhard Werle/Florian Jeßberger*, Principles of International Criminal Law para. 135 (2020).

[284] *Donald K. Piragoff/Darryl Robinson*, Article 30 para. 11 (2022).

[285] *Richard A. Falk*, Bulletin of Peace Proposals, 93 Appendix I (1973).

[286] Id.

[287] *Laurent Neyret*, Des écocrimes à l'écocide: le droit pénal au secours de l'environnement 288 (2015); as cited in *Lay Bronwyn*, et al., Timely and Necessary: Ecocide Law As Urgent and Emerging, 28 J Juris 431, 434, 435 fn. 10 (2015).

haustive lists incorporating a catch-all clause based on the similarity to the acts listed may exclude certain substantial forms of severe environmental harm.

The second possible approach to formulating a crime of ecocide is to define its criminalised conduct more generally without proscribing certain specific activities but rather focusing on the consequences. This, for instance, is the case with the crime of aggression under Article 8 *bis* Rome Statute generally prohibiting the "planning, preparation, initiation or execution [...] of an act of aggression which, by its character, gravity and scale, constitutes a manifest violation of the Charter of the United Nations".

Accordingly, in her proposal to the UN Law Commission to incorporate a fifth crime of ecocide in 2010, Polly Higgins defined ecocide as "the extensive destruction, damage to or loss of ecosystem(s) of a given territory, *whether by human agency or by other causes*, to such an extent that peaceful enjoyment by the inhabitants of that territory has been severely diminished". [288] By prohibiting environmental destruction or damage caused 'whether by human agency or by other causes', Higgins keeps the criminalised conduct very broad covering a variety of environmentally destructive activities which would certainly promote global environmental protection. Nonetheless, due to the cornerstone principle of legality, the criminalised conduct has to be formulated in a clear manner ensuring that possible addressees know which specific conduct is proscribed by the provision.[289] However, the criminalised conduct defined by Higgins requiring environmental damage *whether by human agency or by other causes* suffers from ambiguity, as the meaning of 'by other causes' remains unclear. In her definition Higgins establishes two forms of ecocide: "human caused and naturally occurring ecocide"[290]. According to Higgins, ecocide 'by other causes' refers to "[n]aturally occurring ecocide, whether related to climate change or not".[291] However, in accordance with Article 25 (1) Rome Statute, the ICC can only exert jurisdiction over the actions of natural persons. Although modern climate science has developed methods to attribute certain climate-change related extreme weather conditions indirectly caused by human activities to polluting institutions by determining the institution's contribution to global emissions and thus to climate change, these methods, first, do not work for all extreme weather events, and, second, cannot be attributed to individual perpetrators who could be held criminally liable by the ICC.[292] Hence, as only human agency can evoke criminal liability under international criminal law, Hig-

[288] *Polly Higgins*, Eradicating Ecocide: Laws and Governance to Stop the Destruction of the Planet 63 (2015) (emphasis added).

[289] *Bruce Broomhall*, Article 22, Nullum Crimen Sine Lege, in: Rome Statute of the International Criminal Court para. 9 (Kai Ambos ed., 2022); *Antonio Cassese*, et al., Cassese's International Criminal Law 27, 28 (2013).

[290] *Polly Higgins*, et al., Crime, Law and Social Change 257 (2013).

[291] Id.

[292] See *Michael Burger*, et al., The Law and Science of Climate Change Attribution, 45 (1) Colum. J. Envtl. L. 57, 100 (2020).

gin's definition creates uncertainty and thus cannot serve as a definition for the criminalised conduct.

In conclusion, due to the risk of precluding novel types of grave environmental degradation, the criminalised conduct should not be defined by referring to an exhaustive list of specified activities which hampers the initial goal of promoting environmental protection. Thus, two options remain: (1) establishing a non-exhaustive list of conduct by, for instance, including a catch-all clause or (2) the general description of the criminalised conduct without proscribing specific activities but rather focusing on the environmental impacts. Both alternatives entail advantages and risks which need to be considered. While referring to a non-exhaustive list of activities entails a high level of clarity with regards to the principle of legality, it also poses the risk of precluding certain types of grave environmental harm which are not similar to the activities listed, as evidenced in Neyret's definition above. The determination of whether acts not listed fall within the scope of the catch-all clause is open to interpretation, thereby promoting ambiguity. Thus, even if the list is non-exhaustive, the enumeration of specific proscribed acts always involves the risk of excluding relevant behaviour from criminal liability and therefore hampers environmental protection. Hence, the highest level of environmental protection can be attained by providing a general description of the criminalised conduct without listing specific activities. However, the principle of legality requires a clear and foreseeable proscription of the criminalised conduct entailing the desired deterrent effect.[293] Furthermore, insignificant cases of environmental degradation not rising to the status of a crime under international law need to be excluded. Thus, the objective side has to be further constrained by an additional gravity threshold defining the consequences of the crime and thereby limiting the scope of the crime to grave types of environmental damage in order to avoid the provision becoming too wide. Considering the variety of environmentally destructive activities causing large-scale environmental damage, and the significant need to protect the environment from further abuse, it appears most suitable to keep the criminalised conduct initially broad and constrain the material elements by an additional gravity threshold.

b) The consequences

Furthermore, the definition of a crime of ecocide must contain the consequences, meaning the effects of the criminalised conduct[294], which can either require the existence of materialised harm or the risk of harm (endangerment liability).[295] First, the definition must include a certain gravity threshold to exclude insignificant en-

[293] *Bruce Broomhall*, Article 22 para. 9 (2022).

[294] *Gerhard Werle/Florian Jeßberger*, Principles of International Criminal Law para. 551 (2020); *Albin Eser*, Mental Elements 914 (2002).

[295] *Donald K. Piragoff/Darryl Robinson*, Article 30 para. 11 (2022); *Albin Eser*, Mental Elements 914 (2002).

vironmentally harmful activities which are not serious enough to be elevated to a crime under international law. Second, it has to be considered as to whether the definition should require materialised environmental harm or establish endangerment liability.

aa) The gravity threshold

As mentioned above, the ICC only adjudicates upon "the most serious crimes of international concern"[296]. Pursuant to Article 17 (1) (d) Rome Statute only cases, which are "of sufficient gravity to justify further action by the Court" are admissible to the ICC. Thus, the definition of a crime of ecocide has to exclude insignificant types of environmental harm falling below the threshold of crimes under international law by linking the definition to a certain gravity threshold, such as the damage sustained by the environment. For instance, although contributing to climate change, not every human being emitting carbon dioxide through breathing can be held criminally liable.[297] Similarly, it could be questioned how much deforestation of the Amazon would constitute a crime of ecocide. However, at the same time, the gravity threshold should not be set too high risking the exclusion of severe environmental harm from criminal liability.

For instance, Neyret drew upon Article 7 Rome Statute and required environmentally harmful acts to "threaten the security of the planet and [to be] committed as part of a widespread or systematic action"[298]. However, as with crimes against humanity, under this definition isolated acts of environmental degradation which do not form part of a widespread or systematic action would not constitute a crime. Moreover, it remains unclear when environmental harm exceeds the threshold to threaten the security of the planet. The majority of environmentally destructive activities alone are not capable of destroying the entire globe but rather the accumulation of different acts is likely to threaten the viability of the planet.[299] For this reason, a definition of a crime of ecocide should include both single acts as well as cumulative acts or omissions. However, Neyret did not require a threat to the planet but to the security of the planet. This, in turn, implies that Neyret only intended to include environmental harm posing the threat of causing war. Nevertheless, since most environmental harm is committed during peacetime, Neyret's definition seems too narrow thereby impeding environmental protection.

---

[296] Art. 1 Rome Statute.

[297] See *Anastacia Greene*, Fordham Environmental Law Review 33 (2019).

[298] *Laurent Neyret*, Des écocrimes à l'écocide: le droit pénal au secours de l'environnement (2015); as cited in *Lay Bronwyn*, et al., Timely and Necessary: Ecocide Law as Urgent and Emerging 28 J. Juris. 431, 434 fn. 10 (2015).

[299] *Ricardo Pereira*, Criminal Law Forum 175 (2020); *Regina Rauxloh*, The Role of International Criminal Law in Environmental Protection 447 (2011).

In contrast to Neyret, Higgins required "the extensive destruction, damage to or loss of ecosystem(s) of a given territory, [...], to such an extent that peaceful enjoyment by the inhabitants of that territory has been severely diminished"[300]. According to Higgins, 'damage' is determined by the "[s]ize, duration and significance of impact [...] to a territory"[301]. For the definition of damage to the environment, Higgins borrowed from Article 8 (2) (b) (iv) Rome Statute with a slight modification of the proportionality test by replacing military advantage with community advantage, thus requiring "widespread, long-term and severe damage to the natural environment which would be clearly excessive in relation to the concrete and direct overall *community* advantage anticipated".[302] Nevertheless, Higgin's gravity threshold appears unsuitable for three reasons.

First, similar to Article 8 (2) (b) (iv) Rome Statute, the inclusion of the proportionality test restricts the definition's scope too far by facilitating the justification of environmental harm. It appears even easier to envisage community advantage outweighing environmental harm than military advantage as required in the case of Article 8 (2) (b) (iv) Rome Statute. This proportionality test particularly counteracts the goal of environmental protection, as most environmental harm arises from industrial activities which benefit society in multiple ways by, for instance, providing employment or infrastructure and can thus be easily justified. Second, due to the ubiquitous character of environmental harm, it appears inappropriate to require environmental damage confined to a certain territory, even though due to the absence of a definition the exact meaning of 'territory' remains unclear. Third, Higgins sets the gravity threshold too high by cumulatively requiring 'widespread, long-term and severe' environmental damage. As exemplified by the Kuwait oil spill, the triple standard of 'widespread, long-term and severe' is already deemed inappropriately high in the context of Article 8 (2) (b) (iv) Rome Statute, which, however, is limited to international armed conflicts.[303] Thus, the gravity threshold in the context of a crime of ecocide, applicable both during times of war and peace, must undoubtedly be lowered.

Accordingly, Gray required ecological damage to be "serious and extensive or lasting"[304]. According to Gray, the seriousness of the environmental damage can result from "either the scale of the harm and the numbers of people and species ultimately affected, as in the systematic nature of global rain forest destruction and the trade in endangered species; or its impact on people in terms of social and economic costs, such as those following the Chernobyl nuclear accident, or loss of

---

[300] *Polly Higgins*, Eradicating Ecocide: Laws and Governance to Stop the Destruction of the Planet 63 (2015).

[301] Id.

[302] Id. at 64.

[303] See above Chapter B. IV. 3. a) aa) (2).

[304] *Mark Allan Gray*, Cal. W. Int'l L.J. 216 (1996).

unique natural assets"[305]. Gray further elucidates that the significance of the damage may either arise from vast geographical damage, large numbers of victims, or the irreversibility of the damage sustained.[306] By considering the irreversibility of environmental damage, ecological harm of initially smaller scale which, however, entails irreversible and long-lasting damage for future generations, may be included. At first glance, Gray's trias of 'serious and extensive or lasting, ecological damage' reminds of the triple standard of 'widespread, long-term and severe' damage to the natural environment stipulated under Article 8 (2) (b) (iv) Rome Statute. However, as opposed to Article 8 (2) (b) (iv) Rome Statute, Gray does not require the triple standard in cumulative but in alternative fashion. Thus, it is sufficient if the environmental harm is serious *and* extensive *or* lasting. Hence, by doing so, Gray succeeds in including harm, which is serious and lasting but not extensive, or serious and extensive but not lasting. Particularly with respect to peacetime environmental harm, this alternative triple standard appears much more suitable than the cumulative standard set out in Article 8 (2) (b) (iv) Rome Statute. Furthermore, Gray rightly puts the primary focus on the seriousness of the environmental harm, which is the main characteristic of international criminal law, and only disjunctively requires the environmental damage to be extensive or lasting, as opposed to Article I (1) ENMOD Convention which only alternatively required the damage to be 'widespread, long-lasting or severe'[307] and thus did not focus on the seriousness of the harm.

Nonetheless, Gray required two further criteria: environmental harm must have international consequences and needs to be wasteful.[308] With respect to international consequences, Gray elaborated that environmental damage needs to endanger significant values and interests of the international community, victims and perpetrators originating from more than one state and the need for international cooperation to prevent, reverse or stem the damage.[309] However, the transnational element presupposed by Gray rather relates to the characteristics of crimes under international law than to the material elements of a possible crime of ecocide.

Thus, this criterion seems unnecessary. By including the third criterion, Gray further restricts the definition to cases of environmental damage, which produce "nothing of benefit to society" or cases where "social benefits [...] are greatly outweighed by social costs".[310] Thus, deforestation of the rain forest could be deemed legitimate if considered beneficial to society.[311] Nonetheless, the waste criterion significantly impedes environmental protection by including a propor-

305 Id. at 217.

306 Id.

307 See Art. I (1) ENMOD Convention.

308 *Mark Allan Gray*, Cal. W. Int'l L.J. 216 (1996).

309 Id. at 217.

310 Id. at 218.

311 Id. at 217, 218.

tionality test similar to Higgins' definition which facilitates the justification of large-scale environmental degradation by social benefit.

Hence, irrespective of the exact wording, whether it is severe or serious, widespread or extensive, or long-term or lasting, a triple standard relating to the geographical scale, the longevity as well as the severity of the harm appears to be a suitable gravity threshold for a future crime of ecocide. However, the prerequisites should not be required cumulatively but rather disjunctively as otherwise the gravity threshold would be set too high. In this vein, borrowing from Article 8 (2) (b) (iv) Rome Statute it appears suitable to require the ecological damage to be *serious* and either *widespread* or *long-term.*

bb) Endangerment liability

It further has to be considered whether to formulate the crime of ecocide as a *crime of conduct* or a *crime of result.*[312] While the mere danger of harm is sufficient to satisfy the material elements of a crime of conduct, also referred to as crimes of endangerment, crimes of result require the materialisation of harm.[313] Thus, instead of criminalising certain materialised harm, crimes of conduct proscribe a certain conduct prior to the occurrence of actual harm and therefore have a highly preventative focus.[314] By doing so, endangerment liability aspires to prevent certain harm from occurring, rather than coming in place when the danger has already materialised. [315] Hence, in the context of environmental harm, creating a crime of conduct would promote global environmental protection by criminalising environmentally destructive conduct prior to the actual materialisation of environmental harm. Furthermore, endangerment liability in the context of environmental harm would assist in overcoming the evidentiary difficulty of proving the causal link with environmental impacts, which sometimes do not manifest themselves for a generation or more.[316] Additionally, in the context of environmental harm, the concept of endangerment liability is not novel to the Rome Statute, as, for instance, Article 8 (2) (b) (iv) Rome Statute does not require actual damage to the natural environment,

[312] *Antonio Cassese*, et al., Cassese's International Criminal Law 38 (2013); *Albin Eser*, Mental Elements 911 (2002); *Donald K. Piragoff/Darryl Robinson*, Article 30 para. 11 (2022); see on crimes of endangerment *Antony Duff/Tatjana Hörnle*, Crimes of Endangerment, in: Core Concepts in Criminal Law and Criminal Justice (Kai Ambos, et al. eds., 2022).

[313] *Antonio Cassese*, et al., Cassese's International Criminal Law 38 (2013); *Antony Duff/Tatjana Hörnle*, Crimes of Endangerment 134 (2022).

[314] *Antonio Cassese*, et al., Cassese's International Criminal Law 38 (2013).

[315] *Andrew Cornford*, Preventive Criminalization, 18 New Criminal Law Review: An International and Interdisciplinary Journal 1, 3 (2015).

[316] *Martin Heger*, Umweltvölkerstrafrecht, in: Strafrecht und Systemunrecht 142 (Florian Jeßberger, et al. eds., 2022); *Emanuela Fronza*, Towards a New Crime of Ecocide 102 (2022); *Frédéric Mégret*, Colum. J. Envtl. L. 236 (2011); *Eric Biber*, Climate Change, Causation, And Delayed Harm, 37 Hofstra L. Rev. 975, 976 (2009).

but rather the mere commission of an attack aimed at destroying the environment suffices.[317].

Hence, from the perspective of striving to attain the highest level of environmental protection possible, the new crime of ecocide should be defined as a crime of conduct. However, at the same time the scope of the crime should not be too wide. In this regard, Article 8 (2) (b) (iv) Rome Statute, for instance, contains a high mental threshold requiring the perpetrator to launch the attack with knowledge and intent of causing disproportionate environmental harm. Thus, if the new crime of ecocide were to be designed as a crime of conduct, the definition would have to be further restricted by a suitable mental threshold, a notion which will be discussed next.

2. The mental elements of the crime

Article 30 (1) Rome Statute, the Rome Statute's general provision concerning the mental elements of a crime, stipulates that "[u]nless otherwise provided, a person shall be criminally responsible and liable for punishment for a crime within the jurisdiction of the Court only if the material elements are committed with intent and knowledge". If a core crime itself does not specify a mental element, Article 30 Rome Statute acts as a "default rule"[318] requiring the commission of the material elements with intent and knowledge.[319] Thus, if a new crime of ecocide did not contain its own built-in mental threshold, Article 30 Rome Statute would have to be applied on the subjective side. In accordance with Article 30 (1) Rome Statute, the perpetrator would therefore have to act with intent and knowledge at the time of committing the environmentally harmful conduct[320]. Hence, in relation to the causation of serious and widespread or long-term environmental damage, the perpetrator would either have to act with direct intent ("means to cause that consequence") or indirect intent ("is aware that it will occur in the ordinary course of events") pursuant to Article 30 (2) (b) Rome Statute.[321]

Nevertheless, the majority of environmental harm is caused by industrial activities *during peacetime*, which occurs for the purpose of economic benefit and not with the 'will or desire' to destroy ecosystems. In most cases environmental harm is

---

[317] *Knut Dörmann*, International Review of the Red Cross 470, 471 (2001).

[318] Prosecutor v. Bemba, ICC-01/05-01/08, Decision Pursuant to Article 61(7)(a) and (b) of the Rome Statute on the Charges of the Prosecutor Against Jean-Pierre Bemba Gombo, ¶ 136, 353 (June 15, 2009).

[319] Art. 30 (1) Rome Statute; see also ICC Elements of Crimes, General Introduction, para. 2; Prosecutor v. Katanga, ICC-01/04-01/07, Judgment Pursuant to Article 74 of the Statute, ¶ 792 (Mar. 7, 2014); *Donald K. Piragoff/Darryl Robinson*, Article 30 paras. 1, 6 (2022).

[320] *Albin Eser*, Mental Elements 930 (2002).

[321] *Donald K. Piragoff/Darryl Robinson*, Article 30 paras. 23–25 (2022).

therefore only a side-effect or collateral damage of industrial activities.[322] Thus, particularly in the case of environmental damage during peacetime, direct intent appears exceedingly unrealistic.

Hence, criminal liability under the new crime of ecocide could only be established if the perpetrators of environmental harm were 'virtually certain' of the occurrence of serious and widespread or long-term environmental damage *at the time of its commission* and thus acted with indirect intent. However, corporate officers would most likely claim in their defence that they could have not foreseen the consequences of their actions with virtual certainty.[323] Nonetheless, the Court would infer from the factual circumstances of the perpetrated conduct whether the perpetrator was aware that their actions would result in serious and widespread or long-term environmental damage environmental harm.[324] Hence, at least in cases where the causation of environmental harm was evident at the time of its commission, this defence would not necessarily be successful.

However, by applying the high mental threshold stipulated in Article 30 Rome Statute, cases of large-scale environmental degradation where the occurrence of serious and widespread or long-term environmental damage was not virtually certain, but rather only probable or highly probable, would be excluded from criminal liability as the concepts of *dolus eventualis* and recklessness are strictly excluded from Article 30 (2) (b) Rome Statute.[325] Furthermore, major environmental accidents, such as the Deepwater Horizon oil spill, would also be excluded form criminal liability[326], as negligence-based criminality is further precluded from the scope of Article 30 (2) (b) Rome Statute.[327] Hence, with respect to the goal of establishing

---

[322] *Regina Rauxloh*, The Role of International Criminal Law in Environmental Protection 449 (2011); *Polly Higgins*, et al., Crime, Law and Social Change 262 (2013).

[323] *Polly Higgins*, et al., Crime, Law and Social Change 262 (2013).

[324] *Antonio Cassese*, et al., Cassese's International Criminal Law 57 (2013).

[325] Prosecutor v. Bemba, ICC-01/05-01/13, Judgment Pursuant to Article 74 of the Statute, ¶ 29 (Oct. 19, 2016); Prosecutor v. Bemba, ICC-01/05-01/08, Decision Pursuant to Article 61(7)(a) and (b) of the Rome Statute on the Charges of the Prosecutor Against Jean-Pierre Bemba Gombo, ¶ 360, 369 (June 15, 2009); Prosecutor v. Lubanga, ICC-01/04-01/06 A 5, Judgment on the Appeal of Mr. Thomas Lubanga Dyilo Against his Conviction, ¶ 449 (Dec. 1, 2014); Prosecutor v. Lubanga, ICC-01/04-01/06, Judgment Pursuant to Article 74 of the Statute, ¶ 1011 (Mar. 14, 2012); *Donald K. Piragoff/Darryl Robinson*, Article 30 para. 26 (2022); *Gerhard Werle/Florian Jeßberger*, Principles of International Criminal Law para. 573 (2020); *William A. Schabas*, The International Criminal Court: A Commentary on the Rome Statute 631, 632 (2016); *Albin Eser*, Mental Elements 915, 916 (2002).

[326] *Ricardo Pereira*, Criminal Law Forum 195 (2020).

[327] Prosecutor v. Bemba, ICC-01/05-01/13, Judgment Pursuant to Article 74 of the Statute, ¶ 29 (Oct. 19, 2016); Prosecutor v. Bemba, ICC-01/05-01/08, Decision Pursuant to Article 61(1)(a) and (b) of the Rome Statute on the Charges of the Prosecutor Against Jean-Pierre Bemba Gombo, ¶ 369 (June 15, 2009); *Donald K. Piragoff/Darryl Robinson*, Article 30 para. 26 (2022); *Gerhard Werle/Florian Jeßberger*, Principles of International Criminal Law para. 573 (2020); *William A. Schabas*, The International Criminal Court: A Commentary on the Rome Statute 631, 632 (2016); *Albin Eser*, Mental Elements 915, 916 (2002).

the highest level of environmental protection possible under the principles of international criminal law, it has to be assessed whether the new crime of ecocide should specify its own mental threshold falling below the 'intent and knowledge' requirement in Article 30 (1) Rome Statute. The phrase 'unless otherwise provided' in Article 30 (1) Rome Statute explicitly permits the provisions under the Rome Statute to deviate from the mental threshold stipulated in Article 30 Rome Statute.[328] Thus, in accordance with Article 30 (1) Rome Statute, the new crime of ecocide could contain a lower mental threshold than 'intent and knowledge' in relation to the risk of serious and widespread or long-term environmental harm (consequence). In the following, it will be assessed whether the mental element of a new crime of ecocide should be lowered to a crime of strict liability, the concept of *dolus eventualis* or even negligence.

a) Crime of strict liability

In this regard, some scholars[329] suggested establishing the crime of ecocide as a crime of strict liability, that is, simply warranting criminal liability on the commission of the material elements without requiring a blameworthy state of mind.[330] However, crimes of strict liability are not, as stated by Higgins, crimes "without intent"[331]. Instead of lacking a mental threshold as a whole, crimes of strict liability only lack a mental requirement relating to a particular material element.[332] In this regard, it could be considered to do without intent and knowledge relating to the causation of severe and either widespread or long-term environmental harm.

Such a crime of strict liability would undoubtedly include environmental accidents, such as nuclear accidents or oil spills. In favour of creating a crime of strict liability, it is predominantly argued that strict liability would better promote the prevention of further ecological harm[333] due to the stronger deterrent effect of

---

[328] *Gerhard Werle/Florian Jeßberger*, JICJ 45 (2005); *Gerhard Werle/Florian Jeßberger*, Principles of International Criminal Law para. 579 (2020); *Robert Cryer*, et al., An Introduction to International Criminal Law and Procedure 367 (2019); *Antonio Cassese*, et al., Cassese's International Criminal Law 56 (2013); *William A. Schabas*, The International Criminal Court: A Commentary on the Rome Statute 629 (2016); *Donald K. Piragoff/Darryl Robinson*, Article 30 paras. 4, 6 (2022).

[329] *Polly Higgins*, Eradicating Ecocide: Laws and Governance to Stop the Destruction of the Planet 68 (2015); *Rosemary Mwanza*, Melb. Journal of International Law 15 (2018); *Mark Allan Gray*, Cal. W. Int'l L.J. 218 (1996).

[330] *Albin Eser*, Mental Elements 902 (2002).

[331] *Polly Higgins*, et al., Crime, Law and Social Change 262 (2013).

[332] See more detailed *Christoph Safferling*, Vorsatz und Schuld, 372–379 (2008).

[333] *Mark Allan Gray*, Cal. W. Int'l L.J. 218 (1996); *Polly Higgins*, Eradicating Ecocide: Laws and Governance to Stop the Destruction of the Planet 68, 69 (2015).

crimes of strict liability resulting from the higher probability of punishment due to the lower prosecutorial burden.[334]

Nonetheless, crimes of strict liability contradict the cornerstone principle in criminal law that criminal culpability requires the commission of certain proscribed conduct accompanied by a blameworthy state of mind[335], which is expressed in the Latin phrase "*actus non facit reum nisi mens sit rea*".[336] In most national criminal justice systems, strict liability concepts have been abolished[337] and, most importantly, the existence of Article 30 Rome Statute proves that the concept is not recognised in international criminal law.[338] Thus, one must concur with Jescheck with regard to the fact that "[e]xceptions from culpability, as would be permitted under the formula 'unless otherwise provided', do not introduce, as one may think, a concept of strict liability"[339]. The formula 'unless otherwise provided' rather relates to mental elements falling below the intent threshold, such as negligence, which is sufficient in the case of Article 28 (a) (i) Rome Statute ("should have known").[340] For these reasons, although, in theory, the phrase 'unless otherwise provided' permits the establishment of a crime of strict liability, it appears highly unlikely that the states would agree to such a provision.[341] Hence, the proposal of establishing a crime of ecocide as a crime of strict liability is to be rejected.

b) Dolus eventualis

However, the mental element of the new crime of ecocide could be lowered to include *dolus eventualis* or recklessness. In the following the terms *dolus eventualis*, recklessness and negligence will briefly be distinguished to shed light on the different forms of culpability the mental threshold could be lowered.

---

[334] *Rosemary Mwanza*, Melb. Journal of International Law 15 (2018).

[335] See Prosecutor v. Delalić, Case No. IT-92-21-T, Judgement, ¶ 424, 425 (Nov. 16, 1998); *Donald K. Piragoff/Darryl Robinson*, Article 30 para. 5 (2022); *Gerhard Werle/Florian Jeßberger*, Principles of International Criminal Law para. 556 (2020); *Robert Cryer*, et al., An Introduction to International Criminal Law and Procedure 365 (2019); *William A. Schabas*, The International Criminal Court: A Commentary on the Rome Statute 626 (2016); *Antonio Cassese*, et al., Cassese's International Criminal Law 39 (2013); *Albin Eser*, Mental Elements 902 (2002).

[336] The Latin maxim translates to: "An act does not make a person guilty of a crime, unless the person's mind be also guilty", *Donald K. Piragoff/Darryl Robinson*, Article 30 para. 5 fn. 14 (2022).

[337] *Albin Eser*, Mental Elements 903 (2002).

[338] *Gerhard Werle/Florian Jeßberger*, JICJ 36 (2005).

[339] *Hans-Heinrich Jescheck*, The General Principles of International Criminal Law Set Out in Nuremberg, as Mirrored in the ICC Statute, 2 (1) JICJ 38, 45 (2004).

[340] Id.

[341] *Albin Eser*, Mental Elements 903 (2002).

While in Anglo-American criminal law four 'kinds of culpability' are distinguished in accordance with the Model Penal Code, namely purpose, knowledge, recklessness and negligence, German criminal law only distinguishes between *Vorsatz* (intention) and *Fahrlässigkeit* (negligence).[342] German criminal law recognises three forms of *Vorsatz* (intention), first-degree *dolus directus*, second-degree *dolus directus* and the concept of *dolus eventualis*, which are to be distinguished from *Fahrlässigkeit*.[343] *Fahrlässigkeit* can further be subdivided into two categories, advertent or inadvertent *Fahrlässigkeit*, depending on whether the perpetrator was aware of the risk of harm he took or created.[344]

If the perpetrator was aware of the risk of harm, they acted with advertent *Fahrlässigkeit* and vice versa. Since in terms of a cognitive element both *dolus eventualis* and advertent *Fahrlässigkeit* require the perpetrator to be aware of the risk of harm which might materialise, the volitional element serves as a distinguisher between both forms of culpability under German criminal law.[345] While a person acting with *dolus eventualis* 'condones', 'accepts', 'approves' or 'comes to terms with' the possible outcome of his conduct, a person acting with advertent *Fahrlässigkeit* 'trusts that the foreseen result will not occur'.[346]

In Anglo-American criminal law a person acts recklessly "when he consciously disregards a substantial and unjustifiable risk that the material element exists or will result from his conduct".[347] In distinction to recklessness, a person acts negligently in relation to a material element of a crime "when he should be aware of a substantial and unjustifiable risk that the material element exists or will result from his conduct".[348] Thus, if a person was aware of the risk of harm they took or created, they acted recklessly and if a person lacked the respective awareness of the risk they took or created, they acted negligently.[349]

Hence, negligence under Anglo-American criminal law corresponds to inadvertent *Fahrlässigkeit* under German criminal law.[350] However, while a person acting in the awareness that his behaviour entails a substantial and unjustifiable risk of

---

[342] *Antony Duff/Tatjana Hörnle*, Crimes of Endangerment 138–140 (2022).

[343] Id. at 139, 140.

[344] Id.

[345] Id. at 140.

[346] Bundesgerichtshof [BGH] [Federal Court of Justice] Jan. 27, 2011, Raub mit Todesfolge – Wegnahme aus Rache; Bedingter Tötungsvorsatz, Neue Zeitschrift für Strafrecht [NStZ] 699, 701, 702 (Ger.); Bundesgerichtshof [BGH] [Federal Court of Justice] Oct. 18, 2007, Heimtückische Tötung eines bewusstlosen Patienten im Krankenhaus, Neue Zeitschrift für Strafrecht [NStZ], 93, 93 (Ger.).

[347] Model Penal Code (MPC), § 2.02. (2) (c), Am. Law Inst., Proposed Official Draft (1962).

[348] Model Penal Code (MPC), § 2.02. (2) (d), Am. Law Inst., Proposed Official Draft (1962).

[349] *Antony Duff/Tatjana Hörnle*, Crimes of Endangerment 138 (2022).

[350] Id. at 140.

harm without any intention to cause such harm acts *recklessly* in Anglo-American criminal law, under German criminal law whether the person acts with *dolus eventualis* or advertent *Fahrlässigkeit* depends on whether he 'condones' the prospective harm or 'trusts the harm will not occur'.[351]

However, in common law jurisdictions the concept of recklessness is further subdivided into *advertent* or *subjective recklessness* entailing a cognitive and a volitional element[352], and *objective recklessness*, which is purely cognitive.[353] Thus, the common law concept of subjective or advertent recklessness is the equivalent to the civil law jurisdictions' concept of *dolus eventualis*.[354]

With respect to Article 30 (2) (b) and (3) Rome Statute, it appears problematic that the civil law jurisdictions require a different level of likelihood that the expected consequence will occur.[355] While some civil law jurisdictions require the awareness of a high probability of the occurrence of the consequence, others consider low probabilities to be sufficient.[356] Thus, some argue that while *dolus eventualis* predicated on low probabilities is excluded, *dolus eventualis* entailing high probabilities is included in Article 30 (2) (b) and (3) Rome Statute.[357] Nonetheless, due to the different notions of the concepts of *dolus eventualis*[358] and the general reluctance to predicate criminal liability on *dolus eventualis* or advertent recklessness[359], the attempt to include these concepts of culpability in Article 30 (2) (b) and (3) Rome Statute was dismissed at an early stage of the deliberations.[360]

---

[351] Id.

[352] *Antonio Cassese*, et al., Cassese's International Criminal Law 46 (2013).

[353] *Kevin Jon Heller*, OpinioJuris (June 23, 2021), https://opiniojuris.org/2021/06/23/skeptical-thoughts-on-the-proposed-crime-of-ecocide-that-isnt/ (last visited Feb. 18, 2025); see more detailed on the two different notions of recklessness *Christoph Safferling*, Vorsatz und Schuld 360–364 (2008).

[354] Prosecutor v. Bemba, ICC-01/05-01/08, Decision Pursuant to Article 61(7)(a) and (b) of the Rome Statute on the Charges of the Prosecutor Against Jean-Pierre Bemba Gombo, ¶ 357 (June 15, 2009); *Antonio Cassese*, et al., Cassese's International Criminal Law 46 (2013); *Gerhard Werle/Florian Jeßberger*, Principles of International Criminal Law para. 575 (2020); *William A. Schabas*, The International Criminal Court: A Commentary on the Rome Statute 629 (2016); *Christoph Safferling*, Vorsatz und Schuld 367, 368 (2008).

[355] *Donald K. Piragoff/Darryl Robinson*, Article 30 para. 26 fn. 56 (2022).

[356] Id.

[357] Id.

[358] Id.; *Gerhard Werle/Florian Jeßberger*, Principles of International Criminal Law para. 576 (2020).

[359] *Roger S. Clark*, Drafting a General Part to a Penal Code: Some Thoughts Inspired by the Negotiations on the Rome Statute of the International Criminal Court and by the Court's First Substantive Law Discussion in the Lubanga Dyilo Confirmation Proceedings, 19 CLF 519, 525 (2008); *Donald K. Piragoff/Darryl Robinson*, Article 30 para. 4 (2022).

[360] Prosecutor v. Bemba, ICC-01/05-01/08, Decision Pursuant to Article 61(7)(a) and (b) of the Rome Statute on the Charges of the Prosecutor Against Jean-Pierre Bemba Gombo, ¶ 366–369 (June 15, 2009).

However, the exclusion of the concepts of *dolus eventualis* (at least with regard to low probabilities[361]) from the scope of Article 30 Rome Statute resulted in a mental standard which is more restrictive than customary international law or civil law jurisdictions.[362] This is due to the fact that in customary international law and civil law jurisdictions, as opposed to common law jurisdictions and the Rome Statute, *dolus eventualis* is treated as intention (*Vorsatz*).[363] Consequently, domestic courts in civil law jurisdictions adjudicating upon crimes under the Rome Statute extend the mental threshold of Article 30 Rome Statute to *dolus eventualis*.[364]

However, although the concept of *dolus eventualis* was excluded from the general provision of Article 30 Rome Statute, this does not impede the inclusion of *dolus eventualis* in a new crime of ecocide under the formula 'unless otherwise provided'.[365] In fact, the Rome Statute itself already contains provisions, such as Article 8 (2) (a) (iv) Rome Statute, under which it is sufficient if the destruction and appropriation of property is committed 'wantonly', meaning recklessly.[366]

Thus, it would be possible to create a new crime of ecocide requiring *dolus eventualis* or advertent recklessness in relation to the severe and either widespread or long-term damage to the environment. In this regard, despite the lack of a uniform definition, *dolus eventualis* may be defined as the "awareness that undertaking a course of conduct carries with it an unreasonable or justifiable risk of producing harmful consequences, and the decision nevertheless to go on to take that risk".[367] Thus, the perpetrator "condones", "comes to terms", "makes peace"[368] or "recon-

---

[361] *Donald K. Piragoff/Darryl Robinson*, Article 30 para. 26 fn. 56 (2022).

[362] Id. at para. 26 fn. 55; *Gerhard Werle/Florian Jeßberger*, Principles of International Criminal Law para. 576 (2020); *Robert Cryer*, et al., An Introduction to International Criminal Law and Procedure 367 (2019); *Antonio Cassese*, et al., Cassese's International Criminal Law 56 (2013); *Albin Eser*, Mental Elements 915, 916 (2002); *Gerhard Werle/Florian Jeßberger*, JICJ 41, 42 (2005).

[363] *Gerhard Werle/Florian Jeßberger*, JICJ 41, 42 (2005); *Gerhard Werle/Florian Jeßberger*, Principles of International Criminal Law para. 576 (2020); *Albin Eser*, Mental Elements 915 (2002).

[364] See, for instance, Code of Crimes against International Law [Völkerstrafgesetzbuch] § 2 (Ger.); *Gerhard Werle/Florian Jeßberger*, JICJ 42 (2005).

[365] *Gerhard Werle/Florian Jeßberger*, JICJ 52 (2005).

[366] *Gerhard Werle/Florian Jeßberger*, Principles of International Criminal Law para. 592 (2020); *William A. Schabas*, The International Criminal Court: A Commentary on the Rome Statute 292 (2016); *Gerhard Werle/Florian Jeßberger*, JICJ 47 (2005); *Albin Eser*, Mental Elements 899 (2002).

[367] *Antonio Cassese*, et al., Cassese's International Criminal Law 41 (2013); see also *Albin Eser*, Mental Elements 932 (2002) (*Dolus eventualis* is defined as "the perpetrator being aware of the risk that might occur and additionally being prepared to accept it should it in fact occur"); *Gerhard Werle/Florian Jeßberger*, Principles of International Criminal Law para. 573 fn. 94 (2020) (defining dolus eventualis as: "if he or she is aware that a material element included in the definition of a crime […] may result from his or her conduct and 'reconciles him[/her]self' or 'makes peace' with this fact").

[368] Prosecutor v. Stakić, Case No. IT-97-24-T, Judgement, ¶ 587 (July 31, 2003).

ciles himself'[369] with the risk of causing the relevant harm.[370] As such, akin to indirect intent, the concepts of *dolus eventualis* or advertent recklessness consist of a cognitive and volitional element, as the perpetrator wilfully takes the risk.[371] However, in contrast to indirect intent pursuant to Article 30 (2) (b) Rome Statute, where the perpetrator has to be aware that the consequence will occur with *virtual certainty*, in the case of *dolus eventualis* or advertent recklessness the perpetrator only envisages the consequence as likely or possible.[372] Hence, under the Rome Statute, the difference between indirect intent and *dolus eventualis* is the level of certainty concerning the occurrence of the consequence.

In the context of environmental harm, where the actual scope, severity and reversibility of damage is often uncertain at the time of the commission, it appears necessary to extend the narrow mental element of Article 30 Rome Statute to include *dolus eventualis* or advertent recklessness, otherwise the Prosecutor will have to prove that the perpetrator was able to foresee the repercussions of their actions with virtual certainty at the time of the environmentally destructive conduct. The uniqueness of environmental damage, particularly the initial delay and uncertainty of the actual damage, justify a different perspective than in the case of the other core crimes, such as, for instance, the crime of genocide, which is incompatible with the concept of *dolus eventualis*.[373]

However, the formula 'unless otherwise provided' in Article 30 (1) Rome Statute explicitly enables lawmakers to do justice to the peculiarities of different types of crimes by adapting their mental thresholds. For this reason, suggestions have been made to lower the mental threshold to *dolus eventualis* or advertent recklessness within the new crime of ecocide, as opposed to amending Article 30 Rome Statute as a whole, which enshrines one of the core principles of international criminal law and appears appropriate with regards to the other core crimes. Furthermore, the fact that, at least in civil law jurisdictions, *dolus eventualis* is deemed a form of intention and thus fully warrants criminal liability, speaks in favour of the extension of the mental element to include *dolus eventualis* or advertent recklessness.

---

[369] Id.; see also Prosecutor v. Lubanga, ICC-01/04-01/06, Decision on the Confirmation of Charges, ¶ 352 (Jan. 29, 2007).

[370] Bundesgerichtshof [BGH] [Federal Court of Justice] Jan. 27, 2011, Raub mit Todesfolge – Wegnahme aus Rache; Bedingter Tötungsvorsatz, Neue Zeitschrift für Strafrecht [NStZ] 699, 701, 702 (Ger.); Bundesgerichtshof [BGH] [Federal Court of Justice] Oct. 18, 2007, Heimtückische Tötung eines bewusstlosen Patienten im Krankenhaus, Neue Zeitschrift für Strafrecht [NStZ], 93, 93 (Ger.); *Antony Duff/Tatjana Hörnle*, Crimes of Endangerment 140 (2022).

[371] *Antonio Cassese*, et al., Cassese's International Criminal Law 46 (2013).

[372] Id.

[373] Similar *Frédéric Mégret*, The Case for a General International Crime Against the Environment 14 (2010).

c) Negligence

Under the formula of 'unless otherwise provided', it is further to be assessed whether the mental threshold of a new crime of ecocide could be lowered to include negligence. Lowering the mental threshold to negligence, and thus to the lowest level of culpability[374] would open the door to imposing criminal liability on serious environmental accidents, such as oil spills or nuclear accidents. The primary argument in favour of introducing negligence-based liability is the effective prevention of future environmental harm. Due to the significantly lower mental threshold, potential perpetrators face a higher risk of prosecution which first leads to a stronger deterrent effect of the provision and, second, promotes prevention of environmental harm. Additionally, in domestic criminal law, the standard of negligence is prevalent in the context of environmental crimes.[375] In the EU, for instance, the 2008 European Crime Directive stipulates in Article 3 that it is sufficient if the environmental offences are committed "at least with serious negligence"[376].

However, as implied by the term 'serious negligence', different levels of negligence can be distinguished. According to Cassese, simple negligence entails the failure to apply the necessary level of care required for a reasonable person in a similar situation[377], whereas gross negligence pertains to the deliberate disregard of the necessary level of care, as in this case the perpetrator is aware of the risk his conduct entails but nevertheless believes that the harmful consequence will not occur.[378] If the perpetrator's conduct was "blatantly at odds with the prescribed standards" he acted with gross negligence.[379] Thus, simple negligence under Anglo-American criminal law corresponds to inadvertent *Fahrlässigkeit* under German criminal law where the perpetrator is unaware of the risk his conduct entails.[380]

The Rome Statute itself contains provisions under which negligent conduct suffices to incur criminal liability. For instance, Article 28 (a) (i) Rome Statute on command liability under which a military commander is not only deemed criminally liable if he knew but also if he "should have known that the forces were committing or about to commit such crimes". This 'should have known' standard mirrors the principle that a commander has an active duty to take all necessary precautions to remain informed on the conduct of his forces.[381] The 'should have known' test is

---

[374] *Antonio Cassese*, et al., Cassese's International Criminal Law 52, 53 (2013).

[375] For instance, under the German Criminal Code (German Criminal Code [StGB], all offences against the environment (§§ 324–330a) can be committed negligently.

[376] Directive 2008/99/EC, art. 3.

[377] *Antonio Cassese*, et al., Cassese's International Criminal Law 52 (2013).

[378] Id.

[379] Id.

[380] *Antony Duff/Tatjana Hörnle*, Crimes of Endangerment 140 (2022).

[381] Prosecutor v. Bemba, ICC-01/05-01/08, Decision Pursuant to Article 61(7)(a) and (b) of the Rome Statute on the Charges of the Prosecutor Against Jean-Pierre Bemba Gombo, ¶ 433 (June 15, 2009).

thus one of simple negligence.[382] Similarly, according to the Elements of Crimes relating to Article 8 (2) (b) (xxvi) Rome Statute on child soldiers, it is sufficient if the perpetrator "knew or should have known that such person or persons were under the age of 15 years"[383] and thus acted negligently.[384] However, it has to be noted that the point of reference of the mental element, namely the fact that the victim is under 15, is in terms of material elements classed as a 'circumstance' and not a 'consequence' of the crime.[385]

Nevertheless, Article 28 (a) (i) Rome Statute stipulating superior responsibility could serve as a role-model for a new crime of ecocide including a standard of negligence, since most perpetrators of environmental harm are expected to be corporate officials failing to take the necessary precautions to avoid large-scale environmental destruction. However, the 'should have known' standard of Article 28 (a) (i) Rome Statute exclusively applies to military commanders, whereas non-miliary commanders have to either know or "consciously disregard information which clearly indicated" the potential commission of crimes by their subordinates pursuant to Article 28 (b) (i) Rome Statute. Thus, the mental threshold for civilian superiors is higher than the one for military commanders[386] and can be referred to as 'wilful blindness', which can be considered a form of *dolus eventualis* or recklessness.[387] The Appeals Chamber of the ICTY elucidated that "sufficiently alarming information putting a superior on notice of the risk that crimes *might* subsequently be carried out by his subordinates and justifying further inquiry is sufficient to hold

[382] *Donald K. Piragoff/Darryl Robinson*, Article 30 para. 44 (2022); *William A. Schabas*, An Introduction to the International Criminal Court 239 (2020); *Albin Eser*, Mental Elements 898, 899 (2002); *Antonio Cassese*, et al., Cassese's International Criminal Law 56 (2013).

[383] ICC Elements of Crimes, Art. 8 (2) (b) (xxvi), para. 3.

[384] Prosecutor v. Lubanga, ICC-01/04-01/06, Decision on the Confirmation of Charges, ¶ 358 (Jan. 29, 2007); *Gerhard Werle/Florian Jeßberger*, Principles of International Criminal Law para. 593 (2020); *Antonio Cassese*, et al., Cassese's International Criminal Law 56 (2013).

[385] *Gerhard Werle/Florian Jeßberger*, Principles of International Criminal Law para. 553 (2020).

[386] *Roberta Arnold/Miles Jackson*, Article 28, Responsibility of Commanders and Other Superiors, in: Rome Statute of the International Criminal Court paras. 82, 83 (Kai Ambos ed., 2022); *Kai Ambos*, Treatise on International Criminal Law, Volume I: Foundations and General Part 319 (2nd ed., 2021); *William A. Schabas*, The International Criminal Court: A Commentary on the Rome Statute 617 (2016); *Antonio Cassese*, et al., Cassese's International Criminal Law 190 (2013); *Kai Ambos*, Superior Responsibility, in: The Rome Statute of the International Criminal Court: A Commentary 870 (Antonio Cassese, et al. eds., 2002).

[387] *Kai Ambos*, Superior Responsibility 870 (2002); *Kai Ambos*, Treatise 319 (2021); *Thomas Weigend*, Bemerkungen zur Vorgesetztenverantwortlichkeit im Völkerstrafrecht, 116 (4) ZStW 999, 1024 (2004); *William A. Schabas*, The International Criminal Court: A Commentary on the Rome Statute 617 (2016); *Gerhard Werle/Florian Jeßberger*, Principles of International Criminal Law para. 699 ('greater degree of negligence') (2020).

a superior liable"[388] on the basis of superior responsibility. The reason behind the lower mental requirement concerning military commanders is to pay tribute to the peculiarities of military command.[389] Since most cases of environmental harm do not involve military agency, Article 28 (a) (i) Rome Statute cannot serve as an argument in favour of lowering the mental threshold of a new crime against the environment to include simple negligence.

In general, due to the serious nature of international criminal law pertaining to macro-criminality, simple negligence or inadvertent *Fahrlässigkeit* is not a generally applicable subjective standard giving rise to individual criminal liability under international criminal law.[390] Instead, only advertent *Fahrlässigkeit*, which will also be referred to as culpable negligence in this thesis, requiring the perpetrator being aware of the risk his or her conduct entails can, in theory, incur individual criminal liability for international crimes.[391] By contrast, it does not come as a surprise that many domestic jurisdictions resort to simple negligence in the context of environmental crimes, as ordinary crimes do not entail the same stigma and consequences as international criminal law.[392]

Nevertheless, although the level of culpability is higher than in the case of simple negligence, there is no suggestion to establish the crime of ecocide as a crime of advertent *Fahrlässigkeit*. While in the case of advertent *Fahrlässigkeit* the perpetrator is aware of the risk but believes the consequence will not occur, in the case of *dolus eventualis* or advertent recklessness the perpetrator is aware of the risk and decides to wilfully take the risk nevertheless.[393] Thus, in the case of *dolus eventualis* the perpetrator is more culpable than in the case of culpable negligence. As international criminal law only pertains to the most serious crimes and a conviction always entails imprisonment, it appears inappropriate to extend criminal liability to the minimum level of culpability.

---

[388] Prosecutor v. Strugar, Case No. IT-01–42-A, Judgement, ¶ 304 (July 17, 2008) (emphasis added).

[389] Prosecutor v. Bemba, ICC-01/05-01/08, Decision Pursuant to Article 61(7)(a) and (b) of the Rome Statute on the Charges of the Prosecutor Against Jean-Pierre Bemba Gombo, ¶ 433 (June 15, 2009); see generally, *Darryl Robinson*, A Justification of Command Responsibility, 28 Criminal Law Forum 633 (2017).

[390] *Antonio Cassese*, et al., Cassese's International Criminal Law 53 (2013); *Robert Cryer*, et al., An Introduction to International Criminal Law and Procedure 366 (2019).

[391] *Antonio Cassese*, et al., Cassese's International Criminal Law 53 (2013).

[392] Id.; *Donald K. Piragoff/Darryl Robinson*, Article 30 para. 1 (2022).

[393] Bundesgerichtshof [BGH] [Federal Court of Justice] Jan. 27, 2011, Raub mit Todesfolge – Wegnahme aus Rache; Bedingter Tötungsvorsatz, Neue Zeitschrift für Strafrecht [NStZ] 699, 701, 702 (Ger.); Bundesgerichtshof [BGH] [Federal Court of Justice] Oct. 18, 2007, Heimtückische Tötung eines bewusstlosen Patienten im Krankenhaus, Neue Zeitschrift für Strafrecht [NStZ], 93, 93 (Ger.); *Antony Duff/Tatjana Hörnle*, Crimes of Endangerment 140 (2022).

Furthermore, it needs to be considered that it was suggested to create the new crime of ecocide as a crime of endangerment, which only requires the substantial risk of environmental damage instead of its materialisation. Due to this lower *objective* threshold of crimes of endangerment liability it appears necessary to require a higher level of culpability by requiring the perpetrator to act with *dolus eventualis* instead of inadvertent *Fahrlässigkeit* to prevent the provision's scope from becoming too wide and thereby risking the loss of political acceptance.[394] In this regard, it is also not advisable to lower the mental threshold to gross negligence, which still entails a lower culpability than *dolus eventualis* or advertent recklessness.

In conclusion, concerning the subjective side of a new crime of ecocide it is suggested to lower the mental threshold to include *dolus eventualis* or advertent recklessness. While the uncertainty of environmental harm justifies lowering the mental threshold of Article 30 (2) (b) Rome Statute, requiring *dolus eventualis* still respects the requisite seriousness of crimes under international law. Furthermore, it is a significant advantage that, at least in civil law jurisdictions, *dolus eventualis* is deemed a form of intention, which might increase the likelihood of a two-thirds majority of the signatory parties voting in favour of the new crime of ecocide.

3. Evaluation of the newly proposed definition

The debate concerning the definition of a crime against the environment was reignited in June 2021 when an International Expert Panel (IEP) proposed a definition for a potential fifth crime of ecocide.[395] In late 2020, the Independent Expert Panel was mandated by the Stop Ecocide Foundation to draft a legal definition of a potential crime of ecocide which could serve as the basis for the inclusion of a fifth core crime in the Rome Statute.[396] The International Expert Panel comprised twelve renowned international jurists from different legal backgrounds, which was co-chaired by UN jurist Dior Fall Sow and Philippe Sands.[397]

Although, it is remarkable that the privately organised Independent Expert Panel produced a potential definition of a crime of ecocide within the short period of only 6 months, compared to the notoriously slow lawmaking processes of the International Law Commission, it has to be noted that the proposed definition did not

[394] See id. at 139.

[395] *Haroon Siddique*, Legal Experts Worldwide Draw Up 'Historic' Definition of Ecocide, The Guardian, 2021.

[396] Stop Ecocide Foundation, Independent Expert Panel for the Legal Definition of Ecocide, Commentary and Core Text (2021).

[397] Id.

emanate from the traditional UN lawmaking process.[398] Nevertheless, the proposed definition could serve the UN lawmaking organs as a basis to seriously consider the drafting of a fifth crime of ecocide.

The International Expert Panel proposed to include a stand-alone crime of ecocide as Article 8 *ter* Rome Statute reading as follows:[399]

Article 8 *ter*: Ecocide

1. For the purpose of this Statute, "ecocide" means unlawful or wanton acts committed with knowledge that there is a substantial likelihood of severe and either widespread or long-term damage to the environment being caused by those acts.
2. For the purpose of paragraph 1:
   a. "Wanton" means with reckless disregard for damage which would be clearly excessive in relation to the social and economic benefits anticipated;
   b. "Severe" means damage which involves very serious adverse changes, disruption or harm to any element of the environment, including grave impacts on human life or natural, cultural or economic resources;
   c. "Widespread" means damage which extends beyond a limited geographic area, crosses state boundaries, or is suffered by an entire ecosystem or species or a large number of human beings;
   d. "Long-term" means damage which is irreversible, or which cannot be redressed through natural recovery within a reasonable period of time;
   e. "Environment" means the earth, its biosphere, cryosphere, lithosphere, hydrosphere and atmosphere, as well as outer space.

Concerning the structure of Article 8 *ter*, the International Expert Panel drew upon Article 7 Rome Statute with a general definition of the crime of ecocide in the first paragraph to be followed by a second paragraph containing the relevant definitions of its core elements.[400] Furthermore, in terms of content, many aspects are borrowed from Article 8 (2) (b) (iv) Rome Statute, including, for instance, the terms 'widespread', 'long-term' and 'severe'.[401] In general, the Panel mostly used familiar language derived from pre-existing international agreements.[402] However, despite the similarities to the pre-existing core crimes, concerning the *ratione materiae* the new crime of ecocide would extend environmental protection under the Rome

---

[398] *Romina Pezzot/Jan-Philip Graf*, Ecocide, Legal Revolution or Symbolism? (2022), https://voelkerrechtsblog.org/de/ecocide-legal-revolution-or-symbolism/ (last visited Feb. 18, 2025).

[399] *Stop Ecocide Foundation*, Independent Expert Panel for the Legal Definition of Ecocide, Commentary and Core Text (2021).

[400] Id.

[401] Id.

[402] Id.

Statute beyond times of international armed conflict.[403] Thus, under this provision environmentally harmful activities would also incur criminal liability if they occurred during non-international armed conflicts, during peacetime or *post bellum*. Although Ambos criticised the lack of reference concerning the relationship of Article 8 *ter* and Article 8 (2) (b) (iv) Rome Statute[404], this is not a valid argument against the inclusion of Article 8 *ter*, as environmentally harmful conduct occurring during international armed conflict could both constitute a war crime and a crime of ecocide. The exact sentence in such a case would be meted out by the ICC and is not a matter of defining the crime.

In the following, the 2021 definition will be evaluated by scrutinising the constituting material and mental elements of the crime.

a) Material Elements

In terms of material elements, the criminalised conduct (*unlawful and wanton acts*), as well as the consequences (*substantial likelihood of severe and either widespread or long-term damage to the environment*) of the crime stipulated in the proposed definition will be evaluated below.

aa) The criminalised conduct

The 2021 proposal proscribes unlawful and wanton *acts* including both single and cumulative acts and omissions.[405] In general, keeping the criminalised conduct broad instead of enumerating certain acts prevents equally destructive activities from being excluded and thus promotes global environmental protection. However, the initially broad scope is significantly restricted by the criteria *unlawful and wanton*. Both terms, *unlawful* and *wanton,* are borrowed from Article 8 (2) (a) (iv) Rome Statute.[406] With regards to the *unlawful* criterion, the Panel stated that due to the scarcity of absolute prohibitions in international environmental law, environmentally harmful conduct is not only considered *unlawful* in case of a breach of international environmental law but also if it violates domestic law.[407] The Panel argued that while lawfulness cannot be determined by national law, international unlawfulness may arise from national illegality, which is also in line with Article 7

---

[403] Id.

[404] *Kai Ambos*, EJIL: Talk! (June 29, 2021), https://www.ejiltalk.org/protecting-the-environment-through-international-criminal-law/ (last visited Feb. 18, 2025).

[405] Stop Ecocide Foundation, Independent Expert Panel for the Legal Definition of Ecocide, Commentary and Core Text (2021).

[406] Id.

[407] Id.

(1) (d) and (e) Rome Statute.[408] Nevertheless, as seen above and argued by the Panel, international environmental law only contains very few absolute prohibitions[409], which is why in the majority of cases the unlawfulness of the environmentally harmful conduct would depend on national law.[410] However, according to the United Nations Preparatory Commission for the International Criminal Court, the criteria *unlawful* or *lawful* as used in several offences under the Rome Statute, as, *inter alia*, Article 8 (2) (a) (iv) Rome Statute, "refer to the lawfulness under international law".[411] With respect to the cornerstone principle of international criminal law, that is its independence of domestic law, it appears highly problematic to predicate international criminal liability on domestic legislation whose scope of application is restricted to a specific territory and people. This is particularly the case in the environmental context, since standards of environmental protection vary greatly amongst national jurisdictions.[412] Thus, the *unlawful* criterion as proposed by the Panel is highly ambiguous rendering it extremely difficult to anticipate the criminalised conduct which contravenes the tantamount principle of legality. For these reasons, it has been advised that the *unlawful* criterion be removed from the definition.

According to the Panel's definition, *lawful* conduct only incurs criminal liability if committed *wantonly*, that is "with reckless disregard for damage which would be clearly excessive in relation to the social and economic benefits anticipated"[413]. The Panel's definition of *wantonly* corresponds to the definition of *wanton* set out by the ICTY in relation to Article 2 (d) ICTY Statute requiring the perpetrator to have acted "with the intent to destroy the protected property or in reckless disregard of the likelihood of its destruction"[414]. The *wanton* criterion as used in the Panel's definition is two-fold: for one, it includes an additional mental element ("reckless disregard"), and second, a proportionality test ("damage which would be clearly excessive in relation to the social and economic benefits anticipated") similar to

---

[408] Id.; see *Robert Cryer*, et al., An Introduction to International Criminal Law and Procedure 246 fn. 146 (2019); *Gerhard Werle/Florian Jeßberger*, Principles of International Criminal Law paras. 1057, 1062 (2020); *William A. Schabas*, The International Criminal Court: A Commentary on the Rome Statute 180 (2016).

[409] *Kai Ambos*, EJIL: Talk! (June 29, 2021), https://www.ejiltalk.org/protecting-the-environment-through-international-criminal-law/ (last visited Feb. 18, 2025).

[410] *Kevin Jon Heller*, Ecocide and Anthropocentric Cost-Benefit Analysis, OpinioJuris (June 26, 2021), http://opiniojuris.org/2021/06/26/ecocide-and-anthropocentric-cost-benefit-analysis/ (last visited Feb. 18, 2025).

[411] United Nations, Preparatory Commission for the International Criminal Court, at 11, U. N. Doc. PCNICC/1999/WGEC/INF.2 (July 14, 1999).

[412] *Kevin Jon Heller*, OpinioJuris (June 26, 2021), http://opiniojuris.org/2021/06/26/ecocide-and-anthropocentric-cost-benefit-analysis/ (last visited Feb. 18, 2025).

[413] Art. 8 ter (2) (a) of the proposed definition.

[414] Prosecutor v. Brdanin, Case No. IT-99-36-T, Judgement, ¶ 589 (Sept. 1, 2004); similar Prosecutor v. Kordič, Case No. IT-95-14/2-T, Judgement, ¶ 341 (Feb. 26, 2001); Prosecutor v. Naletilić, Case No. IT-98-34-T, Judgement, ¶ 577 (Mar. 31, 2003).

Article 8 (2) b) (iv) Rome Statute, where environmental destruction is balanced against the expected military advantage. However, in this part of the thesis only the proportionality test will be assessed, and the additional mental element will be discussed in conjunction with the 'main' mental element below.

According to the Panel, the proportionality test draws upon existing environmental principles, "which balance social and economic benefits with environmental harms through the concept of sustainable development"[415]. In doing so, the Panel intended to exclude certain environmentally destructive activities, such as transportation links and housing developments, likely to cause severe and widespread or long-term environmental damage, which, however, benefit society.[416] Thus, in cases where the social and economic benefit outweighs the environmental harm, these activities must be considered legitimate development not incurring criminal liability.

However, similar to Higgin's definition or Article 8 (2) (b) (iv) Rome Statute, the inclusion of a proportionality test significantly facilitates the justification of environmental degradation. As Heller and Ambos rightly criticised, by permitting large-scale environmental damage to be justified with social and economic benefits, the provision is rendered inherently anthropocentric despite the Panel's proclaimed ecocentric approach.[417] In this regard, Christina Voigt, one of the Panel's members, objected that the proportionality test only applies to lawful acts where "disregard of [the] excessiveness of the damage is the <<criminalizing>> factor"[418]. Voigt further claimed that "[t]he alternative would have been to capture illegal acts only"[419]. Nevertheless, one must concur with Heller that restricting the criminalised conduct to unlawful acts was not the Panel's only alternative, as it could have also criminalised *any* act, both unlawful and lawful, entailing a substantial likelihood of causing severe or either widespread or long-term environmental damage.[420] In this case, the reason behind the criminalisation of ecocide would not be its illegality or disproportionality, but the perpetrator's awareness of the substantial likelihood that their conduct may cause severe or either widespread or long-term environmental

[415] Stop Ecocide Foundation, Independent Expert Panel for the Legal Definition of Ecocide, Commentary and Core Text (2021).

[416] Id.

[417] *Kevin Jon Heller*, OpinioJuris (June 23, 2021), https://opiniojuris.org/2021/06/23/skeptical-thoughts-on-the-proposed-crime-of-ecocide-that-isnt/ (last visited Feb. 18, 2025); *Kevin Jon Heller*, OpinioJuris (June 26, 2021), http://opiniojuris.org/2021/06/26/ecocide-and-anthropocentric-cost-benefit-analysis/ (last visited Feb. 18, 2025); *Kai Ambos*, EJIL: Talk! (June 29, 2021), https://www.ejiltalk.org/protecting-the-environment-through-international-criminal-law/ (last visited Feb. 18, 2025).

[418] Voigt's tweet is cited in *Kevin Jon Heller*, OpinioJuris (June 26, 2021), http://opiniojuris.org/2021/06/26/ecocide-and-anthropocentric-cost-benefit-analysis/ (last visited Feb. 18, 2025).

[419] Id.

[420] Id.

damage.[421] Thus, the main rationale of criminalising ecocide would be to deter potential perpetrators who knowingly take the substantial risk of causing severe and either widespread or long-term environmental damage. The potential deterrent effect would thus be much stronger without the possibility of justifying severe and either widespread or long-term environmental damage with social and economic considerations. Additionally, the lack of absolute prohibitions in international environmental law and the consequence arising that domestic law would, in most cases, determine which conduct would constitute a crime under international law, are compelling reasons to criminalise *any* act, whether lawful or unlawful, which entails the substantial risk of causing severe and either widespread or long-term environmental damage irrespective of anthropocentric considerations.[422] Furthermore, Heller and Ambos rightly stated that only an inherently ecocentric provision, irrespective of anthropocentric considerations, would be consistent with the term *ecocide*.[423] However, for the aforementioned reasons it is not advisable to establish a *crime of ecocide*, but it should rather be resorted to the term *crime against the environment*.[424]

Nevertheless, concerning the proposal to criminalise *any* act Voigt objected that "such 'genuinely ecocentric' approach would then include, for example, every new railroad, motorway, school, hospital, perhaps even wind- or solarpark or hydropower plant that is lawfully developed and be the best guarantee for the 'ecocide' initiative to fail"[425]. Nevertheless, concerning Voigt's assertion Heller rightly objected that *one* hospital or *one* wind park would hardly qualify as ecocide as it would not involve a substantial risk of causing severe and widespread or long-term environmental damage.[426] Requiring a substantial risk of severe and widespread or long-term environmental damage sufficiently excludes ordinary environmental harm arising from isolated infrastructure projects, which, in turn, renders the exclusion of proportionate lawful environmental destruction as intended by the proportionality test obsolete. However, should an isolated infrastructure project entail a substantial risk of causing severe and widespread or long-term damage to the environment, it

---

[421] Id.

[422] Similar id.; see a fictive case study demonstrating the problems the 'wanton' requirement would incur, if it were applied to a case involving the authorisation of a new massive coal field in Australia, *Kevin Jon Heller*, The Crime of Ecocide in Action, OpinioJuris (June 28, 2021), http://opiniojuris.org/2021/06/28/the-crime-of-ecocide-in-action/ (last visited Feb. 18, 2025).

[423] *Kai Ambos*, EJIL: Talk! (June 29, 2021), https://www.ejiltalk.org/protecting-the-environment-through-international-criminal-law/ (last visited Feb. 18, 2025); *Kevin Jon Heller*, OpinioJuris (June 26, 2021), http://opiniojuris.org/2021/06/26/ecocide-and-anthropocentric-cost-benefit-analysis/ (last visited Feb. 18, 2025).

[424] See Chapter C. I.

[425] Voigt's tweet is cited in *Kevin Jon Heller*, OpinioJuris (June 26, 2021), http://opiniojuris.org/2021/06/26/ecocide-and-anthropocentric-cost-benefit-analysis/ (last visited Feb. 18, 2025).

[426] Id.

should face criminal liability for the sake of global environmental protection. Hence, in this thesis it is suggested to create an inherently ecocentric definition by criminalising *any* conduct involving a substantial risk of causing severe and widespread or long-term environmental damage irrespective of economic and social considerations. Establishing such a crime of ecocide inevitably promotes sustainable development, for instance, by forcing the construction industry to explore alternative ways of eco-friendly building. In contrast, the inclusion of a cost-benefit analysis always leaves the door open for legal justification, which seems inappropriate in cases entailing the substantial risk of severe and widespread or long-term environmental damage. Such cost-benefit considerations may, if at all, play a role in cases of low-impact environmental damage but not in the most serious cases of environmental harm.

bb) The consequences

In the following, the consequences of the crime, namely the concept of endangerment liability and the gravity threshold that the Panel chose, will be examined.

(1) Endangerment liability

By having refrained from requiring the actual occurrence of environmental damage and instead letting the substantial likelihood of severe and either widespread or long-term environmental harm suffice, the Panel established endangerment liability rather than creating a crime of material result.[427] In the context of environmental harm it is essential to establish a crime of endangerment, as the environment can only be effectively protected by preventing further environmental destruction. As crimes of conduct criminalise conduct prior to the occurrence of actual harm[428], these types of crimes focus on preventing certain harm from occurring rather than coming into place when the danger has already materialised and are thus highly preventive in nature.[429] Additionally, in the environmental context, endangerment liability assists in overcoming the evidentiary difficulty of proving long-term repercussions, which sometimes do not show for a generation or more.[430] As implied by the Panel's commentary and the existence of Articles 6, 8 (2) (b) (iv) and 8 (2) (b) (i)-(iii)) Rome Statute, the concept of endangerment liability is not

---

[427] *Kai Ambos*, EJIL: Talk! (June 29, 2021), https://www.ejiltalk.org/protecting-the-environment-through-international-criminal-law/ (last visited Feb. 18, 2025); Stop Ecocide Foundation, Independent Expert Panel for the Legal Definition of Ecocide, Commentary and Core Text (2021).

[428] *Antonio Cassese*, et al., Cassese's International Criminal Law 38 (2013).

[429] *Andrew Cornford*, New Criminal Law Review: An International and Interdisciplinary Journal 3 (2015).

[430] *Eric Biber*, Hofstra L. Rev. 976 (2009); *Frédéric Mégret*, Colum. J. Envtl. L. 236 (2011).

novel to the Rome Statute.[431] However, as will be further assessed below[432], Article 8 *ter* does not include a comparably high mental threshold as, for instance, Article 6 Rome Statute which requires genocidal intent or Article 8 (2) (b) (iv) Rome Statute which presupposes knowledge and intent.[433]

(2) Gravity threshold

With the purpose of excluding trivial cases of environmental destruction, in terms of the gravity threshold, the 2021 definition demands a substantial likelihood of "severe and [alternatively] either widespread or long-term"[434] environmental damage. As previously outlined, these terms have already appeared in several other international treaties including Articles 35 (3), 55 AP I, Article 8 (2) (b) (iv) Rome Statute, Article I (1) ENMOD Convention and Article 26 of the 1991 Draft Code. However, the Panel refrained from requiring the three criteria cumulatively, as was done in Articles 35 (3), 55 AP I and Article 8 (2) (b) (iv) Rome Statute or alternatively, as in Article I (1) ENMOD. Instead, the Panel set a new threshold mandating the environmental damage to be severe *and* either widespread *or* long-term. In doing so, the Panel chose a middle-path between both options. While the disjunctive ENMOD threshold was considered too low, as environmental damage must always be sufficiently severe in order to constitute ecocide, the triple-standard in Articles 35 (3), 55 (1) AP I and Article 8 (2) (b) (iv) Rome Statute was deemed unnecessarily high excluding cases of environmental damage which are severe and long-term but not widespread, or severe and widespread but not long-term.[435] In this regard, despite different language, the Panel's definition corresponds to Gray's aforementioned proposed threshold of "serious and extensive or lasting, ecological damage"[436]. Both proposals primarily focus on the seriousness of the environmental harm, which is the main characteristic of international criminal law, and only disjunctively require the damage to be widespread (extensive) or long-term (lasting). The fact that Article 8 *ter* applies to both times of peace and war justifies the lower gravity threshold in contrast to Article 8 (2) (b) (iv) Rome Statute which is restricted to international armed conflicts and which inevitably entail some form of environmental damage.[437] Since the cumulative triple threshold of Article 8

---

[431] Stop Ecocide Foundation, Independent Expert Panel for the Legal Definition of Ecocide, Commentary and Core Text (2021).

[432] See Chapter C. V. 3. b) aa).

[433] *Kai Ambos*, EJIL: Talk! (June 29, 2021), https://www.ejiltalk.org/protecting-the-environment-through-international-criminal-law/ (last visited Feb. 18, 2025).

[434] Stop Ecocide Foundation, Independent Expert Panel for the Legal Definition of Ecocide, Commentary and Core Text (2021).

[435] Id.

[436] *Mark Allan Gray*, Cal. W. Int'l L.J. 216 (1996).

[437] *Kevin Jon Heller*, OpinioJuris (June 23, 2021), https://opiniojuris.org/2021/06/23/skeptical-thoughts-on-the-proposed-crime-of-ecocide-that-isnt/ (last visited Feb. 18, 2025); *Kevin*

(2) (b) (iv) Rome Statute is even considered too high in the case of international armed conflicts[438], a lower gravity threshold is necessary for peacetime activities where serious environmental damage is frequent, yet not ubiquitous.

Besides lowering the gravity threshold, approval must be given to the fact that Article 8 *ter*, as opposed to Article 8 (2) (b) (iv) Rome Statute, provides definitions for all three requirements, which decreases the level of ambiguity in relation to the material elements of the crime. Pursuant to Article 8 *ter* (2) (b) *severe* denotes "damage which involves very serious adverse changes, disruption or harm to any element of the environment, including grave impacts on human life or natural, cultural or economic resources". Similarly, according to an Understanding relating to Article I ENMOD Convention *severe* meant "serious or significant disruption or harm to human life, natural and economic resources or other assets"[439]. However, by replacing *other assets* with *cultural resources* the Panel claimed to stress the cultural value of certain environmental elements, especially to indigenous tribes.[440] In accordance with Article 8 *ter* (2) (e) *environment* means "the earth, its biosphere, cryosphere, lithosphere, hydrosphere and atmosphere, as well as outer space". Due to the lack of an agreed-upon definition of the *environment* hitherto it is commendable that the Panel included a respective definition to avoid ambiguity, as is the case with Article 8 (2) (b) (iv) Rome Statute. Although the Panel's commentary does not shed light on the fact why the Panel decided to use the term *environment* instead of *natural environment,* as deployed in Article 8 (2) (b) (iv) Rome Statute, it is to be assumed that this was done to dispel any doubts concerning the add-on *natural* implying that the term *natural environment* exclusively included natural elements leaving aside the interrelationship to human life. By including the biosphere into the definition, the Panel explicitly included the interrelationship between the environment and the human race.[441] It further appears wise to extend the *severe* criterion to include various impacts on human life, natural, cultural and economic resources, as modern environmental harm is committed in various ways.

In accordance with Article 8 *ter* (2) (c) *widespread* means "damage which extends beyond a limited geographic area, crosses state boundaries, or is suffered by an entire ecosystem or species or a large number of human beings". While in the context of the ENMOD Convention *widespread* was defined as "an area of several hundred square kilometers" [442] and the *travaux préparatoires* to the Additional

---

Jon Heller, OpinioJuris (June 26, 2021), http://opiniojuris.org/2021/06/26/ecocide-and-anthropocentric-cost-benefit-analysis/ (last visited Feb. 18, 2025).

[438] See Chapter B. IV. 3. a) aa) (2).

[439] G.A., Report of the Conference of the Committee on Disarmament, at 91 (Annex I), U. N. Doc. A/31/27 (Vol. I) (1976).

[440] Stop Ecocide Foundation, Independent Expert Panel for the Legal Definition of Ecocide, Commentary and Core Text (2021).

[441] *Emanuela Fronza*, Towards a New Crime of Ecocide 100 (2022).

[442] G.A., Report of the Conference of the Committee on Disarmament, at 91 (Annex I), U. N. Doc. A/31/27 (Vol. I) (1976).

Protocol I indicated that the required scale of damage must, at a minimum, exceed ENMOD's threshold of several hundred square kilometers[443], the Panel refrained from requiring a specific geographical scale. By doing so, they succeeded in avoiding the risk of setting a threshold which excludes acts of environmental destruction affecting thousands of people in a limited geographical area, such as a population centre or city.[444] In this regard, the Bhopal Gas Tragedy in 1984 deserves a mention, which 'only' affected a single city with its neighborhoods yet demanded thousands of deaths.[445] The Panel rightly further claimed that certain harm to climatic systems is not measurable in terms of determining an affected geographical area, which is why requiring a specific geographical area is deemed unsuitable.[446] While the environmental harm sustained by, for instance, oil spills, deforestation, extractive activities is mostly limited to a specific territorial area, air pollution is hardly measurable in terms of locating an affected geographic area due to its gaseous nature. For these reasons, it appears wise of the Panel to require environmental damage to extend *beyond a limited geographic area.*[447] The *widespread* criterion is further satisfied in the case of transboundary harm, if the environmental damage is sustained to an entire ecosystem, or similar to the interpretation of *widespread* under Article 7 (1) Rome Statute, if damage is sustained to a large number of human beings[448], which also appear to be appropriate criteria to determine the geographical scale of environmental harm.

Furthermore, pursuant to Article 8 *ter* (2) (d) *long-term* denotes "damage which is irreversible, or which cannot be redressed through natural recovery within a reasonable period of time". While in the context of the ENMOD environmental damage was deemed *long-lasting* "if it last[ed] for a period of months, or approximately a season" [449], the *travaux préparatoires* to the AP I defined *long-term* as environmental damage lasting at least two or three decades.[450] As the Panel considered both definitions inappropriate, the former being too short whilst the latter was deemed too long and arbitrary, it decided to focus on the irreversibility of the

---

443 *Karen Hulme*, War Torn Environment 92, 98 (2004); *Stefan Wehrenberg*, Article 8 para. 252 (2022).

444 Stop Ecocide Foundation, Independent Expert Panel for the Legal Definition of Ecocide, Commentary and Core Text (2021).

445 Encyclopedia Britannica, Bhopal disaster, https://www.britannica.com/event/Bhopal-di saster (last visited Feb. 18, 2025).

446 Stop Ecocide Foundation, Independent Expert Panel for the Legal Definition of Ecocide, Commentary and Core Text (2021).

447 Similar *Kevin Jon Heller*, OpinioJuris (June 26, 2021), http://opiniojuris.org/2021/06/26/ ecocide-and-anthropocentric-cost-benefit-analysis/ (last visited Feb. 18, 2025).

448 Prosecutor v. Bemba, ICC-01/05-01/08, Decision on the Prosecutor's Application for a Warrant of Arrest against Jean-Pierre Bemba Gombo, ¶ 33 (June 10, 2008).

449 G.A., Report of the Conference of the Committee on Disarmament, at 91 (Annex I), U. N. Doc. A/31/27 (Vol. I) (1976).

450 *Stefan Wehrenberg*, Article 8 para. 252 (2022); *Eliana Teresa Cusato*, JICJ 496 (2017); *Jessica C. Lawrence/Kevin Jon Heller*, Geo. Int'l Envtl. L. Rev. 73 (2007).

damage instead.[451] The Panel concurred that fixed periods of time determining the longevity of environmental harm appear arbitrary and difficult to determine, as some natural elements are more sensitive than others. Thus, it varies as to how fast, or if at all, natural elements can recover. Thus, focusing on the irreversibility of the harm seems more suitable than setting fixed periods of time. In general, it was wise of the IEP to have taken recourse to the pre-existing ENMOD definitions entailing a certain familiarity, albeit having modified and adapted them to the peculiarities of peacetime environmental harm, as ENMOD definitions only apply to wartime.[452] By doing so, the Panel cannot be blamed for having replicated ENMOD's definition which was explicitly banned from being transferred to other international treaties.[453] Furthermore, by providing clear definitions of the three requirements, the gravity threshold in Article 8 *ter* is not subjected to ambiguity, which would impede its effective application and acceptance, in stark contrast to Article 8 (2) (b) (iv) Rome Statute.

b) Mental Elements

Article 8 *ter* includes two mental thresholds, one of which requiring *knowledge that there is a substantial likelihood of severe and either widespread or long-term damage to the environment* and another presupposing reckless disregard (*wanton*) in relation to the excessiveness of the environmental harm, which will both be discussed below.

aa) Knowledge that there is a substantial likelihood of severe and either widespread or long-term damage to the environment

Article 8 *ter* Rome Statute demands that the perpetrator act with *knowledge that there is a substantial likelihood* of severe and either widespread or long-term damage to the environment. With respect to the consequence of the crime, the provision thus deviates from Article 30 (2) (b) second alternative and (3) Rome Statute requiring at least awareness of the *virtual certainty*[454] of the occurrence of

---

[451] Stop Ecocide Foundation, Independent Expert Panel for the Legal Definition of Ecocide, Commentary and Core Text (2021).

[452] However, in its 1996 Advisory Opinion on the Legality of the Threat or Use of Nuclear Weapons the ICJ argued that Art. I (1) ENMOD Convention and Art. 35 (3), 55 (1) AP I "apply at all times, in war as well as in peace" (Legality of the Threat or Use of Nuclear Weapons, Advisory Opinion, 1996 I.C.J. Rep., ¶ 27 (July 8).

[453] G.A., Report of the Conference of the Committee on Disarmament, at 91 (Annex I), U. N. Doc. A/31/27 (Vol. I) (1976) ("It is further understood that the interpretation set forth above is intended exclusively for this Convention and is not intended to prejudice the interpretation of the same or similar terms if used in connexion with any other international agreement.").

[454] Prosecutor v. Bemba, ICC-01/05-01/13, Judgment Pursuant to Article 74 of the Statute, ¶ 29 (Oct. 19, 2016); Prosecutor v. Lubanga, ICC-01/04-01/06 A 5, Judgment on the Appeal

the harm. However, such a deviation is permitted under the *unless otherwise provided* formula in Article 30 (1) Rome Statute. Instead of intent, the Panel lowered the mental threshold to include "recklessness or *dolus eventualis*, requiring awareness of a substantial likelihood of severe and either widespread or long-term damage"[455]. The Panel decided to include the concepts of recklessness or *dolus eventualis*, as it considered indirect intent pursuant to Article 30 (2) (b) second alternative Rome Statute in relation to the consequences of the crime to be too strict, as acts involving merely a *high likelihood* of the occurrence environmental harm would be excluded.[456] In general, the decision to include recklessness or *dolus eventualis* yet exclude negligence-based liability, and thereby require an appropriate level of culpability for a crime under international law, is to be approved of. However, the Panel should have clarified that the mental threshold is lowered to include *advertent recklessness* equating to *dolus eventualis* in order to avoid confusion regarding the numerous different notions of recklessness in common law jurisdictions.[457]

By requiring the *substantial likelihood* of severe and either widespread or long-term environmental damage, the Panel chose an appropriate middle-path between the different notions of *dolus eventualis* in civil law jurisdictions, where some jurisdictions require the awareness of a *high probability*, and others only require the *low probability* of the occurrence of the consequence[458], and indirect intent requiring awareness of the *virtual certainty* of the harm. Since international criminal law only pertains to the most serious atrocities, and the crime of ecocide should be defined as a crime of endangerment, a *substantial* likelihood of the occurrence of harm should be required. Since the mental threshold of Article 8 *ter* was only lowered to include *dolus eventualis* or *advertent recklessness*, which, at least in civil law jurisdictions, is considered a form of intention, the mental threshold appears sufficiently high to be combined with endangerment liability on the objective side.

However, due to the existence of Article 30 (3) Rome Statute which defines knowledge as "the awareness that a circumstance exists in the ordinary course of

of Mr. Thomas Lubanga Dyilo Against His Conviction, ¶ 447 (Dec. 1, 2014); Prosecutor v. Katanga, ICC-01/04-01/07, Judgment Pursuant to Article 74 of the Statute, ¶ 776 (Mar. 7, 2014); Prosecutor v. Bemba, ICC-01/05-01/08, Decision Pursuant to Article 61(7)(a) and (b) of the Rome Statute on the Charges of the Prosecutor Against Jean-Pierre Bemba Gombo, ¶ 362 (June 15, 2009).

[455] Stop Ecocide Foundation, Independent Expert Panel for the Legal Definition of Ecocide, Commentary and Core Text (2021).

[456] Id.

[457] See on the different notions of recklessness and its comparability with the civil law concept of dolus eventualis *Christoph Safferling*, Vorsatz und Schuld 360–368 (2008); *Kevin Jon Heller*, OpinioJuris (June 23, 2021), https://opiniojuris.org/2021/06/23/skeptical-thoughts-on-the-proposed-crime-of-ecocide-that-isnt/ (last visited Feb. 18, 2025).

[458] *Donald K. Piragoff/Darryl Robinson*, Article 30 para. 26 fn. 56 (2022).

events", the Panel should have replaced the term knowledge with *awareness*[459] otherwise confusion arises from the fact that Article 30 (3) Rome Statute requires the *virtual certainty* of the occurrence of harm and thus includes a higher threshold than the *substantial likelihood* threshold set by the Panel.[460] As such, in order to stress the intention to lower the mental threshold set out in Article 30 (2) (b) and (3) Rome Statute, it is suggested to formulate the mental element as *awareness that there is a substantial likelihood of severe and either widespread or long-term damage to the environment.* In terms of language, in *Lubanga* the Pre-Trial Chamber I of the ICC already referred to *dolus eventualis* as "the awareness by the suspect of the substantial likelihood that his or her actions or omissions would result in the realisation of the objective elements of the crime"[461]. However, in this decision the Chamber wrongly claimed that Article 30 (2) (b) and (3) Rome Statute included *dolus eventualis*[462], which was later overturned by several decisions.[463]

bb) Wanton

Article 8 *ter* includes an additional mental element requiring *reckless disregard* with relation to the clear excessiveness of the environmental damage. However, this additional mental threshold is highly confusing[464], as the 'main' mental element ("knowledge that there is a substantial likelihood") already contains the concepts of supposedly advertent recklessness and *dolus eventualis* in relation to the severe and either widespread or long-term environmental damage. Take, for instance, Article 8 (2) (b) (iv) Rome Statute requiring "knowledge that such an attack will cause […] widespread, long-term and severe damage to the natural environment which would be clearly excessive in relation to the concrete and direct overall military advantage anticipated". Under Article 8 (2) (b) (iv) Rome Statute the knowledge and intent requirement clearly both relates to the widespread, long-term and severe nature as well as the excessiveness of the environmental damage. Thus, it remains unclear

---

[459] *Kevin Jon Heller*, OpinioJuris (June 23, 2021), https://opiniojuris.org/2021/06/23/skeptical-thoughts-on-the-proposed-crime-of-ecocide-that-isnt/ (last visited Feb. 18, 2025).

[460] *Kai Ambos*, EJIL: Talk! (June 29, 2021), https://www.ejiltalk.org/protecting-the-environment-through-international-criminal-law/ (last visited Feb. 18, 2025); *Kevin Jon Heller*, OpinioJuris (June 23, 2021), https://opiniojuris.org/2021/06/23/skeptical-thoughts-on-the-proposed-crime-of-ecocide-that-isnt/ (last visited Feb. 18, 2025).

[461] Prosecutor v. Lubanga, ICC-01/04-01/06, Decision on the Confirmation of Charges, ¶ 353 (Jan. 29, 2007).

[462] Id. ¶ 350–352.

[463] Prosecutor v. Bemba, ICC-01/05-01/08, Decision Pursuant to Article 61(7)(a) and (b) of the Rome Statute on the Charges of the Prosecutor Against Jean-Pierre Bemba Gombo, ¶ 357, 358 (June 15, 2009); Prosecutor v. Katanga, ICC-01/04-01/07, Judgment Pursuant to Article 74 of the Statute, ¶ 775, 776 (Mar. 7, 2014); Prosecutor v. Lubanga, ICC-01/04-01/06, Judgment Pursuant to Article 74 of the Statute, ¶ 1011 (Mar. 14, 2012).

[464] *Kevin Jon Heller*, OpinioJuris (June 23, 2021), https://opiniojuris.org/2021/06/23/skeptical-thoughts-on-the-proposed-crime-of-ecocide-that-isnt/ (last visited Feb. 18, 2025).

whether the Panel intended to establish two identical *dolus eventualis* thresholds, one referring to the substantial risk of severe and either widespread or long-term environmental damage and one to its excessiveness, which would undoubtedly be superfluous with regards to Article 8 (2) (b) (iv) Rome Statute stipulating one mental element relating to both thresholds, or if the Panel aimed at creating two different mental thresholds depending on the point of reference. In the latter case, however, it remains unknown which exact meaning the Panel attributes to *recklessness* as there are generally two notions of *recklessness*. For one, *recklessness* is understood as entailing a cognitive as well as a volitional element being classed as advertent or subjective recklessness being the common law equivalent to *dolus eventualis*[465], whereas another notion considers *recklessness* purely cognitively (*objective recklessness*).[466]

Furthermore, it would be difficult to prove that the perpetrator was *ex ante* aware that the anticipated environmental damage would be clearly excessive in relation to the expected social and economic benefits.[467] It is argued that this mental requirement entails a value judgement similar to the one in Article 8 (2) (b) (iv) Rome Statute[468] requiring the perpetrator to be aware of the factual circumstances rendering the severe and either widespread or long-term environmental damage clearly excessive to the social and economic benefits.[469] Thus, if a proportionality test were considered necessary, Heller suggested lowering the evidential burden by only demanding simple negligence with relation to the cost-benefit analysis, leading to the following definition of the crime of ecocide:

"For the purpose of this Statute, 'ecocide' means acts committed with awareness that there is a substantial likelihood of severe and either widespread or long-term damage to the environment being caused by those acts, *where a reasonable person would know that the expected environmental damage would be clearly excessive in relation to the social and economic benefits anticipated*".[470]

However, if a proportionality test were considered necessary, a better alternative to lowering the mental threshold relating to the cost-benefit analysis to include negligence would be to include a simple disproportionality test instead of requiring

[465] *Antonio Cassese*, et al., Cassese's International Criminal Law 46 (2013).

[466] *Kevin Jon Heller*, OpinioJuris (June 23, 2021), https://opiniojuris.org/2021/06/23/skeptical-thoughts-on-the-proposed-crime-of-ecocide-that-isnt/ (last visited Feb. 18, 2025); see more detailed on the two different notions of recklessness *Christoph Safferling*, Vorsatz und Schuld 360–364 (2008).

[467] *Kevin Jon Heller*, OpinioJuris (June 23, 2021), https://opiniojuris.org/2021/06/23/skeptical-thoughts-on-the-proposed-crime-of-ecocide-that-isnt/ (last visited Feb. 18, 2025).

[468] Id.

[469] See *Donald K. Piragoff/Darryl Robinson*, Article 30 para. 34 (2022); *Albin Eser*, Mental Elements 923 (2002).

[470] *Kevin Jon Heller*, OpinioJuris (June 23, 2021), https://opiniojuris.org/2021/06/23/skeptical-thoughts-on-the-proposed-crime-of-ecocide-that-isnt/ (last visited Feb. 18, 2025) (emphasis added).

the environmental damage to be *clearly* excessive. Furthermore, no additional mental element should be included. In this case, the *awareness of a substantial likelihood* threshold would both relate to the severe and either widespread or long-term nature and the excessiveness of the environmental damage. This would both lower the evidentiary burden and at the same time respect that apart from superior responsibility of military commanders in Article 28 (a) (i) Rome Statute simple negligence is not a generally accepted subjective standard under international criminal law[471], which is not comparable to the causation of environmental harm committed by corporate officials. Setting the mental threshold too low jeopardises the political acceptance of the provision and thus further complicates the amendment of the Rome Statute.

Nonetheless, for the above-mentioned reasons, it is preferable to create an inherently ecocentric provision irrespective of anthropocentric considerations. Hence, it is suggested to remove the proportionality test and its corresponding mental element from the ecocide definition altogether.

4. Own proposal

As demonstrated above, the Panel's proposal requires slight modifications to achieve the highest level of global environmental protection within the framework of international criminal law.

Firstly, the crime should not be introduced as a *crime of ecocide* but rather as a *crime against the environment*. Although the reference to the crime of genocide as the 'crime of all crimes' generates attention, it is misleading, as crimes against the environment contain a significantly lower mental threshold and do not entail the destruction of a particular human group.[472]

Secondly, concerning the criminalised conduct there should be no distinction made between unlawful and lawful acts, but rather *any* act exceeding the requisite gravity threshold should qualify as ecocide. Furthermore, a proportionality test rendering the provision anthropocentric and facilitating the legal justification of large-scale environmental harm through social and economic benefits should not form part of the definition. However, should the lawmakers consider the gravity threshold insufficient and therefore deem the inclusion of a proportionality test necessary, the proportionality test should be a simple test not requiring the environmental harm to be *clearly* excessive and no additional mental element relating to the proportionality test should be included. Instead, advertent recklessness or *dolus*

---

[471] *Robert Cryer*, et al., An Introduction to International Criminal Law and Procedure 366 (2019).

[472] *Kevin Jon Heller*, OpinioJuris (June 23, 2021), https://opiniojuris.org/2021/06/23/skeptical-thoughts-on-the-proposed-crime-of-ecocide-that-isnt/ (last visited Feb. 18, 2025); *Kai Ambos*, EJIL: Talk! (June 29, 2021), https://www.ejiltalk.org/protecting-the-environment-through-international-criminal-law/ (last visited Feb. 18, 2025).

eventualis in relation to the excessiveness of the damage would be required. Thus, the definition should only include one 'main' mental element relating both to the substantial risk of severe and either widespread or long-term nature of the environmental harm as well as to the cost-benefit analysis.

Thirdly, in terms of terminology concerning the mental threshold the definition should require the *awareness of a substantial likelihood*, instead of *knowledge* of a substantial likelihood, thereby clarifying that the mental threshold is lowered in contrast to Article 30 (2) (b) and (3) Rome Statute to include the concepts of advertent recklessness and *dolus eventualis*.

Thus, these modifications lead to the following definition of a potential crime against the environment under Article 8 *ter*:

Article 8 *ter*: Crime against the environment

1. For the purpose of this Statute, "crime against the environment" means any act committed with awareness that there is a substantial likelihood of severe and either widespread or long-term environmental damage being caused by those acts.[473]
2. For the purpose of paragraph 1:
   a. "Severe" means damage which involves very serious adverse changes, disruption or harm to any element of the environment, including grave impacts on human life or natural, cultural or economic resources;
   b. "Widespread" means damage which extends beyond a limited geographic area, crosses state boundaries, or is suffered by an entire ecosystem or species or a large number of human beings;
   c. "Long-term" means damage which is irreversible or which cannot be redressed through natural recovery within a reasonable period of time;
   d. "Environment" means the earth, its biosphere, cryosphere, lithosphere, hydrosphere and atmosphere, as well as outer space.

VI. Amendment to the Rome Statute

The incorporation of a fifth crime of ecocide into the Rome Statute would necessitate an amendment to Article 5 Rome Statute as well as the incorporation of an

[473] Similar *Kevin Jon Heller*, OpinioJuris (June 23, 2021), https://opiniojuris.org/2021/06/23/skeptical-thoughts-on-the-proposed-crime-of-ecocide-that-isnt/ (last visited Feb. 18, 2025) ("For the purpose of this Statute, 'ecocide' means acts committed with awareness that there is a substantial likelihood of severe and either widespread or long-term damage to the environment being caused by those acts").

additional core crime. In accordance with Article 121 (1) Rome Statute amendments can be initiated by any signatory state by submitting a proposed amendment to the Secretary-General of the United Nations. Thus, any of the 125 signatory parties could instigate such an amendment.

However, despite at least 24 ICC Member States having expressed support for the inclusion of a fifth crime of ecocide[474], none of them has yet reached out to the Secretary-General of the UN. After having submitted such a proposal, the Assembly of State parties votes on whether to take up the proposal (Article 121 (2) Rome Statute). Pursuant to Article 121 (3) Rome Statute an amendment then requires a two-thirds majority of the signatory parties to vote in favour. Alternatively, the Rome Statute can be amended at a Review Conference convened by the UN Secretary-General upon approval by a majority of State Parties (Article 123 (2) Rome Statute), as occurred in the case of the definition of the crime of aggression.

However, only States formally accepting the amendment to Article 5 of the Rome Statute would be bound by it. Similar to the aggression amendments, it is thus to be feared that countries most likely to perpetrate environmental crimes will refuse to accept the amendment.[475] At this juncture, the ratification of such a fifth crime against the environment is expected to take at least three to seven years[476], yet some lawyers consider a two-thirds majority in favour of a respective amendment to the Rome Statute completely unlikely.[477] The reasons behind the hesitance of some scholars regarding the inclusion of a fifth crime against the environment will be assessed in the following.

VII. Impediments to the enforcement of a fifth crime of ecocide

Despite the potentials of the international criminalisation of environmental destruction, the effective enforcement of a new fifth crime against the environment under the Rome Statute faces significant impediments, primarily flowing from the structure of the ICC, which palpably impede the desired goal of promoting global environmental protection.

[474] Stop Ecocide International, What We Do, https://www.stopecocide.earth/what-we-do (last visited Feb. 18, 2025).

[475] *Kevin Jon Heller*, OpinioJuris (June 23, 2021), https://opiniojuris.org/2021/06/23/skeptical-thoughts-on-the-proposed-crime-of-ecocide-that-isnt/ (last visited Feb. 18, 2025).

[476] *Mélissa Godin*, Lawyers Are Working to Put 'Ecocide' On Par with War Crimes, Could an International Law Hold Major Polluters to Account?, Time, 2021; *Sophie Yeo*, Ecocide, Should Killing Nature Be a Crime?, BBC, 2020.

[477] *Kevin Jon Heller*, OpinioJuris (June 23, 2021), https://opiniojuris.org/2021/06/23/skeptical-thoughts-on-the-proposed-crime-of-ecocide-that-isnt/ (last visited Feb. 18, 2025); *Kai Ambos*, EJIL: Talk! (June 29, 2021), https://www.ejiltalk.org/protecting-the-environment-through-international-criminal-law/ (last visited Feb. 18, 2025).

1. Jurisdictional issues

The enforcement of a fifth crime against the environment under the Rome Statute faces various jurisdictional restrictions limiting its potential to promote global environmental protection. As such, effective enforcement of a new crime of ecocide may be impeded by the temporal (*ratione temporis*) and personal (*ratione personae*) jurisdiction of the ICC.

a) Ratione temporis and the principle of non-retroactivity

Pursuant to Article 11 (1) Rome Statute the ICC "has jurisdiction only with respect to crimes committed after the entry into force of this Statute". Thus, environmentally harmful activities committed before 1 July 2002 fall outside the ICC's temporal jurisdiction. Since the Statute lacks any provision specifying the *ratione temporis* in relation to the addition of new crimes[478], it could be deduced from a literal reading of Article 11 (1) Rome Statute that perpetrators can also be convicted for a new crime of ecocide as of 1 July 2002.[479] When the crime of aggression was included into the Statute, retroactive prosecution was explicitly excluded by the Review Conference[480], as opposed to the inclusion of the new war crimes where a similar regulation was missing, which gave rise to the assumption that these crimes were prosecutable as of 1 July 2002 rather than from the date the amendment entered into force.[481] However, Article 11 (1) Rome Statute stipulating the *ratione temporis* is closely related to Article 24 and Article 22 Rome Statute, which both pertain to the temporal limits of the Statute.[482] Article 24 Rome Statute enshrines the *principle of non-retroactivity* under which a perpetrator cannot be held criminally liable under the Rome Statute for conduct which occurred prior to the Statute's entry into force.[483] Article 22 (1) Rome Statute, in turn, encapsulates the principle of *nullum crimen sine lege* stipulating that no person shall be held criminally liable under the Statute unless the behaviour in question constitutes a *crime within the jurisdiction of the Court* at the time of its commission.[484] By referring to a *crime within the jurisdiction of the Court*, Article 22 (1) Rome Statute relates to the temporal jurisdiction of the Court pursuant to Article 11 (1) Rome Statute.[485]

---

[478] *Rod Rastan/Mohamed Badar*, Article 11, Jurisdiction Ratione Temporis, in: Rome Statute of the International Criminal Court para. 14 (Kai Ambos ed., 2022).

[479] *William A. Schabas*, An Introduction to the International Criminal Court 64 (2020).

[480] Resolution RC/Res.6 of the Review Conference of the Rome Statute, Annex III, at 3, ¶ 4 (June 11, 2010).

[481] *William A. Schabas*, An Introduction to the International Criminal Court 64 (2020).

[482] *William A. Schabas*, The International Criminal Court: A Commentary on the Rome Statute 341 (2016).

[483] *Rod Rastan/Mohamed Badar*, Article 11 para. 2 (2022).

[484] Id.

[485] Id.

Thus, it is to be followed that a new crime of ecocide cannot be enforced retrospectively over environmental harm committed before the amendment entered into force, as this would clash with the *nullum crimen sine lege* maxim. This, however, is an argument that a new crime of ecocide should be incorporated sooner rather than later. Thus, if a new crime of ecocide were included into the Rome Statute, only conduct occurring after the amendment's entry into force would be prosecutable by the ICC. Environmentally destructive activities which occurred prior to the amendment's entry into force or prior to 1 July 2002 could thus only be addressed by an international ad hoc tribunal specifically tasked by the international community to adjudicate upon past conduct.[486]

Nonetheless, in the context of environmental crimes, it appears problematic that environmental degradation is rarely caused by isolated incidents but rather by a gradual accumulation of acts, such as in the case of deforestation, extractive activities, the emission of hazardous substances or greenhouse gases, which often last for decades. Thus, the question arises as to whether the new crime could cover environmentally harmful conduct which commenced prior to the amendment's entry into force and which then continues after the new Article 8 *ter* entered into force. Although, the temporal jurisdiction concerning such "continuing crimes"[487] remains unaddressed in the Rome Statute, the Elements of Crimes specify for the crime of enforced disappearance pursuant to Article 7 (1) (i) Rome Statute that both stages, meaning the individual act of enforced disappearance as a part of a widespread or systematic attack, must occur after the Statute's entry into force.[488] However, Article 8 *ter* is special to the extent that its material elements are fulfilled at the time the perpetrator commits any environmentally harmful act with the awareness that there is a substantial likelihood of severe and either widespread or long-term environmental damage being caused by those acts. Thus, by establishing endangerment liability, the material elements do not require the actual occurrence of severe and either widespread or long-term environmental damage but only the substantial risk thereof. Hence, in terms of temporal jurisdiction the ICC can only prosecute environmentally detrimental conduct which entails a substantial risk of severe and either widespread or long-term environmental damage at the time of the amendment's entry into force. However, regarding the principle of legality, which ensures that possible addressees can anticipate the proscribed conduct[489], the principle demands that at the time of the commission of the crime the perpetrator knew that the conduct in question was proscribed. Thus, if the environmental degradation in question

---

486 See for instance Art. 8 sentence 2 ICTY Statute extending the temporal jurisdiction of the Tribunal to 1 January 1991; *Rod Rastan/Mohamed Badar*, Article 11 para. 15 (2022).

487 *Rod Rastan/Mohamed Badar*, Article 11 para. 16 (2022); *William A. Schabas*, The International Criminal Court: A Commentary on the Rome Statute 342 (2016).

488 ICC Elements of Crimes, Art. 7 (1) (i) para. 1 n. 24; *Rod Rastan/Mohamed Badar*, Article 11 para. 21 (2022).

489 *Antonio Cassese*, et al., Cassese's International Criminal Law 27, 28 (2013); *Bruce Broomhall*, Article 22 para. 9 (2022).

commenced prior to the new crime's entry into force, additional acts entailing a substantial risk of severe and either widespread or long-term environmental harm must occur after Article 8 *ter* came into force. Hence, if continuous environmentally harmful conduct ceases to occur before the new crime enters into force, or if the subsequent acts after the new crime's entry into force do not exceed the threshold of a substantial risk of severe and either widespread or long-term environmental harm, these acts would fall outside the temporal jurisdiction of the ICC.

b) Ratione personae and the lack of state and corporate liability

The foundations of today's scope of personal jurisdiction (*ratione personae*) of the ICC were laid by the International Military Tribunal (*hereinafter* IMT) during the Trial of German Major War Criminals in Nuremberg in 1946, where the following was acknowledged:

> "Crimes against International Law are committed by men, not by abstract entities, and only by punishing individuals who commit such crimes can the provisions of International Law be enforced."[490]

This attitude towards the *ratione personae* was introduced into Article 25 (1) Rome Statute stipulating that the ICC "shall only have jurisdiction over natural persons". Thus, the ICC may only hold individual persons criminally liable and explicitly lacks jurisdiction over legal entities such as states or corporations.[491] In the following, it will be examined whether the lack of state and corporate criminal liability under the current Rome Statute would impede the effective enforcement of a new crime of ecocide.

aa) Exclusion of state liability

In accordance with Article 25 (1) Rome Statute, states are excluded from criminal liability under international criminal law. Article 25 (4) Rome Statute clarifies that "no provision in this Statute relating to individual criminal responsibility shall affect the responsibility of states under international law". Article 25 (4) Rome Statute therefore mirrors the clear distinction between state responsibility and individual criminal liability and emphasises that individual liability under international criminal law complements state liability under international law. In this regard, it is noteworthy that international criminal law was, at least to some extent,

---

[490] IMT, Judgment of 1 October 1946, The Trial of German Major War Criminals. Proceedings of the International Military Tribunal sitting at Nuremberg, Germany, Part 22, ¶ 447 (Aug. 22 to Oct. 1, 1946).

[491] Furthermore, neither the ICTY nor the ICTR had jurisdiction over legal persons, see Article 6 ICTY and Article 5 ICTR.

established to respond to the inadequacy of state liability.[492] In 1976, the ILC contemplated establishing state criminal responsibility for "a serious breach of an international obligation of essential importance for the safeguarding and preservation of the human environment, such as those prohibiting massive pollution of the atmosphere or of the seas".[493] However, due to a lack of consensus and conceptual problems, the idea of creating international criminal liability of states was ultimately rejected.[494] In general, criminal liability for states has always been an extremely controversial topic.[495] However, in accordance with Article 25 (4) Rome Statute, the exclusion of states from criminal liability under international criminal law does not curb other forms of state responsibility.[496] Thus, states can only be responsible for transboundary environmental harm under civil or public law. However, as explored above, state responsibility for transboundary environmental harm is very limited under current international environmental law.[497] Nevertheless, although states often contribute to environmental harm, the majority of large-scale environmental harm is caused by multinational corporations.[498] Thus, in the environmental context, the effective enforcement of a new crime of ecocide is not to the same extent impeded by the lack of state criminal liability as it may be by the lack of corporate criminal liability, which will be discussed next.

bb) Exclusion of corporate criminal liability

Besides having excluded state criminal liability in 1976, the French proposal[499] to include responsibility over legal persons into the Rome Statute was also rejected

---

[492] *Frédéric Mégret*, Les angles morts de la responsabilité pénale individuelle en droit international, 71 R.I.E.J. 83, 85 (2013); *Carsten Stahn*, A Critical Introduction to International Criminal Law 119 (2019).

[493] Report of the Commission to the General Assembly on the Work of its Twenty-Eighth Session, [1976] 2 Y.B. Int'l L. Comm'n 96, U.N. Doc. A/CN.4/SER.A/1976/Add.1 (Part 2).

[494] Report of the Commission to the General Assembly on the Work of its Fiftieth Session, [1998] 2 Y.B. Int'l L. Comm'n 77 ¶ 331, U.N. Doc. A/CN.4/SER.A/1998/Add.1 (Part 2).

[495] *Cherif M. Bassiouni*, International Crimes: The Ratione Materiae of International Criminal Law 1034 (2008); see *Sean Fleming*, Leviathan on Trial: Should States Be Held Criminally Responsible?, 13 (3) International Theory 427 (2021).

[496] *Albin Eser*, Individual Criminal Responsibility, in: The Rome Statute of the International Criminal Court: A Commentary 779 (Antonio Cassese, et al. eds., 2002).

[497] See Chapter B. I. 2. c).

[498] EUROPOL, Environmental Crime in the Age of Climate Change 7 (2022); *Emanuela Fronza*, Towards a New Crime of Ecocide 101 (2022); *Ricardo Pereira*, Criminal Law Forum 219 (2020); *Frédéric Mégret*, Colum. J. Envtl. L. 225, 226 (2011).

[499] Draft Article 23(5) of the French proposal read as follows:

"5. Without prejudice to any individual criminal responsibility of natural persons under this Statute, the Court may also have jurisdiction over a juridical person for a crime under this Statute. Charges may be filed by the Prosecutor against a juridical person, and the Court may render a judgement over a juridical person for the crime charged, if (a) The charges filed by the Prosecutor against the natural person and the juridical person allege the matters referred to in

at the 1998 Rome Conference.[500] The final proposal to include corporate criminal liability by the French delegation was restricted to private corporations, thereby precluding states and other public entities as well as non-profit organisations from criminal liability.[501] Corporate criminal liability, as proposed by the French delegation, was closely linked to individual criminal liability requiring the conviction of a leading member who exerts control over the corporation and who committed the crime on behalf of and with the consent of the corporation in the course of the company's activities.[502] Thus, the French proposal was predicated on the assumption that legal persons cannot act for themselves but only through their organs, which is why the conduct and mental element of the natural person were attributed to the corporation.[503] Despite this very limited scope of corporate liability, the French proposal was rejected due to time constraints regarding the major differences concerning corporate criminal liability in domestic criminal systems as well as a lack of political will.[504] First, it was argued that corporate criminal liability is not compatible with the ICC's inherent focus on individual criminal liability.[505]

---

subparagraphs (b) and (c); and (b) The natural person charged was in a position of control within the juridical person under the national law of the State where the juridical person was registered at the time the crime was committed; and (c) The crime was committed by the natural person acting on behalf of and with the explicit consent of that juridical person and in the course of its activities; and (d) The natural person has been convicted of the crime charged. For the purpose of this Statute, 'juridical person' means a corporation whose concrete, real or dominant objective is seeking private profit or benefit, and not a State or other public body in the exercise of State authority, a public international body or an organization registered, and acting under the national law of a state as a non-profit organization." (See U.N. Diplomatic Conference of Plenipotentiaries on the Establishment of an International Criminal Court, Working Paper on Article 23, Paragraphs 5 and 6, U.N. Doc. A/Conf.183/C.1/WGGP/L.5/Rev.2 (1998)); see for an analysis of the French proposal, *Harmen Van der Wilt*, Corporate Criminal Responsibility for International Crimes: Exploring the Possibilities, 12 (1) Chinese J. INT'l L. 43 (2013).

[500] U.N. Nations Diplomatic Conference of Plenipotentiaries on the Establishment of an International Criminal Court, Report of the Preparatory Committee on the Establishment of an International Criminal Court, at paras. 48–50, U.N. Doc. A/Conf.183/2/Add.1 (1998); *Gerhard Werle/Florian Jeßberger*, Principles of International Criminal Law para. 145 (2020); see *Andrew Clapham*, The Question of Jurisdiction under International Criminal Law Over Legal Persons: Lessons from the Rome Conference on an International Criminal Court, in: Liability of Multinational Corporations Under International Law 139 (Menno T. Kamminga/Zia-Zarifi Saman eds., 2000).

[501] U.N. Diplomatic Conference of Plenipotentiaries on the Establishment of an International Criminal Court, Working Paper on Article 23, Paragraphs 5 and 6, U.N. Doc. A/Conf.183/C.1/WGGP/L.5/Rev.2 (1998); *Kai Ambos*, Article 25, Individual Criminal Responsibility, in: Rome Statute of the International Criminal Court para. 4 (Kai Ambos ed., 2022).

[502] U.N. Diplomatic Conference of Plenipotentiaries on the Establishment of an International Criminal Court, Working Paper on Article 23, Paragraphs 5 and 6, U.N. Doc. A/Conf.183/C.1/WGGP/L.5/Rev.2 (1998); *Kai Ambos*, Article 25 para. 4 (2022).

[503] *Harmen Van der Wilt*, Chinese J. INT'l L., 47 (2013).

[504] *Kai Ambos*, Wirtschaftsvölkerstrafrecht 32, 33 (2018).

[505] *Kai Ambos*, Article 25 para. 4 (2022).

Second, the inclusion of corporate criminal liability would evoke significant evidentiary problems.[506] Third, and most importantly, it was argued that corporate criminal liability is not a commonly recognised concept, in fact, some domestic criminal law systems still do not recognise this concept, which would render the principle of complementarity obsolete.[507] Although corporate criminal liability was, once again, on the agenda at the Kampala Review Conference in 2010, the ICC Member States were too preoccupied with deciding on a definition of the crime of aggression than to re-address the matter of corporate criminal liability.[508]

(1) Individual criminal liability of business leaders

Due to the lack of corporate criminal liability under the current Rome Statute, the ICC can only prosecute business leaders for having engaged in criminal conduct on behalf of the company, whereas the company itself goes unpunished. The post-Second World War trials, including the *I.G. Farben* trial, where Nazi corporate officers such as Carl Krauch and a further 22 officials of *I.G. Farbenindustrie* were held criminally liable for war crimes, serve as a precedent for the establishment of individual criminal liability of business leaders.[509] Similarly, the ICTR held corporate executives of a media company liable for public incitement of the Rwandan genocide in 1994 instead of prosecuting the two media companies themselves.[510] In the same vein, but more recently, the ICC charged a key broadcaster of a media company in Kenya, Mr. Sang, with crimes against humanity.[511]

In attempting to translate collective responsibility into individual liability, the five most relevant modes of liability concerning individual criminal liability of business leaders are joint criminal enterprise, co-perpetration, aiding and abetting, common purpose and superior responsibility. These modes of attribution are particularly important in the corporate context as they permit the conviction of business

[506] Id.; *Albin Eser*, Individual Criminal Responsibility 779 (2002).

[507] *Kai Ambos*, Article 25 para. 4 (2022); *Albin Eser*, Individual Criminal Responsibility 779 (2002); *William A. Schabas*, The International Criminal Court: A Commentary on the Rome Statute 564–566 (2016); *David Scheffer*, Corporate Liability under the Rome Statute, 57, Harvard International Law Journal 35, 38 (2016).

[508] *Harmen Van der Wilt*, Chinese J. INT'l L., 45 (2013).

[509] US Military Tribunal Nuremberg, Judgment of 30 July 1948, in: Trials of War Criminals Before the Nuernberg Military Tribunals, Vol. VIII; see further on the IG Farben Trial as the first trial to impose individual criminal liability on corporate managers, *Florian Jeßberger*, On the Origins of Individual Criminal Responsibility under International Law for Business Activity, 8 (3) JICJ 783 (2010); see for further post-Second World War trials against Nazi business leaders *Harmen Van der Wilt*, Chinese J. INT'l L., 50–66 (2013).

[510] See Prosecutor v. Nahimana, Case No. ICTR-99–52-A, Judgment (Nov. 28, 2007).

[511] Prosecutor v. Ruto, ICC-01/09-01/11, Decision on the Confirmation of Charges Pursuant to Article 61(7)(a) and (b) of the Rome Statute, ¶ 22 (Jan. 23, 2012); however, on 5 April 2016, the charges were dropped based on evidentiary grounds. See Prosecutor v. Ruto, ICC-01/09-01/11, Decision on Defence Applications for Judgments of Acquittal, ¶ 127, 131 (Apr. 5, 2016).

leaders who remotely contributed to the commission of a crime. In the context of environmental harm, remoteness of business leaders to the crime scene plays a significant role as the bulk of environmental harm is committed by multinational corporations. As EUROPOL stated in its Threat Assessment on environmental crime in 2022: "The majority of environmental crime actors are opportunistic legal business owners/operators who decide to increase their chances of profit by establishing a criminal venture. These networks are mainly composed of low-level associates who operate under the command of few leaders, who are located far from the criminal activities"[512]. While most multinational corporations are headquartered in the Global North, the exploitation of natural resources is largely perpetrated by subsidiary companies in the Global South.[513] In the following, the suitability of these five modes of liability concerning the individual criminal liability of business leaders for environmental harm will be assessed.

(a) Joint criminal enterprise

The first relevant mode of liability in the context of individual criminal liability of business leaders is the concept of joint criminal enterprise (*hereinafter* JCE)[514], which was developed and further subdivided into three categories by the ICTY and the ICTR.[515] Although the ICC refrained from including the concept of JCE into the Rome Statute[516], this specific mode of liability deserves mentioning in the context of attributing collective criminality to individuals. The basic form of JCE, which is the only of relevance in the context of environmental harm, pertains to collective criminal activity perpetrated by a plurality of people acting together on the basis of a common plan.[517] On the objective side, *any* type of assistance[518], including an omission in case of a legal obligation to act[519], is sufficient and direct involvement

[512] EUROPOL, Environmental Crime in the Age of Climate Change 7 (2022).

[513] *Ingeborg Zerbes/Mark Pieth*, Unternehmerische Verantwortlichkeit für Völkerrechtsverbrechen im Ausland, 51 (1) Kritische Justiz 67, 67 (2018).

[514] *Kai Ambos*, Wirtschaftsvölkerstrafrecht 60 (2018); *Norman Farrell*, JICJ 878 (2010); *Hans Vest*, Business Leaders and the Modes of Individual Criminal Responsibility under International Law, 8 (3) JICJ 851, 868 (2010).

[515] Prosecutor v. Tadić, Case No. IT-94-1-A, Judgement, ¶ 185–228 (July 15, 1999).

[516] *Christoph Safferling*, Internationales Strafrecht § 5 para. 77 (2011).

[517] Prosecutor v. Tadić, Case No. IT-94-1-A, Judgement, ¶ 227, 228 (July 15, 1999); *Kai Ambos*, Article 25 para. 10 (2022).

[518] The ad hoc Tribunals opined that "although the contribution need not be necessary or substantial, it should at least be a significant contribution to the crimes for which the accused is to be found responsible" (Prosecutor v. Brdanin, Case No. IT-99-36-A, Judgement, ¶ 430 (Apr. 3, 2007); see also Prosecutor v. Prlić, IT-04-74-A, Judgement, Volume II, ¶ 2768 (Nov. 29, 2017); *Gerhard Werle/Florian Jeßberger*, Principles of International Criminal Law para. 627 (2020).

[519] Prosecutor v. Milutinović, Case No. IT-05-87-T, Judgement, Volume 1 of 4, ¶ 103 (Feb. 26, 2009); Prosecutor v. Prlić, Case No. IT-04-74-A, Judgement, Volume II, ¶ 1394 (Nov. 29, 2017).

of the participant is not necessarily required.[520] However, on the subjective side the basic form of joint criminal enterprise entails a high mental threshold presupposing the shared intent of all co-perpetrators to commit the underlying crimes according to the common plan.[521] If both material and mental elements are fulfilled, each participant is held criminally liable as a perpetrator of the crime irrespective of his or her level of contribution.[522] In the context of environmental harm, the concept of JCE may, for instance, become relevant in cases where corporate agents colluded with government officials to impede the clean-up of large areas contaminated by oil and gas extraction activities; a scenario which has been occurring in the Niger Delta for decades.[523] However, the main challenge of securing a conviction of a business leader on the basic form of JCE is to prove the direct intent of all co-perpetrators to commit the underlying crimes according to the common plan. Due to the high mental threshold, which is significantly higher than the one for aiders and abettors, convicting corporate officials for engaging in a joint criminal enterprise appears rather unlikely.[524]

(b) Co-perpetration, Article 25 (3) (a) second alternative Rome Statute

Furthermore, corporate officials could be prosecuted for co-perpetration pursuant to Article 25 (3) (a) second alternative Rome Statute. In contrast to mere accessories under Article 25 (3) (b), (c), (d) Rome Statute, co-perpetrators are principals exerting 'joint control' over the crime. [525] Co-perpetration requires the functional distribution of tasks between at least two co-perpetrators usually on the basis of a common plan.[526] Besides the existence of a common plan or agreement of at least two persons, on the objective side, co-perpetration further requires an 'essential contribution' of each co-perpetrator to the crime requiring that "each co-perpetrator could frustrate the joint commission of the crime by not carrying out his

[520] Prosecutor v. Milutinović, Case No. IT-05-87-T, Judgement, Volume 1 of 4, ¶ 103 (Feb. 26, 2009); Prosecutor v. Krajišnik, Case No. IT-00-39-A, Judgement, ¶ 663 (Mar. 17, 2009).

[521] Prosecutor v. Tadić, Case No. IT-94-1-A, Judgement, ¶ 196, 220 (July 15, 1999); Prosecutor v. Prlić, Case No. IT-04-74-A, Judgement, Volume II, ¶ 2008 (Nov. 29, 2017); *Kai Ambos*, Article 25 para. 10 (2022); *Gerhard Werle/Florian Jeßberger*, Principles of International Criminal Law para. 629 (2020).

[522] *Gerhard Werle/Florian Jeßberger*, Principles of International Criminal Law para. 629 (2020).

[523] Amnesty International, No clean up, no justice: Shell's oil pollution in the Niger Delta (2020), https://www.amnesty.org/en/latest/news/2020/06/no-clean-up-no-justice-shell-oil-pollution-in-the-niger-delta/ (last visited Feb. 18, 2025).

[524] Similar *Norman Farrell*, JICJ 879 (2010); *Hans Vest*, JICJ 869 (2010).

[525] Prosecutor v. Katanga, Decision on the Confirmation of Charges, ICC-01/04-01/07, ¶ 480–484 (Sept. 30, 2008); Prosecutor v. Lubanga, ICC-01/04-01/06, Decision on the Confirmation of Charges, ¶ 338, 341 (Jan. 29, 2007); Prosecutor v. Katanga, ICC-01/04-01/07, Decision on the Confirmation of Charges, ¶ 486 (Sept. 30, 2008).

[526] *Kai Ambos*, Article 25 para. 9 (2022).

or her task"[527]. Thus, the requisite 'joint control' over the commission of the crime distinguishes perpetration under Article 25 (3) (a) Rome Statute from mere assistance under Article 25 (3) (b) to (d) Rome Statute.[528] On the subjective side, each co-perpetrator has to personally satisfy all mental elements required by the envisaged crime.[529] If the material and mental elements are met, objective contributions forming part of the common plan are reciprocally attributed to the other co-perpetrators ensuring that all co-perpetrators can be held liable for the entire crime.[530] Nonetheless, in the context of multinational corporations, it appears unlikely from a legal and evidentiary perspective that corporate officials exert the requisite control over the crime, which would distinguish them from mere assistants.[531]

In the case of *Katanga and Ngudjolo Chui*, the Pre-Trial Chamber combined the concepts of co-perpetration and indirect perpetration, so called 'indirect co-perpetration'.[532] This mode of liability relates to cases "in which the perpetrator behind the perpetrator commits the crime through another by means of 'control over an organisation' (*Organisationsherrschaft*)".[533] As elaborated by the Pre-Trial Chamber, this mode of attribution requires a hierarchical organisation where the indirect perpetrator's orders are automatically abided by interchangeable executors.[534] This type of liability was originally established to create individual criminal liability for high-ranking leaders, especially heads of states, by replacing the concept of joint criminal enterprise through a new mode of liability.[535]

---

[527] *Gerhard Werle/Florian Jeßberger*, Principles of International Criminal Law para. 640 (2020).

[528] Prosecutor v. Lubanga, ICC-01/04-01/06, Judgment Pursuant to Article 74 of the Statute, ¶ 996–1000 (Mar. 14, 2012); Prosecutor v. Lubanga, ICC-01/04-01/06 A 5, Judgment on the Appeal of Mr. Thomas Lubanga Dyilo Against His Conviction, ¶ 469 (Dec. 1, 2014).

[529] Prosecutor v. Lubanga, ICC-01/04-01/06, Decision on the Confirmation of Charges, ¶ 349 (Jan. 29, 2007).

[530] Id. at ¶ 326; *Kai Ambos*, Article 25 para. 9 (2022).

[531] Similar *Norman Farrell*, JICJ 880 (2010); *Hans Vest*, JICJ 869 (2010); *Frank Meyer*, Schweizerische Zeitschrift für Strafrecht 69 (2013); *Kai Ambos*, Wirtschaftsvölkerstrafrecht 60 (2018).

[532] Prosecutor v. Katanga, ICC-01/04-01/07, Decision on the Confirmation of Charges, ¶ 494–518 (Sept. 30, 2008); confirmed in Prosecutor v. Ongwen, ICC-02/04-01/15, Trial Judgment, ¶ 2786 (Feb. 4, 2021); see further on 'indirect perpetration' *Kai Ambos*, Article 25 paras. 14–19 (2022); *William A. Schabas*, The International Criminal Court: A Commentary on the Rome Statute 572 (2016); *Joanna Kyriakakis*, Developments in International Criminal Law and the Case of Business Involvement in International Crimes, 94 (887) IRRC 981, 992–997 (2012); *Stefano Manacorda/Chantal Meloni*, Indirect Perpetration versus Joint Criminal Enterprise, 9 (1) JICJ 159 (2011).

[533] Prosecutor v. Katanga, ICC-01/04-01/07, Decision on the Confirmation of Charges, ¶ 498 (Sept. 30, 2008).

[534] Id. at ¶ 512–517; *Kai Ambos*, Article 25 para. 14 (2022).

[535] See *Stefano Manacorda/Chantal Meloni*, JICJ (2011).

However, it appears difficult to read legal entities into the term "through another person" in Article 25 (3) (a) third alternative Rome Statute.[536] Furthermore, similar to 'normal' co-perpetration, this type of liability is predicated on the 'control over the crime' doctrine.[537] Any doctrine of indirect perpetration over completely responsible direct perpetrators, including the *Organisationsherrschaftslehre* developed by German law theorist Claus Roxin, faces the challenge of determining whether the indirect perpetrator exercised the requisite degree of control, similar to the one in Article 28 Rome Statute, over the fully responsible direct perpetrator.[538] Particularly in the context of corporations, depending on the vertical organisational structure of the corporation, it appears unlikely that business leaders exercise the necessary degree of control over the employees directly perpetrating the crime.[539] In particular, multinational corporations tend to be organised horizontally rather than vertically encompassing numerous legally independent business entities.[540]

Thus, due to the control requirement both alternatives of co-perpetration, direct and indirect co-perpetration, under Article 25 (3) (a) Rome Statute are not suitable modes of liability to establish individual criminal liability for business leaders.

(c) Assistance, Article 25 (3) (c) Rome Statute

Instead of exercising joint control over the crime, it seems more likely that business leaders of the parent company remotely assist the commission of the crime, which is directly perpetrated by employees of the subsidiary company located somewhere in the Global South. In this regard, the International Commission of Jurists Expert Legal Panel on Corporate Complicity in International Crimes held that "a company official who knows that his acts will facilitate, encourage or provide moral support for the commission of a crime and nonetheless proceeds, will be in grave danger of being held criminally accountable for aiding and abetting".[541] Thus, managers of the partner company (assistants) assisting employees of a subsidiary company (principals) to commit environmental harm could be held criminally liable for assistance under Article 25 (3) (c) Rome Statute. On the objective side, the wording of Article 25 (3) (c) Rome Statute implies that assistance under Article 25 (3) (c) Rome Statute includes *any* act assisting the crime committed by a

---

[536] Prosecutor v. Ngudjolo, ICC-01/04-02/12, Judgment Pursuant to Article 74 of the Statute, Concurring Opinion of Judge Christine Van den Wyngaert, ¶ 52, 53 (Dec. 18, 2012).

[537] Prosecutor v. Katanga, ICC-01/04-01/07, Decision on the Confirmation of Charges, ¶ 494 (Sept. 30, 2008).

[538] *Kai Ambos*, Article 25 para. 18 (2022); *Joanna Kyriakakis*, IRRC, 995 (2012).

[539] *Kai Ambos*, Wirtschaftsvölkerstrafrecht 60 (2018); *Joanna Kyriakakis*, IRRC, 995 (2012); *Kai Ambos*, Article 25 para. 19 (2022) (advocating the modification of the current modes of individual attribution under the Rome Statute by establishing a system of 'organizational domination in stages').

[540] *Joanna Kyriakakis*, IRRC, 995 (2012).

[541] International Commission of Jurists, Report of the International Commission of Jurists Expert Legal Panel on Corporate Complicity in International Crimes, Volume 2, 22 (2008).

principal. While the ad hoc tribunals required the act of assistance to have a *substantial* effect on the commission of the crime[542], it is disputed whether this substantiality requirement should be read into Article 25 (3) (c) Rome Statute, which itself does not contain such an objective limitation.[543] However, scholars widely concur that the act of assistance must have a *substantial effect* due to Article 17 (1) (d) Rome Statute, which requires the act of assistance to be sufficiently grave.[544] By contrast, the ICC recently denied the necessity of the substantiality requirement for two reasons on several occasions: first, lawmakers explicitly refrained from including a substantiality threshold into Article 25 (3) (c) Rome Statute, and, second, the scope of Article 25 (3) (c) Rome Statute is sufficiently restricted by the high mental threshold ('for the purpose of') and thus does not need further objective limitation in the sense of a substantiality requirement.[545] Thus, the objective pre-

[542] Prosecutor v. Blagojević, Case No. IT-02-60-A, Judgement, ¶ 127 (May 9, 2007); Prosecutor v. Simić, Case No. IT-95-9-A, Judgement, ¶ 85 (Nov. 28, 2006); Prosecutor v. Blaškić, Case No. IT-95-14-A, Judgement, ¶ 45, 46 (July 29, 2004); Prosecutor v. Vasiljević, Case No. IT-98-32-A, Judgement, ¶ 102 (Feb. 25, 2004); Prosecutor v. Ntagerura, Case No. ICTR-99-46-A, Judgement, ¶ 370 (July 7, 2006).

[543] In favour Prosecutor v. Lubanga, ICC-01/04-01/06, Judgment Pursuant to Article 74 of the Statute, ¶ 997 (Mar. 14, 2012); Prosecutor v. Mbarushimana, ICC-01/04-01/10, Decision on the Confirmation of Charges, ¶ 281 (Dec. 16, 2011); Prosecutor v. Ruto, ICC-01/09-01/11, Decision on the Confirmation of Charges Pursuant to Article 61 (7)(a) and (b) of the Rome Statute, ¶ 354 (Jan. 23, 2012); contra Prosecutor v. Bemba, ICC-01/05-01/13, Judgment Pursuant to Article 74 of the Statute, ¶ 93–95 (Oct. 19, 2016) (however, the Chamber referred to 'substantial contribution' instead of 'substantial effect'); Prosecutor v. Bemba, ICC-01/05-01/13 A A2 A3 A4 A5, Judgment on the Appeals of Mr. Jean-Pierre Bemba Gombo, Mr. Aimé Kilolo Musamba, Mr. Jean-Jacques Mangenda Kabongo, Mr. Fidèle Babala Wandu and Mr. Narcisse Arido Against the Decision of Trial Chamber VII Entitled "Judgment Pursuant to Article 74 of the Statute", ¶ 1326 (Mar. 8, 2018); pro *Kai Ambos*, Article 25 paras. 25–33 (2022) ("At any rate, taking all case law together, it is safe to say that aiding and abetting encompasses, […] any assistance […], that has a substantial effect on the commission of the crime", para. 32); pro *Gerhard Werle*, Individual Criminal Responsibility in Article 25 ICC Statute, 5 JICJ 953, 969 (2007) ("The wording of Article 25 (3) (c) does not require that the assistance has a substantial effect on the commission of the crime. However, within the ICC Statute's framework of modes of participation, it is reasonable to interpret the actus reus of assistance in this way"); pro *Albin Eser*, Individual Criminal Responsibility 800, 801 (2002) ("[B]oth the ICTY and the ICTR were prepared to read [the substantiality requirement] into the relevant Statutes. Similarly, the formulation of aiding and abetting in the Rome Statute might be interpreted in the same way", p. 800); pro *Hans Vest*, JICJ 860 (2010) ("Accordingly, this author suggests following the example of the ad hoc tribunals that […] have read the substantial requirement into the respective statutory provisions on individual responsibility"); contra *Christoph Safferling*, Internationales Strafrecht § 5 para. 85 (2011).

[544] *Hans Vest*, JICJ 860 (2010); *Kai Ambos*, Article 25 para. 32 (2022); *Kai Ambos*, Wirtschaftsvölkerstrafrecht 62 (2018); International Commission of Jurists, Report of the International Commission of Jurists Expert Legal Panel on Corporate Complicity in International Crimes, Volume 2, 17–19 (2008).

[545] Prosecutor v. Bemba, ICC-01/05-01/13, Judgment Pursuant to Article 74 of the Statute, ¶ 93–95 (Oct. 19, 2016); Prosecutor v. Ongwen, ICC-02/04-01/15, Decision on the Confirmation of Charges Against Dominic Ongwen, ¶ 43 (Mar. 23, 2016); siminlar *Christoph Safferling*, Internationales Strafrecht § 5 para. 85 (2011).

requisites of Article 25 (3) (c) Rome Statute still remain disputed. Due to the sufficient limitation on the subjective side, it appears necessary to include *any* act of assistance under Article 25 (3) (c) Rome Statute in order to avoid the provision from becoming too narrow. Since assistance under Article 25 (3) (c) Rome Statute does not require the physical presence of the assistant and can be committed through active conduct or an omission[546], corporate officials of the remote partner company headquartered in the Global North could undoubtedly assist the crime through moral support and encouragement or through the lack of action to prevent or cease the environmental harm in question.

On the subjective side, it is necessary that the corporate official knew that his or her act assisted in the perpetration of the crime by the principal. Thus, the corporate official is required to have knowledge of the principal's crime as well as his or her assistance thereto ('double intent').[547] Additionally, Article 25 (3) (c) Rome Statute requires the assistance to occur "[f]or the purpose of facilitating the commission of [the] crime". 'Purpose' in this sense goes beyond mere knowledge requiring the perpetrator to know and wish that his contribution facilitates the commission of the crime.[548] Thus, in deviation to Article 30 (1) Rome Statute, the mental threshold is significantly elevated by requiring direct intent to *facilitate* the commission of the crime.[549] Since most business leaders act for economic purposes and not with the direct intent to facilitate the commission of a crime, such as the destruction of the environment, the majority of prosecutions of business leaders under Article 25 (3) (c) Rome Statute would fail due to the significantly high mental threshold.[550] This holds particularly true for business-related neutral acts[551], which are per se not criminal and exclusively committed for economic purposes.[552] Thus, the purpose

[546] *Kai Ambos*, Article 25 para. 29 (2022); *Gerhard Werle/Florian Jeßberger*, Principles of International Criminal Law para. 671 (2020).

[547] Prosecutor v. Bemba, ICC-01/05-01/13, Judgment Pursuant to Article 74 of the Statute, ¶ 97 (Oct. 19, 2016) ("twofold intent of the accessory").

[548] *Kai Ambos*, Article 25 para. 34 (2022); *Albin Eser*, Individual Criminal Responsibility 801 (2002).

[549] *Kai Ambos*, Article 25 para. 34 (2022); *Christoph Safferling*, Internationales Strafrecht § 5 para. 85 (2011); *Albin Eser*, Individual Criminal Responsibility 801 (2002).

[550] *Hans Vest*, JICJ 862, 863 (2010); *Christoph Burchard*, Ancillary and Neutral Business Contributions to 'Corporate-Political Core Crime', 8 (3) JICJ 919, 939–941 (2010).

[551] See for more detailed analyses of the difficulties concerning individual criminal liability of corporations for neutral acts in international criminal law, *Kai Ambos*, Wirtschaftsvölkerstrafrecht 62–78 (2018); *Christoph Burchard*, JICJ (2010); *Simon M. Meisenberg*, Auf dem Wege zu einem Unternehmensvölkerstrafrecht? 81–86 (2016).

[552] *Frank Meyer*, Schweizerische Zeitschrift für Strafrecht 70 (2013); *Simon M. Meisenberg*, Auf dem Wege zu einem Unternehmensvölkerstrafrecht? 82 (2016); *Christoph Burchard*, JICJ 941 (2010); contra *Kai Ambos*, Article 25 para. 33 (adapting an objective approach by arguing that in order to constitute a crime neutral acts must increase a risk, which causally contributed to the commission of the crime) (2022); similar *Hans Vest*, JICJ 864 (sympathising with the objective approach arguing that neutral acts only constitute a crime if they increase a prohibited risk) (2010).

test renders Article 25 (3) (c) Rome Statute too restrictive, thereby impeding the successful prosecution of business leaders as assistants to environmental crimes.[553]

(d) Contribution to a group crime, Article 25 (3) (d) Rome Statute

However, if the corporate official does not possess the requisite intent to facilitate the commission of the crime under Article 25 (3) (c) Rome Statute, he or she may also be held criminally liable under Article 25 (3) (d) Rome Statute[554], the objectively lowest mode of participation[555] covering any contribution to a group crime predicated on a 'common purpose'.[556] Although referring to a 'common purpose' Article 25 (3) (d) Rome Statute is reminiscent of the ICTY's definition of a joint criminal enterprise, the drafters of the Rome Statute intended to include a new mode of liability[557], which is subsidiary to the other modes of participation, by incorporating Article 25 (3) (d) into the Rome Statute.[558] While in the case of a joint criminal enterprise the participants are liable for all crimes falling within the common purpose, under Article 25 (3) (d) Rome Statute perpetrators can only be held liable for the crimes to whose commission they actually contributed.[559]

On the objective side, the perpetrator must physically or morally assist the (attempted) commission of a group crime acting upon a common purpose.[560] Thus, as opposed to Article 25 (3) (c) Rome Statute, Article 25 (3) (d) Rome Statute only

---

[553] *Kai Ambos*, Wirtschaftsvölkerstrafrecht 71, 72 (2018); *Frank Meyer*, Schweizerische Zeitschrift für Strafrecht 71 (2013); *Christoph Burchard*, JICJ 940, 941 (2010); *Norman Farrell*, JICJ 885–889 (arguing that the purpose test is not acknowledged under international customary law) (2010).

[554] In favour *Norman Farrell*, JICJ 880, 881 (2010); contra *Christoph Burchard*, JICJ 941–945 (2010); contra *Frank Meyer*, Schweizerische Zeitschrift für Strafrecht 70, 71 (2013); see for more sources on the discussion concerning the application of Article 25 (3) (d) Rome Statute to business leaders, *Kai Ambos*, Article 25 para. 36 fn. 255 (2022).

[555] Prosecutor v. Ruto, ICC-01/09-01/11, Decision on the Confirmation of Charges Pursuant to Article 61(7)(a) and (b) of the Rome Statute, ¶ 354 (Jan. 23, 2012); *Gerhard Werle/ Florian Jeßberger*, Principles of International Criminal Law para. 675 (2020); *Kai Ambos*, Article 25 para. 37 (2022).

[556] *Kai Ambos*, Article 25 para. 36 (2022); *Gerhard Werle/Florian Jeßberger*, Principles of International Criminal Law para. 676 (2020).

[557] Prosecutor v. Mbarushimana, ICC-01/04-01/10, Decision on the Confirmation of Charges, ¶ 282 (Dec. 16, 2011).

[558] Prosecutor v. Katanga, ICC-01/04-01/07, Judgment Pursuant to Article 74 of the Statute, ¶ 1618 (Mar. 7, 2014) ("residual form of accessoryship"); Prosecutor v. Lubanga, ICC-01/04-01/06, Decision on the Confirmation of Charges, ¶ 337 (Jan. 29, 2007) ("residual form of accessory liability"); Prosecutor v. Ruto, ICC-01/09-01/11, Decision on the Confirmation of Charges Pursuant to Article 61(7)(a) and (b) of the Rome Statute, ¶ 354 (Jan. 23, 2012) ("residual mode of accessorial liability").

[559] Prosecutor v. Katanga, ICC-01/04-01/07, Judgment Pursuant to Article 74 of the Statute, ¶ 1619 (Mar. 7, 2014).

[560] *Christoph Safferling*, Internationales Strafrecht § 5 para. 87 (2011).

pertains to crimes committed by a group and not by one principal.[561] Although the wording of Article 25 (3) (d) Rome Statute requiring a contribution "[i]n any other way" insinuates that *any* contribution is deemed sufficient under the provision, the ICC clarified that the contribution needs to be "at least significant"[562], meaning that "it had a bearing on the occurrence of the crime and/or the manner of its commission"[563]. Case law further elucidates that Article 25 (3) (d) Rome Statute is a catch-all clause, which is only triggered if Article 25 (3) (a)-(c) Rome Statute are not fulfilled.[564] Thus, the significance standard must be lower than the substantiality standard applied to Article 25 (3) (c) Rome Statute.[565] The mental threshold of Article 25 (3) (d) Rome Statute is two-fold. For one, it requires an 'intentional' contribution, which presupposes intent in the sense of Article 30 (2) (a) Rome Statute, meaning a voluntary act.[566] Additionally, Article 25 (3) (d) Rome Statute requires the perpetrator to act disjunctively either (i) with the aim of furthering the criminal activity or criminal purpose of the group, or (ii) in the knowledge of the intention of the group to commit the crime.

Thus, in contrast to Article 25 (3) (a) Rome Statute, the perpetrator need not have the intent to commit the underlying crime or to personally fulfil the mental elements of the envisaged crime.[567] In distinction to Article 25 (3) (c) Rome Statute, only the second alternative, Article 25 (3) (d) (ii) Rome Statute, becomes relevant. If the perpetrator contributes to the group crime with the aim of furthering the criminal activity or criminal purpose and thus fulfils Article 25 (3) (d) (i) Rome Statute, the perpetrator most likely assisted the crime with the intent to facilitate the commission of the crime and therefore satisfies the mental element of Article 25 (3) (c) Rome

---

561 Id.

562 Prosecutor v. Mbarushimana, ICC-01/04-01/10, Decision on the Confirmation of Charges, ¶ 283 (Dec. 16, 2011); see also Prosecutor v. Katanga, ICC-01/04-01/07, Judgment Pursuant to Article 74 of the Statute, ¶ 1632, 1633 (Mar. 7, 2014).

563 Prosecutor v. Katanga, ICC-01/04-01/07, Judgment Pursuant to Article 74 of the Statute, ¶ 1633 (Mar. 7, 2014); contra Prosecutor v. Mbarushimana, ICC-01/04-01/10 OA 4, Judgment on the Appeal of the Prosecutor Against the Decision of Pre-Trial Chamber I of 16 December 2011 Entitled "Decision on the Confirmation of Charges", Separate Opinion of Judge Silvia Fernández de Gurmendi, ¶ 9 (May 30, 2012) ("The phrase 'in any other way' indicates that there should not be a minimum threshold or level of contribution under this mode of liability").

564 Prosecutor v. Ruto, ICC-01/09-01/11, Decision on the Confirmation of Charges Pursuant to Article 61(7)(a) and (b) of the Rome Statute, ¶ 354 (Jan. 23, 2012).

565 Prosecutor v. Ruto, ICC-01/09-01/11, Decision on the Confirmation of Charges Pursuant to Article 61(7)(a) and (b) of the Rome Statute, ¶ 354 (Jan. 23, 2012); see also Prosecutor v. Mbarushimana, ICC-01/04-01/10, Decision on the Confirmation of Charges, ¶ 282 (Dec. 16, 2011) (arguing that "JCE requires a lower threshold of contribution than aiding and abetting at the *ad hoc* tribunals").

566 *Christoph Safferling*, Internationales Strafrecht § 5 para. 88 (2011).

567 Prosecutor v. Mbarushimana, ICC-01/04-01/10, Decision on the Confirmation of Charges, ¶ 289 (Dec. 16, 2011).

Statute.[568] In this case, the perpetrator can only be convicted for assistance under Article 25 (3) (c) Rome Statute, as Article 25 (3) (d) (i) Rome Statute is subsidiary. However, while assistance under Article 25 (3) (c) Rome Statute always requires intent, mere knowledge is sufficient under Article 25 (3) (d) (ii) Rome Statute.[569] Thus, a perpetrator lacking the requisite specific intent to facilitate the commission of the crime may still be held criminally liable under Article 25 (3) (d) (ii) Rome Statute.[570] Hence, in the context of individual criminal liability of business leaders, Article 25 (3) (d) (ii) Rome Statute appears to be the most relevant mode of liability.[571]

However, although Article 25 (3) (d) Rome Statute establishes a significantly lower mental threshold than Article 25 (3) (c) Rome Statute, it appears unlikely to be able to prove the requisite awareness of a corporate official, who is located thousands of miles away at the partner company somewhere in the Global North, of the intention of the employees at the subsidiary company to cause large-scale environmental harm, particularly in the case of neutral business-related acts.[572] While low-level corporate managers most likely lack the requisite mental element as they are "only a small cog in a large wheel"[573], high-level corporate officials will deny knowledge, claiming that the individuals acted on their own in violation of company rules.[574] In many cases, corporate officials will have only acted with 'wilful blindness' regarding the environmental crimes committed by the subsidiary company, which does not fulfil the mental requirement of Article 25 (3) (d) Rome Statute. Additionally, with regards to Article 25 (3) Rome Statute, Judge Tarfusser rightly observed that "both the legal doctrine, and, more significantly, the relevant case law of the Court show that its interpretation is far from being uncontentious or settled"[575], but rather that the precise requirements of each different mode of liability, the delimitation of perpetration and participation, and thus the existence of a hier-

[568] *Christoph Safferling*, Internationales Strafrecht § 5 para. 88 (2011).

[569] Prosecutor v. Mbarushimana, ICC-01/04-01/10, Decision on the Confirmation of Charges, ¶ 289 (Dec. 16, 2011); *William A. Schabas*, The International Criminal Court: A Commentary on the Rome Statute 582 (2016).

[570] *Kai Ambos*, Article 25 para. 58 (2022); *Hans Vest*, JICJ 865 (2010) (referring to Article 25 (3) (d) (ii) Rome Statute as a 'rescue clause').

[571] Contra *Frank Meyer*, Schweizerische Zeitschrift für Strafrecht 70, 71 (2013); *Christoph Burchard*, JICJ 942–945 (2010).

[572] See *Christoph Burchard*, JICJ 944 (2010).

[573] *Thomas Weigend*, Societas Delinquere Non Potest? A German Perspective, 6 (5) JICJ 927, 932 (2008).

[574] Id.

[575] Prosecutor v. Katanga, ICC-01/04-01/07 OA 13, Judgment on the Appeal of Mr Germain Katanga Against the Decision of Trial Chamber II of 21 November 2012 Entitled "Decision on the Implementation of Regulation 55 of the Regulations of the Court and Severing the Charges Against the Accused Persons", Dissenting Opinion of Judge Cuno Tarfusser, ¶ 15 (Mar. 27, 2013).

archy amongst the different modes of liability presumably with Article 25 (3) (a) Rome Statute at its peak, remain disputed.[576]

(e) Superior responsibility, Article 28 (b) Rome Statute

Besides Article 25 (3) Rome Statute business leaders may further become criminally liable under Article 28 (b) Rome Statute which stipulates superior responsibility for civilian superiors such as business leaders. The concept of superior responsibility is firmly acknowledged in customary international law[577] and has already been reflected in Article 7 (3) ICTY Statute and Article 6 (3) ICTR Statute. Thus, in the following reference will be made both to the case law of the ICC as well as that of the *ad hoc* tribunals in order to outline the peculiarities of superior responsibility. There have already been a number of convictions of business leaders on the basis of superior responsibility, including, for instance, the leader of a tea factory for having failed to control his employees[578], or the operator of a radio station for the hate speech disseminated by his employees.[579]

In the case of superior responsibility, superiors are not punished for the crimes of their subordinates but for their failure to perform their duty to prevent or repress the crimes of their subordinates.[580] While Article 28 Rome Statute clearly establishes omission liability, which is unique to the Rome Statute[581], the legal character of superior responsibility remains contentious.[582] However, in relation to the above-

[576] See for instance Judge Christine Van den Wyngaert criticising the ICC's reliance on the German 'control over the crime' theory to distinguish the different modes of liability, Prosecutor v. Ngudjolo, ICC-01/04-02/12, Judgment Pursuant to Article 74 of the Statute, Concurring Opinion of Judge Christine Van den Wyngaert, ¶ 4–20 (Dec. 18, 2012); similar *Christoph Safferling*, Internationales Strafrecht § 5 para. 77 (criticises that the ICC draws upon the German 'Tatherrschaftslehre', which is not even a recognised doctrine in German jurisprudence, to delimitate co-perpetration from other forms of assistance (2011); *William A. Schabas*, The International Criminal Court: A Commentary on the Rome Statute 567, 568 (2016).

[577] Prosecutor v. Mucić, Case No. IT-96-21-A, Judgement, ¶ 195 (Feb. 20, 2001).

[578] Prosecutor v. Musema, Case No. ICTR-96-13-T, Judgement and Sentence (Jan. 27, 2000).

[579] Prosecutor v. Nahimana, Case No. ICTR-99-52-T, Judgement and Sentence (Dec. 3, 2003).

[580] Prosecutor v. Krnokelac, Case No. IT-97-25-A, Judgement, ¶ 171 (Sept. 17, 2003).

[581] *Roberta Arnold/Miles Jackson*, Article 28 para. 6 (2022); *William A. Schabas*, The International Criminal Court: A Commentary on the Rome Statute 563 (2016); *Albin Eser*, Individual Criminal Responsibility 818, 819 (2002).

[582] *Roberta Arnold/Miles Jackson*, Article 28 paras. 6–16 (2022); *Gerhard Werle/Florian Jeßberger*, Principles of International Criminal Law paras. 683–685 (2020); *Antonio Cassese*, et al., Cassese's International Criminal Law 191, 192 (2013); *William A. Schabas*, The International Criminal Court: A Commentary on the Rome Statute 610, 611 (2016).

mentioned modes of liability under Article 25 (3) Rome Statute, Article 25 (3) Rome Statute takes precedence over Article 28 Rome Statute.[583]

Article 28 (b) Rome Statute entails four prerequisites: (a) the mental element, (b) the superior-subordinate relationship, and (c) the superior's failure to take all necessary and reasonable measures and (d) the commission of crimes by the subordinates as a result of the superior's violation of his duty of control.[584] With respect to business leaders the first two prerequisites appear particularly problematic and thus require further examination.

Firstly, on the subjective side, Article 28 (b) (i) Rome Statute requires that "[t]he superior either knew or consciously disregarded information which clearly indicated, that the subordinates were committing or about to commit such crimes". By presupposing that the superior 'either knew or consciously disregarded' such information, the mental threshold contained in Article 28 (b) Rome Statute is more stringent than the one for military superiors in Article 28 (a) Rome Statute [585] and can be referred to as 'wilful blindness', which can be considered a form of *dolus eventualis* or recklessness.[586] The Appeals Chamber of the ICTY elucidated that "sufficiently alarming information putting a superior on notice of the risk that crimes *might* subsequently be carried out by his subordinates and justifying further inquiry is sufficient to hold a superior liable"[587] on the basis of superior responsibility. Although Article 28 (b) Rome Statute contains the lowest mental threshold of all modes of liability discussed in the context of business leaders falling below the one contained in Article 25 (3) (c) and Article 25 (3) (d) Rome Statute, it still appears difficult to prove that business leaders of transnational corporations working for the partner firm in the Global North either knew or consciously disregarded

[583] See in relation to the Statute of the International Tribunal for the Former Yugoslavia, Prosecutor v. Blaškić, Case No. IT-95-14-A, Judgment, para. 91 (July 29, 2014); Prosecutor v. Kordić, Case No. IT-95-14/2-A, Judgement, ¶ 34 (Dec. 17, 2004); *Gerhard Werle/Florian Jeßberger*, Principles of International Criminal Law para. 685 (2020); *William A. Schabas*, The International Criminal Court: A Commentary on the Rome Statute 611, 612 (2016).

[584] *Gerhard Werle/Florian Jeßberger*, Principles of International Criminal Law para. 686 (2020).

[585] *Roberta Arnold/Miles Jackson*, Article 28 paras. 82, 83 (2022); *Kai Ambos*, Treatise 319 (2021); *Gerhard Werle/Florian Jeßberger*, Principles of International Criminal Law para. 699 (2020); *William A. Schabas*, The International Criminal Court: A Commentary on the Rome Statute 617 (2016); *Antonio Cassese*, et al., Cassese's International Criminal Law 190 (2013); *Hans Vest*, JICJ 870 (2010); *Kai Ambos*, Superior Responsibility 870 (2002).

[586] *Kai Ambos*, Superior Responsibility 870 (2002); *Kai Ambos*, Treatise 319 (2021); *Thomas Weigend*, ZStW 1024 (2004); *William A. Schabas*, The International Criminal Court: A Commentary on the Rome Statute 617 (2016); *Gerhard Werle/Florian Jeßberger*, Principles of International Criminal Law para. 699 ('greater degree of negligence') (2020).

[587] Prosecutor v. Strugar, Case No. IT-01-42-A, Judgement, ¶ 304 (July 17, 2008) (emphasis added).

information indicating the commission of crimes by corporate actors in the Global South.[588]

Secondly, concerning the requisite superior-subordinate relationship, Article 28 (b) Rome Statute requires the subordinates to be under the superior's "effective authority and control". According to Pre-Trial Chamber II 'authority' denotes the "power or right to give orders and enforce obedience"[589]. The concept of 'effective control' presupposes the superior has the "material capacity to prevent or punish the criminal conduct of subordinates"[590]; yet the capacity to exert influence, even if such influence is substantial, is not sufficient.[591] Rather, in order to have effective control the superior must have "the ability *de jure* or *de facto* to issue orders to prevent an offence and to sanction the perpetrators thereof".[592] Thus, civilian superiors have to exert *de facto* control which is comparable to a military superior.[593] However, as a civilian superior does not possess the same disciplinary power as a military commander, the civilian superior's sanctioning power has to be interpreted more widely.[594] Instead of having the actual power to prevent and repress the commission of crimes through their subordinates, it is deemed sufficient if civilian superiors have the duty to report the matter to the responsible authority, thereby initiating the investigation and prosecution thereof.[595] Nevertheless, the precise circumstances under which effective control can be affirmed have not yet been clarified.[596] The question concerning the necessary degree of control of a civilian superior has already been addressed in two cases involving corporations. However,

---

[588] *Kai Ambos*, Wirtschaftsvölkerstrafrecht 62 (2018).

[589] Prosecutor v. Bemba, ICC-01/05-01/08, Decision Pursuant to Article 61 (7)(a) and (b) of the Rome Statute on the Charges of the Prosecutor Against Jean-Pierre Bemba Gombo, ¶ 413 (June 15, 2009).

[590] Prosecutor v. Nahimana, Case No. ICTR-99-52-A, Judgement, ¶ 785 (Nov. 28, 2007); see also Prosecutor v. Bemba, ICC-01/05-01/08, Judgment Pursuant to Article 74 of the Statute, ¶ 183 (Mar. 21, 2016); Prosecutor v. Delalić, Case No. IT-96-21-A, Judgement, ¶ 256 (Feb. 20, 2001); Prosecutor v. Musema, Case No. ICTR-96-13-T, Judgment and Sentence, para. 135 (Jan. 27, 2000).

[591] Prosecutor v. Delalić, Case No. IT-96-21-A, Judgement, ¶ 266 (Feb. 20, 2001); Prosecutor v. Bemba, ICC-01/05-01/08, Judgment Pursuant to Article 74 of the Statute, ¶ 183 (Mar. 21, 2016); *Gerhard Werle/Florian Jeßberger*, Principles of International Criminal Law para. 690 (2020).

[592] Prosecutor v. Aleksovski, Case No. IT-95–14/1-T, Judgement, ¶ 78 (June 25, 1999).

[593] Prosecutor v. Bagilishema, ICTR-95-1 A-A, Judgement, ¶ 52 (July 3, 2002); Prosecutor v. Nahimana, Case No. ICTR-99-52-A, Judgement, ¶ 605, 785 (Nov. 28, 2007).

[594] Prosecutor v. Aleksovski, Case No. IT-95-14/1-T, Judgement, ¶ 78 (June 25, 1999).

[595] Id.

[596] *Gerhard Werle/Florian Jeßberger*, Principles of International Criminal Law para. 693 (2020).

in both precedents the Chamber applied a very extensive interpretation of the superior-subordinate relationship.[597]

In the first precedent, *Alfred Musema*, owner of the Gisovu Tea Factory near Kibuye, was convicted by the ICTR on the basis of superior responsibility for not having prevented the participation of his employees in genocide.[598] In this case, the Chamber argued that "Musema exercised legal and financial control over these employees, particularly through his power to appoint and remove [...] employees from their positions at the Tea Factory"[599]. From his power to appoint, remove or threaten to remove employees at the Tea Factory in the event of their committing a crime, the Chamber deduced that Musema exerted *de jure* authority and control over the employees at the Tea Factory[600] and thus convicted him on the basis of superior responsibility for not having prevented the commission of crimes by his employees[601]. However, since superior responsibility originally emerged from military settings and the fact that superior responsibility already stretches ordinary principles of guilt in international criminal law, it appears rather problematic that the Chamber inferred Musema's effective control over his employees from his substantial social and economic influence.[602] By deducing 'effective control' from the capacity to appoint and dismiss employees, *any* employer with disciplinary power could be held liable as a civilian superior on the basis of superior responsibility for not having prevented or repressed the crimes of his or her employees.[603]

Nonetheless, in the *Media Case*, the Chamber similarly inferred *de facto* authority and control from both Nahimana's and Barayagwiza's status as leading managers of a radio station and convicted both for having failed to prevent genocidal harm caused by the dissemination of Hutu propaganda through their employees.[604]

However, this overly extensive interpretation of the civilian superior-subordinate relationship risks overstretching the principles of culpability.[605] Thus, some advo-

---

[597] Prosecutor v. Musema, Case No. ICTR-96-13-T, Judgement and Sentence, ¶ 868–882 (Jan. 27, 2000); Prosecutor v. Nahimana, Case No. ICTR-99-52-T, Judgement and Sentence, ¶ 567, 970 (Dec. 3, 2003).

[598] Prosecutor v. Musema, Case No. ICTR-96-13-T, Judgement and Sentence, ¶ 895 (Jan. 27, 2000).

[599] Id. at ¶ 880.

[600] Id.

[601] Id. at ¶ 895.

[602] *Hans Vest*, JICJ 871 (2010); *Roberta Arnold/Miles Jackson*, Article 28, 79 (2022); *Thomas Weigend*, ZStW 1012, 1013 (2004).

[603] *Thomas Weigend*, ZStW 1012 (2004).

[604] Prosecutor v. Nahimana, Case No. ICTR-99-52-T, Judgement and Sentence, ¶ 567, 970, 972 (Dec. 3, 2003).

[605] *Thomas Weigend*, ZStW 1011 (advocating a restrictive interpretation of the civilian superior-subordinate relationship closely linked to the military superior-subordinate relationship) (2004).

cate restricting the civilian superior-subordinate relationship in accordance with the rationale of superior liability. It is argued that superior responsibility is predicated on the proposition that superiors have a duty to act due to the underlying high risks they are obliged to control.[606] Thus, concerning civilian superior responsibility, it is advocated to restrict the civilian superior-subordinate relationship to civilians who have a duty to oversee high risks.[607] In the context of corporate involvement, certain business fields, including natural resource extractive industries[608], entail particularly high risks leading to the commission of crimes, which give rise to a sufficient superior-subordinate relationship.[609]

However, this restrictive approach concerning the civilian superior-subordinate relationship appears unnecessary as Article 28 (b) (ii) Rome Statute further restricts the scope of crimes by requiring that "[t]he crimes concerned activities that were within the effective responsibility and control of the superior". Thus, the control authority of civilian superiors is restricted to their official function.[610] In the case of corporate involvement, this means that business leaders only exert effective control over the business-related activities of the subordinates.[611] Hence, the type of business determines the scope of effective control.[612] As a consequence, superiors cannot be held criminally liable for crimes of their subordinates falling outside the scope of their business duties.[613] In the *Musema* case, besides the lack of effective control, the underlying crimes of genocide and crimes against humanity in the form of extermination and rape were also unconnected to the claimed superior's effective control over the tea production.[614]

In conclusion, in the case of corporate involvement, it appears difficult to determine a sufficient superior-subordinate relationship which is similar to the one of a military superior.[615] The question as to whether a business leader has the requisite 'effective authority and control' over his or her employees and whether the crimes

---

[606] Id. at 1013; *Hans Vest*, JICJ 871 (2010).

[607] *Thomas Weigend*, ZStW 1013 (2004); *Hans Vest*, JICJ 871, 872 (2010).

[608] *Hans Vest*, JICJ 872 (2010); see for business fields, which entail a particularly high risk of the commission of crimes International Commission of Jurists, Report of the International Commission of Jurists Expert Legal Panel on Corporate Complicity in International Crimes, Volume 2, 37–43 (2008).

[609] *Thomas Weigend*, ZStW 1013 (2004); *Hans Vest*, JICJ 872 (2010).

[610] *Gerhard Werle/Florian Jeßberger*, Principles of International Criminal Law para. 694 (2020).

[611] *Kai Ambos*, Superior Responsibility 858 (2002).

[612] *Roberta Arnold/Miles Jackson*, Article 28 para. 84 (2022).

[613] *Kai Ambos*, Superior Responsibility 858 (2002); *Hans Vest*, JICJ 871, 872 (2010); *Gerhard Werle/Florian Jeßberger*, Principles of International Criminal Law para. 694 (2020).

[614] *Roberta Arnold/Miles Jackson*, Article 28 para. 84 (2022); *Hans Vest*, JICJ 871, 872 (2010).

[615] *Kai Ambos*, Wirtschaftsvölkerstrafrecht 61 (2018); *Frank Meyer*, Schweizerische Zeitschrift für Strafrecht 69 fn. 61 (2013); *Hans Vest*, JICJ 870, 872 (2010).

concerned were 'within the effective responsibility and control of the superior' rather depends on the type of business. Particularly in the case of multinational corporations, it is to be doubted whether business leaders of the partner company situated in the Global North have 'effective authority and control' over the employees of the subsidiary company in the Global South who perpetrated the crimes, or that the crimes in question were within 'the effective responsibility and control' of the business leaders.[616] However, should a business leader be present at the site of the commission of the crime, the 'effective authority and control' requirement over the employees would most likely be satisfied.[617] Nonetheless, in this case it would be necessary to determine whether the business leader actively instigated the commission of the crime which would incur criminal liability under Article 25 (3) (b) Rome Statute instead.[618]

(f) Impediments concerning the individual criminal liability of business leaders

Irrespective of the mode of liability, whether Article 25 (3) (a)-(d) or Article 28 (b) Rome Statute, establishing individual criminal liability for business leaders faces major evidentiary impediments. In the case of multinational corporations, particularly the discovery of the culpable individual, as well as the production of evidence, appears challenging. Due to the fragmented and hierarchical organisation of multinational corporations it is difficult to trace criminal actions back to particular individual actors.[619] The multiplicity of agents as well as the cross-border distribution and delegation of tasks in multinational corporations render it difficult to identify the individual business agent who causally contributed to the perpetration of the crime.[620] Particularly in the case of multinational corporations, where the crime was directly perpetrated by agents of the subsidiary company, it appears likely that the managers of the parent company did not actively contribute to the perpetration of the crime, but rather failed to control the subsidiary company by omitting to perform their legal duty (*Überwachungsgarantenpflicht*) to prevent the causation of the crime.[621] However, since the Rome Statute lacks any general rule on omission, apart from certain provisions, such as Article 28 Rome Statute, which explicitly stipulates criminal liability for omission, it remains disputed whether, and under what circumstances, the Rome Statute provides criminal liability for omis-

[616] *Kai Ambos*, Wirtschaftsvölkerstrafrecht 61, 62 (2018).

[617] Id. at 62.

[618] Id.

[619] *Mordechai Kremnitzer*, A Possible Case for Imposing Criminal Liability on Corporations in International Criminal Law, 8 (3) JICJ 909, 912 (2010); *Thomas Weigend*, JICJ 932 (2008); *Gabriel Wilhelm Bartalyos Thurner*, Internationales Unternehmensstrafrecht 251, 252 (2012).

[620] *Ingeborg Zerbes/Mark Pieth*, Kritische Justiz 68, 69 (2018).

[621] Id. at 69–74; *Kai Ambos*, Wirtschaftsvölkerstrafrecht 44 (2018).

sion.[622] While most subsidiary companies are legally independent from the parent company, they economically depend on their parent company, which raises the question as to whether, and to what extent, business leaders of the parent company are legally obliged to control (*Überwachungsverschulden*) the subsidiary company.[623] In general, however, such legal duties to control employees can only pertain to conduct within the course of the company's activities.[624] This restriction serves to exclude cases where employees engaged in criminal conduct for their own benefit and not on behalf of the corporation, as in these cases is does not appear appropriate to attribute the employee's conduct to the legal entity.[625]

Hence, at this juncture, criminal conduct involving corporations often goes unpunished. For one, corporate managers continue to hide under the corporate veil due to evidentiary difficulties and due to overly restrictive modes of liability under Article 25 (3) (a)-(d) and Article 28 (b) Rome Statute rendering individual criminal liability for business leaders mostly unsuccessful. At the same time, corporations themselves cannot be held directly criminally liable under the current Rome Statute due to the explicit exclusion of corporate criminal liability in Article 25 (1) Rome Statute. Thus, in the following it will be discussed whether the concept of corporate criminal liability should be introduced into the Rome Statute to remedy this lacuna.

(2) Inclusion of corporate criminal liability into the Rome Statute

Although multinational corporations commit the majority of the gravest environmental crimes and human rights violations, the fact that they operate globally and encompass a multitude of legally independent subsidiary companies particularly enables them to hide beneath their corporate veil. Thus, these multinational conglomerates do not underlie any global governance, which in his report on the issue of human rights and transnational corporations and other business enterprises, UN Special Representative John Ruggie so accurately referred to as the so-called "governance gap"[626] in relation to multinational corporations. To close this 'governance gap' some scholars[627] advocate the establishment of corporate criminal

---

[622] *Kai Ambos*, Article 25 para. 63 (2022); *Gerhard Werle/Florian Jeßberger*, Principles of International Criminal Law paras. 811–819 (2020); *Albin Eser*, Individual Criminal Responsibility 819 (2002).

[623] *Ingeborg Zerbes/Mark Pieth*, Kritische Justiz 72, 73 (2018).

[624] Id. at 74, 75; *Kai Ambos*, Wirtschaftsvölkerstrafrecht 44 (2018).

[625] *Harmen Van der Wilt*, Chinese J. INT'l L., 67, 68 (2013).

[626] U.N. Special Representative of the Secretary-General *John Ruggie*, Promotion and Protection of all Human Rights, Civil, Political, Economic, Social and Cultural Rights, Including the Right to Development, at para. 3, U.N. Doc. A/HRC/8/5 (2008).

[627] *Andrew Clapham*, Extending International Criminal Law Beyond the Individual to Corporations and Armed Opposition Groups, 6 (5) JICJ 899 (2008); *Norman Farrell*, JICJ (2010); *Mordechai Kremnitzer*, JICJ (2010); *Karissa Van den Herik/Jernej Letnar Černič*, Regulating Corporations under International Law: From Human Rights to International Criminal Law and Back Again, 8 (3) JICJ 725 (2010); *Ronald C. Slye*, Corporations, Veils,

liability under the Rome Statute to complement individual criminal responsibility[628], which would permit the ICC to hold corporations directly criminally liable. This would, however, require an amendment to Article 25 (1) Rome Statute. In this context it is to be noted that it follows from Article 10 Rome Statute that it cannot be argued against the renewed interest in including corporate liability into the Rome Statue that the idea of corporate criminal liability was once rejected at the Rome Conference.[629] Due to increasing corporate involvement in international criminal law[630], the debate concerning the establishment of corporate criminal liability under international criminal law has resurfaced. This is particularly relevant in the environmental context, since large-scale environmental harm is mostly committed by multinational corporations exploiting or purchasing natural resources in the resource-rich Global South.[631] In Germany, the discussion concerning whether to introduce corporate criminal liability into international criminal law is conducted under the heading of "*Wirtschaftsvölkerstrafrecht*"[632], literally meaning "international criminal law of business"[633]. In the following, the arguments speaking in favour of and against the inclusion of corporate criminal liability into the Rome Statute will be assessed in order to evaluate the call for the establishment of corporate criminal liability under international criminal law.

And International Criminal Liability, 33 (3) Brook. J. Int'L. 955 (2008); *Caroline Kaeb*, The Shifting Sands of Corporate Liability under International Criminal Law, 49 (2) Geo. Wash. Int'l. Rev. 351 (2016); *Harmen Van der Wilt*, Chinese J. INT'l L. (2013); critical *Thomas Weigend*, JICJ 944–945 (2008).

[628] Most scholars agree that corporate criminal liability should only complement but not replace individual criminal liability in international criminal law, *Caroline Kaeb*, Geo. Wash. Int'l. Rev. 382, 383 (2016); *Gabriel Wilhelm Bartalyos Thurner*, Internationales Unternehmensstrafrecht 252, 253 (2012); *Ronald C. Slye*, Brook. J. Int'L. 960 fn. 20 (2008); *John C. Coffee*, No Soul to Damn: No Body to Kick: An Unscandalized Inquiry into the Problem of Corporate Punishment, 79 (3) Michigan Law Review 386, 407–411 (1981).

[629] *Alexander Heinze*, Article 10 para. 18 (2022).

[630] *Gerhard Werle/Florian Jeßberger*, Principles of International Criminal Law para. 146 fn. 307 (2020); *Norman Farrell*, JICJ 873, 874 (2010); see on corporate involvement in international criminal law *Frank Meyer*, Schweizerische Zeitschrift für Strafrecht (2013).

[631] EUROPOL, Environmental Crime in the Age of Climate Change 7 (2022); *Ricardo Pereira*, Criminal Law Forum 219 (2020); *Frédéric Mégret*, Colum. J. Envtl. L. 225, 226 (2011).

[632] See *Florian Jeßberger*, JICJ (2010); *Florian Jeßberger*, et al., Wirtschaftsvölkerstrafrecht (2015); *Kai Ambos*, Wirtschaftsvölkerstrafrecht (2018); Instead Meisenberg deliberately refers to 'Unternehmensvölkerstrafrecht', literally meaning 'international criminal law of corporations', thereby aiming at emphasising the establishment of criminal liability for corporations, see *Simon M. Meisenberg*, Auf dem Wege zu einem Unternehmensvölkerstrafrecht? 2 (2016).

[633] *Gerhard Werle/Florian Jeßberger*, Principles of International Criminal Law para. 146 (2020).

(a) Arguments in favour of the inclusion of corporate criminal liability

Advocates of corporate criminal liability argue that since business entities are entitled to rights under international law and are already liable under international law, they should also be subjected to international criminal liability.[634] As stated in the European Parliament's report on the liability of companies for environmental damage, "companies should bear the full societal costs of the environmental harm they are directly causing in order to ensure they have incentives to internalise environmental externalities and avoid externalising those costs".[635] Thus, in this regard it is argued that only systematic punishment of corporations may deter the corporations from engaging in criminal conduct by changing the corporate culture.[636] Furthermore, it is rightly observed that translating collective guilt into individual responsibility, which is currently necessary under the Rome Statute, faces multiple challenges and limitations.[637] Moreover, holding a strictly individualist approach bears the risk of disregarding the peculiarities of collective guilt, including the relationship between the corporation and its organs, as in most cases employees do not act for their own purpose but to enrich the company.[638] As the company's success and good reputation depends on the action of its organs, it should also carry the liability of its organs' misdeeds which have occurred on its behalf.[639] Thus, holding corporations as such criminally liable would assist in piercing the corporate culture, which often facilitates, encourages and covers individual criminal conduct under the corporate veil.[640] Additionally, it is claimed that the individual criminal liability of business leaders does not accurately reflect the organisational nature of corporate wrongdoing which often, by far, transcends individual harm.[641] Hence, a

---

[634] *Ronald C. Slye*, Brook. J. Int'L. 958 (2008); *Mordechai Kremnitzer*, JICJ 913 (2010); see on companies as bearers of human rights duties *Karissa Van den Herik/Jernej Letnar Černič*, JICJ (2010).

[635] European Parliament, Report on the Liability of Companies for Environmental Damage, Opinion of the Committee on the Environment, Public Health and Food Safety, Eur. Parl. Doc. 2020/2027(INI) (2021).

[636] *Andrew Clapham*, The Question of Jurisdiction under International Criminal Law Over Legal Persons: Lessons from the Rome Conference on an International Criminal Court 147 (2000); *Gabriel Wilhelm Bartalyos Thurner*, Internationales Unternehmensstrafrecht 237 (2012); *Ronald C. Slye*, Brook. J. Int'L. 963 (2008); *Kai Ambos*, Wirtschaftsvölkerstrafrecht 41, 42 (2018).

[637] See on the challenges and limitations of translating collective guilt into individual responsibility *Cassandra Steer*, Translating Guilt: Identifying Leadership Liability for Mass Atrocity Crimes 12–17 (2017); *George P. Fletcher*, The Storrs Lectures: Liberals and Romantics at War: The Problem of Collective Guilt, 111 (7) The Yale Law Journal 1499 (2002).

[638] *Mordechai Kremnitzer*, JICJ 912 (2010); *Gabriel Wilhelm Bartalyos Thurner*, Internationales Unternehmensstrafrecht 252 (2012).

[639] *Mordechai Kremnitzer*, JICJ 913 (2010).

[640] *Kai Ambos*, Wirtschaftsvölkerstrafrecht 40, 41 (2018); *Gabriel Wilhelm Bartalyos Thurner*, Internationales Unternehmensstrafrecht 247, 248 (2012).

[641] *Caroline Kaeb*, Geo. Wash. Int'l. Rev. 397 (2016); *Ronald C. Slye*, Brook. J. Int'L. 960 (2008).

strict individualist approach risks corporate managers becoming scapegoats for collective guilt[642] and thus "contribute[s] to a myth of collective innocence"[643]. A strict individualist approach further seems to conflict with the nature of international criminal law pertaining to macro-criminality, which is characterised by its collective nature.[644] In this regard, it was rightly observed by Ohlin that international criminal law is divided by two *desiderata*: "recognizing that most atrocities are performed by irreducibly collective endeavours, yet convicting individuals solely for their individual participation in these collective projects".[645]

Furthermore, from a practical perspective concerning the imposition of financial fines it is rightly argued that corporations have larger amounts of money at their disposal than individual business leaders.[646] It is further argued that the inclusion of corporate criminal liability could reinstate the faith of the international community in the ICC as being an unbiased institution, by turning the focus from Africa to the Global North, where most multinational corporations are headquartered.[647] Most importantly, however, the inclusion of corporate criminal liability could resolve the issue of having to prove an individual culpable, such as in the case of individual criminal liability of business leaders, by holding the corporation itself criminally liable. Nevertheless, as will be explained below[648], this depends on the concrete conceptualisation of corporate criminal liability.[649]

(b) Arguments against the inclusion of corporate criminal liability

Nonetheless, despite the obvious governance gap concerning corporate criminal liability under international criminal law, the inclusion of corporate criminal lia-

---

[642] *Carsten Stahn*, A Critical Introduction to International Criminal Law 125 (2019); *Kai Ambos*, Wirtschaftsvölkerstrafrecht 41 (2018).

[643] *Laurel E. Fletcher/Harvey M. Weinstein*, Violence and Social Repair: Rethinking the Contribution of Justice to Reconciliation, 24 Human Rights Quarterly 573, 580 (2002).

[644] As stated in Tadić: "Most of the time [crimes under international law] do not result from the criminal propensity of single individuals but constitute manifestations of collective criminality: the crimes are often carried out by groups of individuals acting in pursuance of a common criminal design" (Prosecutor v. Tadić, Case No. IT-94-1-A, Judgement, ¶ 191 (July 15, 1999); see *Carsten Stahn*, A Critical Introduction to International Criminal Law 128, 129 (2019); *Ronald C. Slye*, Brook. J. Int'L. 961–963 (2008).

[645] *Jens David Ohlin*, Organizational Criminality, in: Pluralism in International Criminal Law 117 (Elies Van Sliedregt/Sergey Vasiliev eds., 2014).

[646] *Mordechai Kremnitzer*, JICJ 913 (2010); *Thomas Weigend*, JICJ 943 (2008); *Kai Ambos*, Wirtschaftsvölkerstrafrecht 42 (2018).

[647] See *Joanna Kyriakakis*, Corporations Before International Criminal Court: Implications for the International Criminal Justice Project, 30 Leiden Journal of International Law 221 (2017).

[648] See Chapter C. VII. 1. b) bb) (2) (b) (bb).

[649] *Gerhard Werle/Florian Jeßberger*, Principles of International Criminal Law para. 149 (2020).

bility in the Rome Statute faces major impediments which will be discussed in the following.

(aa) Doctrinal challenges: Principle of individual criminal guilt

Particularly German law theorists voice doctrinal challenges concerning the establishment of corporate criminal liability. While corporate criminal liability is well-established in common law jurisdictions, it is a fairly new concept in civil law jurisdictions.[650] Although an increasing number of civil law jurisdictions have, to date, incorporated corporate criminal liability into their domestic criminal codes[651], German law still only provides administrative responsibility for corporations. Section 30 of the Act on Regulatory Offences (*Gesetz über Ordnungswidrigkeiten*) permits the imposition of a monetary fines on corporations if a representative, organ or other person with control over the legal person perpetrated a criminal or regulatory offence by which a duty of the legal person was infringed, or the legal person was enriched.[652] Thus, under German law, exclusively administrative sanctions can be imposed on corporations holding them responsible for offences perpetrated by their agents on their behalf.[653] However, on 16 June 2020, the German government proposed a draft law (*Verbandssanktionengesetz – VerSanG*) directed at sanctioning corporations for criminal conduct.[654] Nevertheless, although the German government explicitly acknowledged the inadequacy of administrative responsibility in addressing corporate criminality, the proposed sanctions are not 'criminal' per se but rather *sui generis*, as the government expressly considered the introduction of criminal sanctions as unnecessary at this point in time.[655] With regard to corporate criminal liability, the traditional German law doctrine is very restrictive and still holds the view that "corporations cannot act, corporations cannot be blamed, and corporations cannot be subject to criminal punishment"[656]. These doctrinal chal-

---

[650] *Thomas Weigend*, JICJ 928 (2008).

[651] See for an overview over corporate criminal liability in the EU Deutscher Bundestag, Eine Übersicht zum Unternehmensstrafrecht in einzelnen Mitgliedstaaten der Europäischen Union, Az. WD 7-3000-070/17 (2017).

[652] See Gesetz über Ordnungswidrigkeiten [OWiG] [Act on Regulatory Offences], Feb. 19, 1987, BGBl. at 602, last amended by Gesetz [G], Mar. 14, 2023, BGBl. No. 73, art. 30 (1) (Ger.).

[653] *Thomas Weigend*, JICJ 931, 932 (2008).

[654] Gesetzesentwurf der Bundesregierung [Government Draft], Entwurf eines Gesetzes zur Stärkung der Integrität in der Wirtschaft, Drucksache [BT] 19/23568 (Ger.).

[655] Gesetzesentwurf der Bundesregierung [Government Draft], Entwurf eines Gesetzes zur Stärkung der Integrität in der Wirtschaft, at 2, 128, Drucksache [BT] 19/23568 (Ger.). According to the *Bundesregierung* the new law requires reevaluation after a period of five years including the evaluation as to whether the proposed sanctions constitute adequate means to address corporate criminality or if the introduction of corporate criminal liability is necessary; see for an evaluation of the proposed draft law *Friederike Rotsch*, et al., Der Regierungsentwurf zum Verbandssanktionengesetz, Kritische Analyse und Ausblick, CCZ 169 (2020).

[656] *Thomas Weigend*, JICJ 936 (2008).

lenges are predicated on the Latin maxim *societas delinquere non potest*, literally meaning that 'companies cannot commit crimes'.[657] This traditional view is based on the guilt principle inherent in the German law doctrine under which criminal liability, as opposed to civil or administrative responsibility, is based on moral blame, which, in turn, requires a moral agent who voluntarily decides to perpetrate a wrongdoing.[658] However, even though legal persons are bearers of legal rights and duties, they lack a moral conscience and thus can neither volitionally act for themselves, nor be subject of moral blame.[659]

Nonetheless, some argue that while these doctrinal concerns are prevalent in German criminal law, they only play a subordinate role in international criminal law as corporate criminal liability is widely accepted particularly in common law jurisdictions.[660] Apart from Germany, which is proclaimed as the "'bastion' of the traditional principle *societas delinquere non potest*"[661], in domestic legal systems there is a clear inclination in favour of corporate criminal liability these days.[662] Similarly, at the regional and international level, all recent treaties include rules on corporate criminal liability.[663] In the EU, a proliferating number of conventions entail corporate criminal liability in case of violations, including, for instance the 2008 Crime Directive.[664] Furthermore, the Malabo Protocol, which has not yet entered into force due to a lack ratifications, explicitly extends the jurisdiction of the African Court of Justice and Human Rights (ACJHR) to "legal persons, with the exception of States"[665] in relation to transnational crimes.[666] Thus, at the domestic and regional level, the maxim *societas delinquere non potest* is clearly being erod-

[657] *Andrew Clapham*, JICJ 900 (2008).

[658] *Thomas Weigend*, JICJ 936 (2008).

[659] Id. at 936–942.

[660] *Kai Ambos*, Wirtschaftsvölkerstrafrecht 45, 46 (2018).

[661] *Caroline Kaeb*, Geo. Wash. Int'l. Rev. 381 (2016).

[662] *Frank Meyer*, Diskussionsbeitrag: "Verbandsverantwortung im Völkerstrafrecht", 126 (1) ZStW 122, 124 (2014); *Gerhard Werle/Florian Jeßberger*, Principles of International Criminal Law para. 147 (2020); *Joanna Kyriakakis*, Corporate Criminal Liability and the ICC Statute: The Comparative Law Challenge, NILR 333, 336–348 (2009); *Caroline Kaeb*, Geo. Wash. Int'l. Rev. 380 (2016).

[663] Prosecutor v. New TV S.A.L., Case No. STL-14-05/PT/AP/AR126.1, Decision on Interlocutory Appeal Concerning Personal Jurisdiction in Contempt Proceedings, para. 66 (Oct. 2, 2014) ("[…] there have been a varied number of international treaties recognising criminal liability for legal entities which does not suggest that they enjoy impunity for their actions"); *Gerhard Werle/Florian Jeßberger*, Principles of International Criminal Law para. 147 (2020); *Frank Meyer*, ZStW 124 (2014).

[664] Directive 2008/99/EC, art. 6.

[665] Protocol on Amendments to the Protocol on the Statute of the African Court of Justice and Human Rights, art. 46C (1) (June 27, 2014).

[666] Id. art. 28 A (1).

ed.[667] In this regard, the International Commission of Jurists stated in its Report on Corporate Complicity in International Crimes that the fact that an increasing number of domestic jurisdictions having established corporate criminal liability proves that all impediments concerning corporate criminal liability can be overcome.[668]

Nevertheless, since international criminal law pertains to macro-criminality as opposed to ordinary criminal law, it is to be doubted that the domestic and regional inclination towards corporate criminal liability can justify the inclusion of corporate criminal liability at the *international* level. However, in 2014, in *Al-Jadeed*, the Special Tribunal for Lebanon (*hereinafter* STL), as the first international criminal tribunal to do so, charged a corporation with contempt of court.[669] In the *Al-Jadeed Case*, the STL charged a Lebanese corporation, New TV S.A.L., and its Deputy Head of News and Political Programs, Al Khayat, with contempt of court pursuant to Article 60 bis (a) of the STL Statute.[670] In terms of personal jurisdiction, the Appeals Panel affirmed the STL's jurisdiction over legal persons arguing that "there is an emerging shared international understanding on the need to address corporate responsibility".[671] The Appeals Panel further elaborated on this stating that "corporate criminal liability is on the verge of attaining, at the very least, the status of a general principle of law applicable under international law"[672]. While some heralded the decision as a "foundation for further development of liability of corporate entities in international criminal law"[673], the Appeals Panel's decision faces major

[667] *Gerhard Werle/Florian Jeßberger*, Principles of International Criminal Law para. 148 (2020).

[668] *International Commission of Jurists*, Report of the International Commission of Jurists Expert Legal Panel on Corporate Complicity in International Crimes, Volume 2, 58 (2008).

[669] Prosecutor v. New TV S.A.L., Case No. STL-14-05/PT/AP/AR126.1, Decision on Interlocutory Appeal Concerning Personal Jurisdiction in Contempt Proceedings, ¶ 67 (Oct. 2, 2014); see more detailed on the Al-Jadeed case *Caroline Kaeb*, Geo. Wash. Int'l. Rev. 364–371 (2016); *Nadia Bernaz*, Corporate Criminal Liability under International Law, 13 JICJ 313 (2015); *Simon M. Meisenberg*, Auf dem Wege zu einem Unternehmensvölkerstrafrecht? (2016).

[670] See Prosecutor v. Al Jadeed, Case No. STL-14-05/A/AP, Public Redacted Version of Judgment on Appeal (Mar. 8, 2016).

[671] Prosecutor v. New TV S.A.L., Case No. STL-14-05/PT/AP/AR126.1, Decision on Interlocutory Appeal Concerning Personal Jurisdiction in Contempt Proceedings, ¶ 46 (Oct. 2, 2014); see more detailed on the Appeals Panel's argumentation, *Simon M. Meisenberg*, Auf dem Wege zu einem Unternehmensvölkerstrafrecht? 21–33 (2016).

[672] Prosecutor v. New TV S.A.L., Case No. STL-14-05/PT/AP/AR126.1, Decision on Interlocutory Appeal Concerning Personal Jurisdiction in Contempt Proceedings, ¶ 67 (Oct. 2, 2014).

[673] *Karlijn Van der Voort*, Contempt Case Against Lebanese Journalists at the STL (2014), http://lebanontribunal.blogspot.com/2014/04/contempt-case-against-lebanese_30.html (last visited Feb. 18, 2025).

criticism.[674] It is rightly criticised that the Appeals Panel based its decision to extend the personal jurisdiction over legal persons, *inter alia*, on gross human rights violations, even though the crime at issue of the proceedings was not an international core crime, but the crime of contempt of court.[675] In this vein, it is particularly noteworthy that the subject-matter jurisdiction of the STL is limited to provisions of the Lebanese Criminal Code.[676] Thus, the charge was based on Lebanese criminal law. Additionally, one has to concur with the contempt judge claiming that "there is no relevant international convention with respect to the elements of corporate liability, nor international custom or general principles of law (there is indeed nothing approaching a universal model or a consensus across national systems)".[677] In general, the lack of consensus regarding the conceptualisation of corporate criminal liability, evidenced by the existence of differing models of corporate criminal liability in domestic jurisdictions, refutes the assumption of a general principle under international law.[678] In this vein, despite having acknowledged personal jurisdiction for corporations, the Panel did not elaborate on the challenge of how to conceptualise corporate criminal liability in international criminal law.[679]

Furthermore, despite the tendency towards corporate criminal liability at the domestic and regional, it is particularly noteworthy that the principle of individual guilt is not only inherent in traditional German law doctrine but is also a core foundation of international criminal law.[680] The IMT first stated that in international

---

[674] See *Simon M. Meisenberg*, Auf dem Wege zu einem Unternehmensvölkerstrafrecht? 35–69 (2016); *Gerhard Werle/Florian Jeßberger*, Principles of International Criminal Law para. 148 (2020).

[675] *Gerhard Werle/Florian Jeßberger*, Principles of International Criminal Law para. 148 (2020); *Simon M. Meisenberg*, Auf dem Wege zu einem Unternehmensvölkerstrafrecht? 41 (2016).

[676] *Simon M. Meisenberg*, Auf dem Wege zu einem Unternehmensvölkerstrafrecht? 8 (2016); see generally on the subject-matter jurisdiction of the STL *Nidal Nabil Jurdi*, The Subject-Matter Jurisdiction of the Special Tribunal for Lebanon, 5 (5) JICJ 1125 (2007).

[677] Prosecutor v. Al Jadeed, Case No. STL-14-05/T/CJ, Public Redacted Version of Judgment, ¶ 61 (Sept. 18, 2015).

[678] *Frank Meyer*, Schweizerische Zeitschrift für Strafrecht 77–86 (2013); *Gerhard Werle/Florian Jeßberger*, Principles of International Criminal Law para. 148 fn. 317 (2020); similar *Simon M. Meisenberg*, Auf dem Wege zu einem Unternehmensvölkerstrafrecht? 66, 67 (2016).

[679] See the contempt judge arguing that "[t]he Appeals Panel, however, provided no clear guidance as to the applicable material elements in attributing liability to legal persons" (Prosecutor v. New TV S.A.L., Case No. STL-14-05/T/CJ, Public Redacted Version of Judgment, ¶ 55 (Sep 18, 2015)); *Gerhard Werle/Florian Jeßberger*, Principles of International Criminal Law para. 148 (2020); *Simon M. Meisenberg*, Auf dem Wege zu einem Unternehmensvölkerstrafrecht? 62–66 (2016).

[680] Report of the Commission to the General Assembly on the Work of its Forty-Eighth Session, [1996] 2 Y.B. Int'l L. Comm'n 19 ¶ 1, U.N. Doc. A/CN.4/SER.A/1996/Add.1 (Part 2); *Kai Ambos*, Article 25 para. 1 (2022); *Gerhard Werle/Florian Jeßberger*, Principles of International Criminal Law para. 141 (2020); *William A. Schabas*, The International Criminal Court: A Commentary on the Rome Statute 566 (2016).

criminal law "one of the most important [principles] is that criminal guilt is personal".[681] The principle of personal culpability also includes the principle of individual criminal responsibility which is expressed in Article 25 (1) and (2) Rome Statute[682], which was initially acknowledged by the IMT stating that "[c]rimes against International Law are committed by men, not by abstract entities"[683], which was later reiterated by the ICTY.[684] The principle of individual criminal responsibility is predicated on the traditional proposition in international criminal law that individuals bear obligations under international law, which necessitates the imposition of individual sanctions linked to personal culpability.[685] By imposing sanctions on individuals, it is ensured that perpetrators are not penalised for the wrongdoing of others but only for their own malfeasance.[686] Hence, although there is a clear tendency towards corporate criminal liability at the domestic and regional level, this concept detracts from the traditional focus on individual guilt inherent in international criminal law since its establishment in Nuremberg.[687] With regards to the STL's effort to extend its personal jurisdiction to legal persons, it should be emphasised that other international criminal tribunals are not bound by the STL's decision to extend its personal jurisdiction to legal persons.[688] In fact, the ICC could not even be bound by the STL due to the explicit exclusion of corporate criminal liability in Article 25 (1) Rome Statute. Furthermore, it should be noted that the STL's extension of its personal jurisdiction exclusively applies to the crime of contempt of court under Lebanese criminal law and not the international core crimes as such.

Hence, although there is a clear tendency towards corporate criminal law at the domestic and regional level, it should be considered that individual guilt is still a cornerstone principle under international criminal law.

---

[681] IMT, Judgment of 1 October 1946, The Trial of German Major War Criminals. Proceedings of the International Military Tribunal sitting at Nuremberg, Germany, Part 22, ¶ 469 (Aug. 22 to Oct. 1, 1946).

[682] *Kai Ambos*, Article 25 para. 1 (2022); *William A. Schabas*, The International Criminal Court: A Commentary on the Rome Statute 566 (2016).

[683] IMT, Judgment of 1 October 1946, The Trial of German Major War Criminals. Proceedings of the International Military Tribunal sitting at Nuremberg, Germany, Part 22, ¶ 447 (Aug. 22 to Oct. 1, 1946).

[684] Prosecutor v. Tadić, Case No. IT-94-1, Decision on the Defence Motion for Interlocutory Appeal on Jurisdiction, ¶ 128–137 (Oct. 2, 1995).

[685] *Carsten Stahn*, A Critical Introduction to International Criminal Law 117, 119 (2019).

[686] Id. at 145.

[687] *Kai Ambos*, Wirtschaftsvölkerstrafrecht 42 (2018).

[688] See Prosecutor v. Delalić, Case No. IT-96-21-A, Judgement, ¶ 24 (Feb. 20, 2001) ("Although the Appeals Chamber will necessarily take into consideration other decisions of international courts, it may, after careful consideration, come to a different conclusion"); Prosecutor v. Kupreskić, Case No. IT-95-16-T, Judgement, ¶ 540 (Jan. 14, 2000).

(bb) Practical challenges of conceptualising corporate criminal liability

Despite the clear inclination towards corporate criminal liability, there is no consensus regarding the constituting elements thereof. Instead, the concepts of corporate criminal liability vary greatly amongst the different domestic jurisdictions.[689] However, the existing concepts of corporate criminal liability in domestic jurisdictions can be divided into two main models, which are also discussed in the debate concerning the conceptualisation of corporate criminal liability in international criminal law. Under the first model, which predominates in Anglo-American jurisdictions, the corporation is held criminally liable for the crimes committed by an employee in the course of corporate duties, while under the second model, which is prevalent in German speaking jurisdictions, the corporation is punished for its own organisational deficiency.[690] Thus, while the first model is based upon the assumption that corporations can only act through their organs and, therefore, individual guilt needs to be imputed to the corporation, under the second model the corporation itself is considered blameworthy.

However, under the first model the view in domestic jurisdictions differs as to whose criminal conduct is attributable to the corporation. Whilst in the US the criminal conduct of *any* employee (vicarious liability or *respondeat superior* theory[691]) is imputable, in the UK only criminal behaviour of *directing minds* can be attributed (identification theory[692]). Particularly in the context of individual criminal law where individual criminal responsibility is one of the core principles, its similarity to individual criminal liability, due to it being tied to individual guilt, can be argued in favour of the first model.[693] Nevertheless, the first model requires the identification of a culpable individual whose guilt can be ascribed to the corporation. Thus, this concept of corporate criminal liability faces the same evidentiary obstacles as individual criminal responsibility of business leaders which initially

[689] See the different approaches of conceptualising corporate criminal liability in domestic jurisdictions, *Gabriel Wilhelm Bartalyos Thurner*, Internationales Unternehmensstrafrecht 252–275 (2012).

[690] *Ingeborg Zerbes/Mark Pieth*, Kritische Justiz 78, 79 (2018); *Frank Meyer*, Schweizerische Zeitschrift für Strafrecht 79–82 (2013); *Thomas Weigend*, JICJ 933–935 (2008); *Kai Ambos*, Wirtschaftsvölkerstrafrecht 46–58 (2018); *Gerhard Werle/Florian Jeßberger*, Principles of International Criminal Law para. 148 fn. 317 (2020); see Slye distinguishing four approaches within these two main models, *Ronald C. Slye*, Brook. J. Int'L. 964–969 (2008).

[691] *Ingeborg Zerbes/Mark Pieth*, Kritische Justiz 78 (2018); *Gabriel Wilhelm Bartalyos Thurner*, Internationales Unternehmensstrafrecht 254, 255 (2012); *Kai Ambos*, Wirtschaftsvölkerstrafrecht 54 (2018); *Frank Meyer*, Schweizerische Zeitschrift für Strafrecht 79 (2013); *Caroline Kaeb*, Geo. Wash. Int'l. Rev. 384 (2016).

[692] *Gabriel Wilhelm Bartalyos Thurner*, Internationales Unternehmensstrafrecht 256, 257 (2012); *Ingeborg Zerbes/Mark Pieth*, Kritische Justiz 79 (2018); *Kai Ambos*, Wirtschaftsvölkerstrafrecht 54 (2018); *Frank Meyer*, Schweizerische Zeitschrift für Strafrecht 79 (2013).

[693] *Kai Ambos*, Wirtschaftsvölkerstrafrecht 57 (2018).

gave rise to considering the establishment of corporate criminal liability.[694] Particularly in the case of multinational corporations operating transnationally, it will be almost impossible to trace back the criminal conduct to a culpable individual.[695] In this regard, however, it is noteworthy that a different version of the first model allows the attribution of guilt from an unknown agent.[696] Nonetheless, imputing the guilt of a fictional person to a corporation renders this model a mere fiction which appears to conflict with the rationale of this model to attribute individual guilt to a corporation.[697] Besides the difficulty of tracing individual conduct back to an individual, as demonstrated above[698], it is further difficult to prove the individual guilt of a business leader under the current modes of liability available under the Rome Statute.[699] Additionally, this first model would incentivise corporations to conceal employees' individual guilt to evade (transferred) liability.[700] Furthermore, the attribution of individual guilt leads to a duplication of liability by not only holding the culpable individual criminally liable for his personal guilt, but also establishing corporate criminal liability for the *same* conduct.[701]

Alternatively, one could resort to the second model, the collective "corporate approach"[702], which is predicated on the organisational failure of the corporation itself, irrespective of the attribution of any individual guilt.[703] Under this model the fault lies in the corporation's deficient organisation as well as the paucity of any proper supervision of its employees.[704] Thus, while the corporation's deficient organisation gives reason for punishment, the individual perpetration of a crime, which in fact does not even have to be proven, would only trigger the prosecution of the corporation.[705] Hence, under this model it is sufficient if there is proof that a lack

---

[694] *Frank Meyer*, Schweizerische Zeitschrift für Strafrecht 81 (2013); *Thomas Weigend*, JICJ 933 (2008); *Kai Ambos*, Wirtschaftsvölkerstrafrecht 57, 58 (2018).

[695] *Frank Meyer*, ZStW 128 (2014).

[696] *Frank Meyer*, Schweizerische Zeitschrift für Strafrecht 79 (2013); *Thomas Weigend*, JICJ 934 (2008).

[697] *Thomas Weigend*, JICJ 934 (2008).

[698] Chapter C. VII. 1. b) bb) (1).

[699] *Frank Meyer*, ZStW 128 (2014).

[700] *Thomas Weigend*, JICJ 933, 934 (2008).

[701] *Kai Ambos*, Wirtschaftsvölkerstrafrecht 53 (2018); *Thomas Weigend*, JICJ 933 (2008).

[702] See *Kai Ambos*, Wirtschaftsvölkerstrafrecht 40–45 (2018).

[703] *Frank Meyer*, ZStW 129 (2014); *Thomas Weigend*, JICJ 934 (2008); explicitly in favour of transferring this collective model of corporate criminal liability to international criminal law *Gabriel Wilhelm Bartalyos Thurner*, Internationales Unternehmensstrafrecht 264, 276–278 (2012).

[704] *Thomas Weigend*, JICJ 934 (2008).

[705] *Frank Meyer*, Schweizerische Zeitschrift für Strafrecht 79 (2013); *Thomas Weigend*, JICJ 934 (2008).

of supervision resulted in damage caused by the company, which could have been prevented by proper supervision.[706]

Hence, only the second model decreases evidentiary problems which arise from the necessity of having to identify an individual who is responsible.[707] However, this model disregards the fact that corporations cannot act for themselves but only through natural persons.[708] Thus, concerning the objective side, this second model is based on a mere fiction presuming a corporate personality which can act and organise itself.[709] With respect to the subjective side, the collective approach is based on another fiction by presuming 'corporate knowledge' or 'corporate intent' and thus attributing aggregate knowledge of all employees to the corporation.[710] Besides these doctrinal concerns voiced in the domestic debate, collective corporate criminal liability faces even greater criticism in the context of international criminal law. With respect to the principle of complementarity all Member States of the ICC would have to incorporate a similar model of collective corporate criminal liability as otherwise the principle of complementarity would be rendered obsolete.[711] However, as evidenced by the existence of the two models of corporate criminal liability, so far there has been no consensus amongst the Member States concerning the conceptualisation of corporate criminal liability. Some states, such as Germany, still refuse to establish corporate criminal liability. Thus, regarding the already fragile legitimation of individual criminal law, which is predicated on core principles such as the principle of individual criminal guilt, it appears highly problematic to experiment with such an innovative mode of collective corporate criminal liability.[712] It rather appears arbitrary to punish corporations based on a mere fiction simply to satisfy the need to fill 'governance gaps' concerning corporate criminality.[713]

(cc) Lack of appropriate sanctions

However, besides doctrinal concerns and the lack of consensus regarding the conceptualisation of corporate criminal liability, particularly the paucity of appro-

[706] *Thomas Weigend*, JICJ 934 (2008).

[707] Id.

[708] *Kai Ambos*, Wirtschaftsvölkerstrafrecht 47 (2018); *Thomas Weigend*, JICJ 934 (2008); *Ben Swart*, International Trends towards Establishing Some Form of Punishment for Corporations, 6 (5) JICJ 947, 951 (2008); *Marie Kuntz*, Conceptualising Transnational Corporate Groups for International Criminal Law 30, 31 (2017).

[709] *Thomas Weigend*, JICJ 934 (2008); *Kai Ambos*, Wirtschaftsvölkerstrafrecht 49, 50 (2018).

[710] *Frank Meyer*, Schweizerische Zeitschrift für Strafrecht 81 (2013); *Caroline Kaeb*, Geo. Wash. Int'l. Rev. 385 (2016).

[711] *Frank Meyer*, Schweizerische Zeitschrift für Strafrecht 83 (2013).

[712] Similar *Frank Meyer*, ZStW 130 (2014); *Frank Meyer*, Schweizerische Zeitschrift für Strafrecht 85 (2013).

[713] *Frank Meyer*, Schweizerische Zeitschrift für Strafrecht 84 (2013).

priate sanctions for corporations under the Rome Statute speaks against the inclusion of corporate criminal liability in the Rome Statute.[714] Article 77 Rome Statute limits the available sanctions to imprisonment as the primary sanction, which can only be complemented by fines or the forfeiture of proceeds, property and assets.[715] However, corporations cannot be imprisoned. Thus, if corporate criminal liability were to be introduced into the Rome Statute without amending Article 77 Rome Statute, corporations could retain the profits which they have previously obtained through criminal conduct, whereas corporate managers could be sentenced to imprisonment and criminal fines. Hence, the inclusion of corporate criminal liability would inevitably necessitate the amendment of Article 77 Rome Statute by including appropriate penalties tailored to corporate activities, such as monetary fines, injunctions, corporate probation, licence revocation or dissolution.[716]

At first glance, financial sanctions appear to be the perfect fit for profit-driven corporations, which are thus expected to respond to monetary disincentives.[717] However, multinational corporations often have significant economic power, which is why sanctions must be sufficiently high to impact upon the corporation, but at the same time must not be excessively high so as to adversely affect innocent employees.[718] Nonetheless, similar to civil damages, imposing monetary sanctions simply puts a price tag on wrongdoings turning criminal liability into a mere cost-benefit analysis.[719] Thus, as long as corporations are willing to pay the price for their wrongdoings, the imposition of criminal fines will neither deter them from reoffending nor force them to adapt their corporate culture.[720] Hence, financial sanctions alone do not achieve the desired effect of deterring corporations from engaging in criminal conduct. Consequently, in this thesis it is suggested to incorporate non-financial sanctions as primary penalties under Article 77 (1) Rome Statute, which can be complemented by criminal fines under Article 77 (2) (a) Rome Statute.[721]

---

[714] *Eliana Teresa Cusato*, JICJ 504 (2017); *Mark Drumbl*, ILSA J. INT'L & COMP. L. 327, 328 (2000).

[715] *Rolf Einar Fife*, Article 77, Applicable Penalties, in: Rome Statute of the International Criminal Court para. 1 (Kai Ambos ed., 2022).

[716] *Ricardo Pereira*, Criminal Law Forum 220 (2020); *Eliana Teresa Cusato*, JICJ 504 (2017); *Mordechai Kremnitzer*, JICJ 915 (2010); see for an analysis of the different types of sanctions *Ronald C. Slye*, Brook. J. Int'L. 969–973 (2008); see for three approaches of corporate punishment *Caroline Kaeb*, Geo. Wash. Int'l. Rev. 386–396 (2016).

[717] *Caroline Kaeb*, Geo. Wash. Int'l. Rev. 388 (2016).

[718] *Vanessa Schwegeler*, The Disposable Nature: The Case of Ecocide and Corporate Accountability, 9 (3) Amsterdam Law Forum 71, 87 (2017); *Ronald C. Slye*, Brook. J. Int'L. 970 (2008).

[719] *Caroline Kaeb*, Geo. Wash. Int'l. Rev. 388, 389 (2016); *Vanessa Schwegeler*, Amsterdam Law Forum 87 (2017).

[720] *Caroline Kaeb*, Geo. Wash. Int'l. Rev. 388, 389 (2016); *Vanessa Schwegeler*, Amsterdam Law Forum 87 (2017).

[721] Similar *Caroline Kaeb*, Geo. Wash. Int'l. Rev. 389 (2016).

In this regard, Article 77 (1) Rome Statute could be amended to include injunctions which temporally or permanently prohibit corporations from engaging in certain activities.[722] Thus, by imposing injunctions companies can be prevented from operating in a certain country or from engaging in certain activities. For instance, textile companies discharging toxic waste into adjacent rivers or companies in the resource extraction industry exploiting the environment could be either proscribed from operating in the state the damage was caused or, *inter alia*, from discharging their waste into the environment. Thus, particularly in the context of environmental crimes where it is of utmost importance to halt the further causes of environmental destruction, the imposition of injunctions appears to be a promising method in promoting global environmental protection.

In a similar fashion, Article 77 (1) Rome Statute could be extended to include licence revocation as a possible corporate criminal sanction.[723] As such, licences which, for instance, allow corporations to extract natural resources, could be revoked. By doing so, large-scale environmental harm as a side-effect of industrial activities could be halted and a change in corporate culture could be promoted, as companies are expected to limit environmentally destructive practices for fear of losing their licences.

Furthermore, Article 77 (1) Rome Statute could include corporate probation as a possible sanction, meaning that companies' activities are monitored by an independent agency, such as a court, a domestic agency, an international organisation or a non-governmental organisation.[724] By doing so, corporate monitorship could not only establish an efficacious compliance system but also promote a shift in corporate practices.[725] However, corporate probation requires the cooperation with an independent agent. Particularly domestic agencies or governmental organisations bear the risk of being biased in favor of the multinational companies which provide the country with employment and infrastructure.

Additionally, the general confiscation of the corporation's assets could be included as a possible primary sanction.[726] Article 77 (2) (b) Rome Statute currently only allows the forfeiture of assets which are directly or indirectly derived from the crime. More importantly, this sanction can only be imposed to complement an imprisonment sentence but not as a primary sanction. As such, extending Article 77 (1) Rome Statute to include the general confiscation of the company's property as a primary sanction, which is not limited to the assets derived from the crime, would increase its deterrent effect on corporations since the confiscation would bring the

[722] *Ronald C. Slye*, Brook. J. Int'L. 971 (2008).

[723] *Ricardo Pereira*, Criminal Law Forum 220 (2020).

[724] *Ronald C. Slye*, Brook. J. Int'L. 971 (2008); *Caroline Kaeb*, Geo. Wash. Int'l. Rev. 392 (2016); *Mordechai Kremnitzer*, JICJ 915 (2010); *Ricardo Pereira*, Criminal Law Forum 220 (2020).

[725] See *Caroline Kaeb*, Geo. Wash. Int'l. Rev. 391–396 (2016).

[726] Id. at 390; *Mordechai Kremnitzer*, JICJ 915 (2010).

company's business to a standstill. For fear of financial loss this is also expected to alter the corporate practices and thus prevent the future commission of crimes. However, at the enforcement level the confiscation of company assets faces a multitude of political and practical obstacles since it requires the cooperation with the ICC Member States.[727]

As a last resort, Article 77 (1) Rome Statute could include the dissolution of a company, also referred to as "the corporate death penalty"[728]. However, the dissolution of a company is usually limited to corporations which do not pursue a legitimate business at all, but rather whose core purpose is illegal.[729] In the environmental context, the majority of environmental destruction is an unwanted but condoned side-effect of industrial activities. As such, in the environmental context the dissolution of companies is reserved for the most egregious cases of environmental destruction, where companies purposely destroy the environment.

However, in general, with regards to the gravity of the crimes under international law, the dissolution of companies may prove particularly meaningful for the pre-existing core crimes.[730] Nevertheless, despite its strong deterrent effect, it needs to be considered that after the dissolution of a company a new corporation engaging in similar activities may just be reopened.[731]

Since imposing non-financial sanctions, as primary sanctions entail a higher potential deterrent effect, non-financial criminal sanctions seem to be better suited as primary penalties than criminal fines. With regard to the primary goal of promoting global environmental protection in the environmental context, the imposition of injunctions and the revocation of licences seem particularly important. Nonetheless, when speaking of a potential deterrent effect on corporations it needs to be considered that the abovementioned rationales of punishment are tailored to natural persons and it thus appears questionable as to whether these purposes can even be transferred to business entities.[732] In terms of retribution, the fictitious aggregate guilt in the case of corporate criminal liability renders it difficult to mete out a proportionate sanction in relation to the gravity of the criminal conduct and thus provide retributive justice.[733] However, the same concerns exist in the context

[727] *Caroline Kaeb*, Geo. Wash. Int'l. Rev. 390, 391 (2016). See generally on the lack of an effective international enforcement regime, Chapter C. VII. 3.

[728] Id. at 390.

[729] *Ronald C. Slye*, Brook. J. Int'L. 972, 973 (2008).

[730] Similar *Caroline Kaeb*, Geo. Wash. Int'l. Rev. 390 (2016).

[731] *Ronald C. Slye*, Brook. J. Int'L. 972 (2008).

[732] *Kai Ambos*, Wirtschaftsvölkerstrafrecht 42 (2018).

[733] *Frank Meyer*, Schweizerische Zeitschrift für Strafrecht 83 (2013).

of individual criminal liability, where it is doubtful whether the imposition of a custodial sentence matches the egregious gravity of the crimes.[734]

In terms of deterrence, it needs to be considered that as legal entities corporations do not have a conscience and thus cannot be responsive to the threat of criminal sanctions.[735] Instead, the corporate culture only changes if the criminal punishment collaterally affects natural persons, such as officers, shareholders or customers, who then reshape the corporate culture.[736] As with individual criminal responsibility, the deterrent effect of punishment is further complicated by the highly selective enforcement of international criminal law.[737] By contrast, it may be argued that the loss of reputation accompanying a criminal sanction deters corporations from committing crimes and thus incentivises corporations to improve their corporate culture, whereas sanctioning business leaders only renders corporate officials scapegoats while the corporate culture continues to exist.[738] Thus, it is argued that the corporate culture only changes by holding the corporate entity as such criminally liable and not by focusing on the culpable individual.[739] Hence, retributive justice and deterrence may only be attained by holding corporations directly criminally liable.[740] Advocates of corporate criminal liability even go as far as to say that the rationales of criminal punishment align more appropriately with corporate criminal liability concerning the purposes of deterrence and retribution than with individual criminal liability.[741]

In any event, only appropriate sanctions have the potential to attain the desired objectives of criminal punishment. Nevertheless, the current Rome Statute clearly lacks adequate sanctions for corporations. Thus, if corporate criminal liability were incorporated into the Rome Statute, this would necessitate an amendment to Article 77 (1) Rome Statute.

Hence, in this thesis it is proposed to include Article 77 (1) (c) Rome Statute stipulating non-financial sanctions as primary penalties for corporations, including injunctions, licence revocation, corporate probation, the confiscation of company assets and, as a last resort, the dissolution of companies. In the light of the rationales

---

[734] *Mark Drumbl*, We're Exhausting Ourselves, Let's Get Busy Instead 198 (2020); *Frank Neubacher*, Criminology of International Crimes 27 (2020); *Klaus Günther/Vasco Reuss*, Legitimation des Völkerstrafrechts 147 (2014).

[735] *Thomas Weigend*, JICJ 941 (2008).

[736] Id.

[737] *Frank Meyer*, Schweizerische Zeitschrift für Strafrecht 83 (2013).

[738] *Carsten Stahn*, A Critical Introduction to International Criminal Law 125 (2019); International Commission of Jurists, Report of the International Commission of Jurists Expert Legal Panel on Corporate Complicity in International Crimes, Volume 2 59 (2008); *Kai Ambos*, Wirtschaftsvölkerstrafrecht 41 (2018).

[739] *Ronald C. Slye*, Brook. J. Int'L. 963 (2008).

[740] Id.

[741] *Caroline Kaeb*, Geo. Wash. Int'l. Rev. 382 (2016); *Ronald C. Slye*, Brook. J. Int'L. 960 (2008); *Joanna Kyriakakis*, Leiden Journal of International Law 236, 237 (2017).

of punishment, these sanctions are deemed most effective if they were imposed concurrently and complemented by criminal fines under Article 77 (2) Rome Statute. Although it can be disputed whether the traditional purposes of punishment tailored to individual criminal liability can be transferred to corporate criminal liability, it appears very likely that the combination of non-financial sanctions with criminal fines matching the global annual revenue of the corporation has the potential to effectively deter corporations from offending for fear of reputational damage and could further provide retributive justice. Furthermore, establishing corporate criminal liability at the international level would educate the international community that corporations do not go unpunished and thus incentivise corporations to refrain from engaging in criminal conduct in order to comply with international standards (positive general prevention).[742]

(3) Conclusion

The debate concerning the inclusion of corporate criminal liabilityin international criminal law was reignited in the context of a new crime of ecocide. In this regard, the question, which needs to be answered is whether the lack of corporate criminal liability would impede the effective enforcement of a fifth crime of ecocide and would thus necessitate the inclusion of corporate criminal liability into the Rome Statute. Since the majority of large-scale environmental harm is committed by multinational corporations, corporate involvement plays an important role in the context of environmental destruction. However, due to the lack of corporate criminal liability under the current Rome Statute, the ICC's jurisdiction is limited to the individual criminal liability of business leaders.

Yet, proving the individual criminal liability of business leaders under the Rome Statute faces multiple challenges. For one, the material and mental requirements for the different modes of liability in Article 25 (3) (a), (c), (d), and 28 (b) Rome Statute are too restrictive, in particular excluding most cases where business leaders located in the Global North omitted to avoid the causation of large-scale environmental harm perpetrated by employees of their legally independent subsidiary company in the Global South. Additionally, the fragmented and hierarchical organisation of multinational corporations involving a multiplicity of agents operating in a variety of countries renders it difficult to trace back criminal actions to an individual culpable, who causally contributed to the perpetration of the crime. In the environmental context, this is exacerbated by the fact that many environmental crimes are perpetrated by agents of a subsidiary company located in the Global South and only remotely assisted by officials of the parent company situated in the Global North. Due to the legal and evidentiary obstacles concerning individual criminal liability of corporate officials, large parts of the criminal conduct involving corporations go unpunished. While corporate managers continue to hide under their corporate veil, corporations cannot be held directly criminally liable under the current Rome

[742] *Frank Meyer*, Schweizerische Zeitschrift für Strafrecht 84 (2013).

Statute due to the explicit exclusion of corporate criminal liability under Article 25 (1) Rome Statute. In doing so, international criminal law further promotes the "current corporate friendly climate"[743].

Hence, to fill this 'governance gap', a number of scholars advocate the inclusion of corporate criminal liability into Article 25 (1) Rome Statute. Nonetheless, the incorporation of corporate criminal liability faces numerous obstacles under international criminal law. While initially the principle of complementarity was the main reason stated at the Rome Conference for rejecting the inclusion of corporate criminal liability, this reasoning now seems to have lost its significance. Despite a few isolated civil law jurisdictions, there is a clear inclination in favour of corporate criminal liability nowadays.[744] Thus, since the concept of corporate criminal liability is prevalent in most common law as well as civil law jurisdictions, this argument against the inclusion of corporate criminal liability seems to have lost its validity.[745] Nevertheless, in this regard it needs to be considered that although most jurisdictions these days have enshrined corporate criminal liability, no consensus has been reached with respect to the conceptualisation of corporate criminal liability. Thus, as long as the Member States of the ICC do not provide similar concepts of corporate criminal liability, the principle of complementarity will be rendered obsolete.

In conclusion, there are valid arguments against the incorporation of corporate criminal liability into the Rome Statute.

First, although corporate criminal liability is mostly advocated to *complement* individual criminal liability of business leaders, corporate criminal liability detracts from the cornerstone principle of individual criminal responsibility inherent in international criminal law.

Secondly, due to the lack of consensus regarding the constituting elements of corporate criminal liability, two competing models of corporate criminal liability have emerged in domestic jurisdictions, both of which prove inadequate to be transferred to international criminal law. While the first model, which is based on the attribution of individual guilt faces similar evidentiary challenges as establishing individual criminal liability of business leaders, the second collective model, which is based on the mere organisational failure of the corporation, is predicated on a mere fiction which appears to clash with the fragile core principle of individual guilt in international criminal law. Thus, in the author's view, proponents of corporate

---

[743] *Audrey Crasson*, Amsterdam Law Forum 30 (2017).

[744] *Frank Meyer*, ZStW 124, 125 (2014); *Gerhard Werle/Florian Jeßberger*, Principles of International Criminal Law para. 147 (2020); *Joanna Kyriakakis*, NILR, 336–343 (2009); *Caroline Kaeb*, Geo. Wash. Int'l. Rev. 380 (2016).

[745] *Caroline Kaeb*, Geo. Wash. Int'l. Rev. 353, 381 (2016); *David Scheffer*, Harvard International Law Journal 38 (2016); *Simon M. Meisenberg*, Auf dem Wege zu einem Unternehmensvölkerstrafrecht? 77, 78 (2016); more detailed *Gabriel Wilhelm Bartalyos Thurner*, Internationales Unternehmensstrafrecht 243–249 (2012).

criminal liability appear too eager to fill the governance gap concerning corporate criminality thereby disregarding the core principles of international criminal law.

Thirdly, since corporations cannot be imprisoned, the current Rome Statute lacks adequate sanctions to punish corporations, such as non-financial sanctions, including injunctions, licence revocation, corporate probation, the confiscation of company assets or the dissolution of companies. Thus, if the concept of corporate criminal liability were to be included in the Rome Statute, this would inevitably necessitate an amendment to Article 77 (1) Rome Statute. Notwithstanding, amendments to Article 25 (1) and Article 77 (1) Rome Statute appear rather unlikely. As Scheffer rightly observed: "Nations with economies that are fuelled by multinational corporations, either as home states or host states, would likely oppose efforts to expose these companies to criminal liability before the ICC"[746]. In this vein, Werle rightly argued that "it is undisputed that the involvement of corporations in the commission of core crimes is not sufficiently reflected in the practice of international criminal law. As the Nuremberg follow-up trials showed, the importance of corporate activities in the context of crimes under international law may also be expressed in the individual criminal responsibility of specific businesspeople, without necessarily resorting to corporate criminal liability as such".[747] Hence, it is to be followed that corporate involvement in international criminal law is sufficiently addressed by the individual criminal liability of business leaders, without having to resort to the establishment of corporate criminal liability.

In conclusion, it is held that not the lack of corporate criminal liability would impede the effective enforcement of a new crime of ecocide[748], but rather the significantly high and ambiguous prerequisites of Article 25 (3) and 28 (b) Rome Statute complicating the conviction of business leaders. Hence, instead of including corporate criminal liability, the pre-existing modes of liability, in particular Article 25 (3) (d) and 28 (b) Rome Statute should be applied and interpreted less restrictively and more clearly in order to include the criminal conduct of business leaders.[749] Additionally, systems to effectively monitor corporate involvement should be improved and complemented so as to facilitate the discovery of crimes and the identification of individual perpetrators hiding beneath the corporate veil.[750]

c) Lack of universal jurisdiction

The effective enforcement of a new crime of ecocide under the Rome Statute is further impeded by the ICC's lack of universal jurisdiction. At the time the Rome

---

[746] *David Scheffer*, Harvard International Law Journal 38 (2016).

[747] *Gerhard Werle/Florian Jeßberger*, Principles of International Criminal Law para. 149 (2020).

[748] Contra *Emanuela Fronza*, Towards a New Crime of Ecocide 101 (2022).

[749] *Kai Ambos*, Wirtschaftsvölkerstrafrecht 79 (2018); *Frank Meyer*, ZStW 131 (2014).

[750] *Frank Meyer*, Schweizerische Zeitschrift für Strafrecht 72 (2013).

Statute was drafted, Germany proposed, amongst other proposals from other states[751], to ascribe universal jurisdiction to the ICC.[752] In Article 9 (1) of the German proposal it was suggested to authorise the ICC to exercise jurisdiction over the four core crimes listed in Article 5 Rome Statute irrespective of whether, where and by whom they were committed and thus without any direct relation to the crimes.[753] It was argued that it is "well established in customary and conventional international law that certain crimes are against the universal interests, offend against universal public policy and are universally condemned".[754] Thus, any state is permitted to prosecute these crimes in the interest of all states without having a direct connection to the crimes.[755] It was argued that by granting the ICC universal jurisdiction, jurisdictional loopholes limiting the effectiveness of the Court and letting serious crimes go unpunished would be avoided.[756]

Nevertheless, the German proposal was ultimately rejected at the Rome Conference due to political reasons, and instead the states agreed on a compromise – the present Articles 12, 13 Rome Statute.[757]

Article 13 Rome Statute stipulates three 'trigger mechanisms' triggering the jurisdiction of the ICC. Firstly, a situation of alleged crimes can be referred to the Prosecutor by a State Party, so-called *self-referrals* pursuant to Articles 13 (a), 14 Rome Statute. Secondly, the UN Security Council may refer situations to the Prosecutor in accordance with Article 13 (b) Rome Statute and, thirdly, the Prosecutor themself can initiate investigations *proprio motu* under Articles 13 (c) and 15 Rome Statute.

However, a State Party or the Prosecutor acting *proprio motu* can only refer situations which are already within the jurisdiction of the ICC, meaning that the alleged crimes were either committed on the territory of a State Party (Article 12 (2) (a) Rome Statute), or by a national of a State Party (Article 12 (2) (b) Rome Statute). Thus, the jurisdiction of the ICC is predominantly based on the principle of territoriality[758] (Article 12 (a) Rome Statute) and the principle of active personali-

---

[751] See the other proposals concerning the jurisdiction of the ICC, *William Schabas/Giulia Pecorella*, Article 12, Preconditions to the Exercise of Jurisdiction, in: Rome Statute of the International Criminal Court paras. 6–12 (Kai Ambos ed., 2022); *William A. Schabas*, The International Criminal Court: A Commentary on the Rome Statute 346–350 (2016).

[752] *William Schabas/Giulia Pecorella*, Article 12 paras. 5–7 (2022); *William A. Schabas*, The International Criminal Court: A Commentary on the Rome Statute 346 (2016).

[753] *William Schabas/Giulia Pecorella*, Article 12 paras. 6, 7 (2022).

[754] Id. at para. 7.

[755] Id.

[756] Id.; *William A. Schabas*, The International Criminal Court: A Commentary on the Rome Statute 346 (2016).

[757] *William Schabas/Giulia Pecorella*, Article 12 para. 12 (2022); *Gerhard Werle/Florian Jeßberger*, Principles of International Criminal Law para. 274 (2020).

[758] *William Schabas/Giulia Pecorella*, Article 12 para. 16 (2022).

ty[759] (Article 12 (2) (b) Rome Statute), which are both universally accepted principles under international law.[760] In accordance with Article 12 (3) Rome Statute, non-State parties may also accept the jurisdiction of the ICC. Until now, 123 states have ratified the Rome Statute and thereby became States Parties to the Rome Statute of the ICC.[761] In the environmental context, it is particularly noteworthy that the four most polluting countries – China, the US, India and the Russian Federation[762] – are not State Parties to the ICC and are unlikely to accept the Court's jurisdiction.[763] Thus, these countries may only be subjected to the ICC's jurisdiction if environmental harm was committed by one of their nationals on the territory of a Member State.

From Articles 12 (2) and 13 (b) Rome Statute, it follows conversely that irrespective of the site of the crime and the nationality of the perpetrator, the ICC may only exercise jurisdiction if the UN Security Council refers a situation on the basis of Chapter VII of the UN Charter in accordance with Article 13 (b) Rome Statute. Thus, Article 13 (b) Rome Statute is particularly relevant for cases where crimes were committed on the territory of non-member States, thereby extending the territorial jurisdiction of the ICC. Thus, at least in relation to Article 13 (b) Rome Statute the jurisdiction of the ICC is partly based on the principle of universality.[764]

However, so far, the UN Security Council has only referred two cases in total, including the situations in Libya and Sudan.[765] This is mostly due to the fact that all five permanent Member States, including China, France, the Russian Federation, the UK and the US[766] can veto any resolution to refer a situation to the ICC.[767] In the context of environmental harm this is particularly relevant as China the US, and the Russian Federation are amongst the four most polluting countries[768] and are thus

[759] Id. at para. 24.

[760] *Gerhard Werle/Florian Jeßberger*, Principles of International Criminal Law para. 258 (2020).

[761] International Criminal Court, The States Parties to the Rome Statute, https://asp.icc-cpi.int/en_menus/asp/states%20parties/Pages/the%20states%20parties%20to%20the%20rome%20statute.aspx (last visited Feb. 18, 2025).

[762] World Population Review, Pollution by Country 2022, https://worldpopulationreview.com/country-rankings/pollution-by-country (last visited Feb. 18, 2025).

[763] *Martin Heger*, Umweltvölkerstrafrecht 142 (2022); *Liemertje Julia Sieders*, RIDP 45 (2020).

[764] *Gerhard Werle/Florian Jeßberger*, Principles of International Criminal Law para. 274 (2020).

[765] *William Schabas/Giulia Pecorella*, Article 13, Exercise of Jurisdiction, in: Rome Statute of the International Criminal Court paras. 19–23 (Kai Ambos ed., 2022).

[766] U.N. Security Council, Current Members, https://www.un.org/securitycouncil/content/current-members (last visited Feb. 18, 2025).

[767] *William A. Schabas*, An Introduction to the International Criminal Court 160 (2020).

[768] World Population Review, Pollution by Country 2022, https://worldpopulationreview.com/country-rankings/pollution-by-country (last visited Feb. 18, 2025).

likely to veto any referral of a situation involving the allegation of large-scale environmental damage. As such, non-member States, such as China, the US and the Russian Federation may only be subjected to the ICC's jurisdiction if one of their nationals caused environmental harm on the territory of a State Member referring the respective situation or if the Prosecution initiates *proprio motu* investigations in such a situation. Therefore, the ICC's jurisdiction largely depends on the willingness of State Parties or the Prosecutor to refer situations involving large-scale environmental harm which was committed on the territory of a Member State. Hence, particularly in the environmental context, the jurisdiction of the ICC is severely limited by the lack of universal jurisdiction.

Although the majority of environmental harm is caused in the Global South, which mostly consists of Member States of the ICC, multinational corporations exert significant power on the often instable governments in the Global South, which heavily rely upon these corporations for revenue, employment and infrastructure. Thus, it appears rather unlikely that State Parties having sustained environmental harm caused by industrial activities would refer respective situations to the Prosecutor of the ICC. However, at the same time these developing countries, which historically contributed the least to the climate crisis, are the countries most affected by climate change and industrial environmental destruction, whose repercussions are already palpable and threaten everyday life. Thus, if a new crime of ecocide were to be introduced into the Rome Statute, many countries in the Global South which have continuously sustained large-scale environmental harm for the past decades caused by multinational corporations exploiting their countries, may be incentivised to refer these situations to the Prosecutor. If an increasing number of countries in the Global South refrained from submitting to the power of multinational corporations, corporations would be forced to conduct their businesses in an environmentally friendly manner as businesses depend on the resource-rich Global South, particularly in the field of resource exploitation. Nevertheless, in this regard, it has to be considered that many states financially depend on the cooperation with multinational corporations which provide employment and thus secure the survival of these states' nationals.

Hence, although the lack of universal jurisdiction limits the enforcement of a new crime of ecocide, its effectiveness is not fully impeded, as particularly state referrals in the environmental context appear likely to proliferate in the future due to constantly deteriorating environmental conditions in the Global South.

d) Principle of complementarity

For the purpose of protecting state sovereignty[769], the ICC was, as opposed to the Nuremberg Military Tribunal, the ICTY or the ICTR[770], designed to *complement*,

---

[769] *William A. Schabas*, An Introduction to the International Criminal Court 188 (2020).

not *replace* national criminal jurisdictions based on the principle of complementarity.[771] Thus, domestic courts remain the primary judicial bodies to adjudicate upon the core crimes.[772] Hence, a case can only be heard by the ICC if a "[s]tate is unwilling or unable genuinely to carry out the investigation or prosecution".[773] The question as to whether a state is 'unwilling' or 'unable' to investigate or prosecute is determined by the ICC itself. [774] States are, *inter alia*, unable to investigate or prosecute, if they have not transposed a crime under international law into their national criminal system.[775] So far, only 11 states have incorporated a generic crime of ecocide into their domestic criminal codes.[776] Vietnam was the first country which enacted a crime of ecocide into domestic law in 1990 responding to the environmental harm it sustained during the Vietnam War.[777]

Although the Preamble of the Rome Statute affirms that the effective prosecution of the core crimes "must be ensured by taking measures at the national level and by enhancing international cooperation"[778] and recalls "that it is the duty of every State to exercise its criminal jurisdiction over those responsible for international crimes"[779], the Rome Statute lacks any direct legal obligation for Member States to transpose the crimes under international law into their domestic law.[780] Nevertheless, it is the underlying concept of the Rome Statute that all Member States are, similar to the ICC, equally capable of prosecuting the core crimes.[781]

---

[770] *Gerhard Werle/Florian Jeßberger*, Principles of International Criminal Law paras. 307–311 (2020).

[771] Preamble of the Rome Statute (10), Art. 1 and 17 (1) Rome Statute; *Gerhard Werle/Florian Jeßberger*, Principles of International Criminal Law paras. 314 (2020).

[772] *Gerhard Werle/Florian Jeßberger*, Principles of International Criminal Law paras. 314 (2020); *Tim Stephens*, International Courts and Environmental Protection 56 (2009).

[773] Art. 17 (1) (a) Rome Statute.

[774] *Gerhard Werle/Florian Jeßberger*, Principles of International Criminal Law para. 314 (2020).

[775] *Christoph Safferling*, Internationales Strafrecht § 7 para. 23 (2011).

[776] Ecocide law, Ecocide Law in National Jurisdictions, https://ecocidelaw.com/existing-ecocide-laws/ (last visited Feb. 18, 2025).

[777] Penal Code Vietnam (1990) art. 278: "Ecocide or destroying the natural environment", whether committed during war or peace, constitutes a crime against humanity. In 1999 the crime of ecocide was included in Art. 342 of the Penal Code Vietnam, No. 15/1999/QH10 (1999).

[778] Preamble of the Rome Statute (4).

[779] Preamble of the Rome Statute (6).

[780] By contrast, see Convention against Torture and Other Cruel, Inhuman or Degrading Treatment or Punishment art. 4, Dec. 10, 1984, 1465 U.N.T.S. 85 ("Each State Party shall ensure that all acts of torture are offences under its criminal law [...] Each State Party shall make these offences punishable by appropriate penalties which take into account their grave nature").

[781] *Gerhard Werle*, Konturen des deutschen Völkerstrafrechts: Zum Arbeitsentwurf eines Völkerstrafgesetzbuchs, 56 (18) JuristenZeitung 885, 886 (2001); *Gerhard Werle/Florian*

Thus, the establishment of a fifth crime of ecocide would incentivise domestic jurisdictions to criminalise environmental harm, as domestic jurisdictions often mimic international trends by transferring international crimes into national law.[782] By doing so, domestic judicial systems would contribute to the enhancement of global environmental protection.[783] If enough countries criminalise ecocide under national law, the crime of ecocide might, at some point, even be acknowledged as a crime under customary international law.[784] However, if the states that have criminalised environmental harm are willing and genuinely able to carry out the investigation or prosecution, national jurisdictions would take precedence over the ICC with regard to the prosecution of crimes of ecocide. Hence, the enforcement of the fifth crime of ecocide would largely be entrusted to the Member States, which eventually leads to inconsistent environmental standards. By contrast, an International Environmental Court, which would take precedence over national judicial systems, could establish uniform global environmental standards that national courts could be bound by.

Hence, the principle of complementarity impedes the establishment of uniform global environmental standards since the enforcement of a fifth crime of ecocide under the Rome Statute is primarily entrusted to the states which are willing and able to investigate and prosecute environmental crimes. Thus, subsequent to the incorporation of a fifth crime of ecocide, more Member States are likely to enshrine comparable crimes of ecocide into their own domestic laws, withdrawing from the ICC's competence to adjudicate upon crimes of ecocide.

2. Lack of restorative and injunctive sanctions

With respect to the desired purpose of promoting global environmental protection, the sanctions available under the current Rome Statute appear inadequate to bring this goal to fruition. As mentioned above, the penalties available are limited to imprisonment as the primary sanction, which can only be complemented by fines or forfeiture of assets in accordance with Article 77 Rome Statute. Thus, the Rome Statute lacks restorative remedies to reinstate the damaged environment as well as injunctive remedies to prevent environmental harm from occurring.[785]

In terms of reparative justice, Article 75 (1) Rome Statute permits the ICC to grant reparations in the form of restitution, compensation and rehabilitation to vic-

---

Jeßberger, Völkerstrafgesetzbuch, Einleitung, VStGB und Völkerrecht, in: Münchener Kommentar zum StGB para. 36 (Volker Erb/Jürgen Schäfer eds., 2022).

[782] See *Robert Cryer*, et al., An Introduction to International Criminal Law and Procedure 553, 554 (2019); *Mark Drumbl*, Atrocity 123 (2007).

[783] *Frédéric Mégret*, Colum. J. Envtl. L. 237 (2011).

[784] *Anastacia Greene*, Fordham Environmental Law Review 46 (2019).

[785] *Mark Drumbl*, ILSA J. INT'L & COMP. L. 327, 328 (2000); *Anastacia Greene*, Fordham Environmental Law Review 40 (2019).

tims. Thus, as opposed to other international criminal tribunals, the ICC is characterised by establishing not only corrective but also reparative justice.[786] However, in accordance with Article 75 (2) Rome Statute, a reparation order requires the conviction of a person. If a convicted person lacks sufficient assets to satisfy an order for reparations, the reparations may also be withdrawn from a Trust Fund which is financed through voluntary contributions from corporations, individuals, international organisations or governments.[787] Nonetheless, pursuant to Rule 85 of the Rules of Procedure and Evidence, 'victims' are defined as natural persons or organisations and institutions.[788] Thus, the environment as such does not qualify as a victim in the sense of Article 75 Rome Statute.[789] Hence, in the context of environmental harm, under the current Rome Statute reparations may only be granted to natural persons, whose existence depends on the environment.[790] Nonetheless, the lack of restorative sanctions concerning environmental harm is the most daunting impediment to the feasibility of a new crime of ecocide. Effective environmental protection can only be attained through the prevention of further environmental harm as well as the remediation of environmental destruction which has already occurred. Thus, the incorporation of a fifth crime of ecocide would necessitate the introduction of 'reinstatement of the environment' as a complementary sanction into Article 77 (2) Rome Statute. In this regard, the inclusion of a fifth crime of ecocide is inextricably linked to the establishment of a new category of victims, namely the environment as such, requiring a shift from the strictly anthropocentric focus to a biocentric approach. This would be in line with the 1998 Council of Europe's Convention on the Protection of the Environment Through Criminal Law, which contained the reinstatement of the environment as a possible criminal sanction under Article 6.[791] This would further correspond to the 2021 proposed EU Crime Directive which also includes the restoration of the environment as a criminal sanction.[792] The inclusion of the reinstatement of the environment as an additional type of sanction would not only be essential for a new crime of ecocide, but would also be beneficial for the prosecution of environmental harm falling within the ambit of the pre-existing core crimes. Since the adoption of the 2016 OTP policy paper, the ICC is supposed to strengthen its focus on investigating and prosecuting

[786] *Rosemary Mwanza*, Melb. Journal of International Law 23 (2018).

[787] Establishment of a Fund for the Benefit of Victims of Crimes within the Jurisdiction of the Court, and of the Families of such Victims, Resolution ICC-ASP/1/Res.6, para. 8 (Sept. 9, 2002).

[788] See ICC Rules of Procedure and Evidence, Rule 85.

[789] *Mark Drumbl*, ILSA J. INT'L & COMP. L. 328 (2000); *Eliana Teresa Cusato*, JICJ 505, 506 (2017).

[790] *Marcos Orellana*, Geo. Int'l Envtl. L. Rev. 695, 696 (2005).

[791] Convention on the Protection of the Environment through Criminal Law, ETS 172 (Nov. 4, 1998).

[792] European Commission, Question and Answers on the Revised EU Directive on Environmental Crime, https://ec.europa.eu/commission/presscorner/detail/en/QANDA_21_6745 (last visited Feb. 18, 2025).

environmental harm falling within the purview of the pre-existing core crimes. However, the prosecution of environmental destruction only proves meaningful if the environmental harm sustained is reinstated.

Since most convicted perpetrators would most likely be unable to provide sufficient assets to remedy large-scale environmental destruction, it is advised to establish an Environmental Trust Fund providing national environmental organisations located in the country where the environmental destruction was sustained with financial means to perform the environmental rehabilitation.[793] Similar to Article 79 Rome Statute, this Environmental Trust Fund could be financed through fines, forfeitures and voluntary contributions by private donors for the reason of environmental rehabilitation.[794] The idea of establishing environmental funds is not novel. In this regard, the Global Environment Facility (GEF) established in 1991, which is the world's largest global fund to assist developing countries in financing projects for environmental protection, could serve as a precedent.[795] More recently, at the United Nations Climate Change Conference (COP27) in 2022, it was decided to establish a 'loss and damage' fund for developing countries stricken by climate disasters.[796] However, due to the lack of corporate criminal liability, corporations cannot be convicted and thus cannot be ordered to pay criminal fines under the Rome Statute. As such, corporations can only be incentivised and forced by economic means to contribute to the Environmental Trust Fund, depending on their individual contribution to environmental harm.

As already stated above, the Rome Statute further lacks injunctive remedies as primary sanctions under Article 77 (1) to prevent the further occurrence of environmental crimes.[797] Hence, the inclusion of a fifth crime of ecocide would necessitate the incorporation of restorative as well as injunctive remedies into Article 77 Rome Statute.

3. Lack of an effective international enforcement regime

Furthermore, not only the effective enforcement of a new crime of ecocide but also the enforcement of *all* core crimes is impeded by the lack of an international enforcement regime. With regard to the arrest of suspects, the discovery of evidence

[793] Similar *Rosemary Mwanza*, Melb. Journal of International Law 23, 24 (2018); *Mark Drumbl*, ILSA J. INT'L & COMP. L. 331 (2000).

[794] *Mark Drumbl*, ILSA J. INT'L & COMP. L. 331 (2000); *Rosemary Mwanza*, Melb. Journal of International Law 23 (2018).

[795] GEF, Who We Are, https://www.thegef.org/who-we-are (last visited Feb. 18, 2025).

[796] *Fiona Harvey*, et al., Cop27 Agrees Historic 'Loss and Damage' Fund for Climate Impact in Developing Countries, The Guardian, Nov. 20, 2022, https://www.theguardian.com/environment/2022/nov/20/cop27-agrees-to-historic-loss-and-damage-fund-to-compensate-developing-countries-for-climate-impacts.

[797] See Chapter C. VII. 2.

as well as the imprisonment of defendants, the ICC is fully reliant upon its Member States.[798] To put it in a nutshell, there are no 'international police' tasked with the enforcement of international criminal law.[799] Thus, the enforcement of international criminal law is entrusted to domestic authorities, whose jurisdiction the ICC has ousted.[800] However, this lack of an international enforcement regime impedes the deterrent effect of international criminal law, as the probability of a conviction remains low. Nonetheless, this impediment does not derive from the theory of deterrence per se but could be rectified by establishing more institutions and constabulary and increasing the financial means of the ICC thereby elevating the likelihood of a conviction.[801]

Furthermore, the enforcement of international criminal law is highly selective.[802] The case selection depends upon the Prosecutor's discretion[803], whereby the gravity of the situation is the primary case selection criterion.[804] Thus, only the gravest forms of environmental harm can be adjudicated upon by the ICC, excluding less serious cases of environmental destruction from criminal liability. Although the 2016 OTP policy paper emphasised that "the Office [of the Prosecutor] will give particular consideration to prosecuting Rome Statute crimes that are committed by means of, or that result in, *inter alia*, the destruction of the environment, the illegal exploitation of natural resources or the illegal dispossession of land"[805], the enforcement of a new crime of ecocide depends on the willingness of the Prosecutor, who exercises his or her discretion over the selection of cases. This selective enforcement of international crimes impedes the desired theory of deterrence, as only provisions which are effectively enforced have a deterrent effect on potential perpetrators.[806]

4. Conclusion

In conclusion, the enforcement of a fifth crime of ecocide under the Rome Statute would face multiple impediments. Firstly, with respect to the temporal jurisdiction of the ICC, a crime of ecocide cannot be enforced retrospectively over

---

[798] *Robert Cryer*, et al., An Introduction to International Criminal Law and Procedure 558 (2019).

[799] Id. at 551.

[800] *Mark Drumbl*, Atrocity 170 (2007).

[801] Id.

[802] *Gerhard Werle/Florian Jeßberger*, Principles of International Criminal Law para. 113 (2020); in general *Ronen Steinke*, Selektive Strafverfolgung: Über ein wachsendes Problem der internationalen Strafjustiz, 41 (2) Kritische Justiz 207 (2014).

[803] See Art. 53 (1) and (2) Rome Statute.

[804] Office of the Prosecutor, Policy Paper on Case Selection and Prioritisation para. 6 (2016).

[805] Id. at para. 41.

[806] *Christoph Safferling*, Internationales Strafrecht § 4 para. 71 (2011).

environmental destruction which had been committed before the new crime entered into force, as this would clash with the *nullum crimen sine lege* maxim stipulated in Article 22 (1) Rome Statute. Thus, if a new crime of ecocide were included into the Rome Statute, only conduct occurring after the amendment's entry into force would be prosecutable by the ICC. In the event of *continuing crimes*, the ICC can only exercise jurisdiction over environmentally destructive conduct which entails a substantial likelihood of severe and either widespread or long-term environmental damage after Article 8 *ter* Rome Statute entered into force. However, this is not an argument against the inclusion of a fifth crime of ecocide but rather an incentive to establish such a new crime sooner rather than later.

Secondly, and more importantly the requirements of the relevant modes of liability in the environmental context, including Articles 25 (3) (a), (c), (d) and 28 (b) Rome Statute, are too restrictive rendering the conviction of business leaders very unlikely. At the same time, the ICC's personal jurisdiction is restricted to individual criminal liability thereby excluding corporate criminal liability. However, particularly the lack of a suitable concept of corporate criminal liability for international criminal law, as well as the principle of individual guilt in international criminal law speak against the inclusion of corporate criminal liability into the Rome Statute. Thus, not the paucity of corporate criminal liability but rather the inadequately high requirements and ambiguous interpretation of Articles 25 (3) (a), (c), (d) and 28 (b) Rome Statute impede the enforcement of a new crime of ecocide. Hence, instead of establishing corporate criminal liability, the ICC should focus on applying and interpreting the relevant modes of attribution, especially Article 25 (3) (d) and Article 28 (b) Rome Statute, less restrictively in order to cover environmental harm caused by business leaders.

Thirdly, the enforcement of a new crime of ecocide is limited by the lack of universal jurisdiction of the ICC. Since referrals by the UN Security Council would most likely be vetoed by one of the permanent members and most polluting countries China, the US, or the Russian Federation, the prosecution of crimes of ecocide largely depends on the willingness of the Member States to refer respective situations to the Prosecutor (Articles 13 (a), 14 Rome Statute) as well as on the Prosecutor to instigate investigations *proprio motu (*Articles 13 (c), 15 Statute). Due to the principle of territoriality (Article 12 (2) (a) Rome Statute) and the principle of active personality (Article 12 (2) (b) Rome Statute), non-member States may only be subjected to the ICC's jurisdiction through state referrals or *proprio motu* investigations if one of their nationals caused environmental harm on the territory of a State Member. As the bulk of large-scale environmental harm is caused in the resource-rich Global South, self-referrals of Member States experiencing natural exploitation and pollution caused by multinational corporations appear to be the most likely mechanism to trigger the ICC to exercise its jurisdiction. However, although most countries in the Global South are Member States of the ICC and thus could subject nationals of non-member States, including China, the US, India and the Russian Federation, to the jurisdiction of the ICC, these developing countries financially depend on the employment and infrastructure provided by the multinational corporations exploiting them. However, the fact that these countries are the most affected by climate change and environmental destruction may promote self-referrals of environmental crimes. Nevertheless, in terms of territorial jurisdiction state referrals and *proprio motu* investigations are restricted to crimes which were committed on the territory of Member States.

Fourthly, due to the principle of complementarity, the ICC may only assume jurisdiction over crimes of ecocide if states are unwilling or unable to investigate or prosecute environmental crimes. Thus, by transferring crimes of ecocide into their domestic criminal codes national jurisdictions can assume primary jurisdiction over these crimes. However, entrusting the enforcement of the crime of ecocide to national judicial systems results in inconsistent environmental standards. Hence, the principle of complementarity impedes the establishment of uniform global environmental standards.

Fifthly, the enforcement of a new crime of ecocide is severely stymied by the lack of restorative and injunctive remedies under the current Rome Statute. Effective environmental protection necessitates an amendment to Article 77 Rome Statute to include (1) injunctive powers to prevent environmental harm from occurring, and (2) restorative remedies to reinstate the environment coupled with the establishment of an Environmental Trust Fund providing national environmental organisations located in the affected country with the necessary financial means to rehabilitate the environment. The introduction of injunctive and restorative sanctions would not only benefit a new crime of ecocide but also the pre-existing core crimes. Nonetheless, the inclusion of 'remediation of the environment' as an additional sanction would introduce a new category of victims into the Rome Statute shifting the exclusively anthropocentric focus to a biocentric approach.

Sixthly, similar to the pre-existing core crimes, the enforcement of a new crime of ecocide is severely hindered by the absence of an international enforcement regime and the case selection process diminishing the probability for a conviction and thus impeding the potential deterrent effect of crimes.

D. Establishment of an International Environmental Convention

Since the introduction of a fifth crime of ecocide into the Rome Statute faces multiple challenges, primarily flowing from the specific structure of the ICC, the question arises as to whether global environmental protection would better be promoted by adopting an International Environmental Convention which could either be *indirectly* enforced through national courts or *directly* enforced through an International Environmental Court which is yet to be established. Both alternatives will be assessed in the following.

I. Indirect enforcement through national courts

As an alternative to creating a fifth crime of ecocide under the Rome Statute, a transnational crime against the environment could be enshrined in an International Environmental Convention which would be indirectly enforced through national courts.[1] This would necessitate the adoption of a multilateral convention, either on a UN-basis or outside the UN system, containing a generic crime against the environment and mandating the signatory parties to transpose this crime into domestic law. The crime against the environment would thus be prosecuted domestically in domestic courts. The adoption of such an international convention, coupled with indirect enforcement through national courts, would certainly be more expedient than introducing a fifth crime of ecocide into the Rome Statute or creating a new International Environmental Court with distinct Rules of Procedure and jurisdictional mechanisms. Furthermore, being fully funded and readily available, domestic courts are effective adjudicators of environmental disputes.[2]

Nevertheless, the ubiquitous character of environmental crimes and the inadequacy of domestic prosecutions concerning *transboundary* environmental harm requires environmental crimes to be *enforced* through an international court.[3] This is due to the fact that the jurisdiction of domestic courts is restricted to the states'

---

[1] *Anastacia Greene*, Fordham Environmental Law Review 44 (2019).

[2] Documents of the Forty-Eighth Session, [1996] 2 Y.B. Int'l L. Comm'n 22 ¶ 20, U.N. Doc. A/CN.4/SER.A/1996/Add.1 (Part 1); *Sean Murphy*, Geo. Wash. J. Int'l L. & Econ. 342 (2000).

[3] See Cassese arguing that transboundary crimes are best prosecuted by international courts, *Antonio Cassese*, Reflections of International Criminal Justice, 61 (1) MOD. L. REV. 1, 8 (1998).

nationals and their state territories. At the international level, however, states are legal equals.[4] Thus, local courts have limited powers to exercise jurisdiction over foreign polluters, particularly if the polluter is a foreign government or powerful foreign multinational corporation.[5] Examples, such as the Austrian-Swiss case of Chernobyl or the Dutch-French case regarding the salinisation of the river Rhine demonstrate that most prosecutions of *transboundary* environmental harm adjudicated by local courts are unsuccessful.[6] This is further exacerbated by the fact that domestic courts, especially in developing nations, are biased due to political interference and corruption.[7] As the majority of environmental harm is perpetrated by multinational corporations[8], it is likely that they will exert significant influence on local prosecutions, as these multinational corporations provide the respective country with employment and infrastructure, which is why prosecuting these corporations is often not in the state's interest.[9]

For instance, in 2015, as the first country in the world, Guatemala established a specialised environmental court, the Péten Environmental Crimes Court, specifically dealing with the corporate criminal liability of corporations in the Mayan Biosphere.[10] In its first case, the Péten Environmental Crimes Court convicted Guatemalan palm oil company REPSA of ecocide after it had caused a major palm oil effluent overflow into the Pasión River on 6 June 2015.[11] However, a day after the suspension of the company's operations, three human rights activists were allegedly abducted by REPSA and a fourth was shot on the court steps.[12] Subse-

---

[4] *Susan M. Hinde*, Hofstra L. Rev. 746 (2003).

[5] *Sean Murphy*, Geo. Wash. J. Int'l L. & Econ. 342 (2000); *Susan M. Hinde*, Hofstra L. Rev. 741, 746 (2003); *Alfred Rest*, Envtl. Pol'y & L., 36 (1999).

[6] *Alfred Rest*, Envtl. Pol'y & L., 36 (1999).

[7] *Anastacia Greene*, Fordham Environmental Law Review 45 (2019).

[8] EUROPOL, Environmental Crime in the Age of Climate Change 7 (2022); *Ricardo Pereira*, Criminal Law Forum 219 (2020); *Frédéric Mégret*, Colum. J. Envtl. L. 225, 226 (2011).

[9] *Regina Rauxloh*, The Role of International Criminal Law in Environmental Protection 441 (2011).

[10] *Cindy Woods*, The Guatemala Ecocide Case: What It Means for the Business and Human Rights Movement, Blog de la Fundación para el Debido Procesco (DPLF) (Mar. 10, 2016), https://dplfblog.com/2016/03/10/the-guatemala-ecocide-case-what-it-means-for-the-business-and-human-rights-movement/ (last visited Feb. 18, 2025).

[11] Id.; *Jeff Conant*, Justice Delayed Is Justice Denied in Guatemala's Palm Oil-Driven Human Rights Crisis (2016), https://medium.com/economic-policy/justice-delayed-is-justice-denied-in-guatemalas-palm-oil-driven-human-rights-crisis-e2c1f7633412 (last visited Feb. 18, 2025).

[12] *Sandra Cuffe*, Guatemalan Activist Murdered After Court Suspends Palm Oil Company Operations, Mongabay, Sept. 30, 2015, https://news.mongabay.com/2015/09/guatemalan-activist-murdered-after-court-suspends-palm-oil-company-operations/.

quently, although the conviction was upheld by an appellate court in Guatemala[13] the palm oil company resumed work after a brief shutdown and continues to operate now. In its report on the situation of human rights in Guatemala in 2022, the UN High Commissioner for Human Rights confirmed that the Guatemalan justice system faces major structural challenges, including the illegitimate detentions of suspects, the intimidation of suspects, limited access to justice and judicial bias.[14]

Hence, although national courts contribute to the development of environmental law, they cannot promote global environmental protection due to their lack of powers and resources with regards to *transboundary* environmental harm. An international court located outside the affected country and not under the direct influence of multinational corporations is more likely to succeed in prosecuting transboundary environmental harm than national courts.

II. Direct enforcement through an International Environmental Court

As an alternative to establishing a fifth crime of ecocide under the Rome Statute or adopting an International Environmental Convention indirectly enforced through national courts, a number of scholars have suggested the creation of an International Environmental Court (IEC).[15] The idea of establishing an International Environmental Court can be traced back to former Italian Supreme Court Justice and founder of the International Court of the Environment Foundation (ICEF), Amedeo Postiglione, who advocated the establishment of an International Court for the Environment as early as 1990[16] following an international Congress on a More Efficient International Law on the Environment and Setting Up an International Court for the Environment Within the United Nations, which was held in Rome in 1989.[17] This Congress suggested the adoption of a convention establishing a human right to the environment, the creation of an UN environmental agency, the appointment of a UN High Commissioner for the Environment as well as the creation of an Interna-

[13] *Courtney Parker*, Justice in Guatemala: Guatemalan Court Upholds Revolutionary Ruling on Ecocide, Intercontinental Cry, Jan. 1, 2016, https://intercontinentalcry.org/justice-in-guatemala-guatemalan-court-upholds-revolutionary-ruling-on-ecocide/.

[14] G.A., Situation of Human Rights in Guatemala, Report of the United Nations High Commissioner for Human Rights, U.N. Doc. A/HRC/49/20 (2022).

[15] See *Amedeo Postiglione*, A More Efficient International Law on the Environment and Setting Up an International Court for the Environment within the United States, 20 (2) Environmental Law 321 (1990); *Audra E. Dehan*, An International Environmental Court: Should There Be One?, 3 TOURO J. Transnat'l L. 31 (1992); *Lynn Berat*, B.U. INT'l L. J. (1993); *Philippe Sands*, U. Rich. L. Rev. (1999); *Alfred Rest*, Envtl. Pol'y & L. (1999); *Peggy Rodgers Kalas*, Colorado Journal of International Environmenal Law and Policy (2001); *Kenneth F. McCallion*, International Environmental Justice: Rights and Remedies, 26 (3) Hastings International and Comparative Law Review 427 (2003); *Stephen Hockman*, Envtl. L. Rev. (2008).

[16] *Amedeo Postiglione*, Environmental Law (1990).

[17] *Audra E. Dehan*, TOURO J. Transnat'l L. 51 (1992).

tional Court for the Environment within the UN system.[18] The International Court for the Environment was intended to adjudicate upon international environmental disputes as well as human rights to the environment.[19] In 1992, Postiglione presented a Draft Convention for the Establishment of an International Environmental Court to the United Nations Conference on Environment and Development (UNCED) proposing the establishment of an International Court for the Environment which was, however, ultimately removed from its agenda.[20] While the original Draft Convention contained not only the proposal to establish an International Court for the Environment, but also the creation of an international environmental agency as well as the establishment of a human right to the environment, in 1999, the Draft Convention was reduced to a Draft Treaty for the Establishment of an International Court for the Environment exclusively concerning the creation of an International Environmental Court.[21] However, in 1999, former UNEP Deputy Executive Director, Shaqfat Kakakhel, rejected the idea of establishing an International Environmental Court.[22] Nonetheless, at a conference in Washington in 1999, international law scholars suggested the PCA as the interim forum for environmental dispute resolution pending the establishment of an International Environmental Court.[23] In late 2008, the newly founded International Court for the Environment (ICE) Coalition[24] continued the call for the creation of an International Environmental Court.[25] The ICE Coalition established its campaign on the successful experience of the Coalition for the International Criminal Court, which had previously succeeded in having advocated the establishment of the ICC.[26] More recently, in the controversy of whether to incorporate a fifth crime of ecocide into the Rome Statute, the debate regarding the creation of an International Environmental Court was reignited. In the following, it will be examined how such a court could be established and what advantages and disadvantages it would entail in contrast to the pre-existing ICC.

---

[18] Id. at 51–53; *Peggy Rodgers Kalas*, Colorado Journal of International Environmenal Law and Policy 232 (2001).

[19] *Amedeo Postiglione*, Environmental Law 323–326 (1990); *Audra E. Dehan*, TOURO J. Transnat'l L. 52, 53 (1992).

[20] *Jeffrey L. Dunoff*, Institutional Misfits: The GATT, the ICJ & Trade-Environment, 15 (4) Mich. J. Int'l L. 1043, 1107 (1994).

[21] *Peggy Rodgers Kalas*, Colorado Journal of International Environmenal Law and Policy 234 (2001); *Susan M. Hinde*, Hofstra L. Rev. 732 (2003).

[22] *Abraham Lama*, Environment: UNEP Prefers Persuasion over Sanctions, Inter Press Service, Oct. 4, 1999, https://www.ipsnews.net/1999/10/environment-unep-prefers-persuasion-over-sanctions/.

[23] The George Washington University Law School Conference on International Environmental Dispute Resolution (April 15–17, 1999), 32 (3) Geo. Wash. J. Int'l L. & Econ. 325 (2000).

[24] ICE Coalition, http://www.icecoalition.org (last visited Feb. 18, 2025).

[25] *Ole W. Pedersen*, Journal of Environmental Law 549 (2012).

[26] Id.

1. Establishing an International Environmental Court

The establishment of an International Environmental Court would necessitate the adoption of an international convention, such as an "International Convention on Environmental Protection"[27], governing, *inter alia*, the jurisdiction, subject matter scope and relationship of the Court to national courts. In this regard, ITLOS, which was created on the basis of the UNCLOS[28] and Article VI of the Convention on the Prevention and Punishment of the Crime of Genocide providing the possibility to establish an international penal tribunal[29], may serve as precedents. In certain aspects, the 1999 Draft Treaty may serve as a role model for such an International Convention on Environmental Protection, however, the Draft Treaty cannot be approved in its entirity. As proposed by the 1999 Draft Treaty, the International Environmental Court could be established as an independent entity under the auspices of the UN or as an adjunct to another international judicial body such as the PCA.[30] However, due to the lack of compulsory jurisdiction of the PCA, it is not advisable to establish the International Environmental Court as an adjunct thereto. From a financial perspective, the IEC is best established under the auspices of the UN as in this case, similar to the ICJ, the Court is financed through the UN.

As suggested by the Draft Treaty, the Court is best designed to encompass civil as well as criminal jurisdiction over environmental disputes.[31] Thus, the International Environmental Court would be able to issue an order for civil damages as well as to impose criminal sanctions. In terms of criminal jurisdiction, it is necessary to establish a generic crime against the environment under the International Convention on Environmental Protection due to the multitude of subject-specific transnational environmental crimes in international environmental law.[32] Besides civil and criminal jurisdiction, the IEC should further be tasked with enforcing a human right to a clean, healthy and sustainable environment, which would be included in the International Convention for Environmental Protection.[33]

---

[27] *Peggy Rodgers Kalas*, Colorado Journal of International Environmenal Law and Policy 242 (2001).

[28] U.N. Convention on the Law of the Sea annex VI, Dec. 10, 1982, 1833 U.N.T.S. 397.

[29] Convention on the Prevention and Punishment of the Crime of Genocide art. VI, Dec. 9, 1948, 78 U.N.T.S. 277.

[30] *Peggy Rodgers Kalas*, Colorado Journal of International Environmenal Law and Policy 235 (2001); *Susan M. Hinde*, Hofstra L. Rev. 732 (2003).

[31] *Peggy Rodgers Kalas*, Colorado Journal of International Environmenal Law and Policy 236 (2001); similar *Kenneth F. McCallion*, Hastings International and Comparative Law Review 436, 441 (2003); *Anastacia Greene*, Fordham Environmental Law Review 44 (2019).

[32] See for instance Article VIII 8.1 of McCallion's Draft Treaty for the Establishment of an International Court of the Environment *Kenneth F. McCallion*, Hastings International and Comparative Law Review 438–443 (2003).

[33] *Peggy Rodgers Kalas*, Colorado Journal of International Environmenal Law and Policy 242 (2001); *Amedeo Postiglione*, Environmental Law 324–326 (1990).

In relation to national courts, the Draft Treaty suggested that the International Environmental Court be complementary.[34] Thus, similar to the ICC, national judicial systems would take precedence, while the International Environmental Court would only be able to assume jurisdiction if adjudication by domestic courts was unavailable or ineffective.[35] By contrast, Rest suggested that the International Environmental Court take precedence over national judicial systems.[36] As a third alternative, Hey proposed that national courts take precedence and simply ascribe an appeal or referral function to the International Environmental Court.[37] However, due to the limited powers of local courts regarding *transboundary* environmental offences, and the threat of inconsistent environmental standards, national courts should not be given primary jurisdiction over environmental disputes. Instead, the International Environmental Court should take precedence over national jurisdictions and be the primary adjudicator of environmental disputes. Only by assuming primary jurisdiction could the International Environmental Court promote the establishment of uniform global environmental standards which the national courts of the signatory Parties should be bound by. Furthermore, the International Environmental Court should grant states, governmental agencies, individuals, corporations, as well as NGOs standing.[38] Additionally, as proposed in the 1999 Draft Treaty, in terms of temporal jurisdiction the IEC should be able to exercise jurisdiction over crimes committed after the Statute's entry into force, or over civil matters within four years after the Statute's entry into force.[39]

Most importantly, however, the International Environmental Court must be granted compulsory jurisdiction over violations of the underlying International Environmental Convention to prevent dispute parties from forum-shopping.[40] Thus, unlike the ICJ or the PCA, the jurisdiction of the International Environmental Court would arise automatically in the event of a violation of the underlying Convention and would thus not depend on the explicit consent of the parties in each case. Establishing mandatory jurisdiction would also assist in classifying all disputes as 'environmental' which fall under the purview of the underlying Convention and thus clearly distinguishing the Court's jurisdiction from that of other available international forums.[41]

---

[34] *Peggy Rodgers Kalas*, Colorado Journal of International Environmenal Law and Policy 236 (2001); *Susan M. Hinde*, Hofstra L. Rev. 733 (2003).

[35] *Peggy Rodgers Kalas*, Colorado Journal of International Environmenal Law and Policy 238 (2001).

[36] *Alfred Rest*, Envtl. Pol'y & L., 37 (1999).

[37] *Ellen Hey*, Reflections on an International Environmental Court 15, 16, 24, 25 (2000).

[38] Similar *Peggy Rodgers Kalas*, Colorado Journal of International Environmenal Law and Policy 236 (2001); *Alfred Rest*, Envtl. Pol'y & L., 37 (1999).

[39] *Peggy Rodgers Kalas*, Colorado Journal of International Environmenal Law and Policy 236 (2001).

[40] Id. at 241.

[41] Id. at 240, 241.

Furthermore, similar to the UN Convention against Torture and Other Cruel, Inhuman or Degrading Treatment or Punishment, which provides for the establishment of the so-called Committee against Torture[42], the Convention should provide a supervision system, monitoring the implementation and enforcement of the Convention by the states. The Committee against Torture is tasked with considering and commenting on periodic reports from the State Parties on the measures they have taken to give effect to their undertakings under the Convention (Article 19), instigating investigations if reliable information indicating the practice of systematic torture in the territory of a State Party emerges (Article 20) and examining communications by an individual claiming to have fallen victim to a violation of the Convention by a State Party (Article 22). However, the Committee's competences are not compulsory, but rather allow State Parties to "opt out" or to depend on the explicit consent of the State Parties.[43] Thus, borrowing from the Convention against Torture, the underlying Convention should provide for the establishment of an Environmental Committee staffed with environmental experts reviewing periodic reports concerning the implementation and enforcement of the Convention, which the State Parties are obliged to issue on an annual basis. Furthermore, the Committee should have the power to initiate investigations if available information indicates the commission of environmental offences. In contrast to the UN Convention against Torture, an attempt should be made to ascribe compulsory competences to the Environmental Committee.

Hence, ideally, an International Environmental Court would (1) be created under the auspices of the UN, (2) have compulsory jurisdiction, (3) have civil and criminal jurisdiction, (4) enforce a human right to a clean, healthy and sustainable environment, (5) take precedence over national judicial courts, (6) permit states, individuals, corporations as well as NGOs access to the court, and (7) be complemented by a supervision system.

2. International Environmental Court vs. International Criminal Court

After having assessed how a potential International Environmental Court could be established, the advantages and disadvantages of such a new court will be examined in distinction to the pre-existing International Criminal Court. Thus, it will be evaluated whether the creation of an International Convention on Environmental Protection enforced through an International Environmental Court or the incorporation a fifth crime of ecocide into the Rome Statute is better suited to promoting global environmental protection.

---

[42] See Convention against Torture and Other Cruel, Inhuman or Degrading Treatment or Punishment art. 17, Dec. 10, 1984, 1465 U.N.T.S. 85.

[43] See id. art. 28 (1), art. 21 (1), art. 22 (1).

a) Advantages of an International Environmental Court

In contrast to extending the jurisdiction of the ICC to a fifth crime of ecocide, the establishment of an International Environmental Court entails numerous advantages due to the fact that it would not be bound to the rigid structure of the ICC.

Firstly, an International Environmental Court exclusively created to adjudicate upon environmental matters would comprise environmental experts capable of assessing complex environmental matters from a legal, political and scientific perspective.[44] By contrast, none of the 18 judges currently appointed to the ICC is an expert in international environmental law.[45] Thus, if environmental crimes were adjudicated upon by the ICC, this lack of expertise in international environmental law could impede the credibility of the Court.[46] However, a higher level of expertise in the area of environmental law could also be attained by establishing a separate environmental chamber at the ICC[47], which would entail fewer costs and require less time than the creation of a new court.

Secondly, unlike the ICC, where only Member States, the Prosecutor or the UN Security Council may trigger the Court's jurisdiction, the International Environmental Court could be accessed by a multiplicity of actors including states, corporations, NGOs and individuals.[48]

Thirdly, in terms of jurisdiction, the International Environmental Court could exercise civil and criminal jurisdiction over environmental disputes, whereas the ICC can only impose criminal sanctions. The Court's personal jurisdiction with regards to civil liability enabling the International Environmental Court to impose damages should be extended to include individuals, corporations as well as states.[49] Unlike the ICC, the criminal jurisdiction of the International Environmental Court would not be restricted to individual criminal liability but could be extended to include corporate criminal liability. In contrast to international criminal law based upon the core principle of individual guilt, the establishment of corporate criminal liability appears far less problematic with respect to a new international crime against the environment, which is not placed on the same standing as the four core crimes. In fact, outside of the Rome Statute, establishing corporate criminal liability for environmental crimes is rather the rule than the exception in multinational

---

[44] *Anastacia Greene*, Fordham Environmental Law Review 44 (2019); *Tim Stephens*, International Courts and Environmental Protection 58 (2009).

[45] International Criminal Court, Current Judges, https://www.icc-cpi.int/bios-2 (last visited Feb. 18, 2025).

[46] *Anastacia Greene*, Fordham Environmental Law Review 39, 40 (2019).

[47] Id. at 40; *Regina Rauxloh*, The Role of International Criminal Law in Environmental Protection 451 (2011).

[48] *Susan M. Hinde*, Hofstra L. Rev. 738 (2003); *Peggy Rodgers Kalas*, Colorado Journal of International Environmenal Law and Policy 229, 236 (2001).

[49] *Peggy Rodgers Kalas*, Colorado Journal of International Environmenal Law and Policy 236 (2001).

treaties.[50] Furthermore, as the primary criminal sanction available at the International Environmental Court would not be restricted to imposing a term of imprisonment, as opposed to the sanctions under Article 77 (1) Rome Statute, the underlying Convention could provide for non-financial remedies specifically tailored to corporations, such as injunctions, licence revocation, corporate probation, the confiscation of property or the dissolution of a company. In this regard, the 2021 proposal for a new EU Crime Directive, including the withdrawal of licences, disqualifications and the exclusion from public funding as criminal sanctions[51], could serve as a role model. Nevertheless, the challenge pertaining to the conceptualisation of corporate criminal liability persists. Since the attribution of individual guilt requires the identification of a culpable individual, which often proves difficult in the case of multinational corporations operating transnationally, it appears preferable to resort to the abovementioned collective corporate approach based on the organisational failure of the corporation itself. In contrast to the ICC, an International Environmental Court would not be traditionally based on the core principle of individual criminal guilt, which is why it seems far less problematic to establish corporate criminal liability on a fiction than in the context of individual criminal law. The lack of consensus regarding the conceptualisation of corporate criminal liability in national jurisdictions, however, is a further argument in favour of granting primary jurisdiction to the International Environmental Court which would take precedence over national jurisdiction[52] as opposed to establishing complementary jurisdiction as in this case the principle of complementarity would be rendered largely obsolete.

Fourthly, due to it not being bound to Article 30 Rome Statute, the generic crime against the environment enshrined in the International Convention on Environmental Protection could be formulated as a crime of strict liability or a crime of negligence.[53] Since the International Environmental Court would not prosecute macro-criminality and would not have jurisdiction over the core crimes under the Rome Statute, it could also adjudicate upon environmental crimes falling below the gravity threshold of Article 17 (1) (d) Rome Statute and civil claims.[54] Thus, crimes falling within the ambit of the International Convention would not necessarily have to be of the same gravity as the core crimes. The primary argument in favour of including negligence-based liability is the increased likelihood of preventing future environmental harm. Due to the significantly lower mental threshold, potential perpetrators would face a higher risk of prosecution, a fact which first leads to a

---

[50] See for instance Directive 2008/99/EC, art. 6; Protocol on Amendments to the Protocol on the Statute of the African Court of Justice and Human Rights, art. 46C (1) (June 27, 2014).

[51] European Commission, Question and Answers on the Revised EU Directive on Environmental Crime, https://ec.europa.eu/commission/presscorner/detail/en/QANDA_21_6745 (last visited Feb. 18, 2025).

[52] Similar *Alfred Rest*, Envtl. Pol'y & L., 37 (1999).

[53] *Anastacia Greene*, Fordham Environmental Law Review 44 (2019).

[54] Id.

stronger deterrent effect of the provision and, second, promotes the prevention of further environmental harm. Moreover, the lack of a case selection process filtering only the most serious cases of environmental crimes, the risk of being prosecuted and thus the potential deterrent effect of the provision would be higher as opposed to having a fifth crime of ecocide under the Rome Statute. In domestic criminal law the standard of negligence is prevalent in the context of environmental crimes.[55] Even at the regional level, in the EU, in accordance with Article 3 of the 2008 EU Crime Directive, environmental offences may be committed "at least with serious negligence"[56]. Thus, the question arises as to whether the mental threshold suggested above within the proposal for a fifth crime against the environment under the Rome Statute[57] including *dolus eventualis* or advertent recklessness would be appropriate or should be further lowered.

In general, establishing a crime of strict liability under the International Convention is to be rejected as this would clash with the cornerstone principle in criminal law that criminal culpability requires the commission of certain proscribed conduct accompanied by a blameworthy state of mind.[58] Nevertheless, the crime could be defined as a crime of negligence. However, in this regard different levels of negligence or *Fahrlässigkeit* need to be distinguished. While the perpetrator acts with culpable negligence or advertent *Fahrlässigkeit*, if he was aware of the risk of harm he created or took but believed the harm will not occur, the perpetrator acted with simple negligence or inadvertent *Fahrlässigkeit* if he was unaware of the risk he created or took.[59] Thus, while in case of simple negligence or inadvertent *Fahrlässigkeit* the perpetrator failed to apply the necessary level of care required for a reasonable person in a similar situation, in case of culpable negligence or advertent *Fahrlässigkeit* the perpetrator deliberately disregarded the necessary level of care despite being aware of the risk his conduct entailed, but nevertheless believing that the harmful consequence would not occur.[60] If the perpetrator's conduct was "blatantly at odds with the prescribed standards", he acted with gross negligence.[61]

---

[55] For instance, under the German Criminal Code, all offences against the environment can be committed negligently (see Strafgesetzbuch [StGB] [Penal Code], §§ 324–330a).

[56] Directive 2008/99/EC, art. 3.

[57] The fifth crime against the environment as proposed above reads as follows: "any act committed with awareness that there is a substantial likelihood of severe and either widespread or long-term environmental damage being caused by those acts" (see Chapter C. V. 4).

[58] See Prosecutor v. Delalić, Case No. IT-96-21-T, Judgement, ¶ 424, 425 (Nov. 16, 1998); *Donald K. Piragoff/Darryl Robinson*, Article 30 para. 5 (2022); *Gerhard Werle/Florian Jeßberger*, Principles of International Criminal Law para. 556 (2020); *Robert Cryer*, et al., An Introduction to International Criminal Law and Procedure 365 (2019); *William A. Schabas*, The International Criminal Court: A Commentary on the Rome Statute 626 (2016); *Antonio Cassese*, et al., Cassese's International Criminal Law 39 (2013); *Albin Eser*, Mental Elements 902 (2002).

[59] *Antony Duff/Tatjana Hörnle*, Crimes of Endangerment 139, 140 (2022).

[60] *Antonio Cassese*, et al., Cassese's International Criminal Law 52 (2013); *Antony Duff/Tatjana Hörnle*, Crimes of Endangerment 139, 140 (2022).

In defining a possible crime against the environment under the International Convention, a balance needs to be struck. On the one hand, the jurisdiction of the International Environmental Court could cover less severe environmental crimes compared to those under the Rome Statute however, on the other hand, the mental threshold must not be set too low as criminal law, whether at the domestic or international level, is a last resort.[62] Furthermore, for states to transfer their sovereignty over environmental crimes to an international court of law, the crimes in question need to be serious enough to affect the international community as a whole. Thus, environmental accidents caused by a perpetrator who simply lacked the necessary level of care without being aware of the risk of harm his conduct involved (simple negligence or inadvertent *Fahrlässigkeit*) cannot incur criminal liability under international law and thus may only give rise to civil liability. This is in line with the fact that while negligence-based liability is the rule in administrative and civil law, it is the exception in modern criminal law.[63] Thus, if the mental threshold of the proposed crime against the environment under the Rome Statute was at all to be lowered, it could only be lowered from *dolus eventualis* to culpable negligence or advertent *Fahrlässigkeit*. While in the case of *dolus eventualis* or advertent recklessness the perpetrator is aware of the risk and wilfully takes it, advertent *Fahrlässigkeit* covers cases where the perpetrator is aware of the risk but believes the consequence will not occur.[64] Hence, by lowering the mental threshold from *dolus eventualis* to include culpable negligence or advertent *Fahrlässigkeit*, the scope of the crime would be extended to cover cases where the perpetrator was aware of the risk of environmental harm but believed the harm would not materialise, instead of only covering cases where the perpetrator decided to wilfully take the risk of environmental harm. This would also be in line with the 2008 European Crime Directive covering environmental offences committed "at least with serious negligence".[65] Although the exact meaning of 'serious negligence' remains un-

---

[61] *Antonio Cassese*, et al., Cassese's International Criminal Law 52 (2013).

[62] As stated by the Council of Europe: "Considering that while recourse to the criminal law in this field should be a last resort, nevertheless use must be made of it when other measures are not observed or are ineffective or inadequate" (Council of Europe, Committee of Ministers, Resolution (77) 28 on the Contribution of Criminal Law to the Protection of the Environment, Preamble ¶ 3 (Sept. 28, 1977).

[63] See Section 15 of the German Criminal Code: "Unless the law expressly provides for criminal liability for negligent conduct, only intentional conduct attracts criminal liability" (see Strafgesetzbuch [StGB] [Penal Code], §15); *Antony Duff/Tatjana Hörnle*, Crimes of Endangerment 139 (2022); *Mordechai Kremnitzer*, JICJ 911 (2010).

[64] Bundesgerichtshof [BGH] [Federal Court of Justice] Jan. 27, 2011, Raub mit Todesfolge – Wegnahme aus Rache; Bedingter Tötungsvorsatz, Neue Zeitschrift für Strafrecht [NStZ], ¶ 699, 701, 702 (Ger.); Bundesgerichtshof [BGH] [Federal Court of Justice] Oct. 18, 2007, Heimtückische Tötung eines bewusstlosen Patienten im Krankenhaus, Neue Zeitschrift für Strafrecht [NStZ], ¶ 93, 93 (Ger.).; *Antony Duff/Tatjana Hörnle*, Crimes of Endangerment 140 (2022).

[65] Directive 2008/99/EC, art. 3.

known as it could imply culpable negligence or gross negligence, there is a clear distinction between simple negligence and a more serious form of negligence.

Hence, in general, it appears possible to lower the subjective standard to culpable negligence or advertent *Fahrlässigkeit* since the International Environmental Court's jurisdiction would not be limited to the "most serious crimes of international concern"[66] falling within the jurisdiction of the ICC. Nevertheless, from an environmental perspective it appears preferable to keep the *objective* side extensive by establishing a generic crime of endangerment addressing conduct prior to the materialisation of harm and thereby focusing on the prevention of harm. However, establishing a crime of endangerment under which culpable negligence would give rise to criminal liability appears too extensive for an *international crime*. Thus, the definition of the generic crime against the environment should not be further extended to include negligent conduct but should only include *dolus eventualis* or advertent recklessness. In this vein, it is beneficial that the International Environmental Court could exercise both criminal and civil jurisdiction as it could therefore resort to civil liability in the case of negligent conduct.

Thus, in terms of criminal liability, the abovementioned crime against the environment criminalising '*any act committed with awareness that there is a substantial likelihood of severe and either widespread or long-term environmental damage being caused by those acts*'[67], appears to be a suitable definition of a potential generic crime against the environment under the International Convention for Environmental Protection. By including the gravity threshold of *severe and either widespread or long-term* environmental damage, the exclusion of minor cases of environmental harm can be ensured, acts which are not serious enough to be elevated to the status of an international crime. At the same time, by not cumulatively requiring all three criteria, the objective side of the crime is not too restrictive excluding all serious types of environmental harm but the most egregious. Additionally, by creating a crime of endangerment the focus lies upon the prevention of environmental harm. On the subjective side, the scope of the crime is restricted to cases where the perpetrator acted with *dolus eventualis* or advertent recklessness thereby excluding environmental harm, which was committed negligently and should thus only incur civil liability under the International Convention for Environmental Protection.

Fifthly, the criminal sanctions available at the International Environmental Court could be extended to include injunctive and restorative sanctions to address environmental harm, particularly including the 'reinstatement of the environment'.[68] Including the reinstatement of the environment as a primary sanction appears un-

[66] Art. 1 Rome Statute.

[67] See Chapter C. V. 4.

[68] *Anastacia Greene*, Fordham Environmental Law Review 44 (2019), *Peggy Rodgers Kalas*, Colorado Journal of International Environmenal Law and Policy 230 ("increased focus on preventive measures") (2001).

problematic in the case of an International Environmental Court, as this Court holds an inherently ecocentric perspective, as opposed to the ICC. As mentioned above, the reinstatement of the environment as a criminal sanction would be most effective if, at the same time, an Environmental Trust Fund were to be established. In contrast to the ICC, which cannot impose civil or criminal fines on corporations, the Environmental Trust Fund could be financed through civil damages imposed by the International Environmental Court on multinational corporations and states.

b) Disadvantages of an International Environmental Court

Opponents of an International Environmental Court consider the idea of establishing a court unlike any other pre-existing international forum to be "quixotic"[69]. Besides arguing that the establishment of a new International Environmental Court coupled with the development of independent Rules of Procedure and jurisdictional mechanisms would be a very lengthy process[70], two further principal arguments against the establishment of an International Environmental Court have been put forward.

aa) Lack of jurisdiction over non-signatory Parties

First, it is criticised that the majority of states, particularly the world's most polluting states China, the US, India and the Russian Federation are unlikely to ratify the underlying International Convention on Environmental Protection, thereby subjecting themselves to the compulsory jurisdiction of the International Environmental Court.[71] This is due to the fact that states are traditionally reluctant to transfer their sovereignty over state citizens to international courts.[72] For instance, this is evidenced by the United States' failure to ratify the Rome Statute due to its fear of subjecting its own armed forces to criminal liability.[73] It holds true that, as with the incorporation of a fifth crime of ecocide into the Rome Statute, polluting states will be unlikely to ratify the underlying Convention for fear of subjecting their nationals, corporations or themselves to liability for environmental disputes.[74]

Thus, in terms of criminal jurisdiction non-member States could only be subjected to the Court's jurisdiction based upon the principle of territoriality or the

[69] *Tim Stephens*, International Courts and Environmental Protection, 60 (2009).

[70] *Prisca Merz/Cabanes Valérie*, et al., Ending Ecocide, The Next Necessary Step In International Law at 16 (2014).

[71] *Sean Murphy*, Geo. Wash. J. Int'l L. & Econ. 345 (2000); *Philippe Sands/Jacqueline Peel*, Principles of International Environmental Law 180, 190 (2018); *Peggy Rodgers Kalas*, Colorado Journal of International Environmenal Law and Policy 242 (2001).

[72] *Peggy Rodgers Kalas*, Colorado Journal of International Environmenal Law and Policy 239 (2001).

[73] Id. at 239 fn. 205.

[74] Id. at 239.

active or passive personality principle, both of which are well-established principles in international law.[75] However, in this regard, the International Environmental Court would only be able to exercise jurisdiction over environmental crimes which were either committed on the territory of a signatory State, by a national of a signatory State or if the victim was a national of a signatory State. However, this creates jurisdictional loopholes with regards to non-member States impeding the effectiveness of the Court. Thus, a proposal would be to ascribe universal jurisdiction to the International Environmental Court over the crime against the environment, as was already suggested for the ICC at the time the Rome Statute was drafted. If the International Environmental Court were to have universal jurisdiction, the Court would be able to prosecute environmental crimes irrespective of whether the crimes were committed within the territory of a signatory State (principle of territoriality) or whether the crimes were committed by a national of a signatory State (active personality principle) or directed against a national of a signatory State (passive personality principle).[76] Instead, the International Environmental Court would be able to prosecute *any* environmental crime falling within the ambit of the Convention irrespective of the location of its commission and the nationality of the perpetrator or victim.

Nonetheless, so far, the principle of universal jurisdiction has only been acknowledged for genocide, war crimes, crimes against humanity, international piracy on the high seas and slave trading.[77] Thus, this raises the question as to whether universal jurisdiction could also be justified with respect to environmental crimes. With respect to crimes under international law, it is argued that universal jurisdiction over these crimes is necessary as they are "directed against the interests of the international community as a whole".[78] Thus, the universal nature of crimes under international law empowers the international community to prosecute these crimes irrespective of where and by whom and against whom they were committed.[79] However, as outlined above, large-scale environmental harm poses a threat to the international peace and security, violates the universal human right to access to a clean, healthy and sustainable environment and thus violates the universal values of the international community.[80] Nevertheless, the International Environmental Court should only be granted universal jurisdiction over the prosecution of the crime

[75] *Gerhard Werle/Florian Jeßberger*, Principles of International Criminal Law para. 258 (2020).

[76] *Frédéric Mégret*, Colum. J. Envtl. L. 252 (2011).

[77] *Gerhard Werle/Florian Jeßberger*, Principles of International Criminal Law para. 261 (2020); *William Schabas/Giulia Pecorella*, Article 12 para. 7 (2022).

[78] *Gerhard Werle/Florian Jeßberger*, Principles of International Criminal Law para. 259 (2020).

[79] Prosecutor v. Tadić, Case No. IT-94-1, Decision on the Defence Motion for Interlocutory Appeal on Jurisdiction, ¶ 57 (Oct. 2, 1995); *Gerhard Werle/Florian Jeßberger*, Principles of International Criminal Law para. 259 (2020).

[80] See Chapter C. IV. 1. b).

against the environment and not over environmental disputes simply giving rise to civil liability within the ambit of the Convention. Civil liability for environmental disputes covers, *inter alia*, negligent conduct which is certainly not sufficiently serious to justify universal jurisdiction.

Nonetheless, in the context of universal jurisdiction over environmental crimes, the issue of functional immunity needs to be considered. As the International Environmental Court would have criminal jurisdiction over individuals and corporations, the Court would be barred from prosecuting state officials due to their functional immunity. Functional immunity is not limited in time and includes any *official* act of state officials on behalf of the state, including heads of state, ministers, soldiers and police officers.[81] However, it is acknowledged under customary international law that functional immunity does not affect liability for crimes under international law before an international criminal court.[82] The irrelevance of functional immunity concerning crimes under international criminal law before international criminal courts is widely affirmed in international treaties including, for instance, Article 27 (1) Rome Statute, Article 7 IMT Charter, Article 7 (2) ICTY Statute, Article 6 (2) ICTR Statute, Article IV Genocide Convention and Principle III of the Nuremberg Principles.

In this regard, the question arises as to whether a provision exempting state officials of functional immunity with respect to an international environmental crime could be included in the International Convention on Environmental Protection. It could be argued that although the irrelevance of functional immunity with regard to environmental crimes has so far not been acknowledged under customary international law, states could waive functional immunity by ratifying an international treaty establishing an international court.[83] Nonetheless, pursuant to Article 34 Vienna Convention on the Law of the Treaties, international conventions cannot affect third parties.[84] Thus, state officials of third parties which have not ratified the underlying Convention could not be deprived of their functional immunity which is granted under customary international law. Thus, the exemption from functional immunity would only apply to state officials of the signatory Parties of the underlying International Convention on Environmental Protection.

---

[81] *Kai Ambos*, Treatise 530 (2021); *Gerhard Werle/Florian Jeßberger*, Principles of International Criminal Law para. 827 (2020).

[82] Prosecutor v. Blaškić, Case No. IT-95-14-AR108bis, Judgement on the Request of the Republic of Croatia for Review of the Decision of Trial Chamber II of 18 July 1997, ¶ 41 (Oct. 29, 1997); *Gerhard Werle/Florian Jeßberger*, Principles of International Criminal Law para. 828 (2020); *Triffterer Otto/Christoph Burchard*, Article 27, Irrelevance of Official Capacity, in: Rome Statute of the International Criminal Court para. 16 (Kai Ambos ed., 2022).

[83] See *Helmut Kreicker*, Immunität und IStGH, Zur Bedeutung völkerrechtlicher Exemtionen für den Internationalen Strafgerichtshof, 7 ZIS 350 (2009).

[84] See Vienna Convention on the Law of the Treaties art. 34, May 23, 1969, 1155 U.N.T. S. 331 ("A treaty does not create either obligations or rights for a third State without its consent").

However, in this regard, it needs to be noted that on 9 March 2009, the ICC issued an arrest warrant against Sudanese president Al Bashir denying his functional immunity although Sudan has not ratified the Rome Statute.[85] The decision to deny the functional immunity of Al Bashir was based on two main arguments.

Firstly, the Chamber argued that in case of a UN Security Council referral pursuant to Article 13 (b) Rome Statute, functional immunities of state officials are irrelevant.[86] As long as certain people or groups of people are not excluded from prosecution in such a resolution, the UN Security Council authorises the ICC to prosecute the people who are responsible for the crimes even if they are granted functional immunity and irrespective of whether they are nationals of a signatory or non-signatory Party to the Rome Statute.[87] This is due to the fact that, in accordance with Article 24 of the UN Charter, the UN Member States "confer[red] on the Security Council primary responsibility for the maintenance of international peace and security, and agree that in carrying out its duties under this responsibility the Security Council acts on their behalf".[88] Hence, the functional immunity of state officials of non-member States of the ICC is irrelevant in the case of UN Security Council referrals pursuant to Article 13 (b) Rome Statute if the respective country is a UN Member State.[89]

In this regard, the question arises as to whether this argument could be transferred to the International Environmental Court, if the Court's criminal jurisdiction were to be extended to universal jurisdiction. With respect to UN Security Council, referrals under Article 13 (b) Rome Statute the ICC's jurisdiction are at least partly based on the principle of universality. However, the reason as to why the functional immunity of state officials of non-contracting parties can be considered irrelevant in the case of a UN Security Council referral is the very existence of the UN Security Council which was empowered by the UN Member States to maintain international peace and security. Nonetheless, even if the International Environmental Court were created under the auspices of the UN, its jurisdiction, albeit universal, would not be linked to the UN Security Council. Since any of the permanent members of the UN Security Council, who are some of the most polluting countries can veto any resolution, it would not be advisable to include a trigger mechanism similar to Article 13 (b) Rome Statute into the International Convention on Environmental Protection.

Besides the existence of a UN Security Council resolution, the Chamber's decision to deny the functional immunity of Al Bashir was further based on the fact

---

[85] Prosecutor v. Al Bashir, ICC-02/05-01/09, Decision on the Prosecution's Application for a Warrant of Arrest against Omar Hassan Ahmad Al Bashir, ¶ 40 (Mar. 4, 2009); *Helmut Kreicker*, ZIS 351, 352 (2009).

[86] Prosecutor v. Al Bashir, ICC-02/05-01/09, Decision on the Prosecution's Application for a Warrant of Arrest against Omar Hassan Ahmad Al Bashir, ¶ 40, 45 (Mar. 4, 2009).

[87] *Helmut Kreicker*, ZIS 351 (2009).

[88] Id.

[89] Id.

that it is the main goal of the Rome Statute to put a stop to impunity for the most serious crimes of international concern.[90] The Chamber further observed that to attain this goal, Article 27 (1) and (2) Rome Statute provides for the irrelevance of official capacity.[91] The Chamber further elaborated that, in accordance with Article 21 (1) (b) Rome Statute, the functional immunity of state officials recognised under customary international law may only become relevant if there is a lacuna within the Rome Statute which, however, is to be negated due to the existence of Article 27 (1) Rome Statute explicitly stipulating the irrelevance of functional immunity.[92] Although this second line of argumentation appears weak with regard to the fact that, in accordance with Article 34 Vienna Convention on the Law of the Treaties, international treaties may not affect third parties[93], it is widely acknowledged under customary international law that state officials are exempted from functional immunity before *international* criminal courts, such as the ICC, even with respect to state officials from third states.[94] In this regard, several decisions of international criminal courts and tribunals need to be considered. In 1999, the ICTY, which was established as an ad hoc court pursuant to an UN Security Council resolution, preferred charges against the former president of Yugoslavia, Slobodan Milosević. Although at this time Yugoslavia was not a member of the UN, which is why Article 7 (2) ICTY Statute could not deny his functional immunity, the ICTY later waived his functional immunity on the basis that Article 7 (2) ICTY Statute reflected customary international law.[95] Further, in the *Yerodia Case* in 2000, the ICJ held that "an incumbent or former Minister for Foreign Affairs may be subject to criminal proceedings before certain international criminal courts", such as the ICTY, the ICTR and the ICC.[96] In 2003, the Special Court for Sierra Leone denied the functional immunity of the former president of Liberia, Charles Taylor, arguing that functional immunity does not prevent a state official from being prosecuted before international criminal courts and tribunals.[97] In this regard, the Special Court for Sierra Leone elaborated that the principle of functional immunity "derives from the equality of sovereign states and therefore has no relevance to international criminal tribunals which are not organs of a state but derive their mandate from the

---

[90] Prosecutor v. Al Bashir, ICC-02/05-01/09, Decision on the Prosecution's Application for a Warrant of Arrest against Omar Hassan Ahmad Al Bashir, ¶ 42 (Mar. 4, 2009).

[91] Id. at ¶ 43.

[92] Id. at ¶ 44.

[93] *Helmut Kreicker*, ZIS 356 (2009).

[94] *Kai Ambos*, Treatise 536–540 (2021); *Gerhard Werle/Florian Jeßberger*, Principles of International Criminal Law para. 830 (2020); *Helmut Kreicker*, ZIS 356 (2009); *Kai Ambos*, Der Fall Pinochet und das anwendbare Recht, 54 (1) JuristenZeitung 16, 20 (1999).

[95] Prosecutor v. Miloševič, Case No. IT-02-54, Decision on Preliminary Motions, ¶ 28 (Nov. 8, 2001); *Helmut Kreicker*, ZIS 356 (2009).

[96] Case Concerning the Arrest Warrant of 11 April 2000 (Democratic Republic of the Congo v. Belgium), Judgment, 2002 I.C.J. Reports, ¶ 61 (Feb. 2002).

[97] Prosecutor v. Taylor, Decision on Immunity from Jurisdiction, SCSL-2003-01-I, ¶ 51–53 (May 31, 2004).

international community".[98] Thus, the distinction between national and international courts is justified by the fact that before an *international* court, states do not need to be protected from undue interference of another state as an international court is an international judicial institution mandated by the international community acting independently and impartially.[99] As such, the principle of functional immunity is only valid in *interstate* relations and not with regard to an international criminal court or tribunal.[100]

Hence, the same could be argued with respect to the criminal jurisdiction of an International Environmental Court. The International Environmental Court would be mandated by the international community and would operate in an independent and impartial manner. Thus, states would not have to fear undue interference from another state. In sum, it appears likely that even the functional immunity of state officials of *non-contracting* parties could be denied in cases of environmental crimes tried before the International Environmental Court. However, in general, it needs to be considered that functional immunity will not pose a problem in the majority of cases involving large-scale environmental harm which were committed by multinational corporations since functional immunity does not apply to corporate officials.

bb) Institutional fragmentation and 'forum-shopping'

Secondly, it is argued that the establishment of an International Environmental Court exclusively tasked with adjudicating upon environmental disputes further exacerbates the existing institutional fragmentation in international environmental law and thus facilitates 'forum shopping'.[101] In its broadest sense, 'forum shopping' denotes the "exercise of the plaintiff's option to bring a lawsuit in one of several different courts"[102]. 'Forum shopping' is also referred to as "[t]he practice of choosing the most favourable jurisdiction or court in which a claim might be heard"[103]. Due to the lack of hierarchy amongst the international forums and the broad subject matter jurisdiction of the International Environmental Court, a conflict of jurisdiction between the International Environmental Court and the existing international forums capable of hearing environmental offences may arise, a state of affairs which could promote inconsistent judgments.[104] The reason for a potential

[98] Id. at ¶ 51.

[99] *Paola Gaeta*, Ratione Materiae Immunities of Former Heads of State and International Crimes: The Hissène Habré Case, 1 (1) JICJ 186, 194 (2003).

[100] Id.

[101] *Ellen Hey*, Reflections on an International Environmental Court 14, 25 (2000); *Susan M. Hinde*, Hofstra L. Rev. 728 (2003).

[102] *Friedrich K. Juenger*, Forum Shopping, Domestic and International, in: Selected Essays on the Conflict of Laws 110 (Friedrich K. Juenger ed., 2001).

[103] *Bryan A. Garner*, Black's Law Dictionary 291 (2nd pocket ed., 2001).

[104] *Susan M. Hinde*, Hofstra L. Rev. 728, 748 (2003).

conflict of jurisdiction is that most environmental cases are not exclusively environmental but are rather intertwined with various other areas of international law.[105] As Sands rightly stated: "environmental claims are rarely, if ever, raised in isolation of other international legal arguments"[106].

For this reason the panel of judges at the International Environmental Court needs to be a mix of specialised environmental and general experts.[107] For instance, a case combining aspects from trade, environmental and human rights law could be subsequently decided in favour of trade by the WTO Appellate Body, in favour of human rights by the European Court of Human Rights and in favour of the environment by the International Environmental Court.[108] Thus, the creation of an International Environmental Court arguably fragments international environmental law further rather than unifying it.[109]

Nonetheless, instead of considering institutional fragmentation amongst international dispute settlement forums as a problem, others approve of a choice of forum, as long as the coherence of international environmental law is not threatened.[110] As Hey rightly observed: "Either we accept the danger of fragmentation and remedy the unsatisfactory aspects of the system, probably in a piecemeal fashion, or we accept the unsatisfactory nature of current international dispute settlement law and wait for chaos to dictate a complete overhaul of the system"[111]. Due to the existence of a multitude of international adjudicatory forums, fragmentation is part and parcel of the international dispute settlement system.[112]

However, by establishing an International Environmental Court with *compulsory* jurisdiction over disputes arising within the purview of the International Convention on Environmental Protection, it can be ensured that the International Environmental Court has exclusive jurisdiction over environmental disputes within the ambit of the underlying Convention. Thus, a clear hierarchy with regards to environmental disputes falling within the ambit of the Convention would be established with the International Environmental Court at its peak and a respective conflict of jurisdic-

---

105 *Sean Murphy*, Geo. Wash. J. Int'l L. & Econ. 344 (2000); *Philippe Sands*, U. Rich. L. Rev. 1638 (1999); *Ellen Hey*, Reflections on an International Environmental Court 6 (2000); *Ole W. Pedersen*, Journal of Environmental Law 551 (2012).

106 *Philippe Sands*, U. Rich. L. Rev. 1638 (1999).

107 *Ole W. Pedersen*, Journal of Environmental Law 551 (2012); *Philippe Sands*, U. Rich. L. Rev. 1638 (1999).

108 See *Susan M. Hinde*, Hofstra L. Rev. 750, 753 (2003).

109 Id. at 750.

110 See Boyle referring to the establishment of the International Tribunal for the Law of the Sea, *Alan E. Boyle*, Dispute Settlement and the Law of the Sea Convention: Problems of Fragmentation and Jurisdiction, 46 International and Comparative Law Quarterly 37 (1997); see further *Jonathan I. Charney*, The Impact on the International Legal System of the Growth of International Courts and Tribunals, 31 (4) N.Y.U. J. Int'l L. & Pol. 697 (1999).

111 *Ellen Hey*, Reflections on an International Environmental Court 13 (2000).

112 Id.

tion with other international forums could thus be avoided.[113] Hence, due to the lack of a generic environmental crime applicable during times of peace and war, the International Environmental Court would have exclusive jurisdiction over such a crime. However, in the event that the strict objective and subjective requirements of Article 8 (2) (b) (iv) Rome Statute were indeed met, the ICC would have exclusive jurisdiction as the ICC's jurisdiction is compulsory and not based upon consent. In general, by keeping the subject matter jurisdiction of the International Environmental Court broad, uniform jurisprudence regarding environmental disputes is ensured.

Hence, establishing an International Environmental Court with compulsory jurisdiction would be a first step to remedying the voids within the contemporary international dispute settlement system with regards to global environmental protection. Instead of claiming that the establishment of an additional International Environmental Court further fragments international environmental law, it should rather be argued that the current lack of a uniform judicial body fragments the application of international environmental standards.[114] Creating an International Environmental Court would thus be a first step to creating a uniform body of international environmental law.[115] As the primary adjudicator, the International Environmental Court would enforce and monitor the implementation of and compliance with the International Convention on Environmental Protection.

c) Conclusion

In 2023 international environmental law cannot be considered new anymore. Instead, international environmental law consists of more than 500 international treaties and international environmental litigation is steadily on the increase. Nevertheless, global environmental governance still lacks a uniform judicial body and the pre-existing adjudicators, including the ICC, the ICJ and the PCA all prove to be inadequate for different reasons. Thus, while in 1999 Sands stated that "[t]he possibility of an international environmental court should be kept on our radar screens, but the time is clearly not ripe to establish such a body"[116], the time *is* now ripe for the creation of an International Environmental Court. A comparison of both possibilities, (1) incorporating a fifth crime of ecocide into the Rome Statute and (2) adopting an International Convention on Environmental Protection coupled with the creation of an International Environmental Court, has demonstrated that the latter

---

[113] See *Peggy Rodgers Kalas*, Colorado Journal of International Environmenal Law and Policy 240, 241 (2001).

[114] Similar *Philippe Sands*, U. Rich. L. Rev. 1636 (1999).

[115] *Susan M. Hinde*, Hofstra L. Rev. 738 (2003); *Peggy Rodgers Kalas*, Colorado Journal of International Environmenal Law and Policy 229, 230 (2001).

[116] *Philippe Sands*, U. Rich. L. Rev. 1640 (1999).

option is preferable with regards to the goal of promoting global environmental protection through criminal law.

Firstly, unlike the ICC, the International Environmental Court would be accessible by a multiplicity of actors granting states, NGOs, corporations and individuals standing.

Secondly, in contrast to the ICC, the personal jurisdiction of the International Environmental Court would not be limited to individual criminal liability. Instead, the International Environmental Court could be granted individual and corporate criminal jurisdiction as well as civil jurisdiction over individuals and legal entities such as corporations or states. With respect to the individual criminal liability of business leaders, the International Convention on Environmental Protection could include modes of attribution with significantly lower prerequisites than Article 25 (3) and Article 28 (b) Rome Statute. In terms of criminal sanctions, the International Environmental Court would, unlike the ICC, not be limited to imposing terms of imprisonment as the primary sanction but could also impose non-financial criminal penalties tailored to corporations, such as injunctions, licence revocation, corporate probation, the confiscation of assets and the dissolution of companies as well as the reinstatement of the environment. With regard to the reinstatement of the environment, it is particularly beneficial that the International Environmental Court would not only have criminal jurisdiction but also civil jurisdiction, thereby permitting the Court to impose civil damages on multinational corporations, which could finance the Environmental Trust Fund thus providing a financial basis for environmental organisations to reinstate the affected environment. Furthermore, the International Environmental Court could also serve as an international adjudicator for the human right to access to a clean, healthy and sustainable environment.

Thirdly, unlike a potential fifth crime of ecocide under the Rome Statute, the mental threshold of a generic crime against the environment enshrined in the International Convention on Environmental Protection could be lowered to include *dolus eventualis* or advertent *Fahrlässigkeit*. Since the International Environmental Court would not prosecute macro-criminality and would not have jurisdiction over the core crimes under the Rome Statute, it could also adjudicate upon environmental crimes falling below the gravity threshold of Article 17 (1) (d) Rome Statute and also civil claims. However, the mental element may not be set too low as otherwise states may refrain from transferring their sovereignty to the International Environmental Court. Thus, environmental accidents caused by a perpetrator, who simply lacked the necessary level of care without being aware of the risk of harm his conduct involved (simple negligence or inadvertent *Fahrlässigkeit*) may not incur criminal liability under international law and thus may only give rise to civil liability. Nevertheless, the generic crime against the environment could include cases of culpable negligence thereby covering cases where the perpetrator was aware of the risk of environmental harm but believed the harm would not materialise. Nonetheless, enhancing global environmental protection is best attained by keeping the *objective* side broad by establishing a generic crime of endangerment addressing conduct prior to the materialisation of harm and keeping the *subjective* side inclusive by requiring *dolus eventualis*. Thus, the definition of the generic crime against the environment should not be further extended to include negligent conduct but should only include *dolus eventualis* or advertent recklessness.

Fourthly, similar to the UN Convention against Torture, the International Convention on Environmental Protection could provide for the establishment of an Environmental Committee which has compulsory competence to review periodic reports by the signatory States concerning the implementation and enforcement of the Convention and to initiate investigations if the formation available indicates the commission of environmental offences.

For these reasons, the author of this thesis advocates the establishment of an International Environmental Court as opposed to incorporating a fifth crime of ecocide into the Rome Statute and establishing a separate environmental chamber at the ICC. Although the establishment of a separate environmental chamber would be less cost-intensive than the creation of a new court, the impediments to the enforcement of a fifth crime of ecocide flowing from the nature of international criminal law and the structure of the ICC speak against the inclusion of such a crime. Due to the broader accessibility and the lower gravity threshold, the International Environmental Court is likely to attract more lawsuits than the ICC and thus could induce corporations "to engage in environmentally sound practices abroad"[117].

[117] *Peggy Rodgers Kalas*, Colorado Journal of International Environmenal Law and Policy 230 (2001).

E. Final considerations

Although global environmental protection is afforded by several fields of international law, including international environmental law, international humanitarian law, international human rights law as well as international criminal law, the current global environmental governance system is not sufficiently well-equipped to halt environmental destruction occurring at an ever-increasing pace, predominantly caused by industrial activities. While international environmental law lacks both a single consolidated framework which includes a generic transnational environmental crime and an international judicial system to develop consistent international environmental standards, international humanitarian law only affords environmental protection during wartime. Although the UN General Assembly recently declared access to a clean, healthy and sustainable environment a universal human right, human rights law lacks an international court to enforce environmental human rights. Ultimately, international criminal law affords environmental protection only to the extent environmentally destructive behaviour falls within the purview of war crimes, crimes against humanity or genocide. However, prosecuting environmental harm as genocide will mostly fail due to the significantly high mental threshold of having to prove the perpetrator's intent to destroy a particular group. Even though war crimes and crimes against humanity carry a considerably lower mental threshold, the environmental war crime under Article 8 (2) (b) (iv) Rome Statute is restricted to international armed conflicts leaving the most prevalent forms of environmental harm, which occur during non-international armed conflicts and peacetime, wholly unaddressed. Although crimes against humanity could, in theory, cover environmental degradation during non-international armed conflicts and peacetime, crimes against humanity hold a strictly anthropocentric perspective only prohibiting environmentally destructive conduct *directly* causing human harm and thus leaving the environment as such unprotected.

In this thesis it has been adjudged that this lack of effective global environmental protection is best remedied by adopting an International Convention on Environmental Protection enforced through an International Environmental Court, which is yet to be established, as opposed to including a fifth crime of ecocide into the Rome Statute. Ideally, such an International Environmental Court (1) would be created under the auspices of the UN, (2) be compulsory, (3) would have civil and criminal jurisdiction, (4) would enforce a human right to a clean, healthy and sustainable environment, (5) take precedence over national judicial courts, (6) would permit states, individuals, corporations as well as NGOs access to the court, and (7) would be complemented by a supervision system. In doing so, it is acknowledged that the mere criminalisation of environmental harm under international criminal law by incorporating a fifth crime of ecocide into the Rome Statute is not sufficient.[1]

Instead, a multifaceted approach is to be preferred. Although criminal sanctions have a different moral overtone by expressing the societal condemnation of certain conduct as opposed to civil remedies, the actual extent of their potential negative and positive deterrent effect on individuals and corporations remains unknown. As Drumbl rightly stated: "The preference for incarceration following what liberal international lawyers deem to be an acceptable criminal trial on the whole falls short of its penological objectives, in particular retribution and deterrence. This may be because those objectives are too ambitious. It may also be because the criminal law, standing alone, simply is not enough nor can ever be enough".[2]

Thus, by ascribing both civil and criminal jurisdiction to the International Environmental Court, the Court may act as the main adjudicator of international environmental law, enforce a human right to access to a clean, healthy and sustainable environment as well as impose individual and corporate criminal liability for committing crimes against the environment.

In doing so, several birds are killed with one stone. Firstly, the lack of an international judicial system in international environmental law and environmental human rights law would be remedied. Secondly, global environmental protection would be promoted by establishing corporate and individual criminal liability for environmental harm. Creating a generic crime against the environment would eventually fill the voids caused by the plethora of subject-specific environmental treaties in international environmental law. Thirdly, an Environmental Trust Fund could be established, which could be financed through civil damages imposed on corporations and states, and an Environmental Committee similar to the Committee against Torture could monitor the implementation of and compliance with the underlying International Convention on Environmental Protection. These *legal* means should further be complemented by economic incentives for corporations which would encourage environmentally friendly corporate behaviour to promote global environmental protection. Nevertheless, all these means to fill the existing legal lacunae in current global environmental protection require political will. What may seem as a naïve and unrealistic idea now, is the future of tomorrow. All great developments start with a bold idea. Take, by way of example, Rafael Lemkin who spent his lifetime fighting for the criminalisation of genocide or Arthur Galston who created the idea of ecocide in response to the environmental atrocities committed during the Vietnam War. The time is *now* ripe to promote global environmental protection through the establishment of an International Environmental Court and to safeguard the future of the next generations.

---

[1] Similar, *Eliana Teresa Cusato*, JICJ 507 (2017) ("it is crystal clear that the ICC will never be able to do justice to all forms of environmental destruction, as it is evident that criminal accountability is just one dimension of 'environmental justice'").

[2] *Mark Drumbl*, Atrocity 180 (2007).

Bibliography

Primary Sources

Deutscher Bundestag, Eine Übersicht zum Unternehmensstrafrecht in einzelnen Mitgliedstaaten der Europäischen Union, Az. WD 7-3000-070/17 (2017)

European Commission, European Green Deal: Strengthening EU Law to Combat Environmental Crime (2021)

European Court of Human Rights, Factsheet, Environment and the Eurpoean Convention on Human Rights (2022)

European Court of Human rights, Guide to the Case-Law of the European Court of Human Rights (2022)

European Parliament, Report on the Liability of Companies for Environmental Damage, Opinion of the Committee on the Environment, Public Health and Food Safety, Eur. Parl. Doc. 2020/2027(INI) (2021)

EUROPOL, Environmental Crime in the Age of Climate Change (2022)

Fafo and International Peace Academy, Business and International Crimes: Assessing the Liability of Business Entities for Grave Violations of International Law, Fafo-Report 467 (2005)

G.A., Report of the Conference of the Committee on Disarmament, U.N. Doc. A/31/27 (Vol. I) (1976)

G.A., Report of the Special Rapporteur on the Issue of Human Rights Obligations Relating to the Enjoyment of a Safe, Clean, Healthy and Sustainable Environment, U.N. Doc. A/HRC/ 43/53 (2019)

G.A., Situation of Human Rights in Guatemala, Report of the United Nations High Commissioner for Human Rights, U.N. Doc. A/HRC/49/20 (2022)

Government of the Republic of Vanuatu, General Debate of the 18th Session of the Assembly of States Parties to the Rome Statute of the International Criminal Court, Statement by H.E. John H. Licht (2019)

ICTY, Final Report to the Prosecutor by the Committee Established to Review the Nato Bombing Campaign Against the Federal Republic of Yugoslavia (2000)

International Commission of Jurists, Report of the International Commission of Jurists Expert Legal Panel on Corporate Complicity in International Crimes, Volume 2 (2008)

International Commission of Jurists, Report of the International Commission of Jurists Expert Legal Panel on Corporate Complicity in International Crimes, Volume 3 (2008)

Office of the Prosecutor, Policy Paper on Case Selection and Prioritisation (2016)

Republic of Maldives, 18th Session of the Assembly of State Parties to the Rome Statute of the International Criminal Court, Written Statement of the Republic of Maldives (2019)

Ruggie, John (U.N. Special Representative of the Secretary-General), Promotion and Protection of all Human Rights, Civil, Political, Economic, Social and Cultural Rights, Including the Right to Development, U.N. Doc. A/HRC/8/5 (2008)

Ruhashyankiko, Nicodème (Special Rapporteur on Prevention and Punishment of the Crime of Genocide), Study of the Question of the Prevention and Punishment of the Crime of Genocide, U.N. Doc. E/CN.4/Sub.2/416 (1978)

Stop Ecocide Foundation, Independent Expert Panel for the Legal Definition of Ecocide, Commentary and Core Text (2021)

The George Washington University Law School Conference on International Environmental Dispute Resolution (April 15–17, 1999), 32 (3) Geo. Wash. J. Int'l L. & Econ. 325 (2000)

The Office of the Prosecutor, Report on Preliminary Examination Activities (2016)

The Office of the Prosecutor, Report on Preliminary Examination Activities (2017)

The Office of the Prosecutor, Report on Preliminary Examination Activities (2018)

The Office of the Prosecutor, Report on Preliminary Examination Activities (2019)

The Office of the Prosecutor, Report on Preliminary Examination Activities (2020)

UNEP, From Conflict to Peacebuilding: The Role of Natural Resources and the Environment (2009)

UNEP, Protecting the Environment During Armed Conflict: An Inventory and Analysis of International Law (2009)

UNEP, The Rise of Environmental Crime, A Growing Threat to Natural Resources, Peace, Development and Security (2016)

U.N. Diplomatic Conference of Plenipotentiaries on the Establishment of an International Criminal Court, Report of the Preparatory Committee on the Establishment of an International Criminal Court, U.N. Doc. A/Conf.183/2/Add.1 (1998)

U.N. Diplomatic Conference of Plenipotentiaries on the Establishment of an International Criminal Court, Working Paper on Article 23, Paragraphs 5 and 6, U.N. Doc. A/Conf.183/C.1/WGGP/L.5/Rev.2 (1998)

U.N., Report of the United Nations Conference on Environment and Development, U.N. Doc. A/CONF.151/26/Rev.1 (Vol. I) (1992)

U.N., Report of the UN Conference on the Human Environment, U.N. Doc. A/CONF.48/Rev.1 (1972)

U.N. Secretary-General, Gaps in International Environmental Law and Environmental-Related Instruments, Towards a Global Pact for the Environment, U.N. Doc. A/73/419 (2018)

U.N. Security Council, Letter Dated 24 February 2022 from the Permanent Representative of the Russian Federation to the United Nations Addressed to the Secretary-General, U.N. Doc. S/2022/154 (2022)

U.N. Security Council, Report of the Secretary-General Pursuant to Paragraph 2 of Security Council Resolution 808, U.N. Doc. S/25704 (1993)

U.N. Subcommission on Prevention of Discrimination and Protection of Minorities, Report of the Sub-Commission on Prevention of Discrimination and Protection of Minorities on its Thirty-Eight Session, U.N. Doc. E/CN.4/1986/5 (1985)

United States Department of Defense, Report to Congress on the Conduct of the Persian Gulf War – Appendix on the Role of the Law of War, 31 (3) International Legal Materials 612 (1992)

Whitaker, Benjamin (Special Rapporteur on Prevention and Punishment of the Crime of Genocide), Revised and Updated Report on the Question of the Prevention and Punishment of the Crime of Genocide, U.N. Doc. E/CN.4/Sub.2/1985/6 (1985)

Secondary Sources

Alderman, Liz/*Méheut*, Constant, Going Green, or Greenwashing? A Proposed Climate Law Divides France, The New York Times (May 19, 2021)

Amann, Diane Marie, Group Mentality, Expressivism, and Genocide, 2 (2) International Criminal Law Review 93 (2002)

Ambos, Kai, Der Fall Pinochet und das anwendbare Recht, 54 (1) JuristenZeitung 16 (1999)

Ambos, Kai, Rome Statute of the International Criminal Court (2022)

Ambos, Kai, Treatise on International Criminal Law, Volume I: Foundations and General Part (2nd ed., 2021)

Ambos, Kai, Wirtschaftsvölkerstrafrecht (2018)

Ambos Kai/*Duff*, Antony, et al., Core Concepts in Criminal Law and Criminal Justice, Vol. II (2022)

Bassiouni, Cherif M., International Criminal Law (2008)

Berat, Lynn, Defending the Right to a Healthy Environment: Toward a Crime of Geocide in International Law, B.U. INT'l L. J. 327 (1993)

Bernaz, Nadia, Corporate Criminal Liability under International Law, 13 JICJ 313 (2015)

Biber, Eric, Climate Change, Causation, And Delayed Harm, 37 Hofstra L. Rev. 975 (2009)

Bodansky, Daniel, Customary (and Not So Customary) International Environmental Law, 3 (1) Indiana Journal of Global Studies 105 (1995)

Botchway, Francis N., Natural Resource Investment and Africa's Development (2011)

Bourke, India, Philippe Sands on why "Ecocide" Should Be a Crime, The New Statesman (Feb. 16, 2021)

Boyle, Alan E., Dispute Settlement and the Law of the Sea Convention: Problems of Fragmentation and Jurisdiction, 46 International and Comparative Law Quarterly 37 (1997)

Bronwyn, Lay, et al., Timely and Necessary: Ecocide Law as Urgent and Emerging 28 J. Juris. 431 (2015)

Bruch, Carl E., All's Not Fair in (Civil) War: Criminal Liability for Environmental Damage in Internal Armed Conflict, 25 (3) Vermont Law Review 695 (2001)

Burchard, Christoph, Ancillary and Neutral Business Contributions to 'Corporate-Political Core Crime', 8 (3) JICJ 919 (2010)

Burger, Michael/*Wentz*, Jessica, et al., The Law and Science of Climate Change Attribution, 45 (1) Colum. J. Envtl. L. 57 (2020)

Byung-Sun, Cho, Emergence of an International Environmental Criminal Law?, 19 (1) UCLA Journal of Environmental Law and Policy 11 (2000)

Çakmak, Cenap, A Brief History of International Criminal Law and International Criminal Court (2017)

Carrington, Damian, Test Trial Convicts Fossil Fuel Bosses of 'Ecocide', The Guardian (Oct. 5, 2011)

Cassese, Antonio, Reflections of International Criminal Justice, 61 (1) MOD. L. REV. 1 (1998)

Cassese, Antonio/*Gaeta*, Paola, et al., Cassese's International Criminal Law (3rd ed., 2013)

Cassese, Antonio/*Gaeta*, Paola, et al., The Rome Statute of the International Criminal Court: A Commentary (2002)

Charney, Jonathan I., The Impact on the International Legal System of the Growth of International Courts and Tribunals, 31 (4) N.Y.U. J. Int'l L. & Pol. 697 (1999)

Clapham, Andrew, Extending International Criminal Law Beyond the Individual to Corporations and Armed Opposition Groups, 6 (5) JICJ 899 (2008)

Clark, Roger S., Drafting a General Part to a Penal Code: Some Thoughts Inspired by the Negotiations on the Rome Statute of the International Criminal Court and by the Court's First Substantive Law Discussion in the Lubanga Dyilo Confirmation Proceedings, 19 CLF 519 (2008)

Coffee, John C., No Soul to Damn: No Body to Kick: An Unscandalized Inquiry into the Problem of Corporate Punishment, 79 (3) Michigan Law Review 386 (1981)

Colacurci, Marco, The Draft Convention Ecocide and the Role for Corporate Remediation, Some Insights from the International Monsanto Tribunal and a Recent Research Proposal, 21 International Criminal Law Review 154 (2021)

Cornford, Andrew, Preventive Criminalization, 18 New Criminal Law Review: An International and Interdisciplinary Journal 1 (2015)

Crasson, Audrey, The Case of Chevron in Ecuador: The Need for an International Crime Against the Environment?, 9 (3) Amsterdam Law Forum 29 (2017)

Cryer, Robert, et al., An Introduction to International Criminal Law and Procedure (4th ed., 2019)

Cuffe, Sandra, Guatemalan Activist Murdered After Court Suspends Palm Oil Company Operations, Mongabay (Sept. 30, 2015)

Cusato, Eliana Teresa, Beyond Symbolism, 15 JICJ 491 (2017)

Decaux, Emmanuel, The Place of Human Rights Courts and International Criminal Courts in the International System, 9 (3) JICJ 597 (2011)

Dehan, Audra E., An International Environmental Court: Should There Be One?, 3 TOURO J. Transnat'l L. 31 (1992)

Dinstein, Yoram, Protection of the Environment in International Armed Conflict, 5 Max Planck Yearbook of United Nations Law 523 (2001)

Dölling, Dieter, Generalprävention durch Strafrecht: Realität oder Illusion?, 1 (102) ZStW 1 (1990)

Dörmann, Knut, Preparatory Commission for the International Criminal Court: The Elements of War Crimes, Part II, 83 International Review of the Red Cross 461 (2001)

Drumbl, Mark, Atrocity, Punishment and International Law (2007)

Drumbl, Mark, International Human Rights, International Humanitarian Law and Environmental Security: Can the International Criminal Court Bridge the Gaps?, 6 (2) ILSA J. INT'L & COMP. L. 305 (2000)

Drumbl, Mark A., Accountability for Property Crimes and Environmental War Crimes: Prosecution, Litigation, and Development, ICTJ 1 (2009)

Dunoff, Jeffrey L., Institutional Misfits: The GATT, the ICJ & Trade-Environment, 15 (4) Mich. J. Int'l L. 1043 (1994)

Einarsen, Terje, The Concept of Universal Crimes in International Law (2012)

Erb, Volker/*Schäfer*, Jürgen, Münchener Kommentar zum Strafgesetzbuch, Nebenstafrecht III, Völkerstrafgesetzbuch (4th ed., 2022)

Falk, Richard A., Environmental Warfare and Ecocide, 4 (1) Bulletin of Peace Proposals 80 (1973)

Farrell, Norman, Attributing Criminal Liability to Corporate Actors: Some Lessons from the International Tribunals, 8 (3) JICJ 873 (2010)

Feinberg, Joel, The Expressive Function of Punishment, 49 (3) The Monist 397 (1970)

Fleck, Dieter, The Handbook of International Humanitarian Law (4th ed., 2021)

Fleming, Sean, Leviathan on Trial: Should States Be Held Criminally Responsible?, 13 (3) International Theory 427 (2021)

Fletcher, George P., The Storrs Lectures: Liberals and Romantics at War: The Problem of Collective Guilt, 111 (7) The Yale Law Journal 1499 (2002)

Fletcher, Laurel E./*Weinstein*, Harvey M., Violence and Social Repair: Rethinking the Contribution of Justice to Reconciliation, 24 Human Rights Quarterly 573 (2002)

Freestone, David, The Road from Rio: International Environmental Law After the Earth Summit, 6 (2) Journal of Environmental Law 193 (1994)

Gaeta, Paola, Ratione Materiae Immunities of Former Heads of State and International Crimes: The Hissène Habré Case, 1 (1) JICJ 186 (2003)

Garner, Bryan A., Black's Law Dictionary (2nd pocket ed., 2001)

Gauger, Anja, et al., The Ecocide Project – Ecocide Is the Missing 5th Crime Against Peace (2012)

Geis, Gilbert, On White-Collar Crime (1982)

Godin, Mélissa, Lawyers Are Working to Put 'Ecocide' On Par with War Crimes, Could an International Law Hold Major Polluters to Account?, Time (Feb. 19, 2021)

Gray, Mark Allan, The International Crime of Ecocide, 26 Cal. W. Int'l L.J. 215 (1996)

Greenawalt, Alexander K. A., International Criminal Law for Retributivists, 35 (4) University of Pennsylvania Journal of International Law 969 (2014)

Greene, Anastacia, The Campaign to Make Ecocide an International Crime: Quixotic Quest or Moral Imperative?, 30 (3) Fordham Environmental Law Review 1 (2019)

Haenen, Iris, Classifying Acts as Crimes Against Humanity in the Rome Statute of the International Criminal Court, 14 (7) German American Law Journal 796 (2013)

Harvey, Fiona/*Carrington*, Damian, World is on 'Highway to Climate Hell', UN Chief Warns at Cop27 Summit, The Guardian (Nov. 7, 2022)

Harvey, Fiona/*Lakhani*, Nina, et al., Cop27 Agrees Historic 'Loss and Damage' Fund for Climate Impact in Developing Countries, The Guardian (Nov. 20, 2022)

Hedman, Susan, Expressive Functions of Criminal Sanctions in Environmental Law, 59 (4) Geo. Wash. Int'l. Rev. 889 (1990)

Hey, Ellen, Reflections on an International Environmental Court (2000)

Higgins, Polly, Eradicating Ecocide: Laws and Governance to Stop the Destruction of the Planet (2nd ed., 2015)

Higgins, Polly/*Short*, Damien, et al., Protecting the Planet: A Proposal for a Law of Ecocide, 59 Crime, Law and Social Change 251 (2013)

Hinde, Susan M., The International Environmental Court: Its Broad Jurisdiction as a Possible Fatal Flaw, 32 Hofstra L. Rev. 727 (2003)

Hockman, Stephen, An International Court for the Environment, 11 Envtl. L. Rev. 1 (2008)

Hulme, Karen, War Torn Environment: Interpreting the Legal Threshold (2004)

INTERPOL/UNEP, Strategic Report, Environment, Peace and Security, A Convergence of Threats (2016)

Jacobs, Rebecca Elizabeth, Treading Deep Waters: Substantive Law Issues in Tuvalu's Threat to Sue the United States in the International Court of Justice, 14 Pac. Rim L & Pol'y J. 103 (2005)

Jäger, Herbert, Makrokriminalität (1989)

Jennings, Robert/*Watts*, Arthur, Oppenheim's International Law (9th ed., 2008)

Jescheck, Hans-Heinrich, The General Principles of International Criminal Law Set Out in Nuremberg, as Mirrored in the ICC Statute, 2 (1) JICJ 38 (2004)

Jeßberger, Florian, On the Origins of Individual Criminal Responsibility under International Law for Business Activity, 8 (3) JICJ 783 (2010)

Jeßberger, Florian/*Geneuss*, Julia, Why Punish Perpetrators of Mass Atrocities? Purposes of Punishment in International Criminal Law (Florian Jeßberger and Julia Geneuss eds., 2020)

Jeßberger, Florian/*Kalleck*, Wolfgang, et al., Wirtschaftsvölkerstrafrecht (2015)

Jeßberger, Florian/*Vormbaum*, Moritz, et al., Strafrecht und Systemunrecht (2022)

Johnston, Ian, Campaign to Out Ecocide on a Par with Genocide in Attempt to Curb Environmental Destruction, The Independent (Oct. 12, 2014)

Juenger, Friedrich K., Selected Essays on the Conflict of Laws (2001)

Jurdi, Nidal Nabil, The Subject-Matter Jurisdiction of the Special Tribunal for Lebanon, 5 (5) JICJ 1125 (2007)

Kaeb, Caroline, The Shifting Sands of Corporate Liability under International Criminal Law, 49 (2) Geo. Wash. Int'l. Rev. 351 (2016)

Kalas, Peggy Rodgers, International Environmental Dispute Resolution and the Need for Access by Non-State Entities, 12 Colorado Journal of International Environmenal Law and Policy 191 (2001)

Kamminga, Menno T./*Zia-Zarifi*, Saman, Liability of Multinational Corporations Under International Law (2000)

Killean, Rachel, From Ecocide to Eco-Sensitivity: 'Greening' Reparations at the International Criminal Court, 25 (2) International Journal of Human Rights 323 (2021)

Kreicker, Helmut, Immunität und IStGH, Zur Bedeutung völkerrechtlicher Exemtionen für den Internationalen Strafgerichtshof, 7 ZIS 350 (2009)

Kremnitzer, Mordechai, A Possible Case for Imposing Criminal Liability on Corporations in International Criminal Law, 8 (3) JICJ 909 (2010)

Kuntz, Marie, Conceptualising Transnational Corporate Groups for International Criminal Law (2017)

Kyriakakis, Joanna, Corporate Criminal Liability and the ICC Statute: The Comparative Law Challenge, NILR 333 (2009)

Kyriakakis, Joanna, Corporations Before International Criminal Court: Implications for the International Criminal Justice Project, 30 Leiden Journal of International Law 221 (2017)

Kyriakakis, Joanna, Developments in International Criminal Law and the Case of Business Involvement in International Crimes, 94 (887) IRRC 981 (2012)

Lama, Abraham, Environment: UNEP Prefers Persuasion over Sanctions, Inter Press Service (Oct. 4, 1999)

Lambert, Caitlin, Environmental Destruction in Ecuador: Crimes Against Humanity Under the Rome Statute?, 30 Leiden Journal of International Law 707 (2017)

Lawrence, Jessica C./*Heller*, Kevin Jon, The First Ecocentric Environmental War Crime: The Limits of Article 8 (2) (b) (iv) of the Rome Statute, 20 (1) Geo. Int'l Envtl. L. Rev. 61 (2007)

Leahy, Stephen, This Is The World's Most Destructive Oil Operation – And It's Growing, National Geographic (Apr. 11, 2019)

Lemkin, Raphael, Axis Rule in Occupied Europe (1944)

Manacorda, Stefano/*Meloni*, Chantal, Indirect Perpetration versus Joint Criminal Enterprise, 9 (1) JICJ 159 (2011)

McCallion, Kenneth F., International Environmental Justice: Rights and Remedies, 26 (3) Hastings International and Comparative Law Review 427 (2003)

McCallion, Kenneth F./*Sharma*, H. Rajan, Environmental Justice Without Borders: The Need for an International Court of the Environment to Protect Fundamental Environmental Rights, 32 (3) Geo. Wash. J. Int'l L. & Econ. 351 (2000)

Mégret, Frédéric, Les angles morts de la responsabilité pénale individuelle en droit international, 71 R.I.E.J. 83 (2013)

Mégret, Frédéric, The Case for a General International Crime Against the Environment (2010)

Mégret, Frédéric, The Problem of an International Criminal Law of the Environment, 36 Colum. J. Envtl. L. 195 (2011)

Meisenberg, Simon M., Auf dem Wege zu einem Unternehmensvölkerstrafrecht? Eine kritische Würdigung der "New TV S.A.L"-Entscheidung des Sondergerichtshofs für den Libanon (2016)

Merz, Prisca, Ecocide: Prisca Merz Argues It Is Now Time to Act Against the Large-Scale Damage or Destruction of Ecosystems, Socialist Lawyer 16 (2014)

Merz, Prisca/*Cabanes*, Valérie, et al., Ending Ecocide – the next necessary step in international law (2014)

Meyer, Frank, Diskussionsbeitrag: "Verbandsverantwortung im Völkerstrafrecht", 126 (1) ZStW 122 (2014)

Meyer, Frank, Multinationale Unternehmen und das Völkerstrafrecht, 131 (1) Schweizerische Zeitschrift für Strafrecht 56 (2013)

Milanović, Marko, Is the Rome Statute Binding on Individuals? (And Why We Should Care), 9 (1) JICJ 25 (2011)

Milhorance, Flàvia, Jair Bolsonaro Could Face Charges in The Hague Over Amazon Rainforest, The Guardian (Jan. 23, 2021)

Mistura, Alessandra, Is There Space for Environmental Crimes Under International Criminal Law? The Impact of the Office of the Prosecutor Policy Paper on Case Selection and Prioritization on the Current Legal Framework, Colum. J. Envtl. L. 181 (2018)

Möller, Christina, Völkerstrafrecht und Internationaler Strafgerichtshof (2003)

Moules, Richard, Significant EU Environmental Cases: 2019, 32 (1) Journal of Environmental Law 161 (2020)

Mulgrew, Roisin/*Abels*, Denis, Research Handbook on the International Penal System (2016)

Murphy, Sean, Does the World Need a New International Environmental Court?, 32 (3) Geo. Wash. J. Int'l L. & Econ. 333 (2000)

Mwanza, Rosemary, Enhancing Accountability For Environmental Damage Under International Law: Ecocide As a Legal Fulfillment of Ecological Integrity, 19 (2) Melb. Journal of International Law 1 (2018)

Neubacher, Frank, Kriminologische Grundlagen einer internationalen Strafgerichtsbarkeit (2005)

Neubacher, Frank, Strafzwecke und Völkerstrafrecht, NJW 966 (2006)

Neyret, Laurent, Des écocrimes à l'écocide: le droit pénal au secours de l'environnement (2015)

Notaras, Mark, Should Ecocide Be Deemed a Crime Against Peace?, Our World (Mar. 5, 2010)

Oehm, Franziska Maria, Land Grabbing in Cambodia as a Crime Against Humanity, Approaches in International Criminal Law, 48 (4) Verfassung und Recht in Übersee 469 (2015)

Orellana, Marcos, Criminal Punishment for Environmental Damage: Individual and State Responsibility at a Crossroad, 17 (4) Geo. Int'l Envtl. L. Rev. 673 (2005)

Pallemaerts, Marc, International Environmental Law from Stockholm to Rio: Back to the Future, 1 (3) Rev. Eur. Comp. & Int'l Envtl. L. 254 (1992)

Palme, Olof, Outrage of Ecocide, Bulletin of the Atomic Scientists 44 (1972)

Palmer, Geoffrey, New Ways to Make International Environmental Law, 86 (2) The American Journal of International Law 259 (1992)

Palmer, Michael G., The Case of Agent Orange, 29 Contemporary Southeast Asia 172 (2007)

Parker, Courtney, Justice in Guatemala: Guatemalan Court Upholds Revolutionary Ruling on Ecocide, Intercontinental Cry (Jan. 1, 2016)

Pearce, Jeremy, Arthur Galston, Agent Orange Researcher, Is Dead at 88, The New York Times (June 23, 2008)

Pedersen, Ole W., An International Environmental Court and International Legalism, 24 (3) Journal of Environmental Law 547 (2012)

Pereira, Ricardo, After the ICC Office of the Prosecutor's 2016 Policy Paper on Case Selection and Prioritisation: Towards an International Crime of Ecocide?, 31 Criminal Law Forum 179 (2020)

Pereira, Ricardo, Towards Effective Implementation of the EU Environmental Crime Directive? The Case of Illegal Waste Management and Trafficking Offences, 26 (2) Rev. Eur. Comp. & Int'l Envtl. L. 147 (2017)

Peterson, Ines, The Natural Environment in Times of Armed Conflict: A Concern for International War Crimes Law?, 22 (2) Leiden Journal of International Law 325 (2009)

Pilloud, Claude/*Sandoz*, Yves, et al., Commentary on the Additional Protocols of 8 June 1977 to the Geneva Conventions of 12 August 1949 (1987)

Postiglione, Amedeo, A More Efficient International Law on the Environment and Setting Up an International Court for the Environment within the United States, 20 (2) Environmental Law 321 (1990)

Prosperi, Luigi/*Terrosi*, Jacopo, Embracing the 'Human Factor': Is There New Impetus at the ICC for Conceiving and Prioritizing International Environmental Harms as Crimes Against Humanity?, 15 (3) JICJ 509 (2017)

Rannard, Georgina, Amazon Deforestation, Record High Destruction of Trees in January, BBC News (Feb. 11, 2022)

Rauscher, Michael, On Ecological Dumping, 46 Oxford Economic Papers 822 (1994)

Rest, Alfred, Enhanced Implementation of the Biological Diversity Convention by Judicial Control, 29 (1) Envtl. Pol'y & L. 32 (1999)

Reuss, Vasco, Zivilcourage als Strafzweck des Völkerstrafrechts (2012)

Robinson, Darryl, A Justification of Command Responsibility, 28 Criminal Law Forum 633 (2017)

Roch, Philippe/*Perrez*, Franz Xaver, International Environmental Governance: The Strive Towards a Comprehensive, Coherent, Effective and Efficient International Environmental Regime, 16 (1) Colorado Journal of International Environmenal Law and Policy 1 (2005)

Rotsch, Friederike, et al., Der Regierungsentwurf zum Verbandssanktionengesetz, Kritische Analyse und Ausblick, CCZ 169 (2020)

Saadoun, Sarah, The Coal Mine Next Door, How the US Government's Deregulation of Mountaintop Removal Threatens Public Health, Human Rights Watch (Dec. 10, 2018)

Safferling, Christoph, Internationales Strafrecht (2011)

Safferling, Christoph, Vorsatz und Schuld (2008)

Safferling, Christoph/*Kirsch*, Stefan, Völkerstrafrechtspolitik (2014)

Sands, Philippe, International Environmental Litigation and its Future, 32 (5) U. Rich. L. Rev. 1619 (1999)

Sands, Philippe/*Peel*, Jacqueline, Principles of International Environmental Law (4th ed., 2018)

Sandy, Matt, The Amazon Rainforest Is Nearly Gone, We Went to the Front Lines to See If It Could Be Saved, Time (Sept. 12, 2019)

Schabas, William A., An Introduction to the International Criminal Court (6th ed., 2020)

Schabas, William A., Genocide in International Law: The Crime of Crimes (2nd ed., 2009)

Schabas, William A., The International Criminal Court: A Commentary on the Rome Statute (2nd ed., 2016)

Scheffer, David, Corporate Liability under the Rome Statute, 57 Harvard International Law Journal 35 (2016)

Schmitt, Michael N., Green War: An Assessment of the Environmental Law of International Armed Conflict, 22 Yale Journal of International Law 1 (1997)

Schneider, Keith, The Nation, The New York Times (Mar. 17, 1991)

Schwegeler, Vanessa, The Disposable Nature: The Case of Ecocide and Corporate Accountability, 9 (3) Amsterdam Law Forum 71 (2017)

Scoville, Ryan M., Finding Customary International Law, 101 Iowa L. Rev. 1893 (2016)

Sharp, Peter, Prospects for Environmental Liability in the International Criminal Court, 18 (2) Virginia Environmental Law Journal 217 (1999)

Short, Damien, Redefining Genocide, Settler Colonialism, Social Death and Ecocide (2016)

Shukla, Ashutosh, Bhopal Gas Tragedy Convict Dead, 37 Years Later, Court Fight Drags On, The Times of India (Oct. 12, 2021)

Siddique, Haroon, Legal Experts Worldwide Draw Up 'Historic' Definition of Ecocide, The Guardian (June 22, 2021)

Sieders, Liemertje Julia, The Battle of Realities: The Case for and Against the Inclusion of 'Ecocide' in the ICC Rome Statute, RIDP 29 (2020)

Sloane, Robert, The Expressive Capacity of International Punishment: The Limits of the National Law Analogy and the Potential of International Criminal Law, 43 Stanford Journal of International Law 39 (2007)

Slye, Ronald C., Corporations, Veils, And International Criminal Liability, 33 (3) Brook. J. Int'L. 955 (2008)

Smith, Wesley, Ecocide: A Crime Against Peace?, The Weekly Standard (May 10, 2010)

Sohn, Louis B., The Stockholm Declaration on the Human Environment, 14 Harvard International Law Journal 423 (1973)

Stahn, Carsten, A Critical Introduction to International Criminal Law (2019)

Stahn, Carsten/*Iverson*, Jens, et al., Environmental Protection and Transitions from Conflict to Peace: Clarifying Norms, Principles, and Practices (2017)

Steer, Cassandra, Translating Guilt: Identifying Leadership Liability for Mass Atrocity Crimes (2017)

Steinke, Ronen, Selektive Strafverfolgung: Über ein wachsendes Problem der internationalen Strafjustiz, 41 (2) Kritische Justiz 207 (2014)

Stempel, Jonathan, No Prison Terms for Gulf Spill As Final Defendant Gets Probation, Reuters (Apr. 6, 2016)

Stephens, Tim, International Courts and Environmental Protection (2009)

Swart, Ben, International Trends towards Establishing Some Form of Punishment for Corporations, 6 (5) JICJ 947 (2008)

Thurner, Gabriel Wilhelm Bartalyos, Internationales Unternehmensstrafrecht (2012)

Tomuschat, Christian, Crimes Against the Environment, 26 (6) Envtl. Pol'y & L. 242 (1996)

Van den Herik, Karissa/*Letnar*, Černič Jernej, Regulating Corporations under International Law: From Human Rights to International Criminal Law and Back Again, 8 (3) JICJ 725 (2010)

Van der Wilt, Harmen, Corporate Criminal Responsibility for International Crimes: Exploring the Possibilities, 12 (1) Chinese J. INT'l L. 43 (2013)

Van Sliedregt, Elies/*Vasiliev*, Sergey, Pluralism in International Criminal Law (2014)

Vest, Hans, Business Leaders and the Modes of Individual Criminal Responsibility under International Law, 8 (3) JICJ 851 (2010)

Vest, Hans, Humanitätsverbrechen – Herausforderung für das Individualstrafrecht?, 113 (3) ZStW 457 (2001)

Victor, David G./*Raustiala*, Kal, et al., The Implementation and Effectiveness of International Environmental Commitments, Theory and Practice (1998)

Wang, Yating, Fukushima Nuclear Disaster Aftermath: No One Was Found Criminally Liable, Fordham Environmental Law Review (Dec. 3, 2019)

Watson, Michael, The Enforcement of Environmental Law: Civil or Criminal Penalties?, 17 (1) Environmental Law and Management 3 (2005)

Wattad, Mohammed Saif-Alden, Is Terrorism a Crime or an Aggravating Factor in Sentencing?, 4 (5) JICJ 1017 (2006)

Wattad, Mohammed Saif-Alden, The Rome Statute & Captain Planet: What Lies Between 'Crimes Against Humanity' and the 'Natural Environment'?, 19 (2) Fordham Environmental Law Review 265 (2009)

Weigend, Thomas, Bemerkungen zur Vorgesetztenverantwortlichkeit im Völkerstrafrecht, 116 (4) ZStW 999 (2004)

Weigend, Thomas, Societas Delinquere Non Potest? A German Perspective, 6 (5) JICJ 927 (2008)

Weinstein, Tara, Prosecuting Attacks that Destroy the Environment: Environmental Crimes or Humanitarian Atrocities, 17 (4) Geo. Int'l Envtl. L. Rev. 697 (2005)

Weisberg, Barry, Ecocide in Indochina, The Ecology of War (1970)

Welch, Craig, Earth Now has 8 Billion People – and Counting, Where Do We Go From Here?, National Geographic (Nov. 14, 2022)

Werle, Gerhard, Individual Criminal Responsibility in Article 25 ICC Statute, 5 JICJ 953 (2007)

Werle, Gerhard, Konturen des deutschen Völkerstrafrechts: Zum Arbeitsentwurf eines Völkerstrafgesetzbuchs, 56 (18) JuristenZeitung 885 (2001)

Werle, Gerhard, Menschenrechtsschutz durch Völkerstrafrecht, 109 (4) ZStW 808 (1997)

Werle, Gerhard/*Jeßberger*, Florian, Principles of International Criminal Law (4th ed., 2020)

Werle, Gerhard/*Jeßberger*, Florian, 'Unless Otherwise Provided': Article 30 of the ICC Statute and the Mental Element of Crimes under International Criminal Law, 3 (1) JICJ 35 (2005)

Wirth, David A., The Rio Declaration on Environment and Development: Two Steps Forward and One Back, or Vice Versa, 29 (3) Georgia Law Review 599 (1995)

Wong, Edward/*Buckley*, Chris, U.S. Says China's Repression of Uighurs Is 'Genocide', The New York Times (Jan. 19, 2021)

Yeo, Sophie, Ecocide, Should Killing Nature Be a Crime?, BBC (Nov. 6, 2020)

Zerbes, Ingeborg/*Pieth*, Mark, Unternehmerische Verantwortlichkeit für Völkerrechtsverbrechen im Ausland, 51 (1) Kritische Justiz 67 (2018)

Websites

Akande, Dapo, Customary International Law and the Addition of New War Crimes to the Statute of the ICC, EJIL: Talk! (Jan. 2, 2018), https://www.ejiltalk.org/customary-international-law-and-the-addition-of-new-war-crimes-to-the-statute-of-the-icc/ (last visited Feb. 18, 2025)

Ambos, Kai, Protecting the Environment Through International Criminal Law?, EJIL: Talk! (June 29, 2021), https://www.ejiltalk.org/protecting-the-environment-through-international-criminal-law/ (last visited Feb. 18, 2025)

Amnesty International, No clean up, no justice: Shell's oil pollution in the Niger Delta (2020), https://www.amnesty.org/en/latest/news/2020/06/no-clean-up-no-justice-shell-oil-pollution-in-the-niger-delta/ (last visited Feb. 18, 2025)

Conant, Jeff, Justice Delayed Is Justice Denied in Guatemala's Palm Oil-Driven Human Rights Crisis (2016), https://medium.com/economic-policy/justice-delayed-is-justice-denied-in-guatemalas-palm-oil-driven-human-rights-crisis-e2c1f7633412 (last visited Feb. 18, 2025)

Ecocide Law, Ecocide Law in National Jurisdictions, https://ecocidelaw.com/existing-ecocide-laws/ (last visited Feb. 18, 2025)

ECOLEX, https://www.ecolex.org (last visited Feb. 18, 2025)

Encyclopedia Britannica, Bhopal disaster, https://www.britannica.com/event/Bhopal-disaster (last visited Feb. 18, 2025)

Encyclopedia Britannica, Environmental Law, https://www.britannica.com/topic/environmental-law (last visited Feb. 18, 2025)

EU, Court of Justice of the European Union (CJEU), https://european-union.europa.eu/institutions-law-budget/institutions-and-bodies/institutions-and-bodies-profiles/court-justice-european-union-cjeu_en (last visited Feb. 18, 2025)

European Citizens' Initiative, End Ecocide in Europe: A Citizens' Initiative to Give the Earth Rights, https://europa.eu/citizens-initiative/initiatives/details/2012/000012_en (last visited Feb. 18, 2025)

European Commission, A European Green Deal, https://ec.europa.eu/info/strategy/priorities-2019-2024/european-green-deal_en (last visited Feb. 18, 2025)

European Commission, Question and Answers on the Revised EU Directive on Environmental Crime, https://ec.europa.eu/commission/presscorner/detail/en/QANDA_21_6745 (last visited Feb. 18, 2025)

European Council, Council Agrees Its Negotiating Mandate on the Environmental Crime Directive (2022), https://www.consilium.europa.eu/en/press/press-releases/2022/12/09/council-agrees-its-negotiating-mandate-on-the-environmental-crime-directive/ (last visited Feb. 18, 2025)

European Parliament, A Universal Right to a Healthy Environment (2021), https://www.europarl.europa.eu/RegData/etudes/ATAG/2021/698846/EPRS_ATA(2021)698846_EN.pdf (last visited Feb. 18, 2025)

Federal Foreign Office, G7 Foreign Minister's Statement on Climate, Environment, Peace and Security (2022), https://www.auswaertiges-amt.de/en/newsroom/news/-/2531240 (last visited Feb. 18, 2025)

GEF, Who We Are, https://www.thegef.org/who-we-are (last visited Feb. 18, 2025)

Global Diligence, Communication under Article 15 of the Rome Statute of the International Criminal Court (2020), https://www.fidh.org/IMG/pdf/executive_summary-2.pdf (last visited Feb. 18, 2025)

Heller, Kevin Jon, Belgium Set to Criminalise Ecocide (Kinda Sorta), Opinio Juris (Nov. 8, 2022), http://opiniojuris.org/2022/11/08/belgium-set-to-criminalise-ecocide-kinda-sorta/ (last visited Feb. 18, 2025)

Heller, Kevin Jon, Ecocide and Anthropocentric Cost-Benefit Analysis, OpinioJuris (June 26, 2021), http://opiniojuris.org/2021/06/26/ecocide-and-anthropocentric-cost-benefit-analysis/ (last visited Feb. 18, 2025)

Heller, Kevin Jon, Skeptical Thoughts on the Proposed Crime of "Ecocide" (That Isn't), OpinioJuris (June 23, 2021), https://opiniojuris.org/2021/06/23/skeptical-thoughts-on-the-proposed-crime-of-ecocide-that-isnt/ (last visited Feb. 18, 2025)

Heller, Kevin Jon, The Crime of Ecocide in Action, OpinioJuris (June 28, 2021), http://opiniojuris.org/2021/06/28/the-crime-of-ecocide-in-action/ (last visited Feb. 18, 2025)

ICE Coalition, http://www.icecoalition.org (last visited Feb. 18, 2025)

ICRC, Advisory Service on International Humanitarian Law (2004), https://www.icrc.org/en/doc/assets/files/other/what_is_ihl.pdf (last visited Feb. 18, 2025)

International Court of Justice, Chambers and Committees, https://www.icj-cij.org/en/chambers-and-committees (last visited Feb. 18, 2025)

International Court of Justice, Obligations of States in Respect of Climate Change, Press Release No. 2023/44 (2023), https://www.icj-cij.org/sites/default/files/case-related/187/187-20230901-pre-01-00-en.pdf (last visited Feb. 18, 2025)

International Criminal Court, Al Bashir Case, https://www.icc-cpi.int/darfur/albashir (last visited Feb. 18, 2025)

International Criminal Court, Preliminary Examinations, https://www.icc-cpi.int/situations-preliminary-examinations (last visited Feb. 18, 2025)

International Criminal Court, The States Parties to the Rome Statute, https://asp.icc-cpi.int/en_menus/asp/states%20parties/Pages/the%20states%20parties%20to%20the%20rome%20statute.aspx (last visited Feb. 18, 2025)

INTERPOL, Interpol Makes Public Appeal to Help Track Environmental Fugitives (2019), https://www.interpol.int/News-and-Events/News/2019/INTERPOL-makes-public-appeal-to-help-track-environmental-fugitives (last visited Feb. 18, 2025)

Khattabi, Zakia, Zakia Khattabi Gets the Crime of Ecocide Written into the Criminal Code (2022), https://khattabi.belgium.be/en/pr-zakia-khattabi-gets-crime-ecocide-written-criminal-code (last visited Feb. 18, 2025)

Kreß, Claus, International Criminal Law (2009), https://opil.ouplaw.com/view/10.1093/law:epil/9780199231690/law-9780199231690-e1423#law-9780199231690-e1423 (last visited Feb. 18, 2025)

Mendoza, Pablo Fajardo/*Toledo*, Eduardo Bernabé, Communication, Situation in Ecuador, https://chevroninecuador.org/assets/docs/2014-icc-complaint.pdf (last visited Feb. 18, 2025)

Parliamentary Assembly Council of Europe, The Right to a Healthy Environment: PACE Proposes Draft of a New Protocol to the European Convention on Human Rights (2021), https://pace.coe.int/en/news/8452/the-right-to-a-healthy-environment-pace-proposes-draft-of-a-new-protocol-to-the-european-convention-on-human-rights- (last visited Feb. 18, 2025)

Permanent Court of Arbitration, Contracting Parties, https://pca-cpa.org/en/about/introduction/contracting-parties/ (last visited Feb. 18, 2025)

Permanent Court of Arbitration, Dispute Resolution Services, https://pca-cpa.org/en/services/ (last visited Feb. 18, 2025)

Permanent Court of Arbitration, Environmental Dispute Resolution, https://pca-cpa.org/en/services/arbitration-services/environmental-dispute-resolution/ (last visited Feb. 18, 2025)

Pezzot, Romina/*Graf*, Jan-Philip, Ecocide, Legal Revolution or Symbolism? (2022), https://voelkerrechtsblog.org/de/ecocide-legal-revolution-or-symbolism/ (last visited Feb. 18, 2025)

Stop Ecocide International, What is Ecocide? , https://www.stopecocide.earth/what-is-ecocide (last visited Feb. 18, 2025)

Stop Ecocide International, What We Do, https://www.stopecocide.earth/what-we-do (last visited Feb. 18, 2025)

Umweltbundesamt, Resource Use and Its Consequences (2019), https://www.umweltbundesamt.de/en/topics/waste-resources/resource-use-its-consequences (last visited Feb. 18, 2025)

U.N. Security Council, Current Members, https://www.un.org/securitycouncil/content/current-members (last visited Feb. 18, 2025)

UNEP, About UN Environment Programme, https://www.unep.org/about-un-environment (last visited Feb. 18, 2025)

United Nations, Briefing UN Security Council on Humanitarian Effects of Environmental Degradation on Peace and Security (2020), https://www.unccd.int/news-stories/statements/briefing-un-security-council-humanitarian-effects-environmental-degradation (last visited Feb. 18, 2025)

United Nations, Day of Eight Billion, https://www.un.org/en/dayof8billion (last visited Feb. 18, 2025)

United Nations, General Assembly Adopts Resolution Requesting International Court of Justice Provide Advisory Opinion on States' Obligations Concerning Climate Change (2023), https://press.un.org/en/2023/ga12497.doc.htm (last visited Feb. 18, 2025)

United Nations, Security Council Holds First-Ever Debate on Impact of Climate Change on Peace, Security, Hearing over 50 Speakers (2007), https://press.un.org/en/2007/sc9000.doc.htm (last visited Feb. 18, 2025)

United Nations, UN General Assembly Declares Access to Clean and Healthy Environment a Universal Human Right (2022), https://news.un.org/en/story/2022/07/1123482 (last visited Feb. 18, 2025)

Woods, Cindy, The Guatemala Ecocide Case: What It Means for the Business and Human Rights Movement, Blog de la Fundación para el Debido Procesco (DPLF) (Mar. 10, 2016), https://dplfblog.com/2016/03/10/the-guatemala-ecocide-case-what-it-means-for-the-business-and-human-rights-movement/ (last visited Feb. 18, 2025)

World Population Review, Pollution by Country 2022, https://worldpopulationreview.com/country-rankings/pollution-by-country (last visited Feb. 18, 2025)

Index